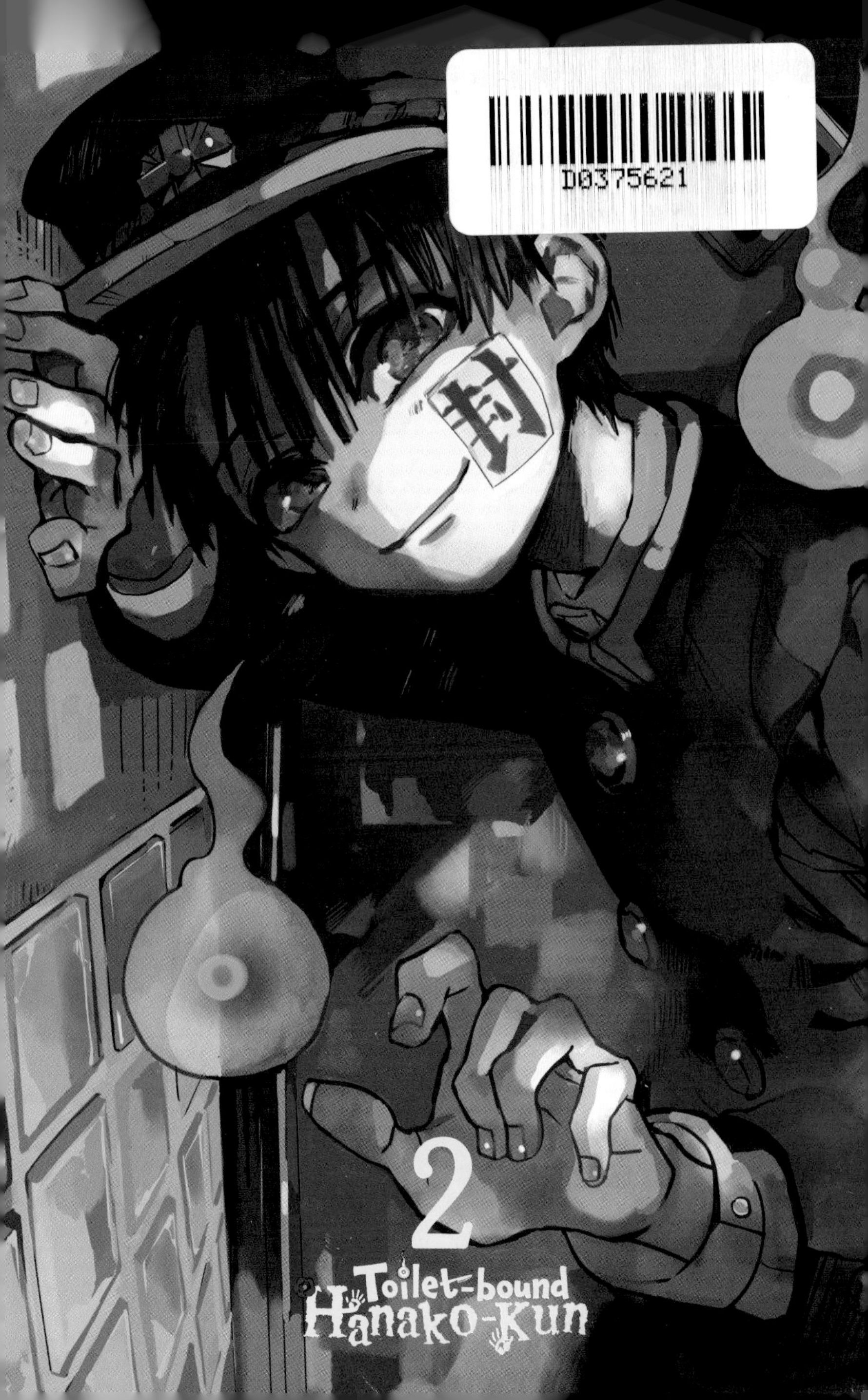
2
Toilet-bound
Hanako-Kun

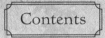

Contents

SPOOK 6 THE MISAKI STAIRS (PART 3)

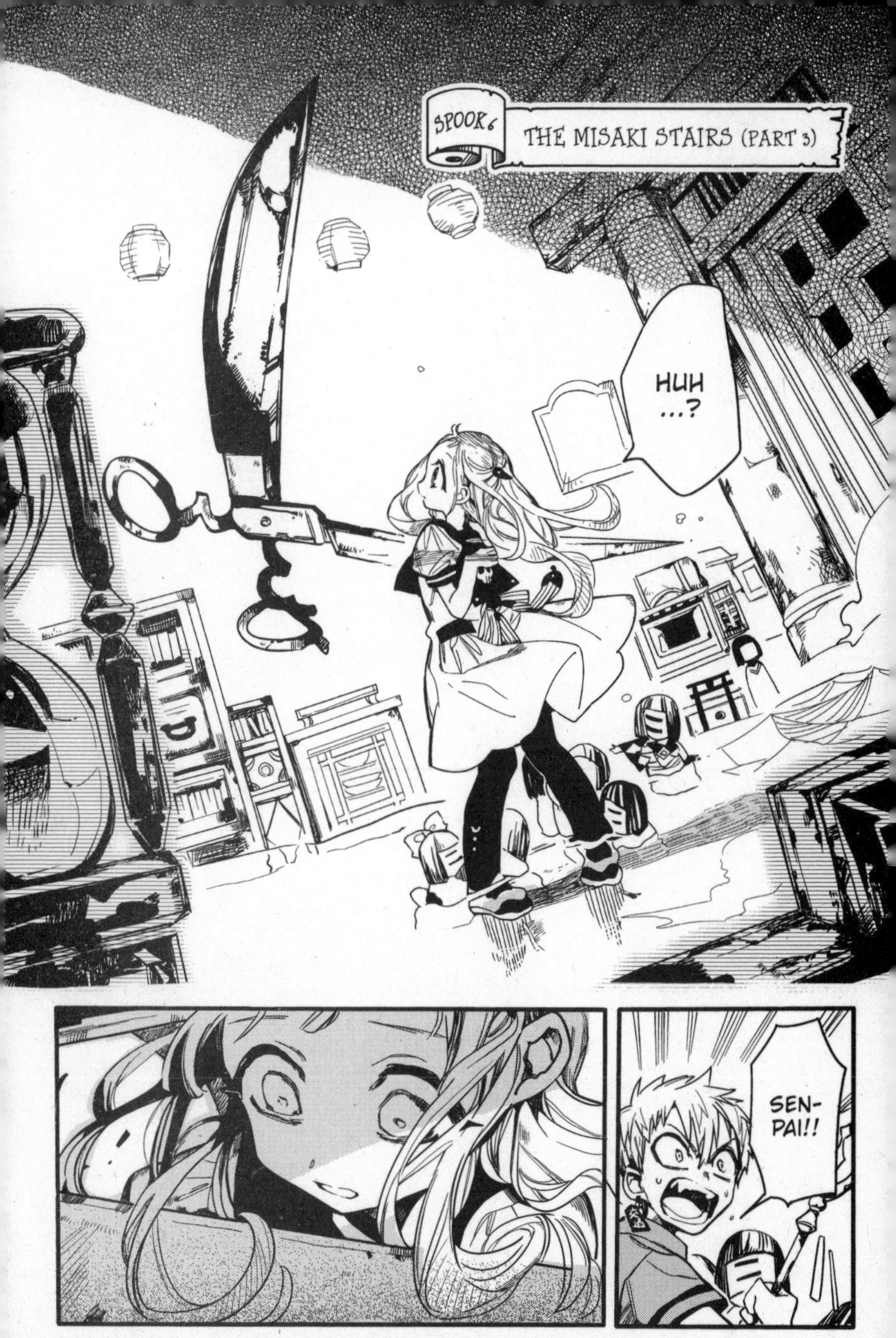
HUH ...?
SEN-PAI!!

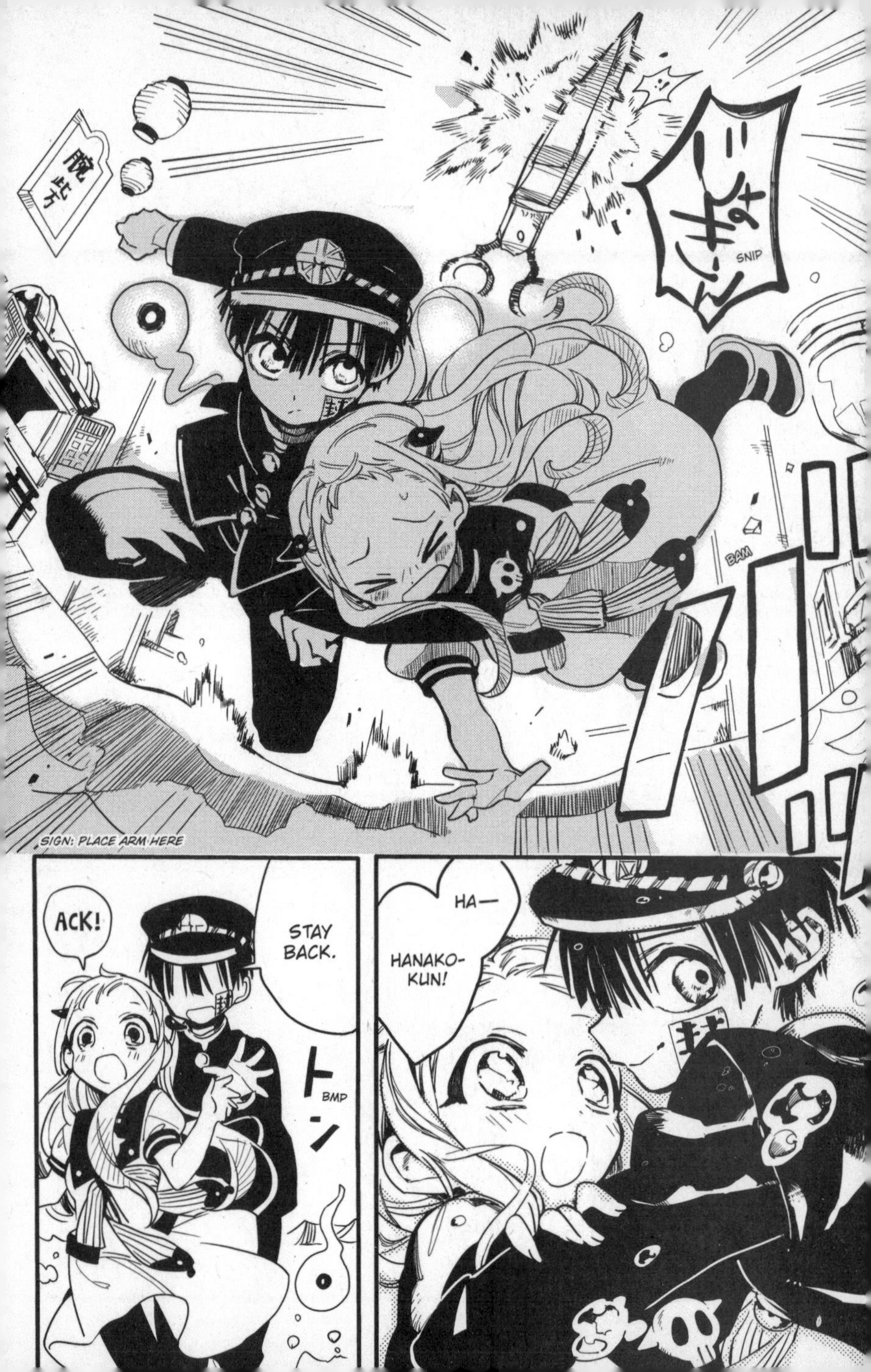
SNIP
BAM
SIGN: PLACE ARM HERE
HA—
HANAKO-KUN!
STAY BACK.
BMP
ACK!

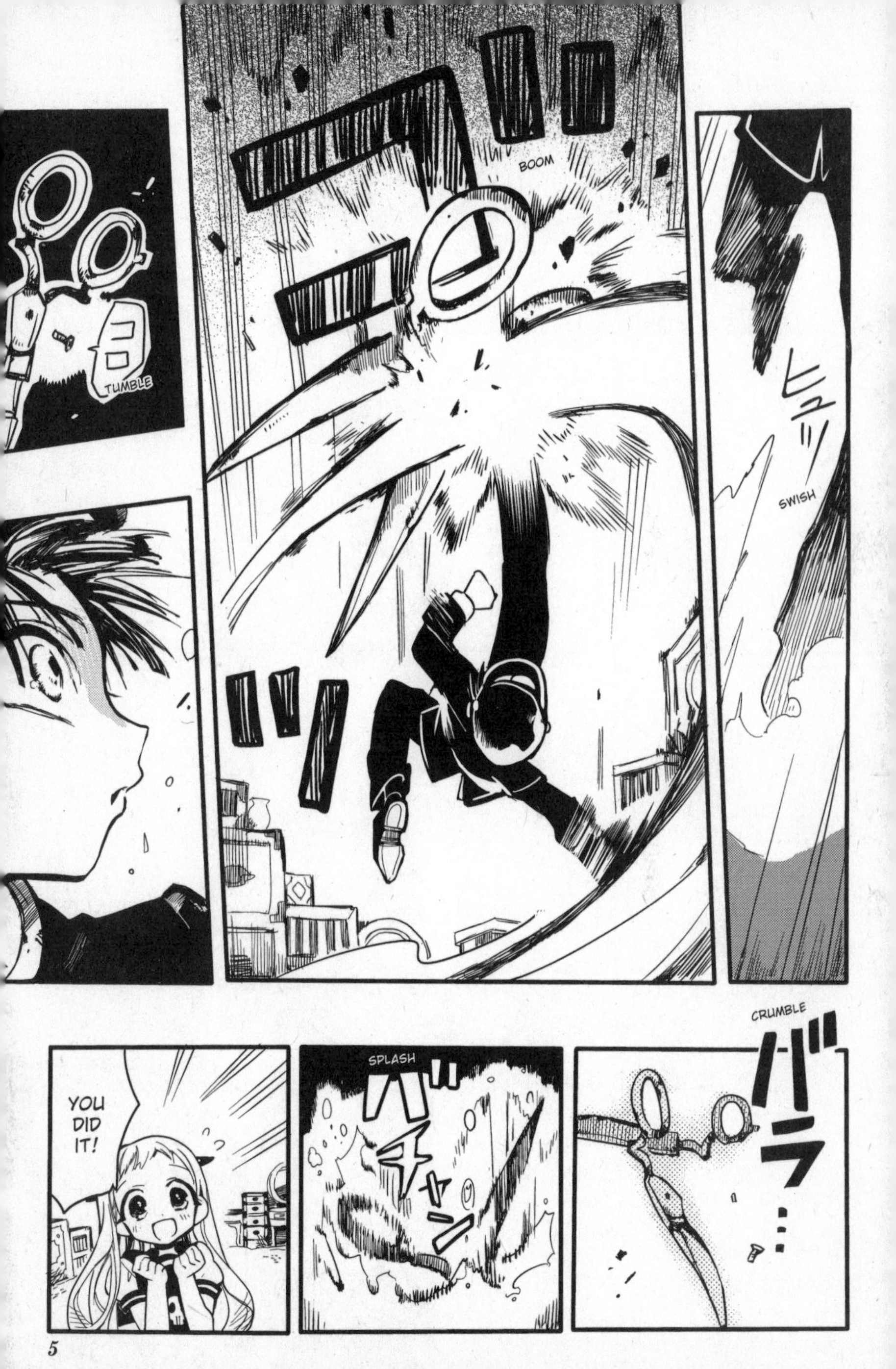
SWISH
BOOM
TUMBLE
CRUMBLE
SPLASH
YOU DID IT!

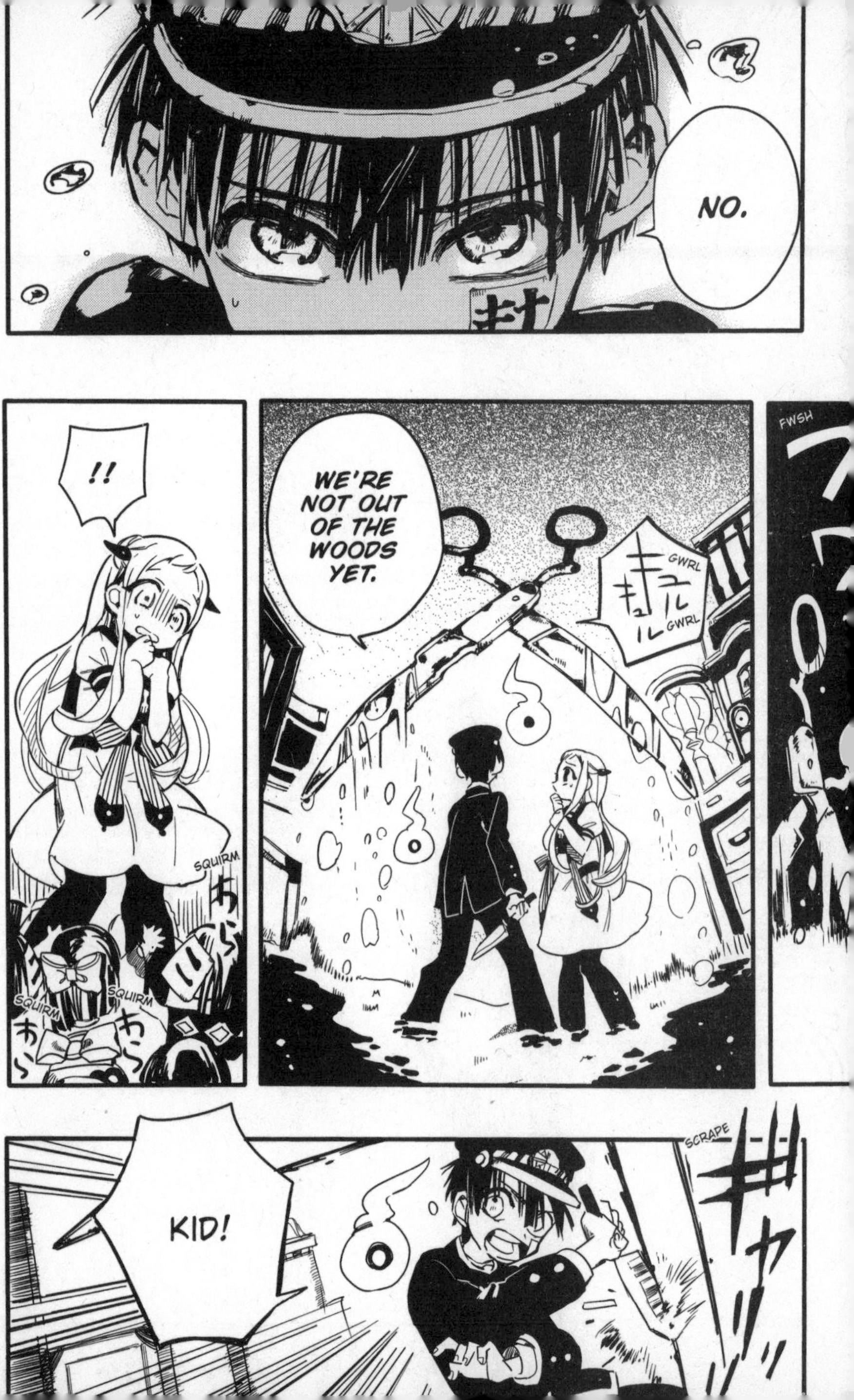
NO.
FWSH
WE'RE NOT OUT OF THE WOODS YET.
GWRL
GWRL
!!
SQUIRM
SQUIRM
SQUIRM
SCRAPE
KID!

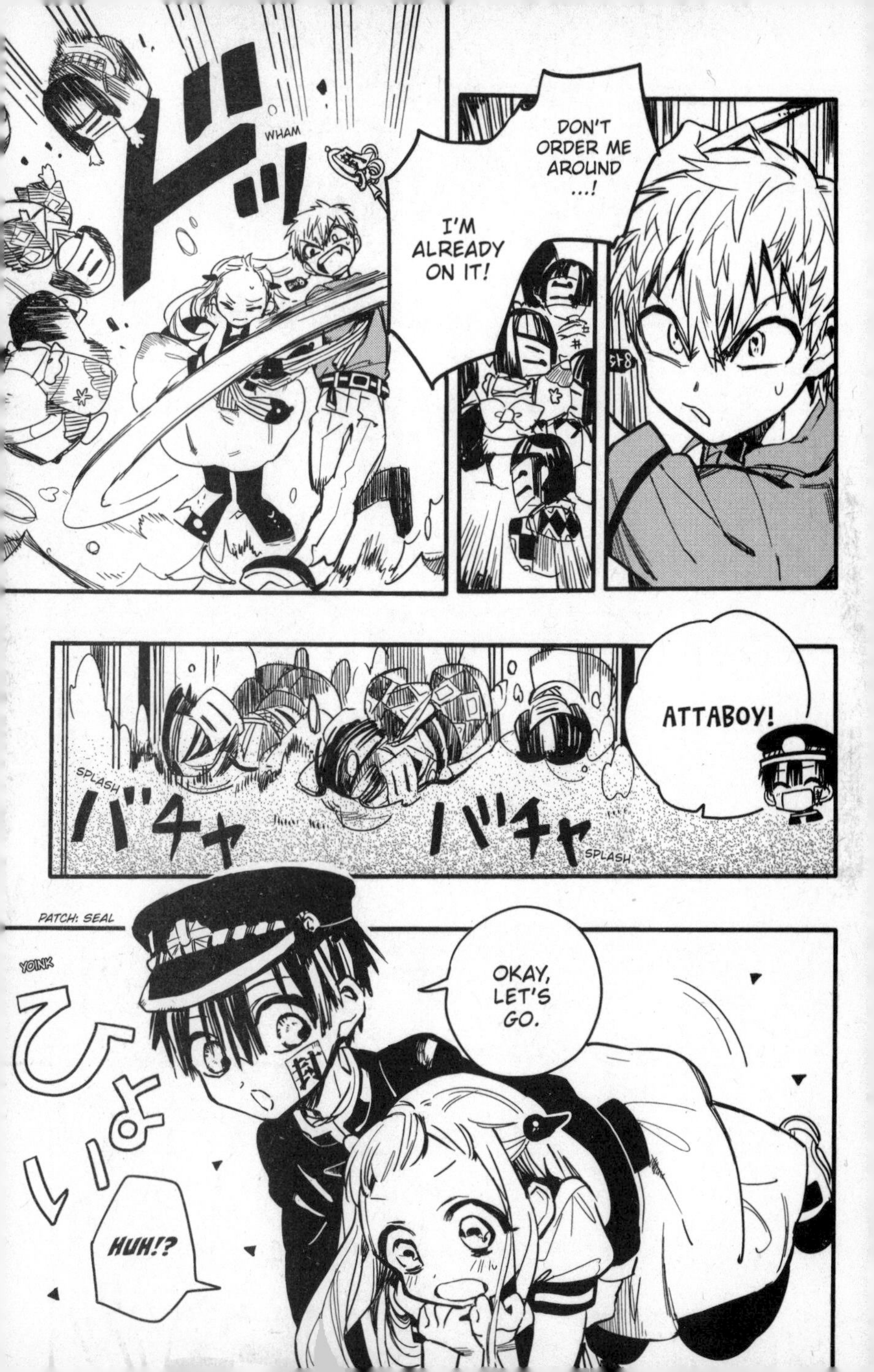
DON'T ORDER ME AROUND ...!
I'M ALREADY ON IT!
ドッ
WHAM
ATTABOY!
バチャ
SPLASH
バチャ
SPLASH
PATCH: SEAL
OKAY, LET'S GO.
ひょい
YOINK
HUH!?

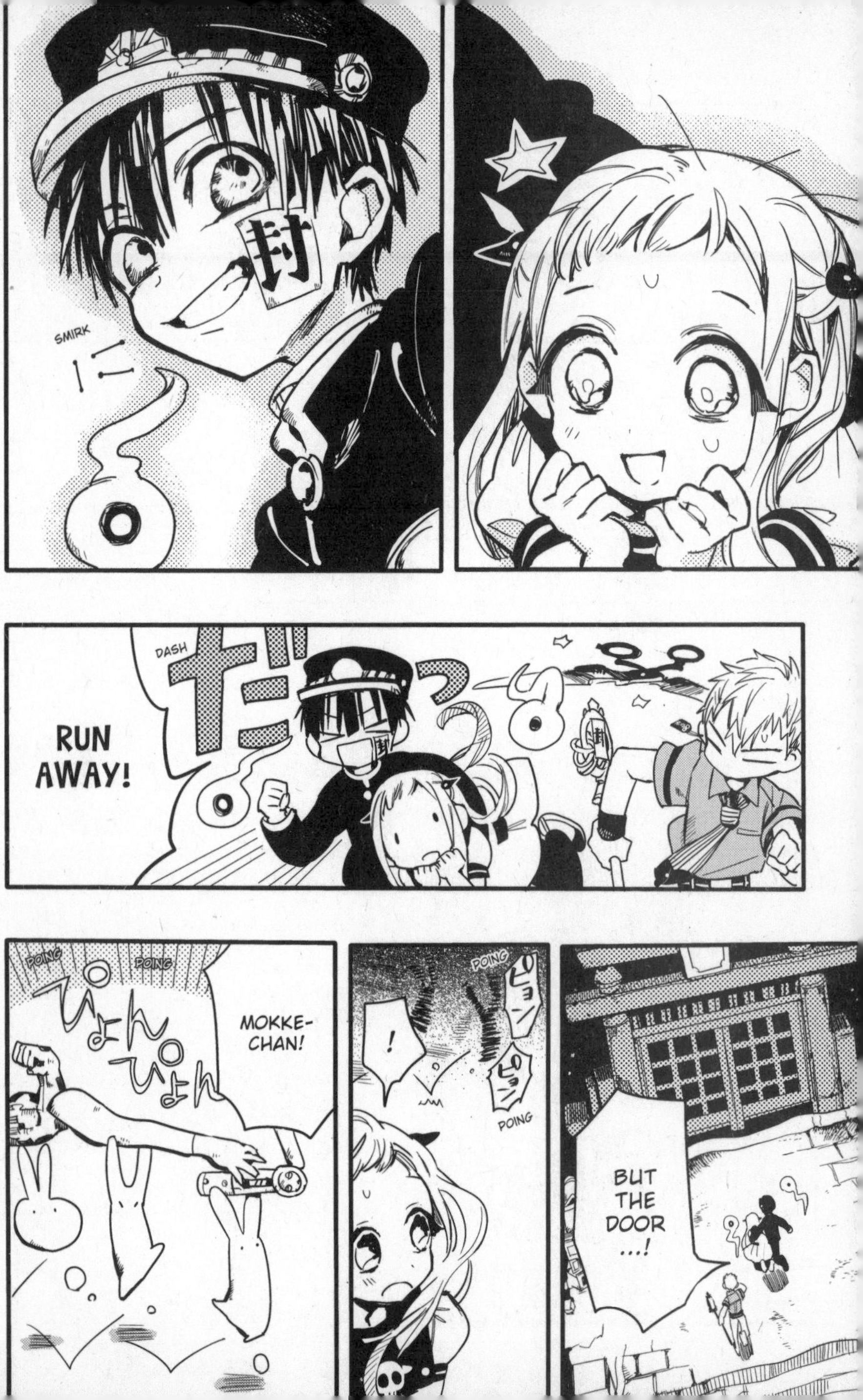
SMIRK
DASH
RUN AWAY!
BUT THE DOOR ...!
POING
!
POING
POING
POING
MOKKE-CHAN!

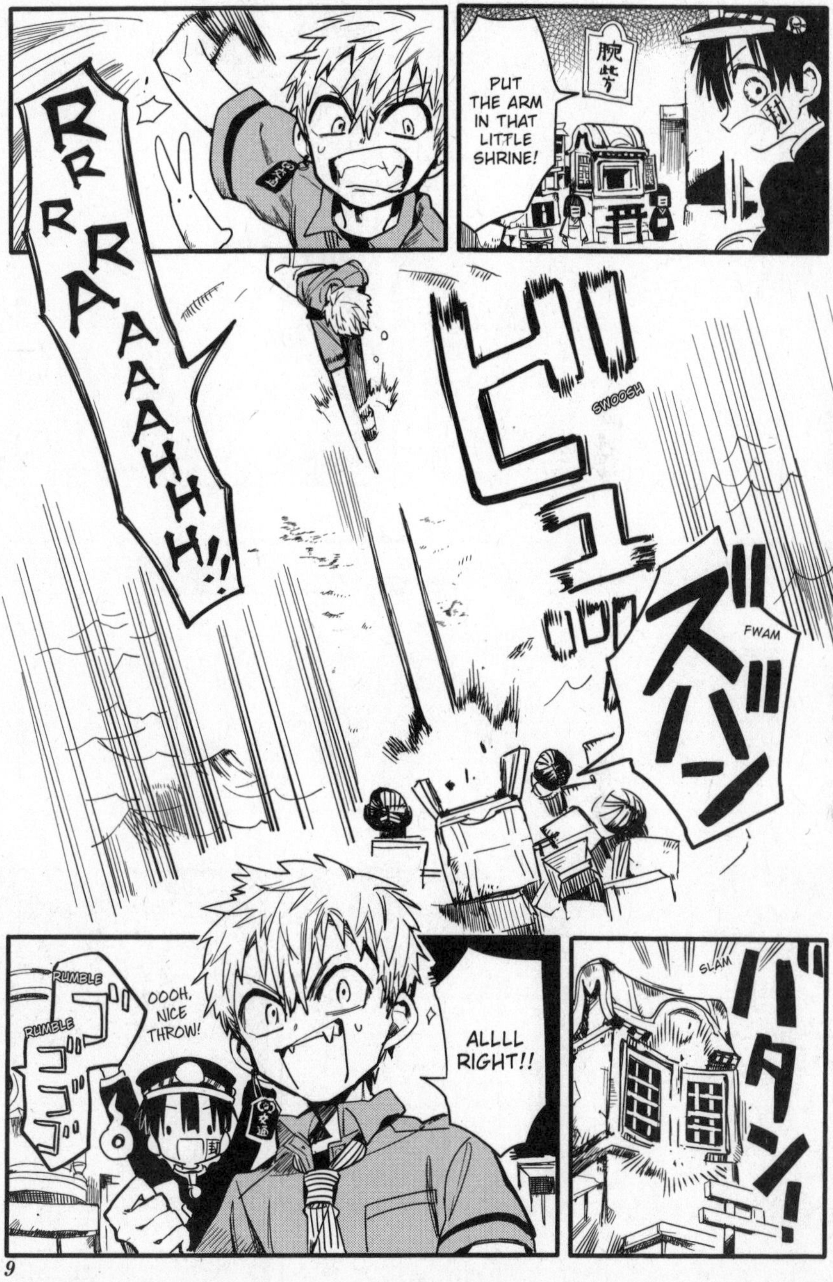
PUT THE ARM IN THAT LITTLE SHRINE!
RRRRAAAAHHH!!
SWOOSH
FWAM
SLAM
ALLLL RIGHT!!
OOOH, NICE THROW!
RUMBLE
RUMBLE

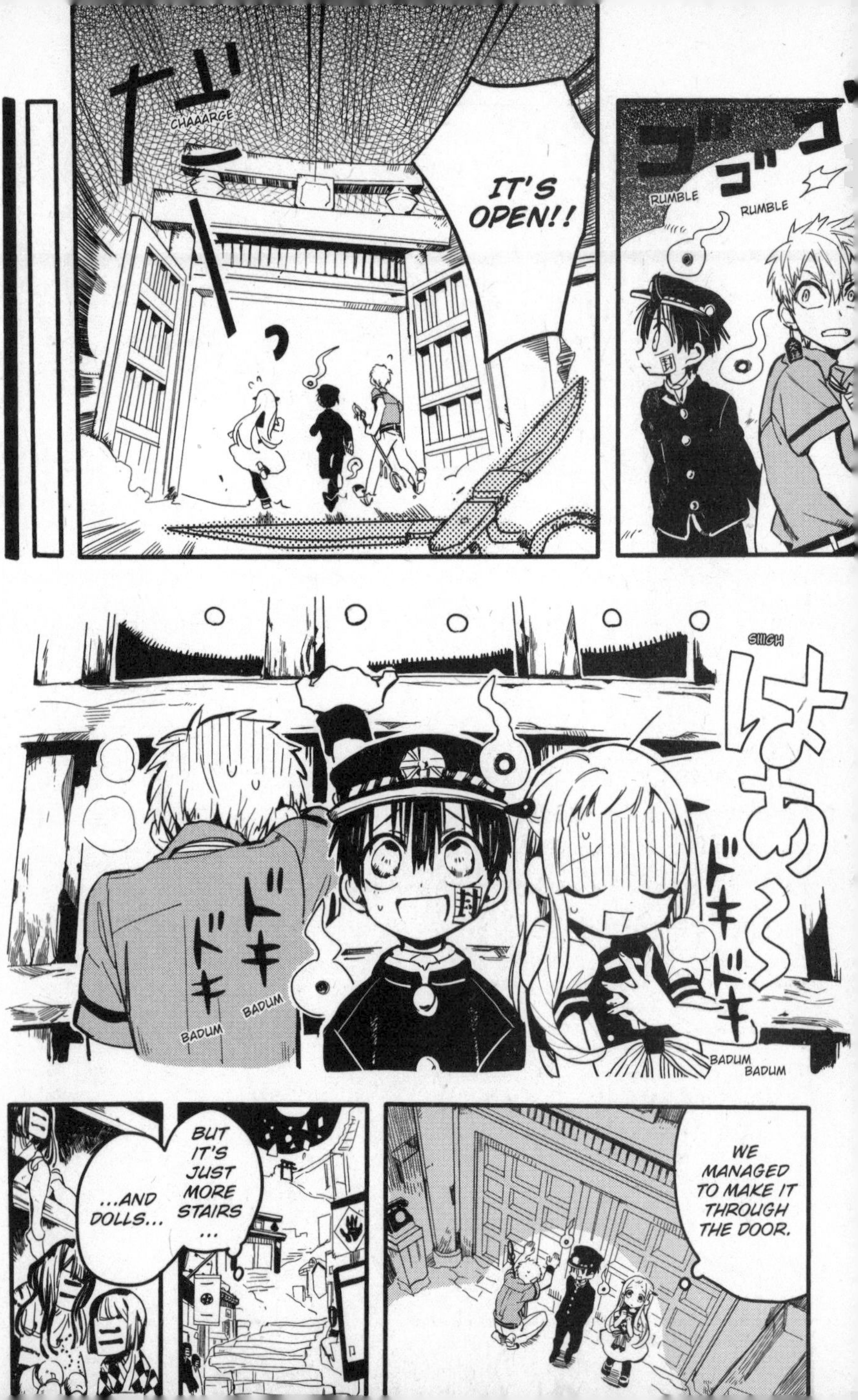
RUMBLE
RUMBLE
CHAAARGE
IT'S OPEN!!
SIIIGH
BADUM
BADUM
BADUM
BADUM
WE MANAGED TO MAKE IT THROUGH THE DOOR.
BUT IT'S JUST MORE STAIRS...
...AND DOLLS...

AND THERE'S NOBODY HERE.
NOT AOI, NOT ANY OF THE OTHER KIDS...
IF WE KEEP GOING, WE WILL FIND THEM...WON'T WE?
RIIING
JUMP
RIIING
RIIING
ANOTHER ONE...
SFF
YOU'RE GONNA ANSWER IT, HANAKO-KUN?
A-YELLO?
AHEM...
My left arm ...

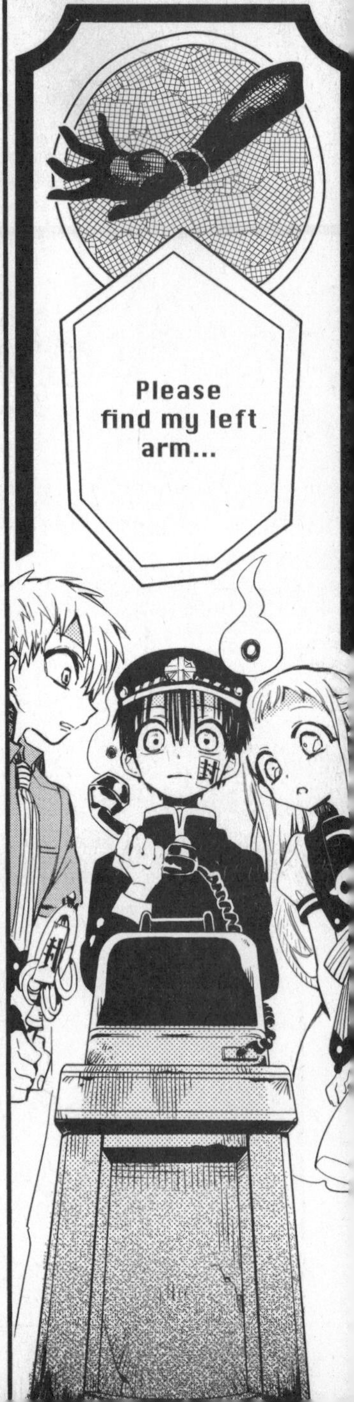
Please find my left arm...

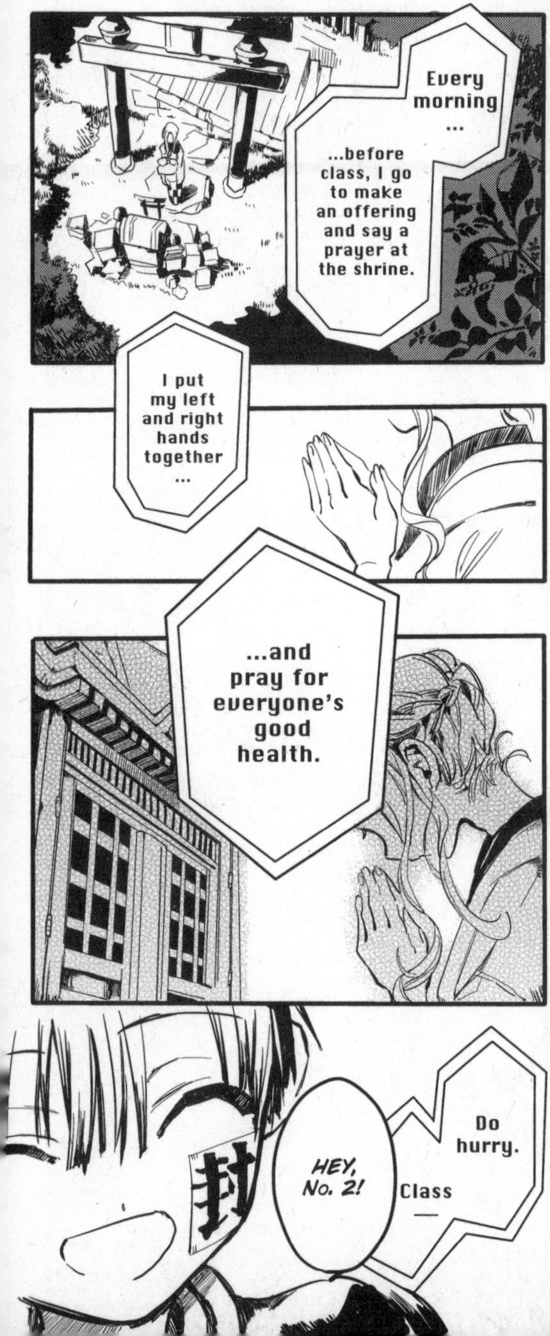
Every morning...
...before class, I go to make an offering and say a prayer at the shrine.
I put my left and right hands together...
...and pray for everyone's good health.
Do hurry.
Class —
HEY, No. 2!

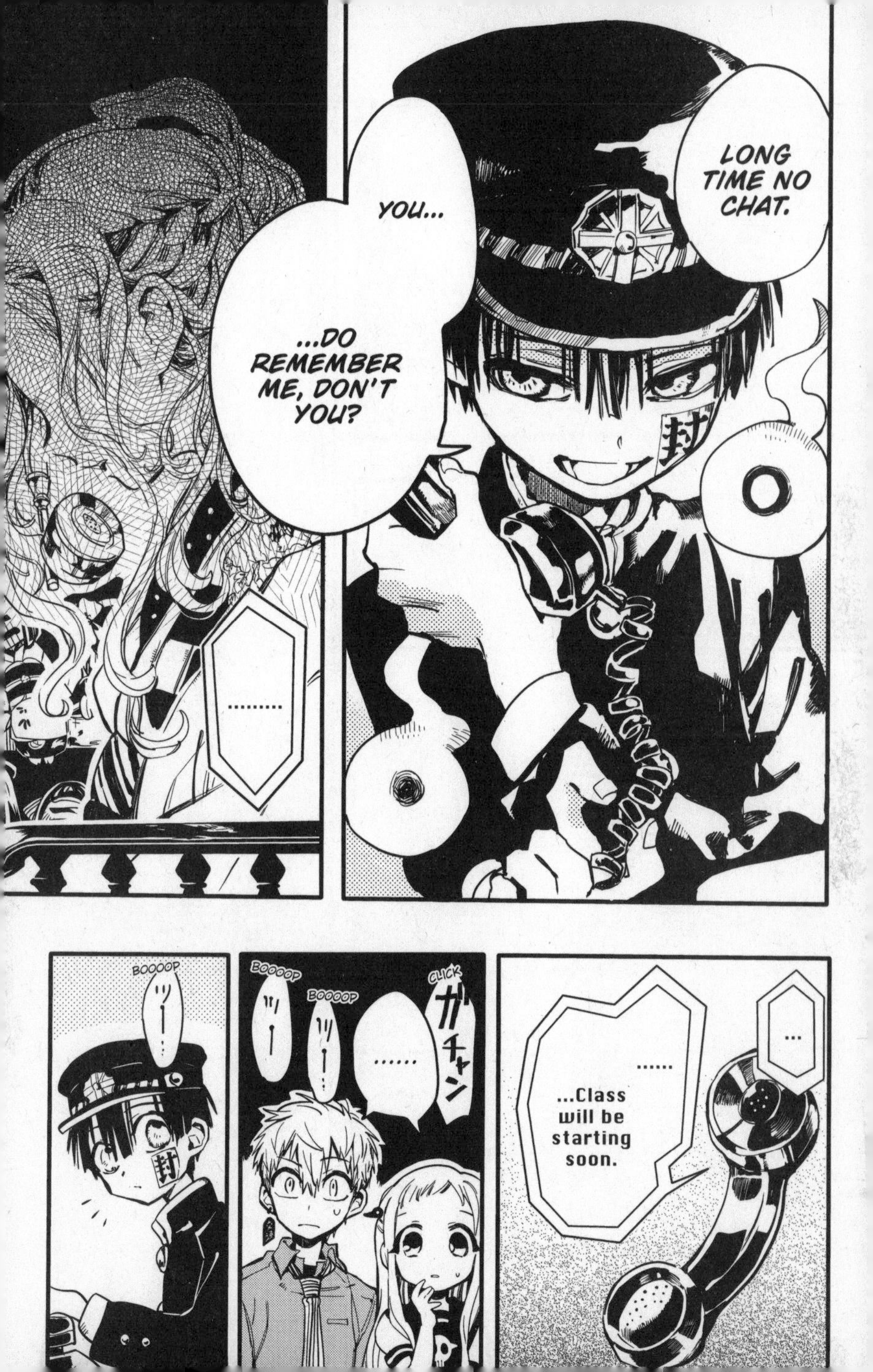
LONG TIME NO CHAT.
YOU...
...DO REMEMBER ME, DON'T YOU?
....
...
......
...Class will be starting soon.
CLICK
ガチャン
......
BOOOOP
ツー…
BOOOOP
ツー
BOOOOP
ツー…

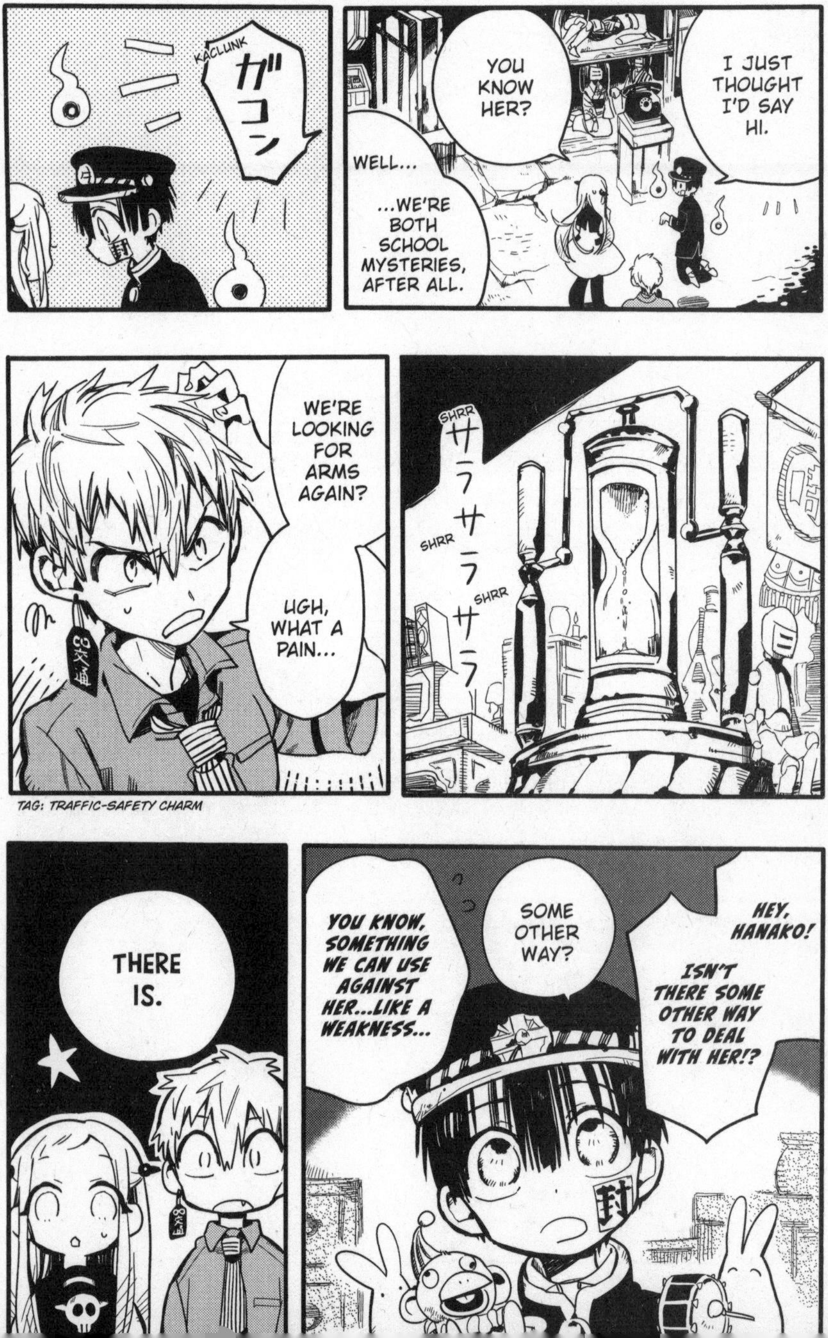
I JUST THOUGHT I'D SAY HI.
YOU KNOW HER?
WELL...
...WE'RE BOTH SCHOOL MYSTERIES, AFTER ALL.
KACLUNK
ガコン
SHRR
サラサラサラ
SHRR
SHRR
WE'RE LOOKING FOR ARMS AGAIN?
UGH, WHAT A PAIN...
HEY, HANAKO!
ISN'T THERE SOME OTHER WAY TO DEAL WITH HER!?
SOME OTHER WAY?
YOU KNOW, SOMETHING WE CAN USE AGAINST HER...LIKE A WEAKNESS...
THERE IS.

TAG: TRAFFIC-SAFETY CHARM

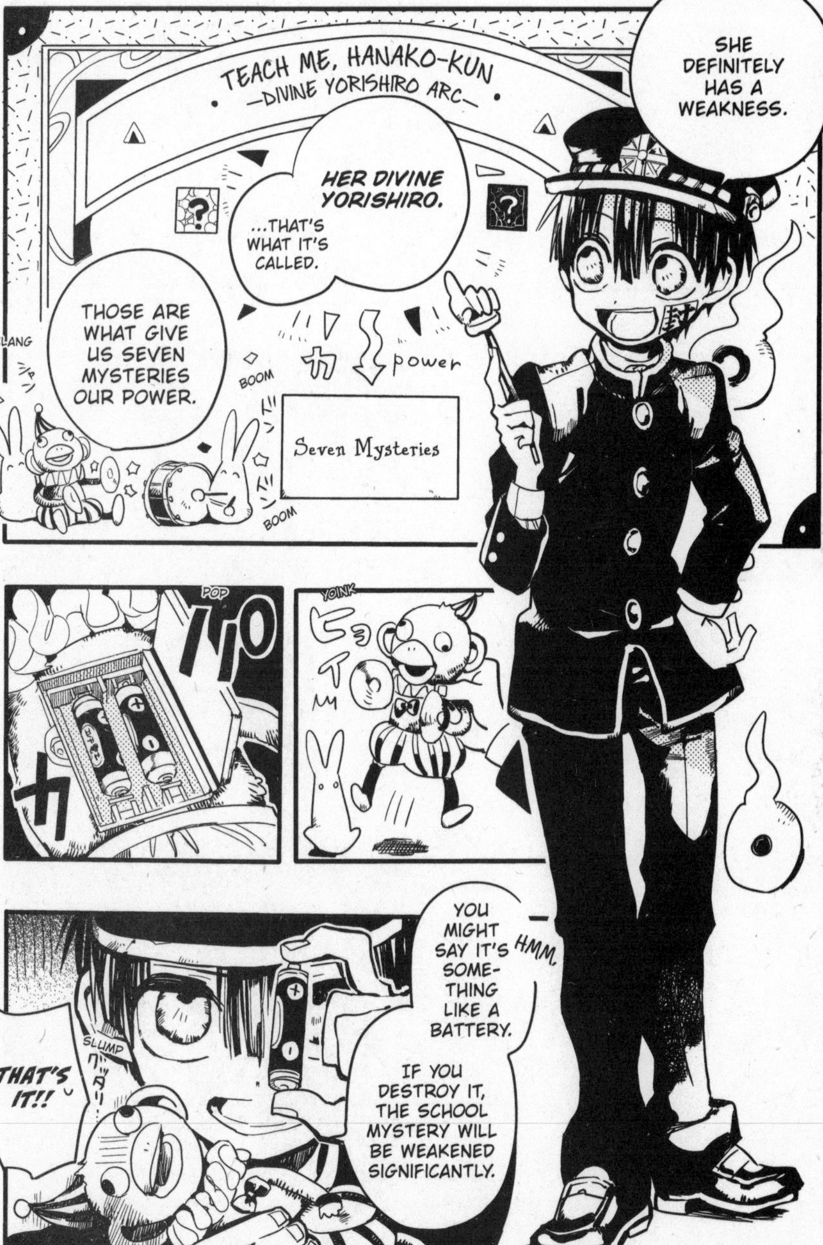
TEACH ME, HANAKO-KUN
—DIVINE YORISHIRO ARC—
SHE DEFINITELY HAS A WEAKNESS.
HER DIVINE YORISHIRO.
...THAT'S WHAT IT'S CALLED.
power
Seven Mysteries
THOSE ARE WHAT GIVE US SEVEN MYSTERIES OUR POWER.
BOOM
BOOM
CLANG
CLANG
YOINK
POP
YOU MIGHT SAY IT'S SOME-THING LIKE A BATTERY.
HMM.
IF YOU DESTROY IT, THE SCHOOL MYSTERY WILL BE WEAKENED SIGNIFICANTLY.
SLUMP
THAT'S IT!!

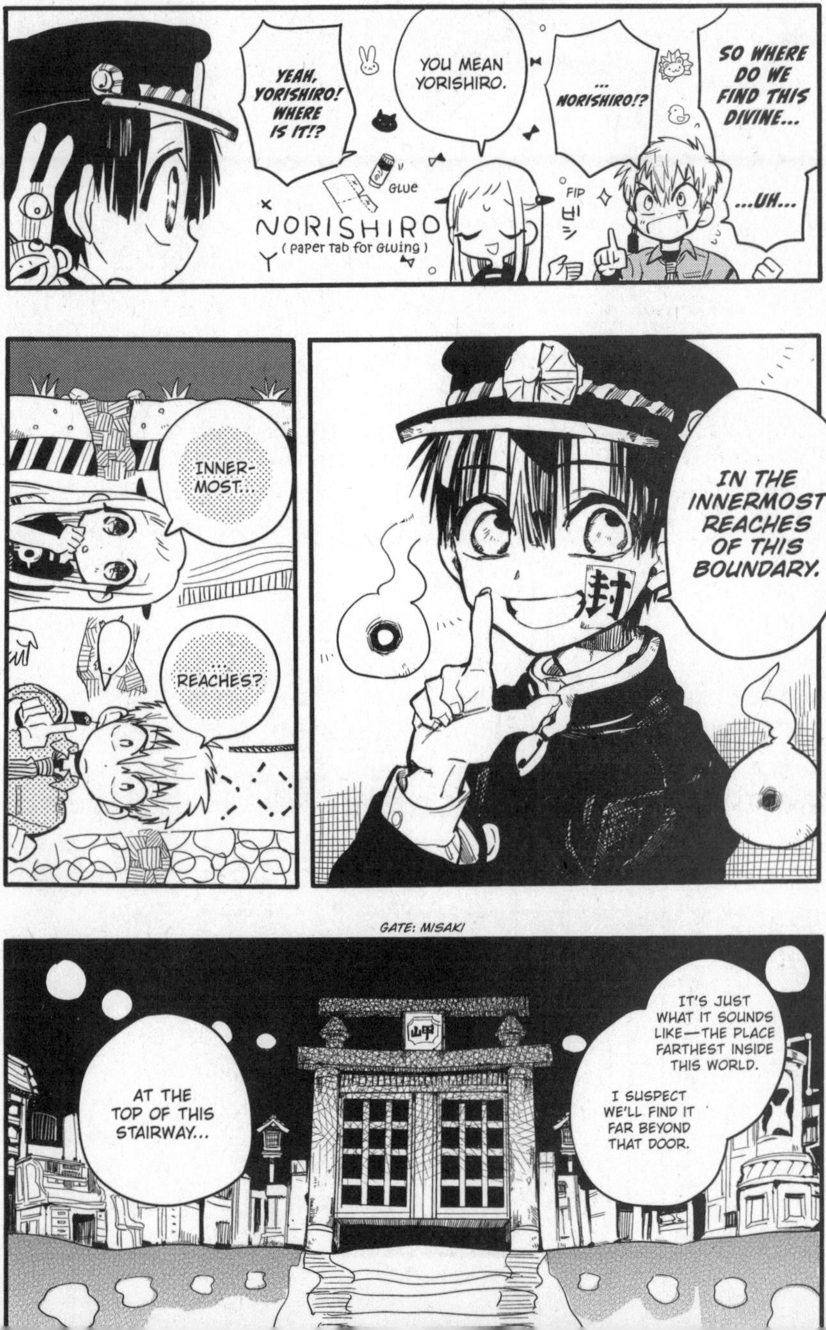
SO WHERE DO WE FIND THIS DIVINE...
...UH...
...NORISHIRO!?
FIP
YOU MEAN YORISHIRO.
YEAH, YORISHIRO! WHERE IS IT!?
GLUE
NORISHIRO
(paper tab for gluing)
IN THE INNERMOST REACHES OF THIS BOUNDARY.
INNER-MOST...
...REACHES?
GATE: MISAKI
岬
IT'S JUST WHAT IT SOUNDS LIKE—THE PLACE FARTHEST INSIDE THIS WORLD.
I SUSPECT WE'LL FIND IT FAR BEYOND THAT DOOR.
AT THE TOP OF THIS STAIRWAY...

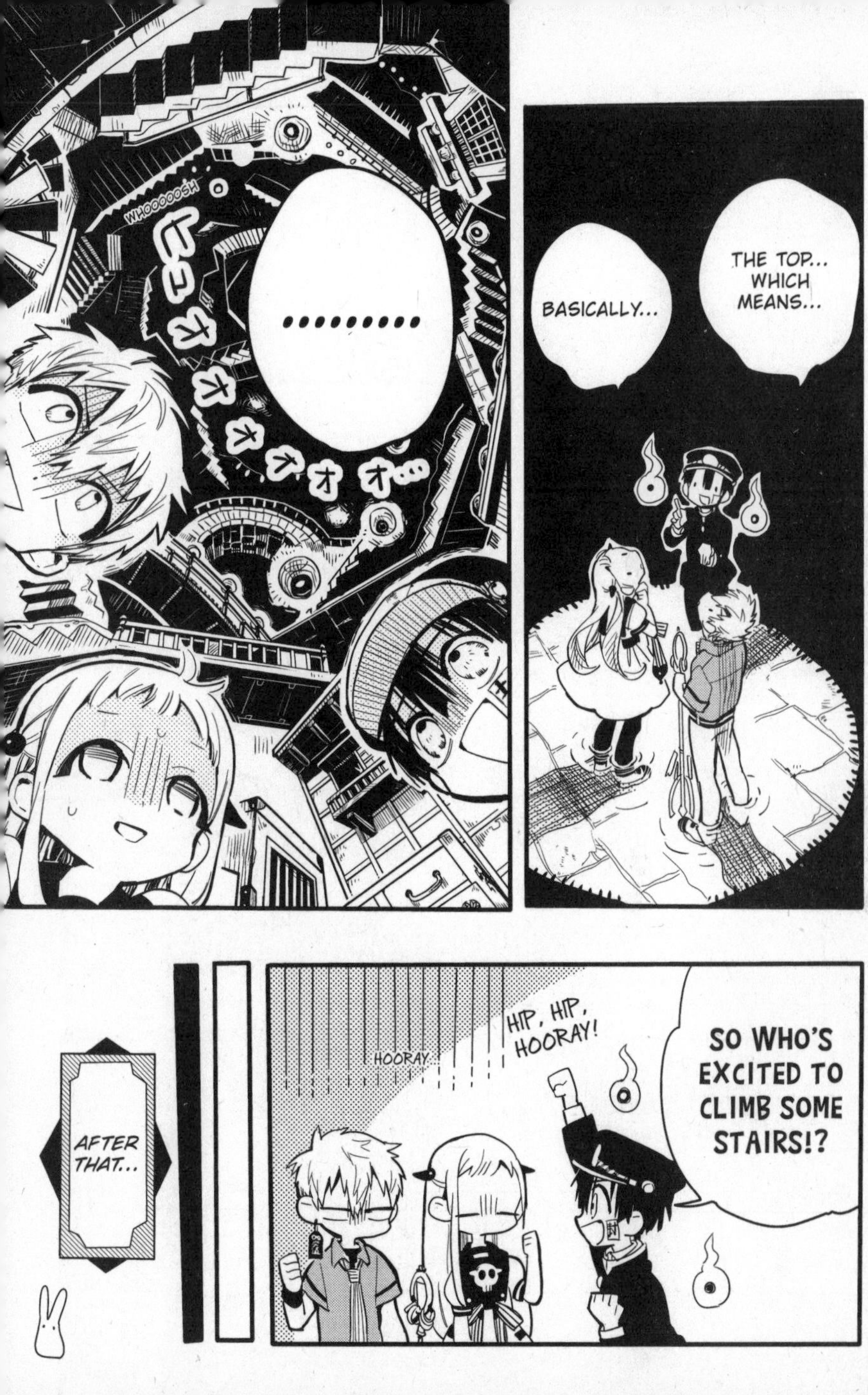
THE TOP... WHICH MEANS...
BASICALLY...
WHOOOOOSH
ヒュオオオオオ…
....
SO WHO'S EXCITED TO CLIMB SOME STAIRS!?
HIP, HIP, HOORAY!
HOORAY
AFTER THAT...

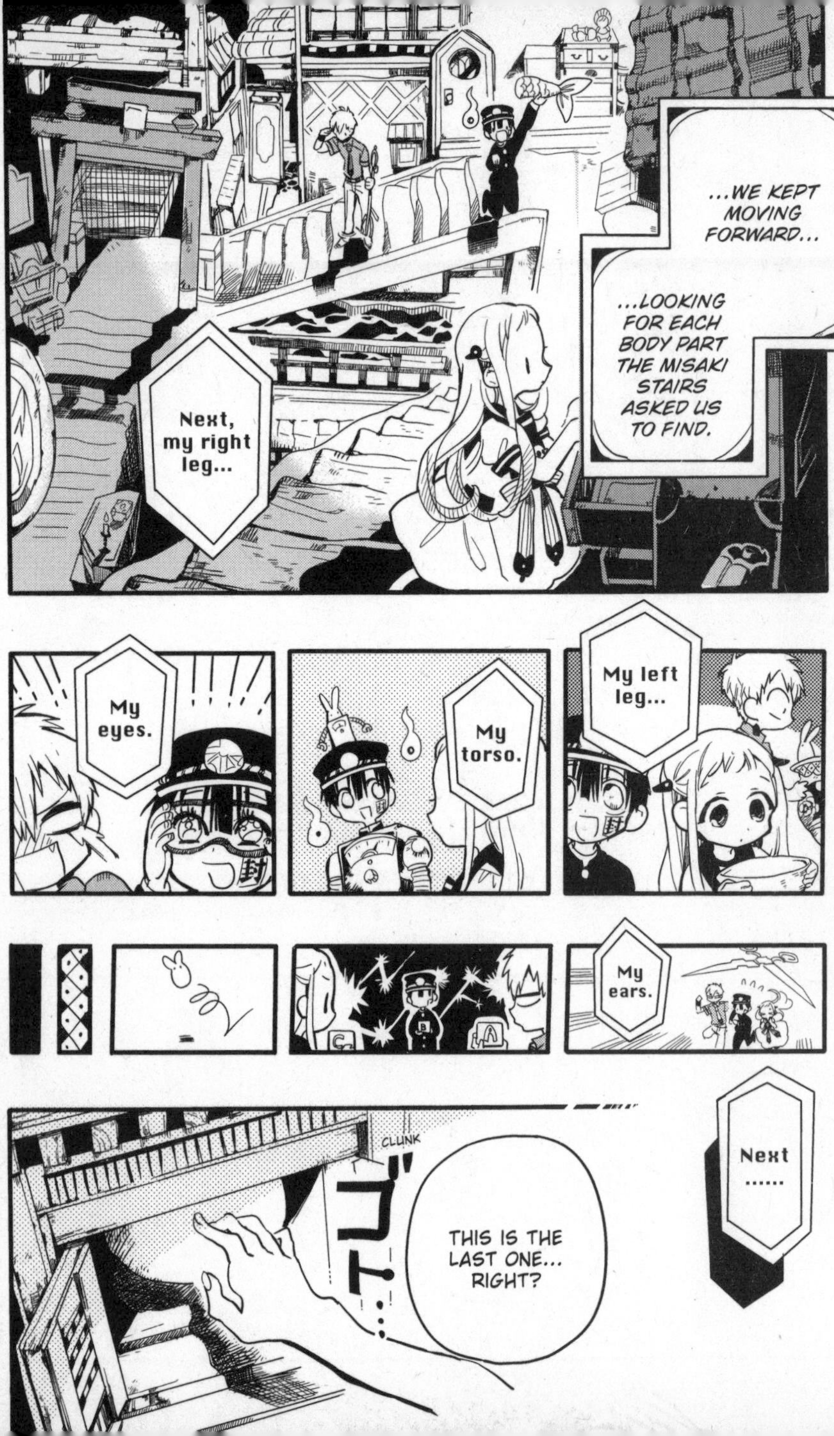
...WE KEPT MOVING FORWARD...
...LOOKING FOR EACH BODY PART THE MISAKI STAIRS ASKED US TO FIND.
Next, my right leg...
My left leg...
My torso.
My eyes.
My ears.
Next......
THIS IS THE LAST ONE... RIGHT?
CLUNK

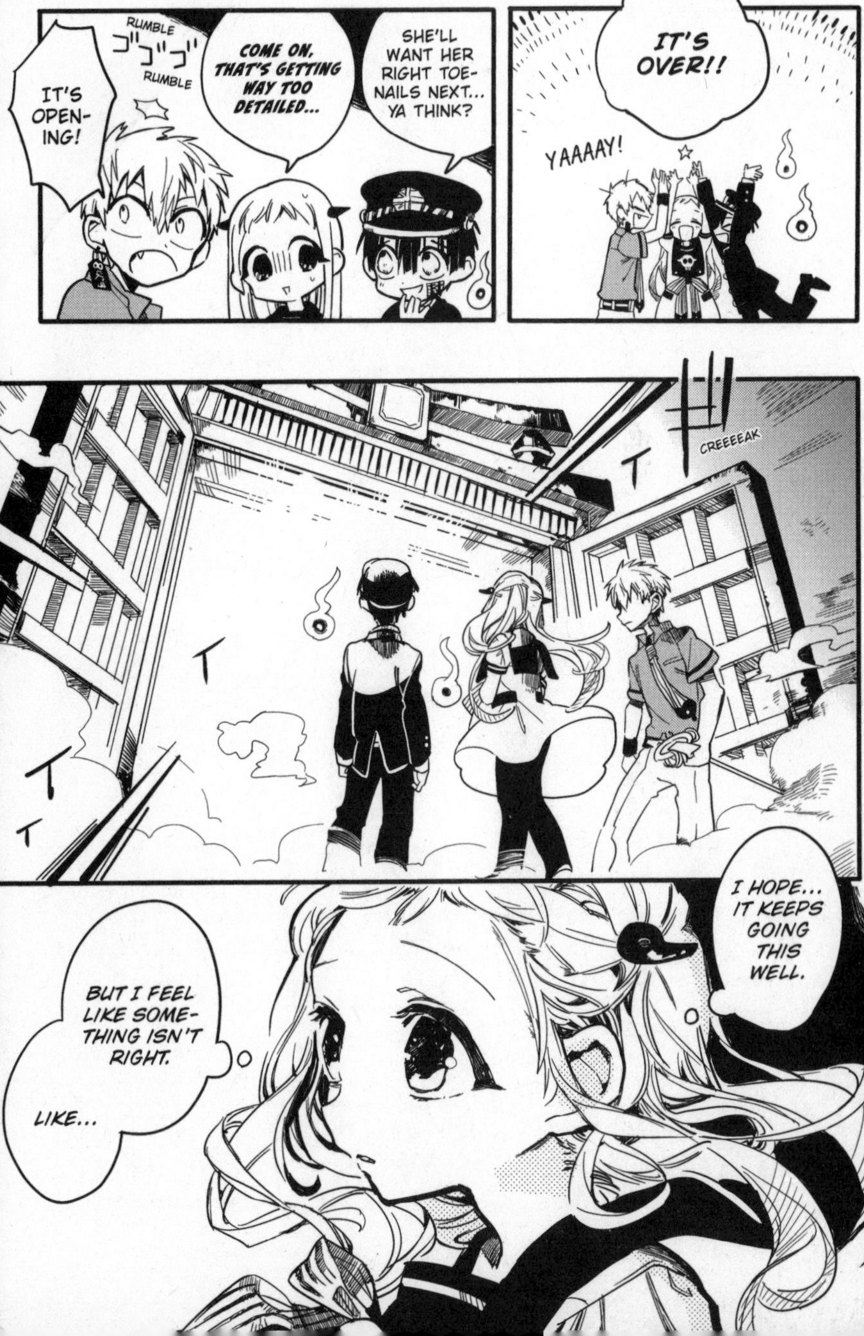
IT'S OVER!!
YAAAAY!
SHE'LL WANT HER RIGHT TOE-NAILS NEXT... YA THINK?
COME ON, THAT'S GETTING WAY TOO DETAILED...
ゴゴゴ
RUMBLE RUMBLE
IT'S OPEN-ING!
CREEEEAK
I HOPE... IT KEEPS GOING THIS WELL.
BUT I FEEL LIKE SOME-THING ISN'T RIGHT.
LIKE...

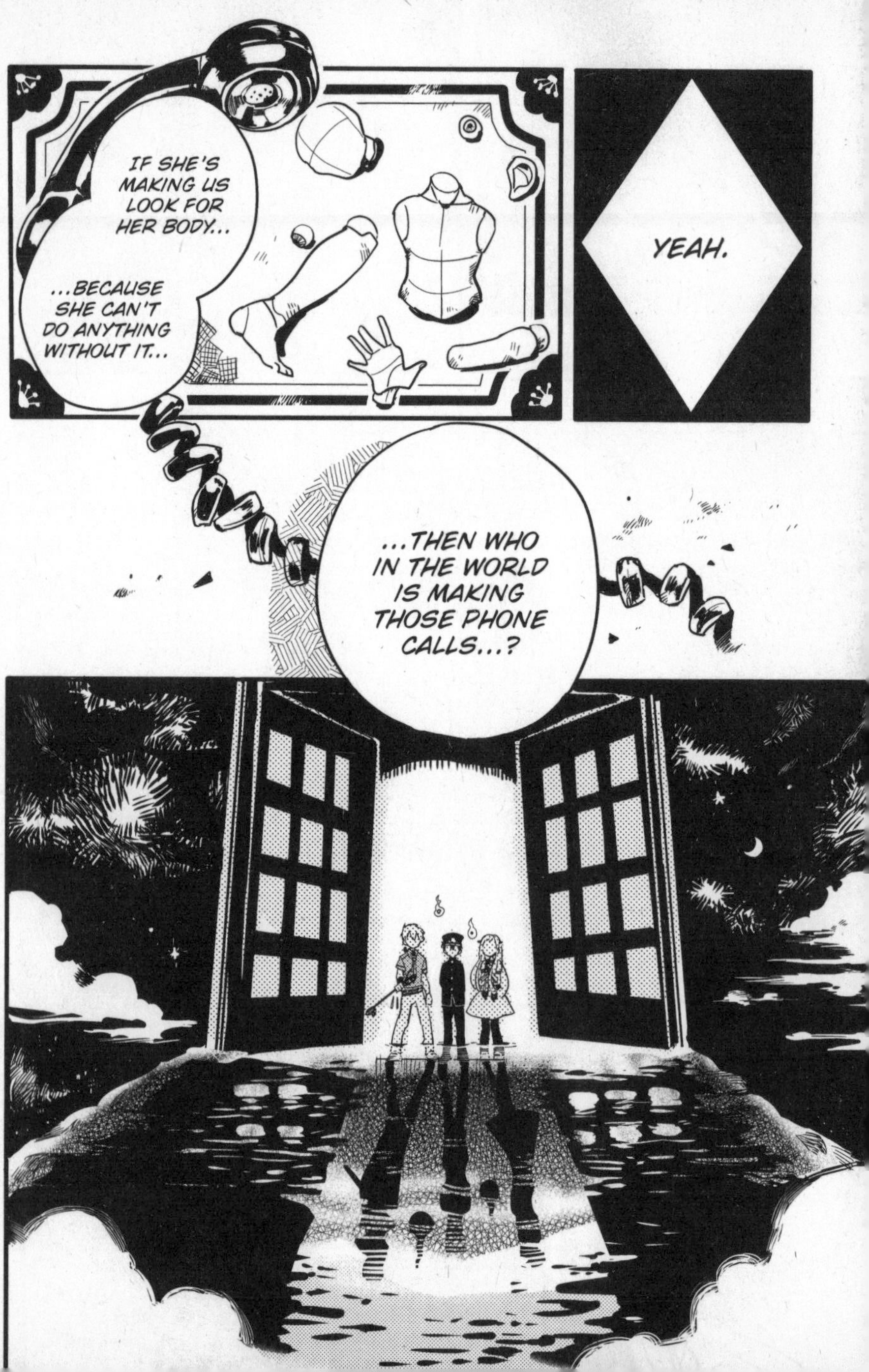
YEAH.
IF SHE'S MAKING US LOOK FOR HER BODY...
...BECAUSE SHE CAN'T DO ANYTHING WITHOUT IT...
...THEN WHO IN THE WORLD IS MAKING THOSE PHONE CALLS...?

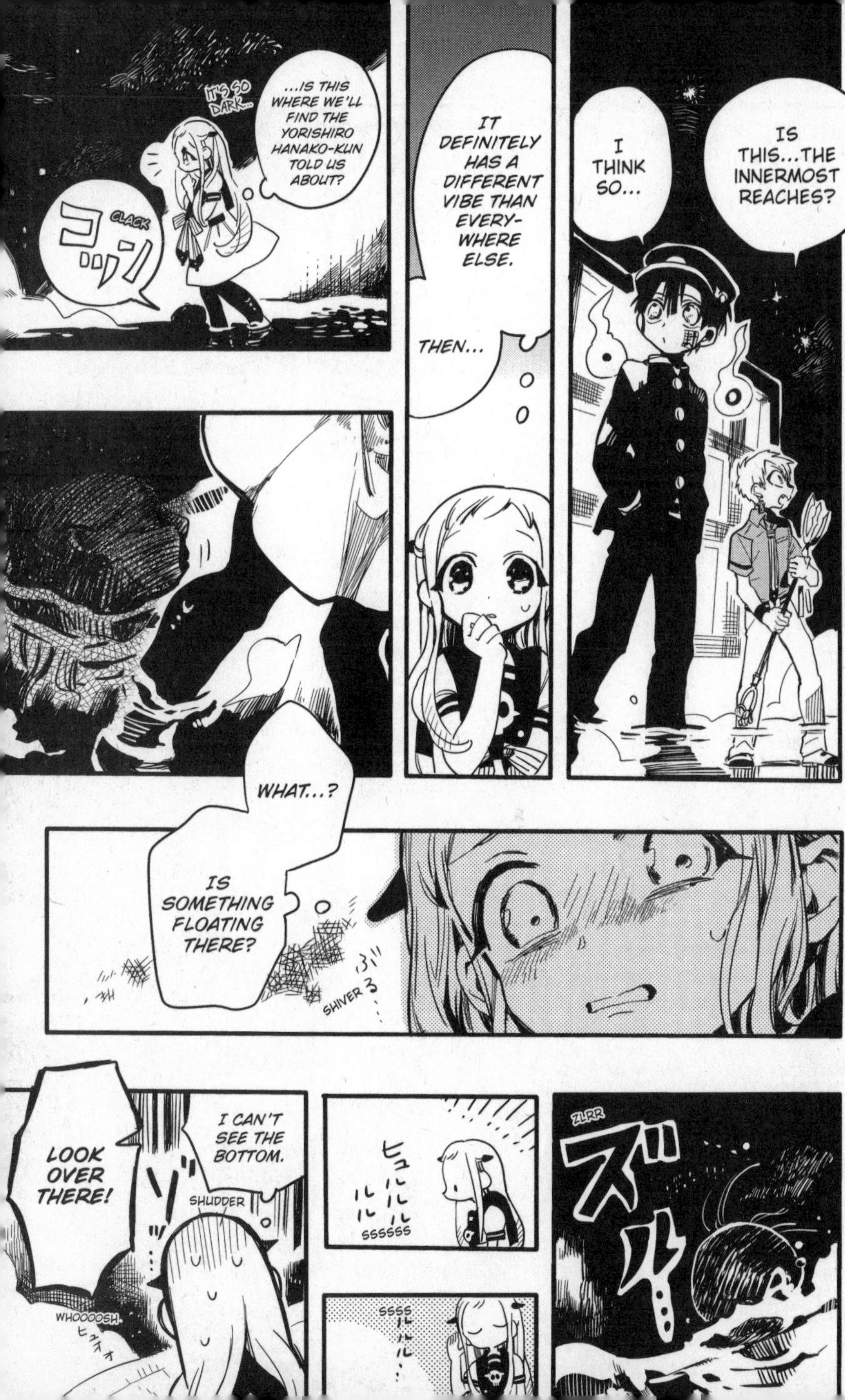
IS THIS...THE INNERMOST REACHES?
I THINK SO...
IT DEFINITELY HAS A DIFFERENT VIBE THAN EVERY-WHERE ELSE.
THEN...
IT'S SO DARK...
...IS THIS WHERE WE'LL FIND THE YORISHIRO HANAKO-KUN TOLD US ABOUT?
CLACK
WHAT...?
IS SOMETHING FLOATING THERE?
SHIVER
ZLRR
ズル
SSSSSS
SSSS
I CAN'T SEE THE BOTTOM.
LOOK OVER THERE!
SHUDDER
WHOOOOSH

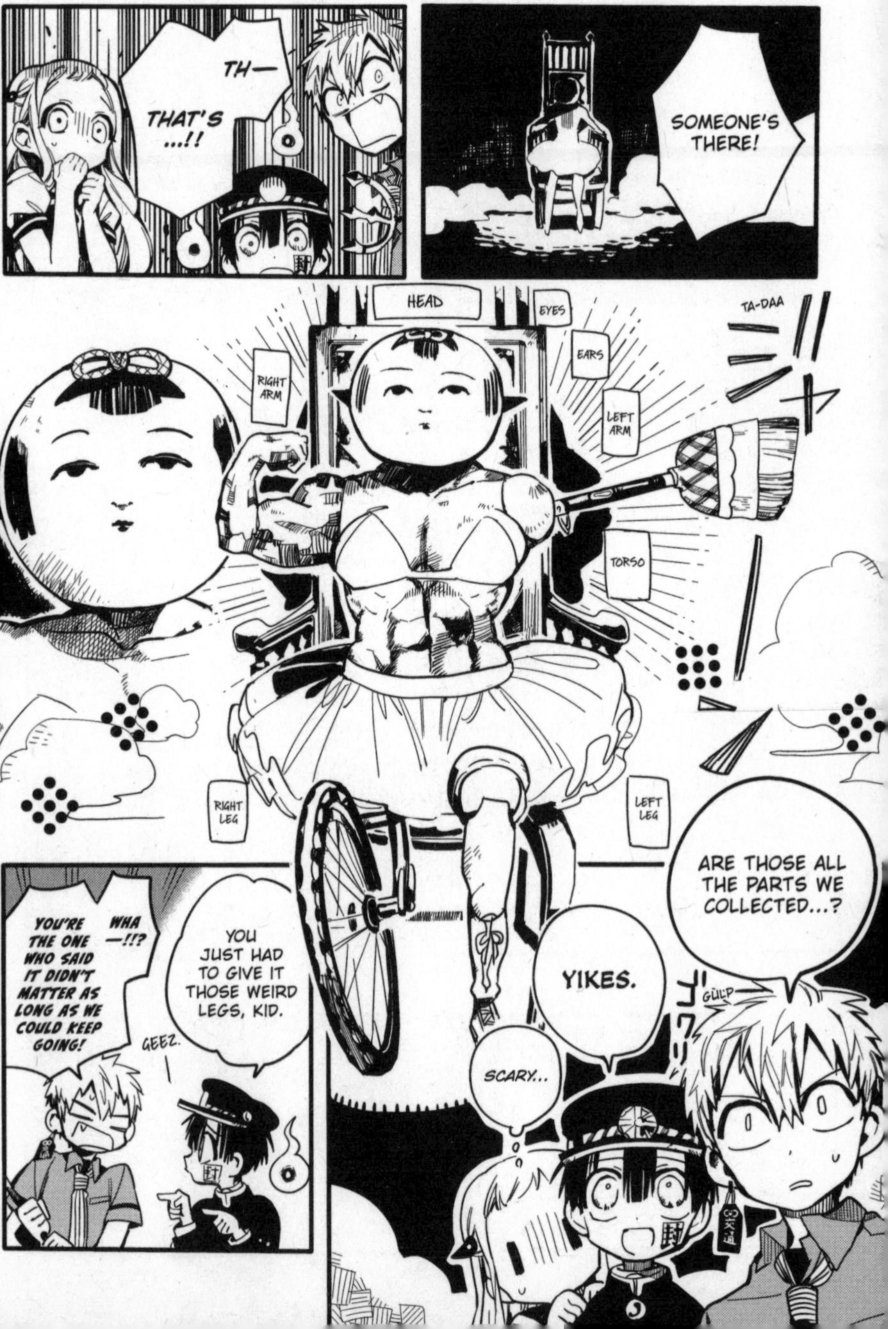
SOMEONE'S THERE!
TH—
THAT'S ...!!
TA-DAA
HEAD
EYES
EARS
RIGHT ARM
LEFT ARM
TORSO
LEFT LEG
RIGHT LEG
ARE THOSE ALL THE PARTS WE COLLECTED...?
GULP
YIKES.
SCARY...
YOU JUST HAD TO GIVE IT THOSE WEIRD LEGS, KID.
WHA—!!?
YOU'RE THE ONE WHO SAID IT DIDN'T MATTER AS LONG AS WE COULD KEEP GOING!
GEEZ.

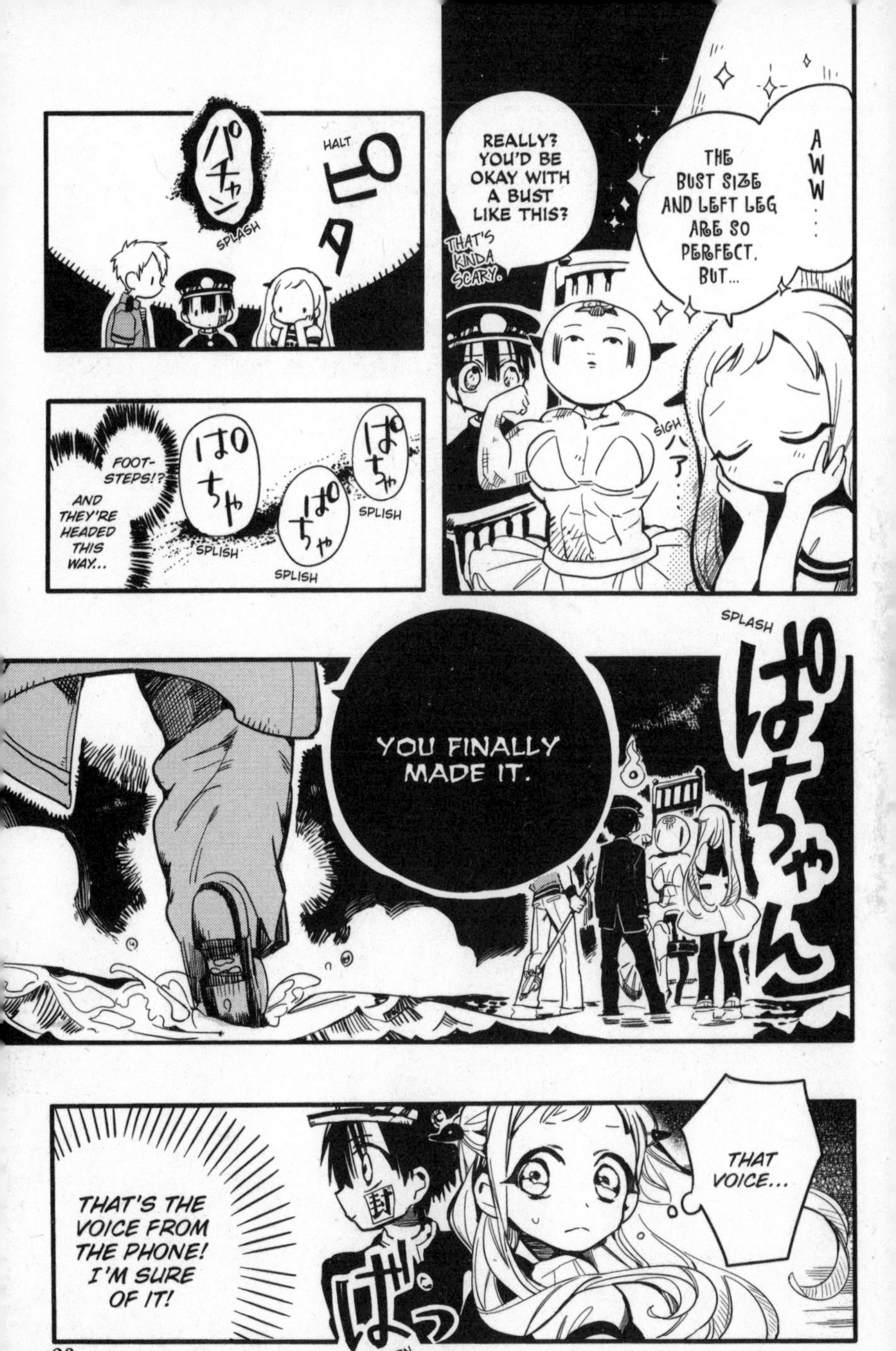
AWW...
THE BUST SIZE AND LEFT LEG ARE SO PERFECT, BUT...
REALLY? YOU'D BE OKAY WITH A BUST LIKE THIS?
THAT'S KINDA SCARY.
ハア
SIGH
ピタ
HALT
パチャン
SPLASH
ぱちゃ
SPLISH
ぱちゃ
SPLISH
ぱちゃ
SPLISH
FOOT-STEPS!?
AND THEY'RE HEADED THIS WAY...
ぱちゃん
SPLASH
YOU FINALLY MADE IT.
THAT VOICE...
ぱっ
TURN
THAT'S THE VOICE FROM THE PHONE! I'M SURE OF IT!

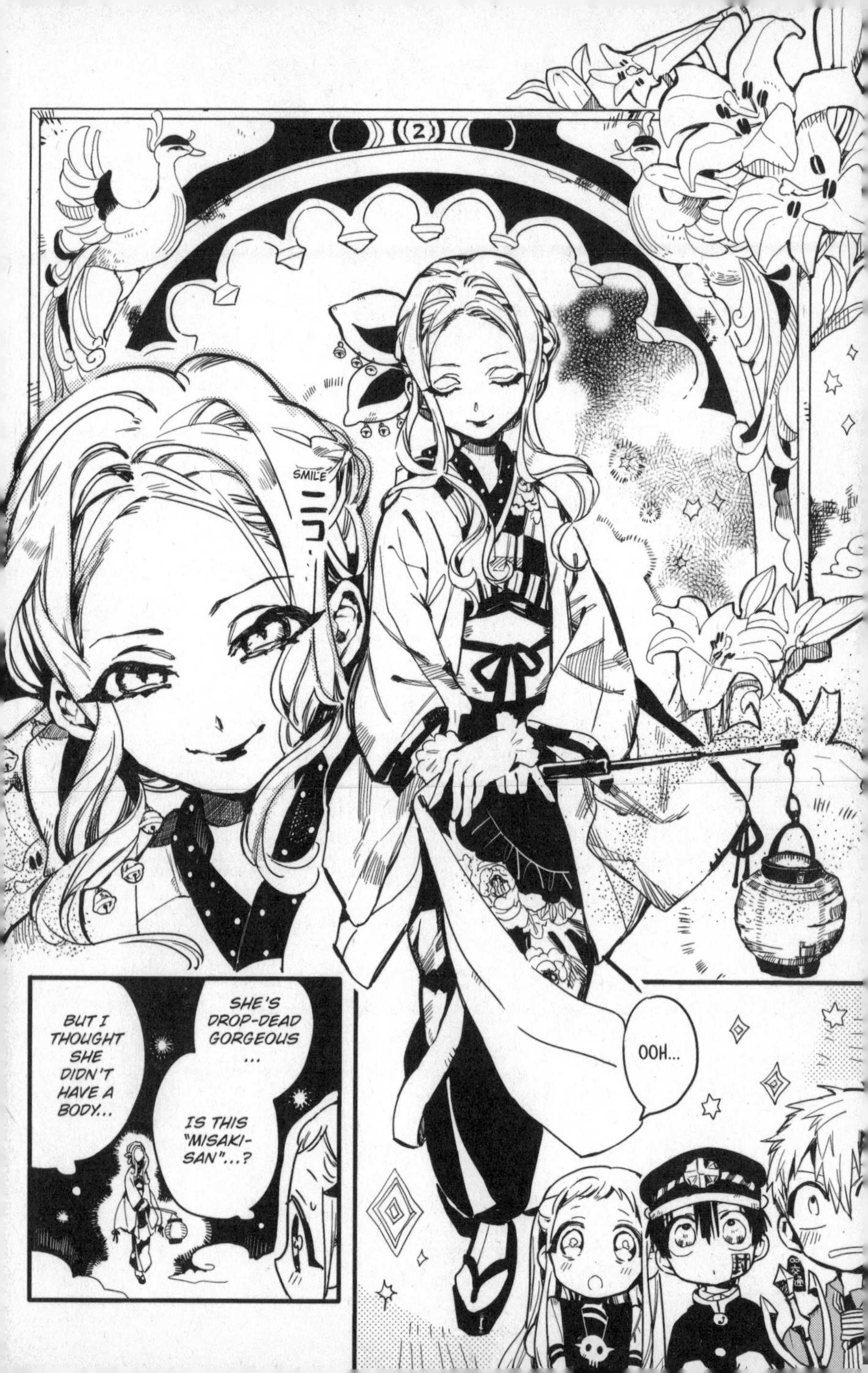
SMILE
ニコ
OOH...
SHE'S DROP-DEAD GORGEOUS...
BUT I THOUGHT SHE DIDN'T HAVE A BODY...
IS THIS "MISAKI-SAN"...?

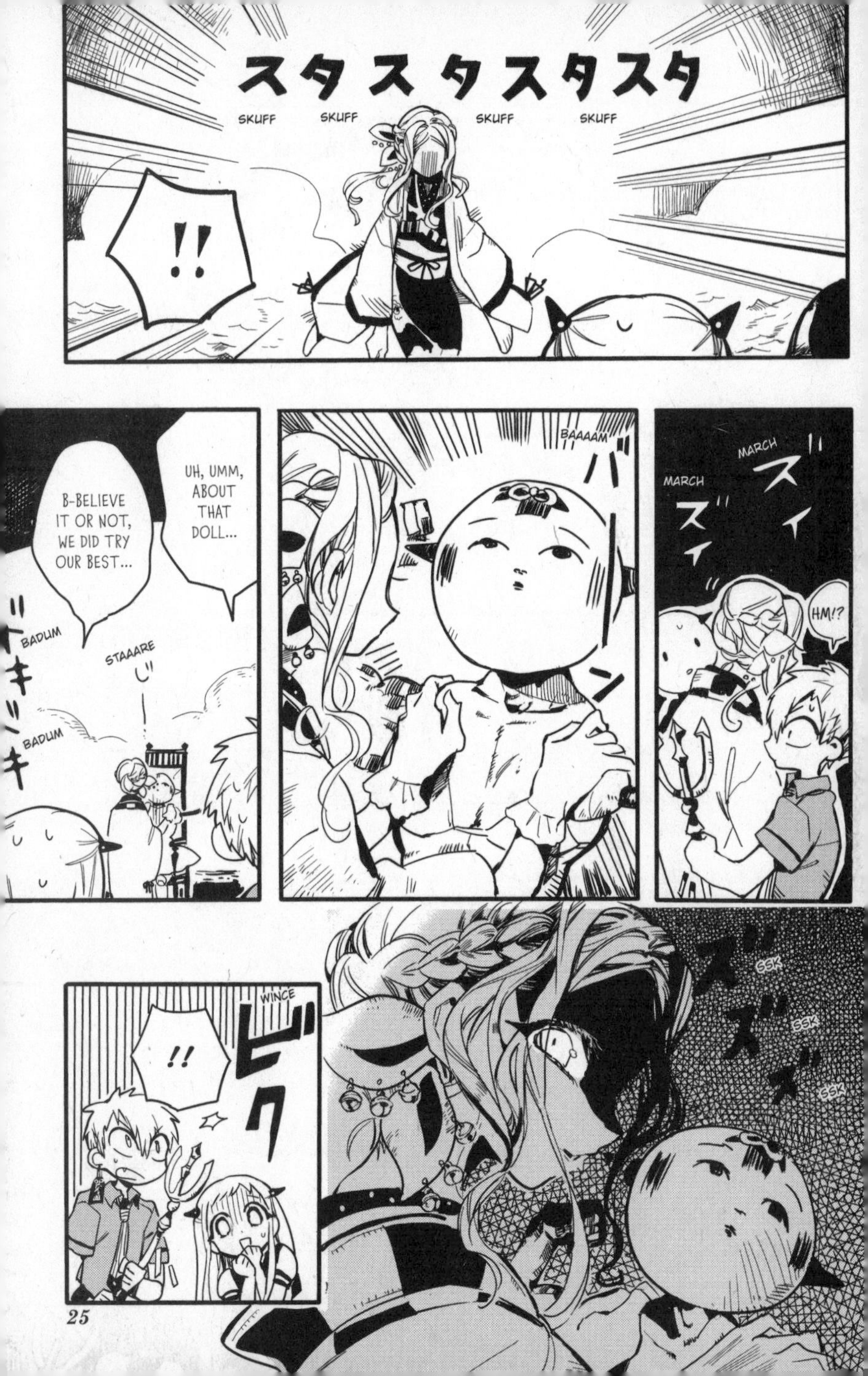
スタスタスタスタ
SKUFF
SKUFF
SKUFF
SKUFF
!!
MARCH
ズイ
MARCH
ズイ
HM!?
BAAAAM
バーン
UH, UMM, ABOUT THAT DOLL...
B-BELIEVE IT OR NOT, WE DID TRY OUR BEST...
ドキドキ
BADUM
BADUM
STAAARE
じー
SSK
SSK
SSK
ズズズ
WINCE
ビク
!!

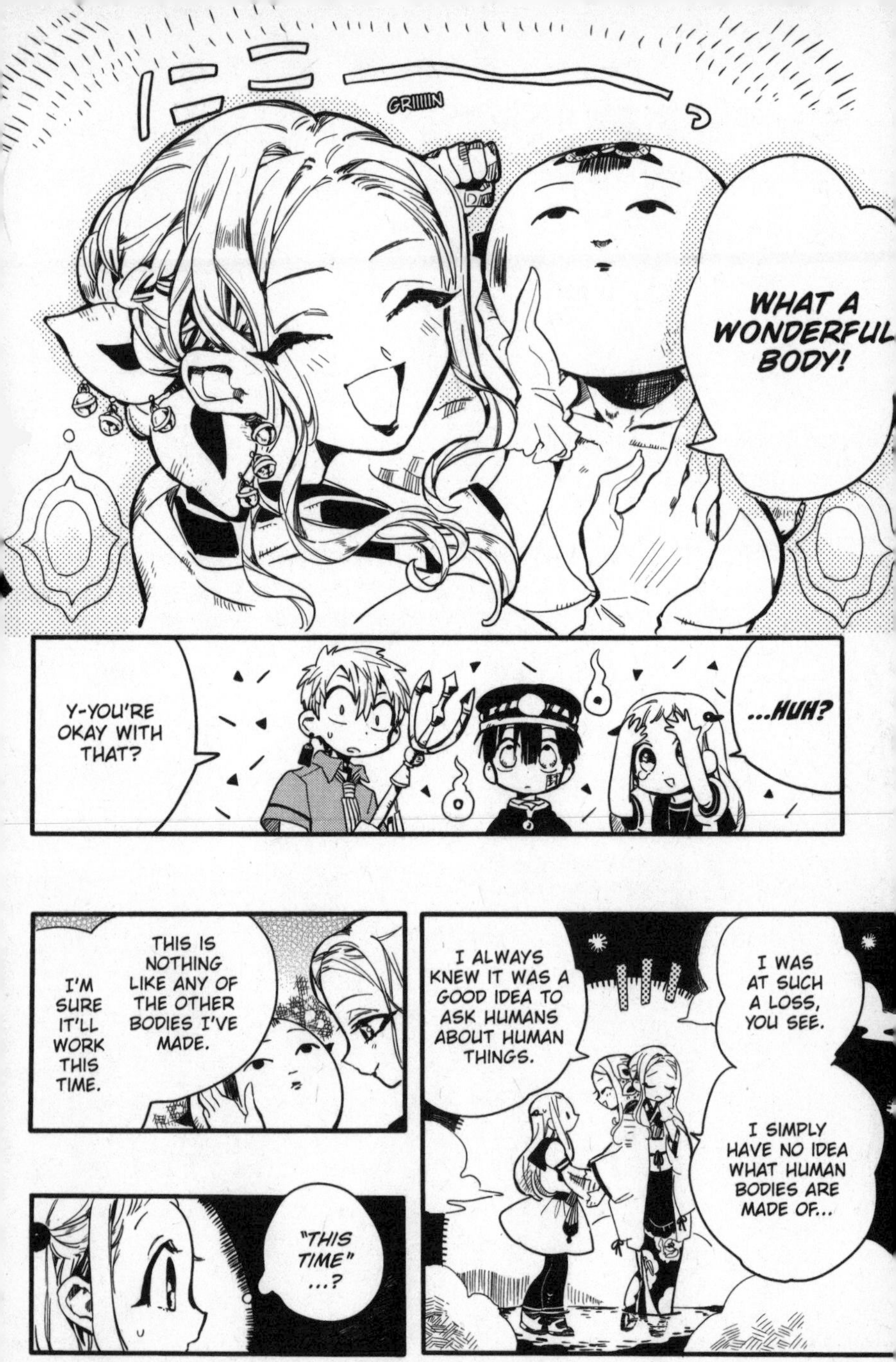
GRIIIIN
WHAT A WONDERFUL BODY!
...HUH?
Y-YOU'RE OKAY WITH THAT?
I WAS AT SUCH A LOSS, YOU SEE.
I SIMPLY HAVE NO IDEA WHAT HUMAN BODIES ARE MADE OF...
I ALWAYS KNEW IT WAS A GOOD IDEA TO ASK HUMANS ABOUT HUMAN THINGS.
THIS IS NOTHING LIKE ANY OF THE OTHER BODIES I'VE MADE.
I'M SURE IT'LL WORK THIS TIME.
"THIS TIME" ...?

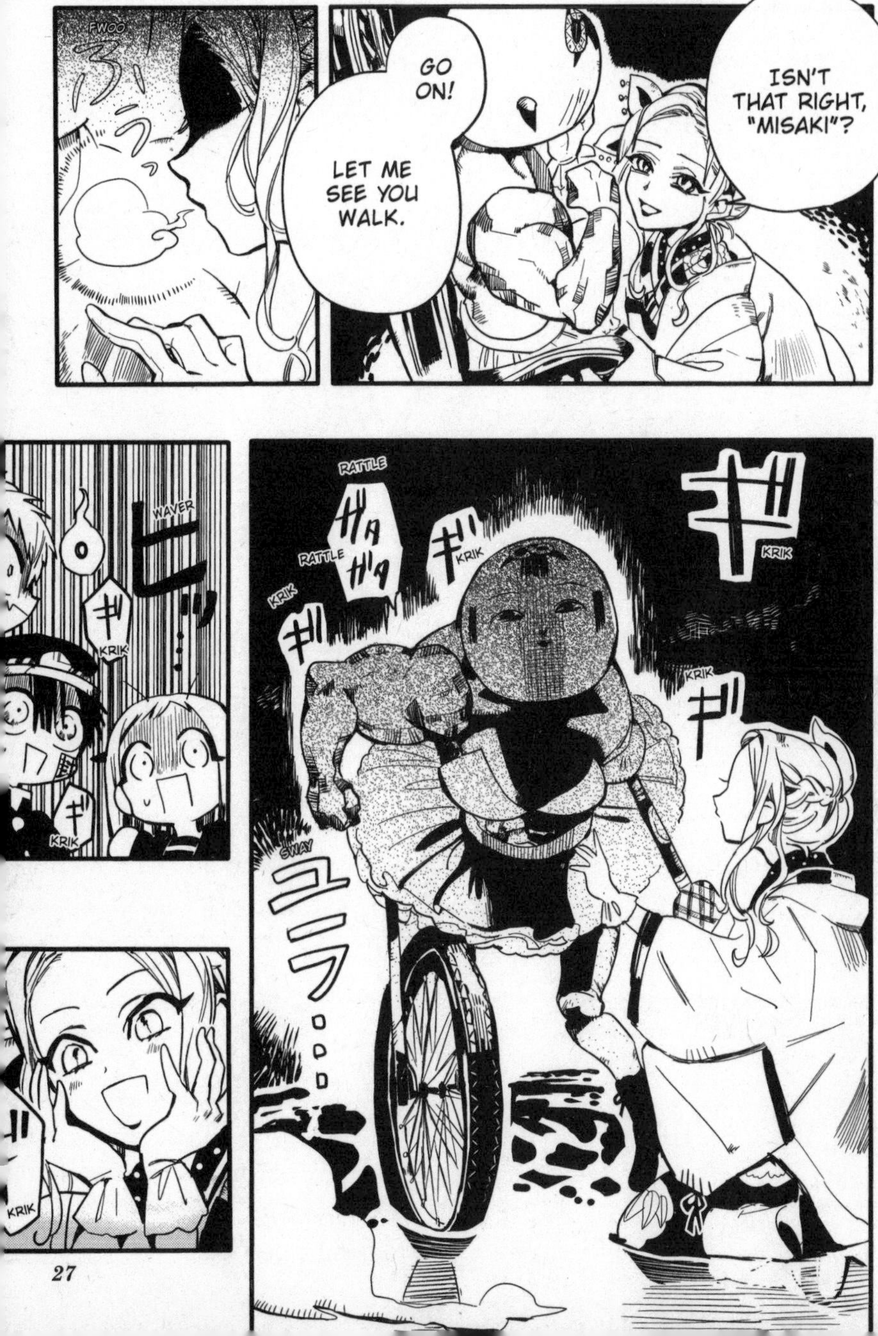

ISN'T THAT RIGHT, "MISAKI"?
GO ON!
LET ME SEE YOU WALK.
FWOO
KRIK
KRIK
KRIK
RATTLE
RATTLE
KRIK
SWAY
WAVER
KRIK
KRIK
KRIK

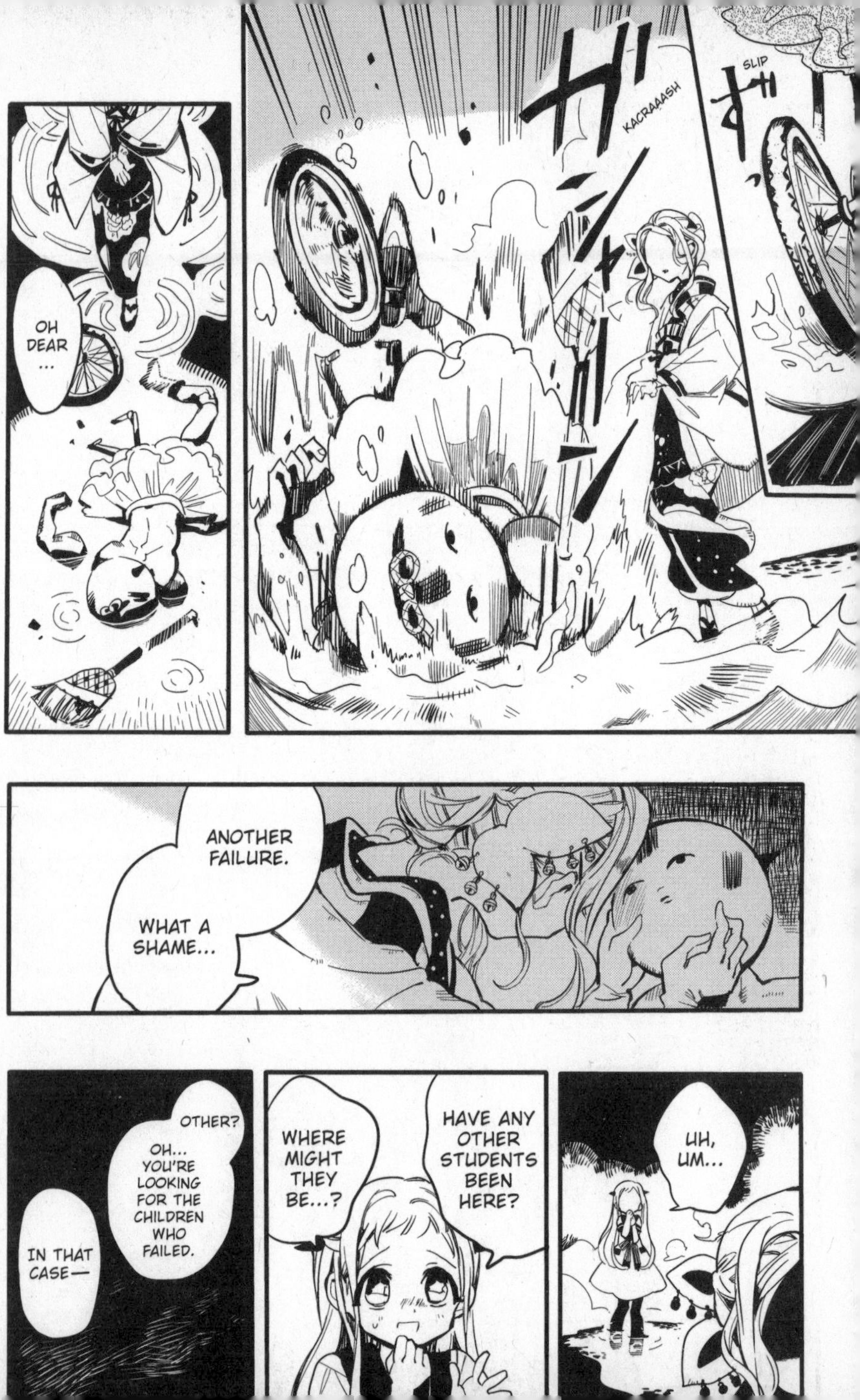
SLIP
KACRAAASH
OH DEAR ...
ANOTHER FAILURE.
WHAT A SHAME...
UH, UM...
HAVE ANY OTHER STUDENTS BEEN HERE?
WHERE MIGHT THEY BE...?
OTHER?
OH... YOU'RE LOOKING FOR THE CHILDREN WHO FAILED.
IN THAT CASE—

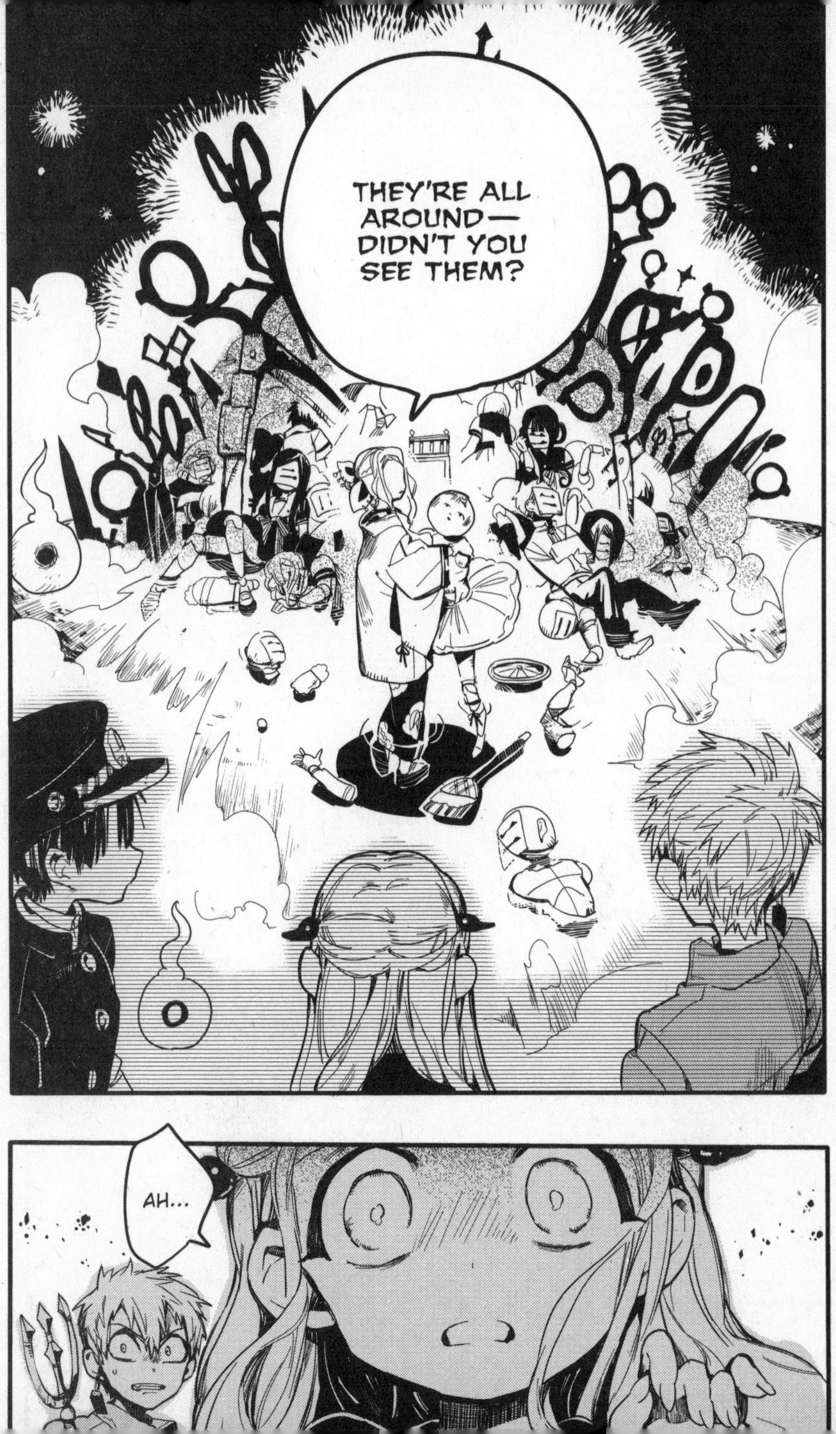
THEY'RE ALL AROUND—DIDN'T YOU SEE THEM?
AH...

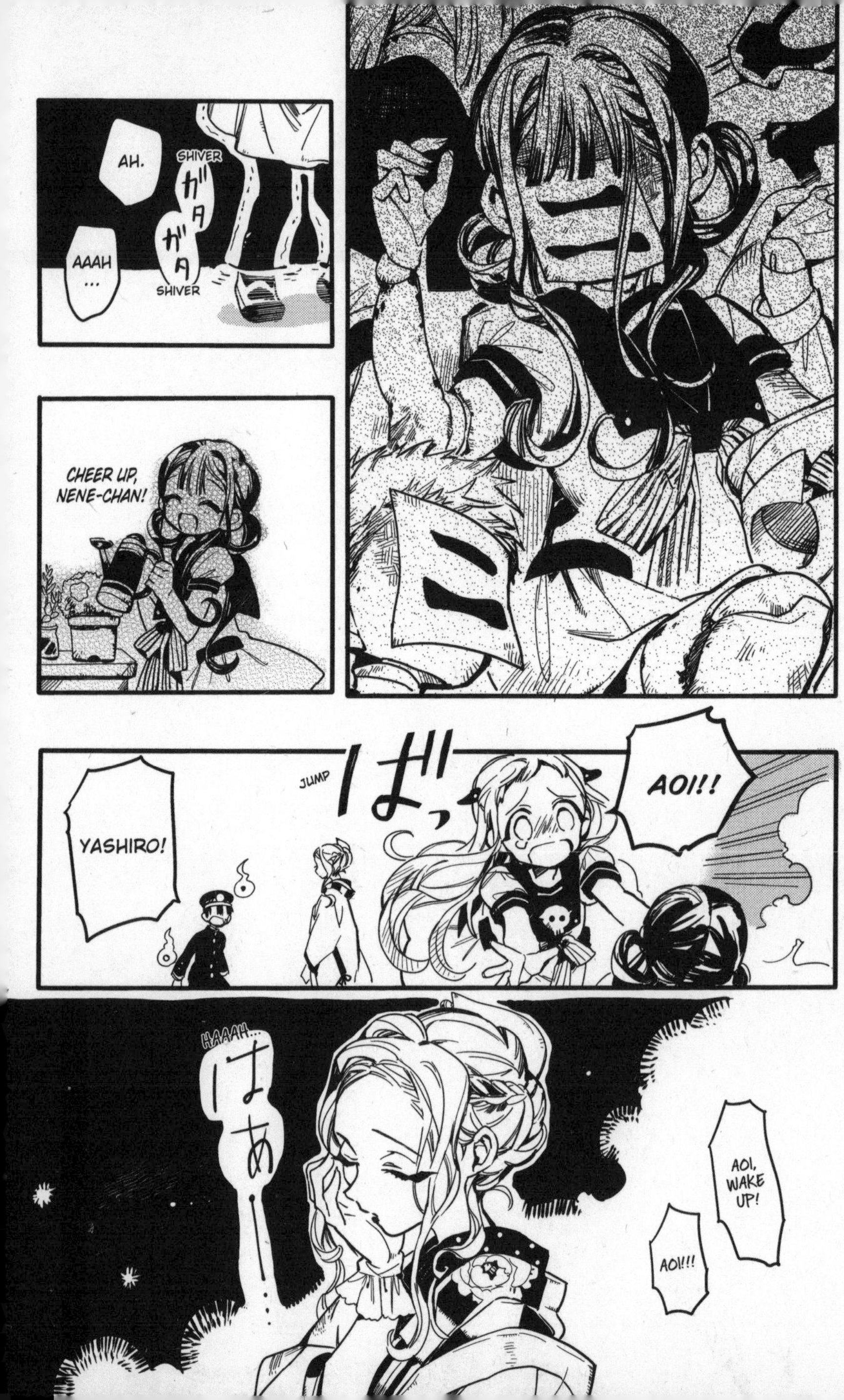
AH.
SHIVER
ガタガタ
SHIVER
AAAH ...
CHEER UP, NENE-CHAN!
AOI!!
JUMP
ぱっ
YASHIRO!
AOI, WAKE UP!
AOI!!!
HAAAH...
はあ…

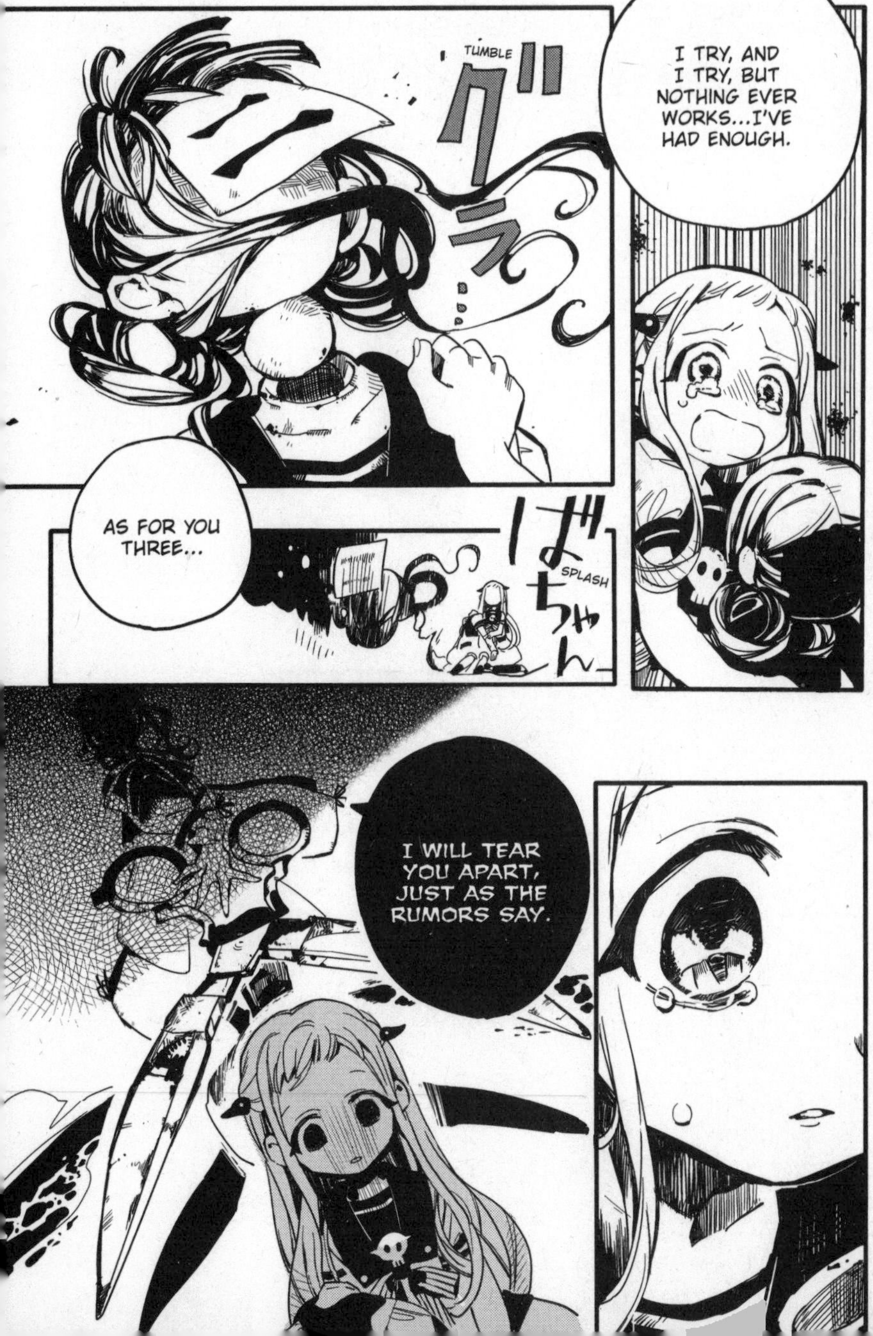
I TRY, AND I TRY, BUT NOTHING EVER WORKS...I'VE HAD ENOUGH.
グラ
TUMBLE
AS FOR YOU THREE...
ばちゃん
SPLASH
I WILL TEAR YOU APART, JUST AS THE RUMORS SAY.

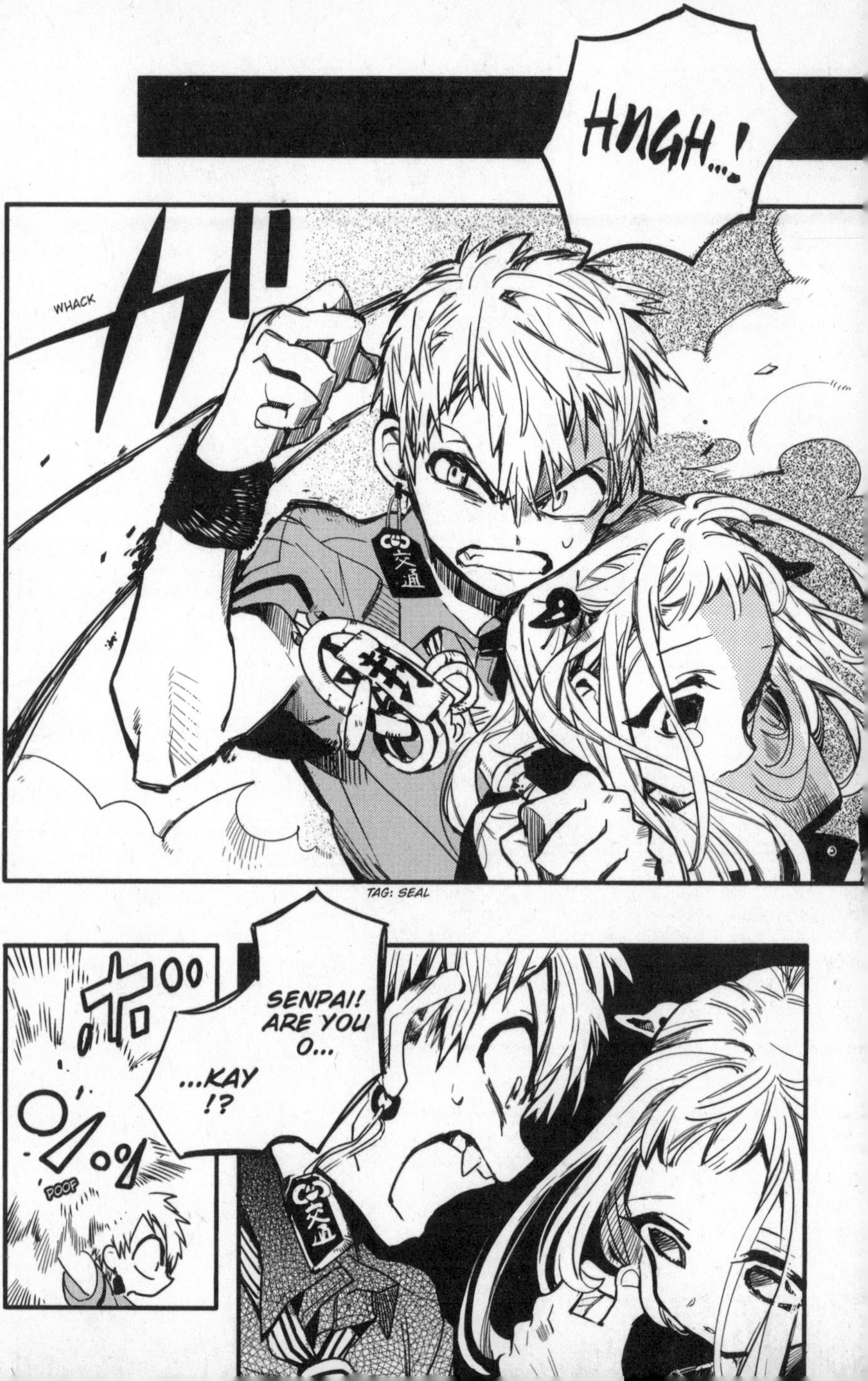
HNGH...!
WHACK
TAG: SEAL
SENPAI! ARE YOU O...
...KAY!?
POOP

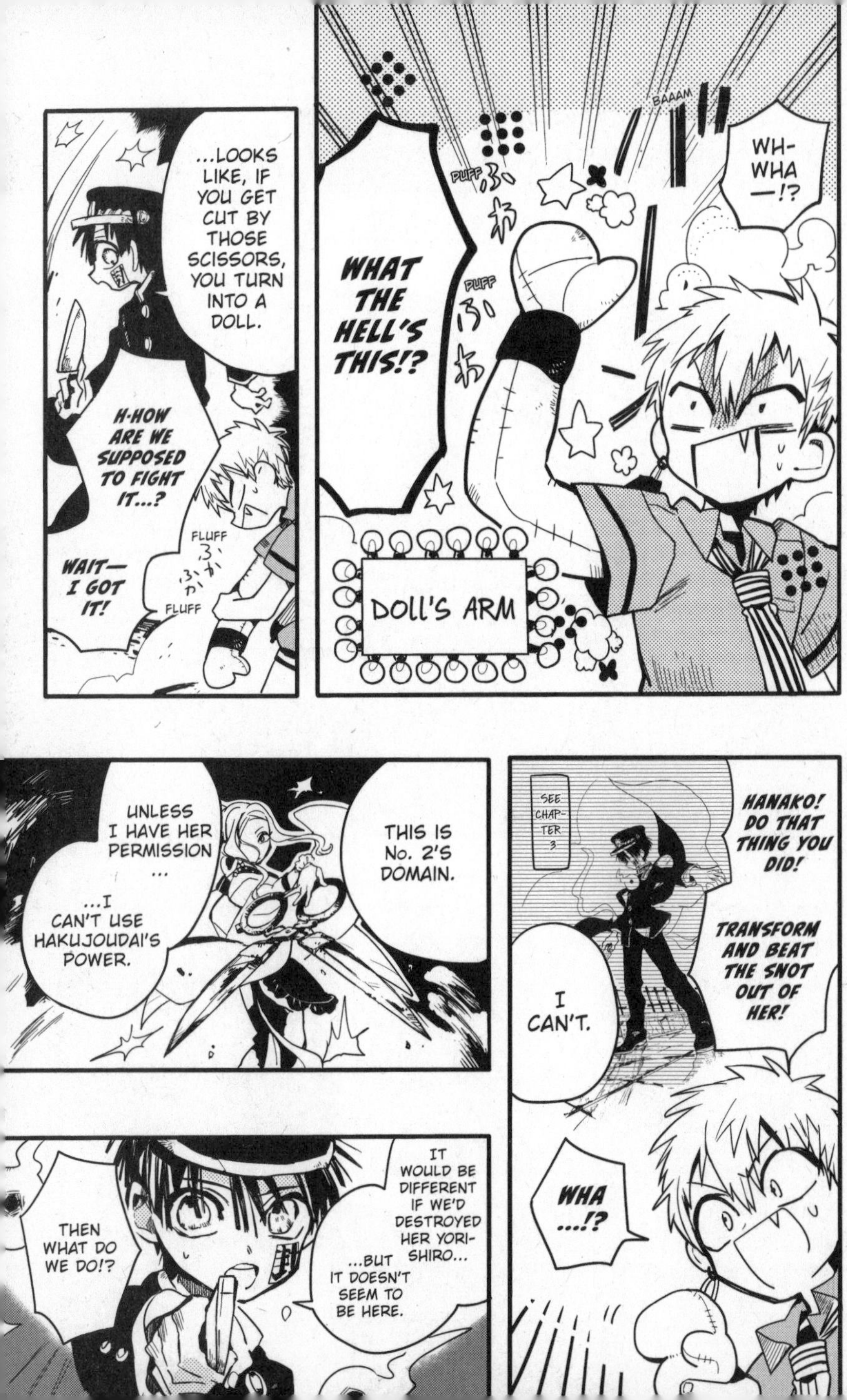
BAAAM
WH-WHA—!?
PUFF ふわ
WHAT THE HELL'S THIS!?
PUFF ふわ
DOLL'S ARM
...LOOKS LIKE, IF YOU GET CUT BY THOSE SCISSORS, YOU TURN INTO A DOLL.
H-HOW ARE WE SUPPOSED TO FIGHT IT...?
FLUFF ふか ふか FLUFF
WAIT— I GOT IT!
HANAKO! DO THAT THING YOU DID!
TRANSFORM AND BEAT THE SNOT OUT OF HER!
SEE CHAPTER 3
I CAN'T.
WHA ...!?
THIS IS No. 2'S DOMAIN.
UNLESS I HAVE HER PERMISSION ...
...I CAN'T USE HAKUJOUDAI'S POWER.
IT WOULD BE DIFFERENT IF WE'D DESTROYED HER YORI-SHIRO...
...BUT IT DOESN'T SEEM TO BE HERE.
THEN WHAT DO WE DO!?

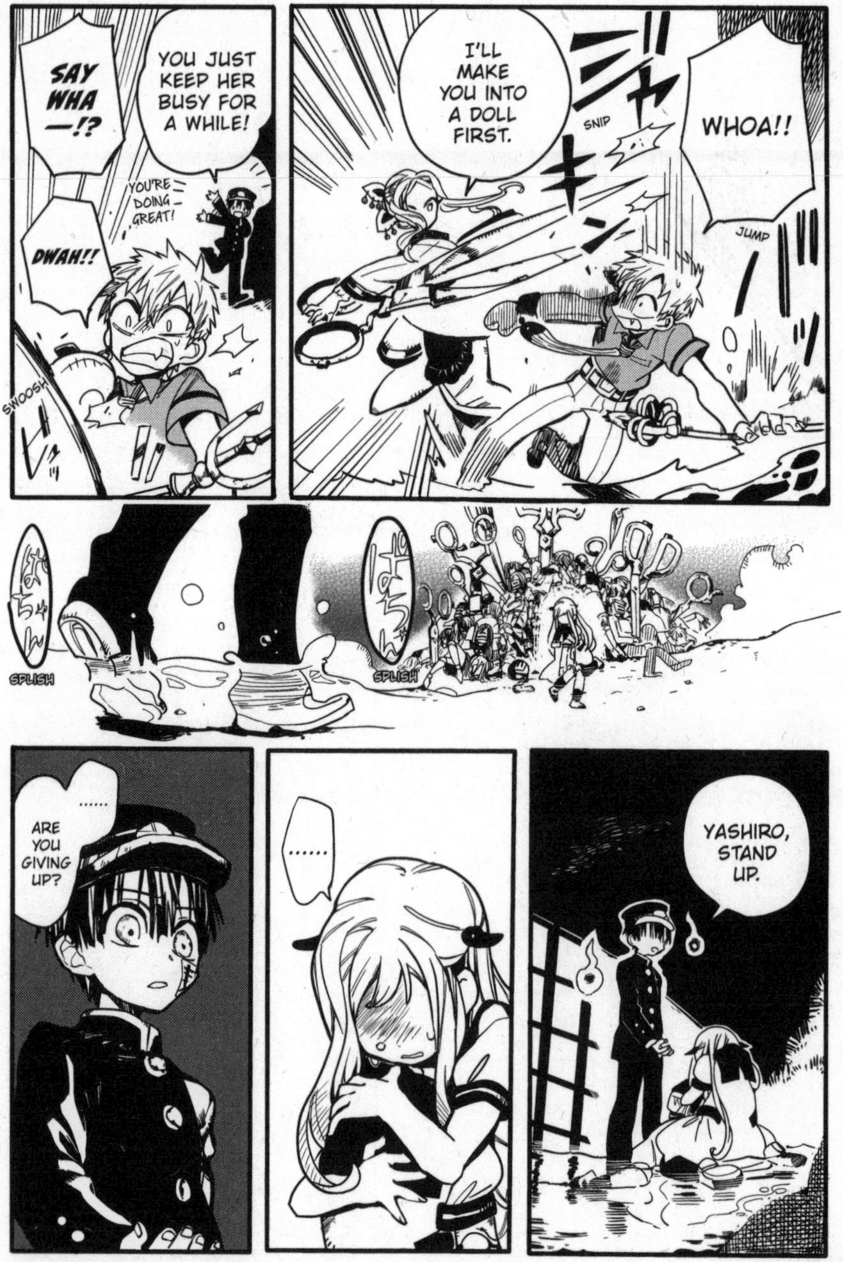
WHOA!!
I'LL MAKE YOU INTO A DOLL FIRST.
SNIP
JUMP
YOU JUST KEEP HER BUSY FOR A WHILE!
SAY WHA—!?
YOU'RE DOING GREAT!
DWAH!!
SWOOSH
SPLISH
SPLISH
YASHIRO, STAND UP.
....
......
ARE YOU GIVING UP?

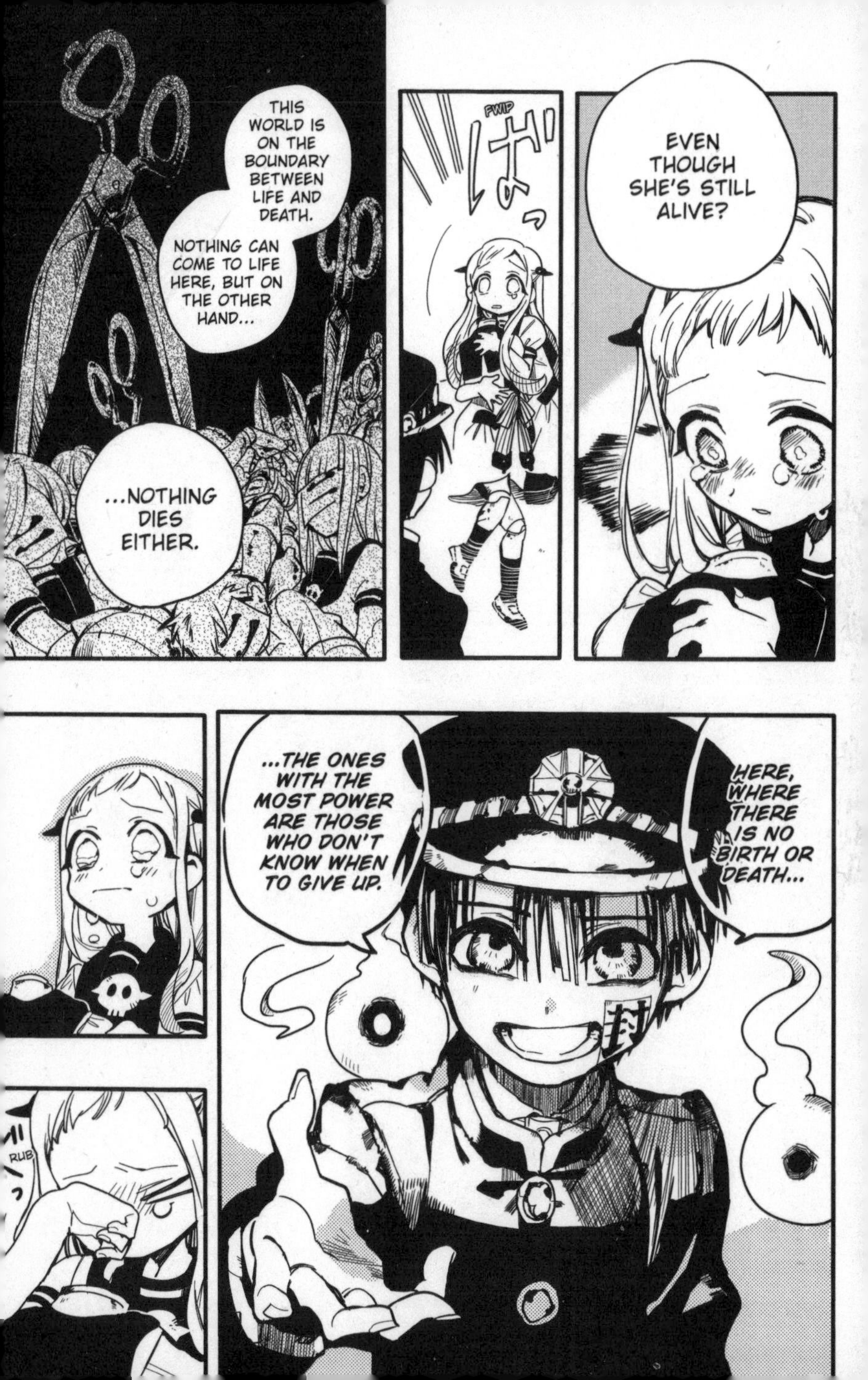
EVEN THOUGH SHE'S STILL ALIVE?
FWIP
THIS WORLD IS ON THE BOUNDARY BETWEEN LIFE AND DEATH.
NOTHING CAN COME TO LIFE HERE, BUT ON THE OTHER HAND...
...NOTHING DIES EITHER.
HERE, WHERE THERE IS NO BIRTH OR DEATH...
...THE ONES WITH THE MOST POWER ARE THOSE WHO DON'T KNOW WHEN TO GIVE UP.
RUB

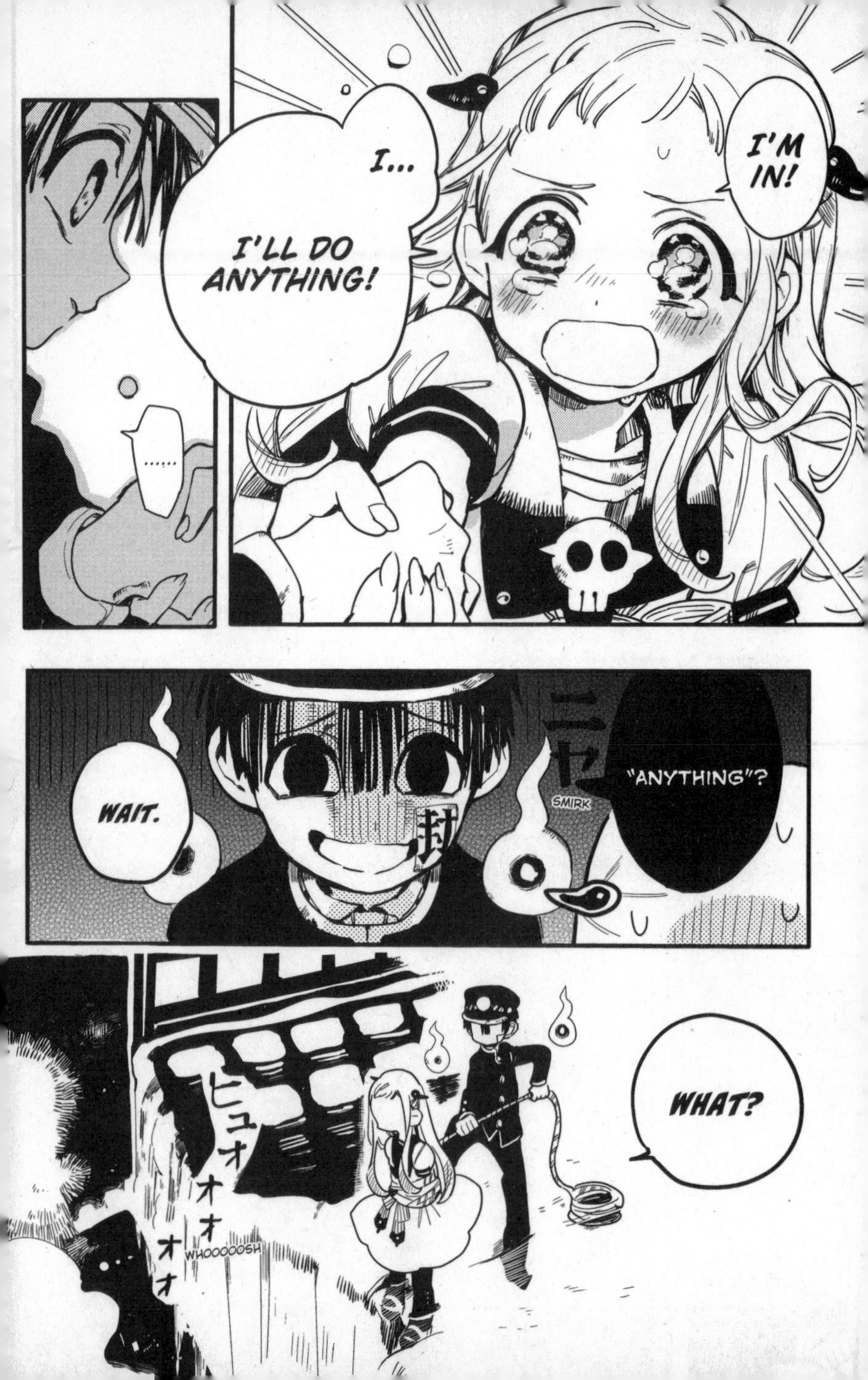

I'M IN!
I...
I'LL DO ANYTHING!
......
ニヤ
SMIRK
"ANYTHING"?
WAIT.
WHAT?
ヒュオオオオオ
WHOOOOOSH

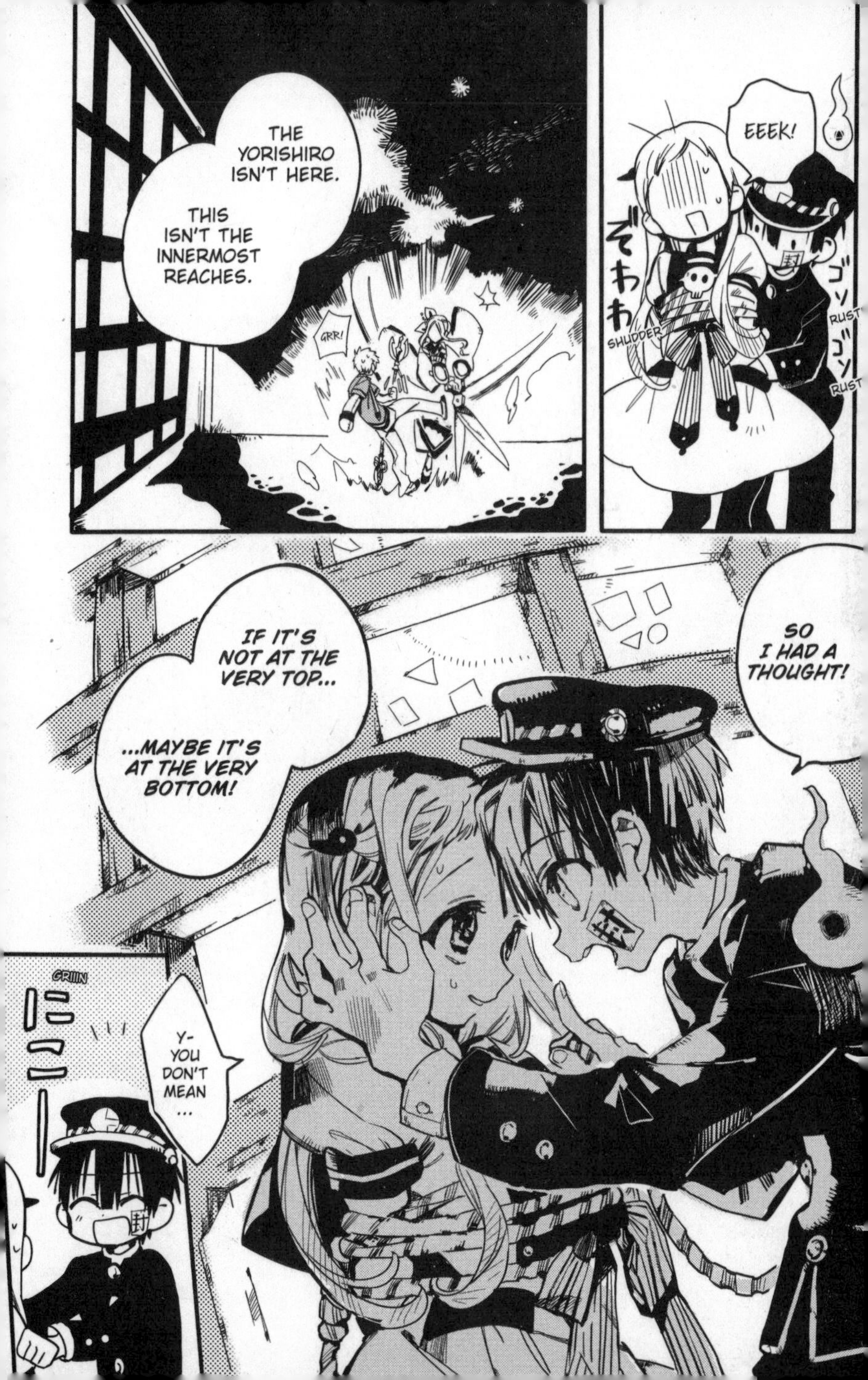
EEEK!
ざわわ
SHUDDER
ゴソゴソ
RUST
RUST
THE YORISHIRO ISN'T HERE.
THIS ISN'T THE INNERMOST REACHES.
GRR!
SO I HAD A THOUGHT!
IF IT'S NOT AT THE VERY TOP...
...MAYBE IT'S AT THE VERY BOTTOM!
GRIIN
Y-YOU DON'T MEAN ...

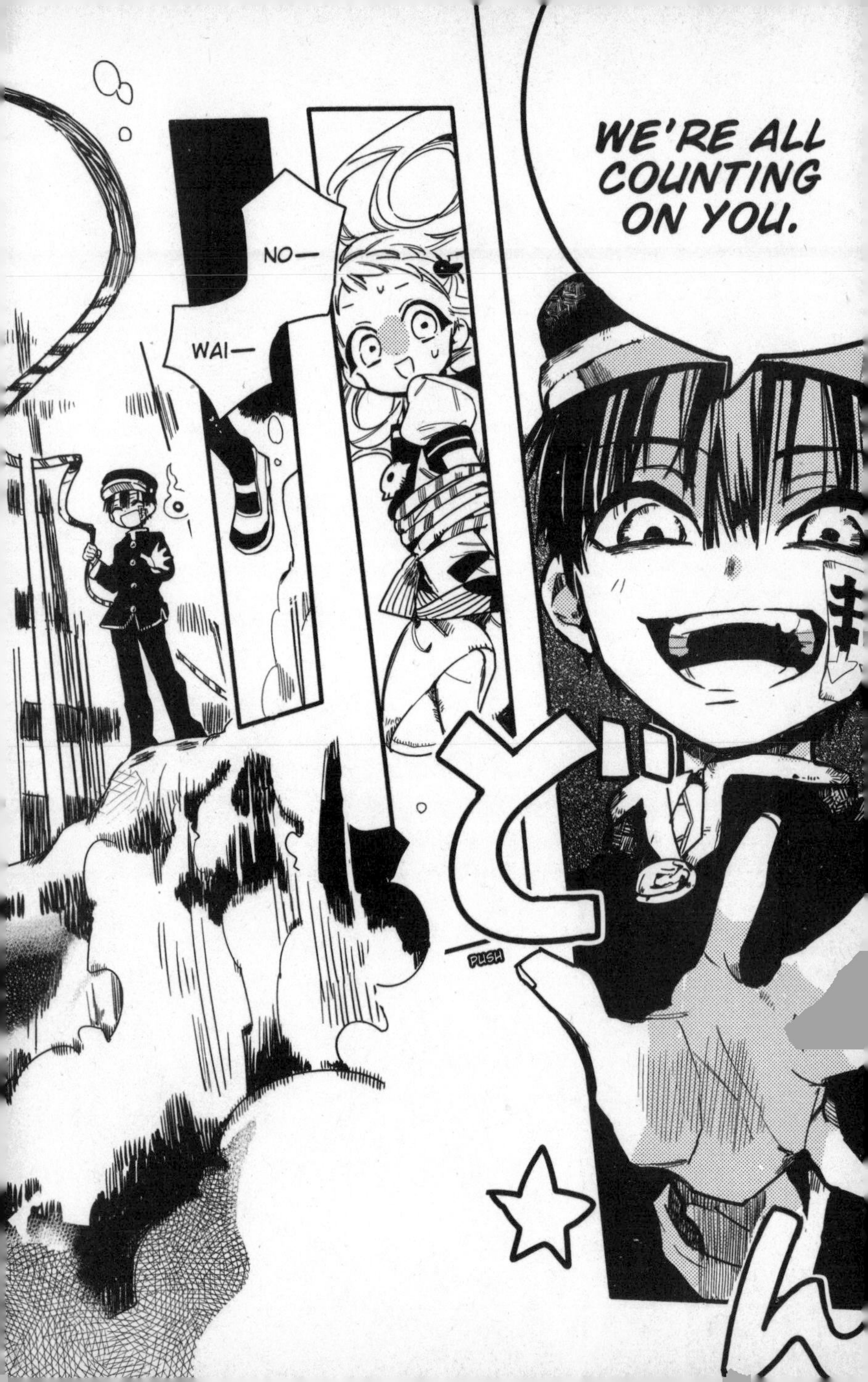
WE'RE ALL COUNTING ON YOU.
NO—
WAI—
PUSH

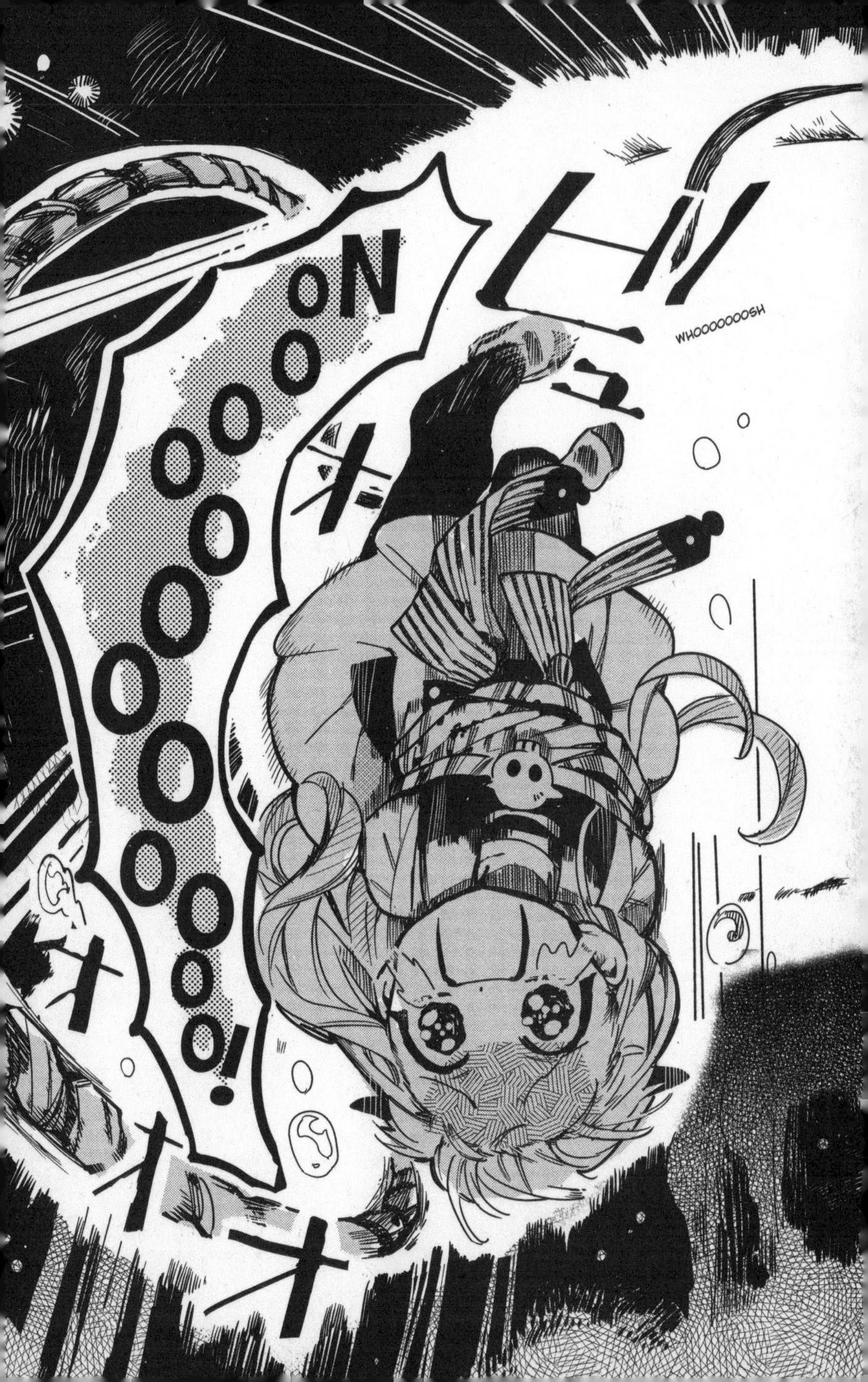
NOOOOOOOOOOOOOO!
WHOOOOOOOSH

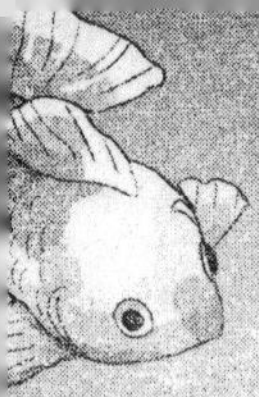

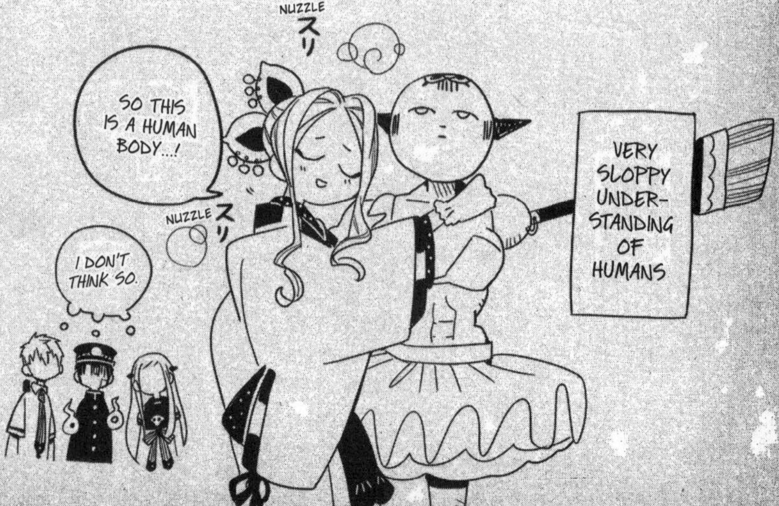
VERY SLOPPY UNDER-STANDING OF HUMANS
NUZZLE スリ
SO THIS IS A HUMAN BODY...!
NUZZLE スリ
I DON'T THINK SO.

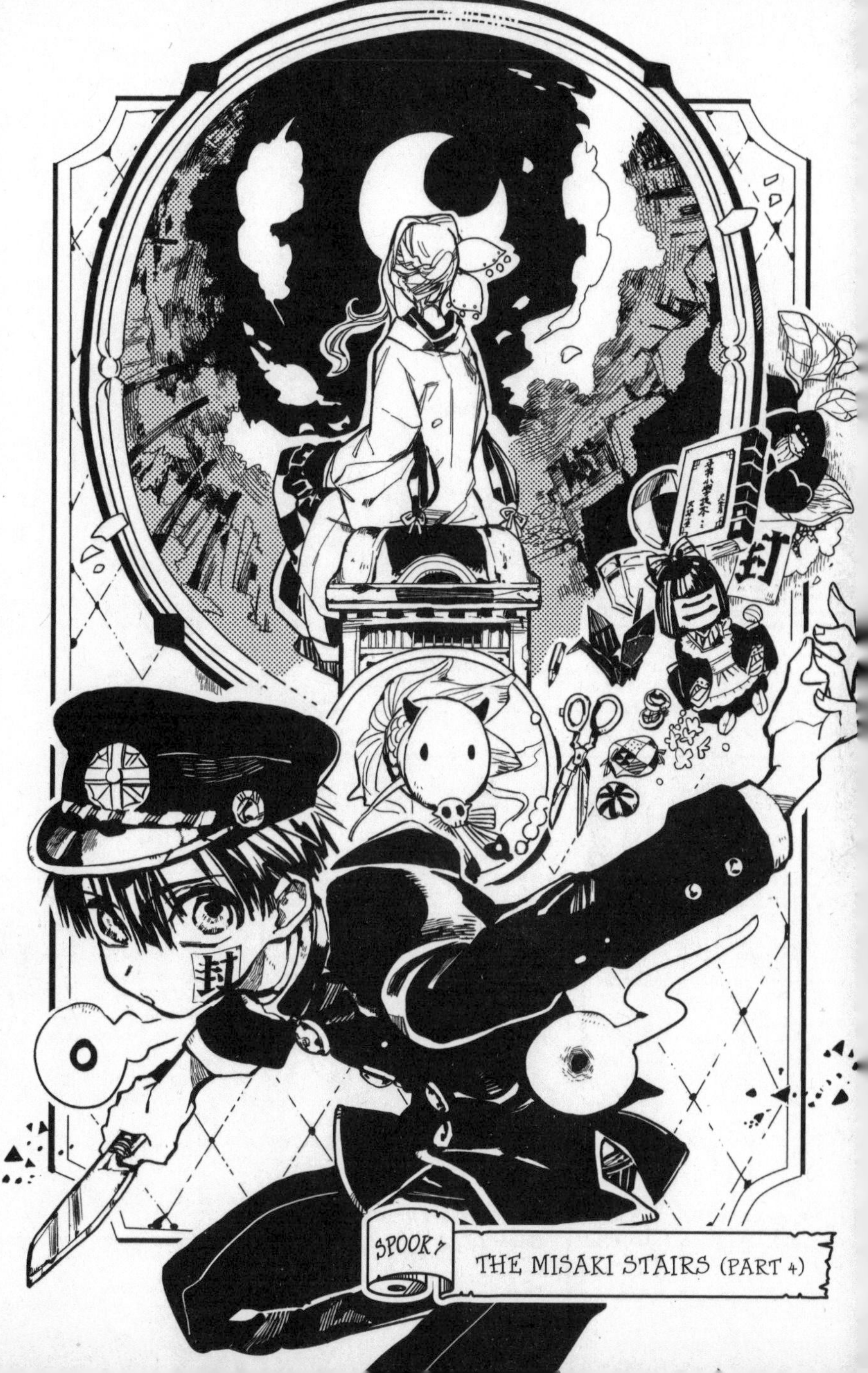
SPOOK 7
THE MISAKI STAIRS (PART 4)

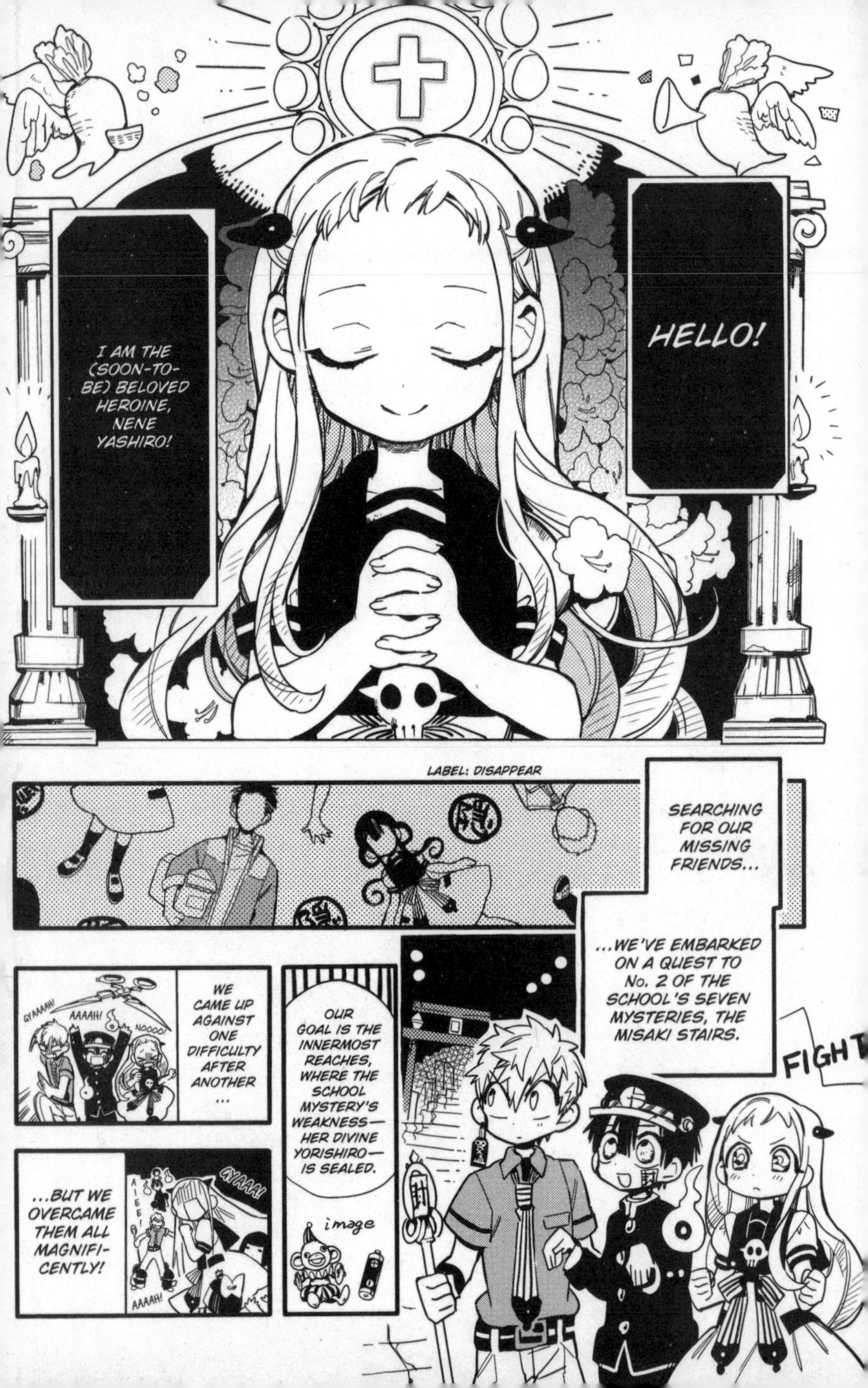
HELLO!
I AM THE (SOON-TO-BE) BELOVED HEROINE, NENE YASHIRO!
SEARCHING FOR OUR MISSING FRIENDS...
LABEL: DISAPPEAR
...WE'VE EMBARKED ON A QUEST TO No. 2 OF THE SCHOOL'S SEVEN MYSTERIES, THE MISAKI STAIRS.
FIGHT
OUR GOAL IS THE INNERMOST REACHES, WHERE THE SCHOOL MYSTERY'S WEAKNESS—HER DIVINE YORISHIRO—IS SEALED.
image
WE CAME UP AGAINST ONE DIFFICULTY AFTER ANOTHER...
NOOOO!
AAAAH!
GYAAAH!
GYAAA!
AIEEE!
AAAAH!
...BUT WE OVERCAME THEM ALL MAGNIFICENTLY!

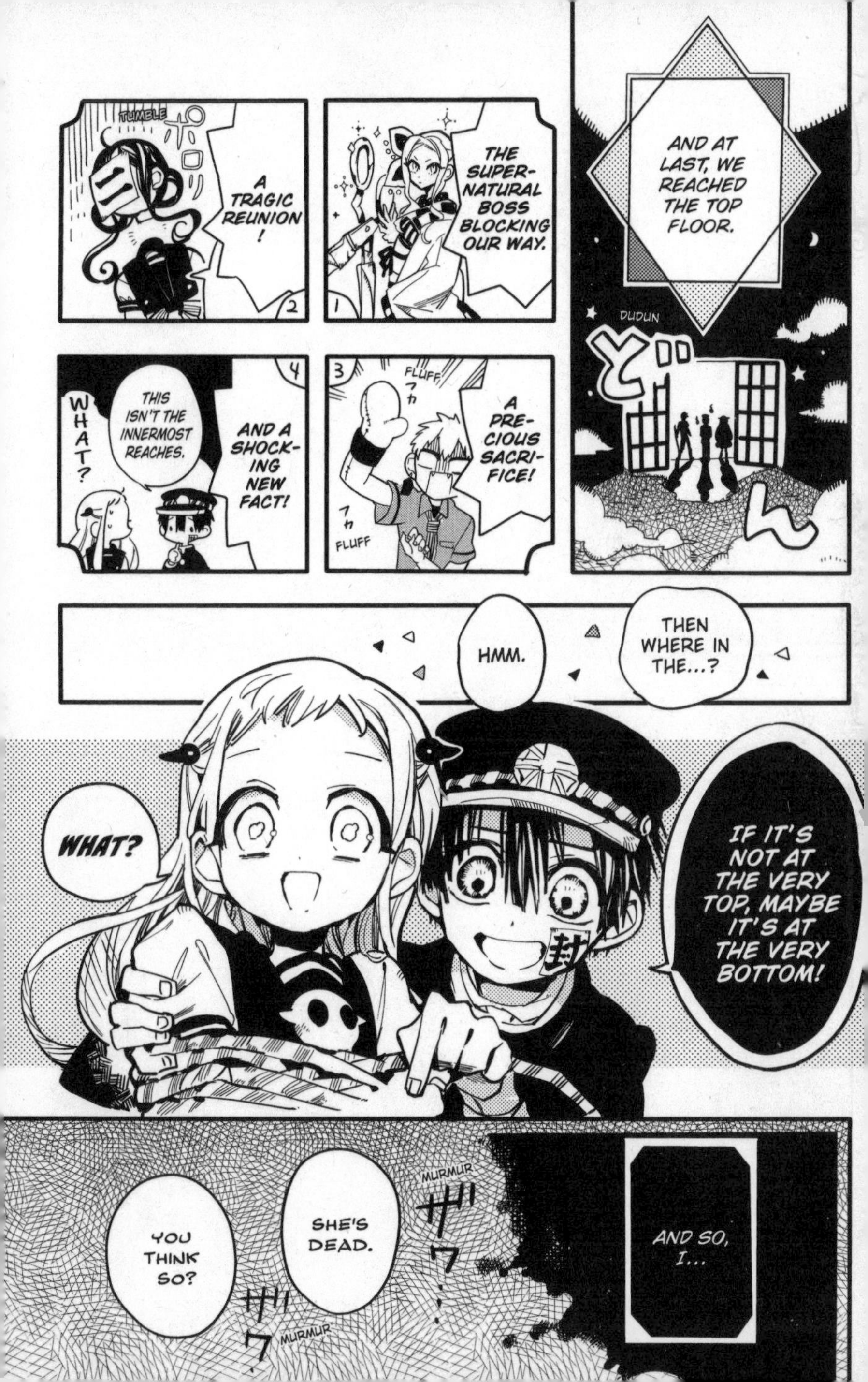
AND AT LAST, WE REACHED THE TOP FLOOR.
DUDUN
THE SUPER-NATURAL BOSS BLOCKING OUR WAY.
TUMBLE
A TRAGIC REUNION!
FLUFF
A PRECIOUS SACRIFICE!
FLUFF
AND A SHOCKING NEW FACT!
THIS ISN'T THE INNERMOST REACHES.
WHAT?
THEN WHERE IN THE...?
HMM.
IF IT'S NOT AT THE VERY TOP, MAYBE IT'S AT THE VERY BOTTOM!
WHAT?
AND SO, I...
MURMUR
SHE'S DEAD.
YOU THINK SO?
MURMUR

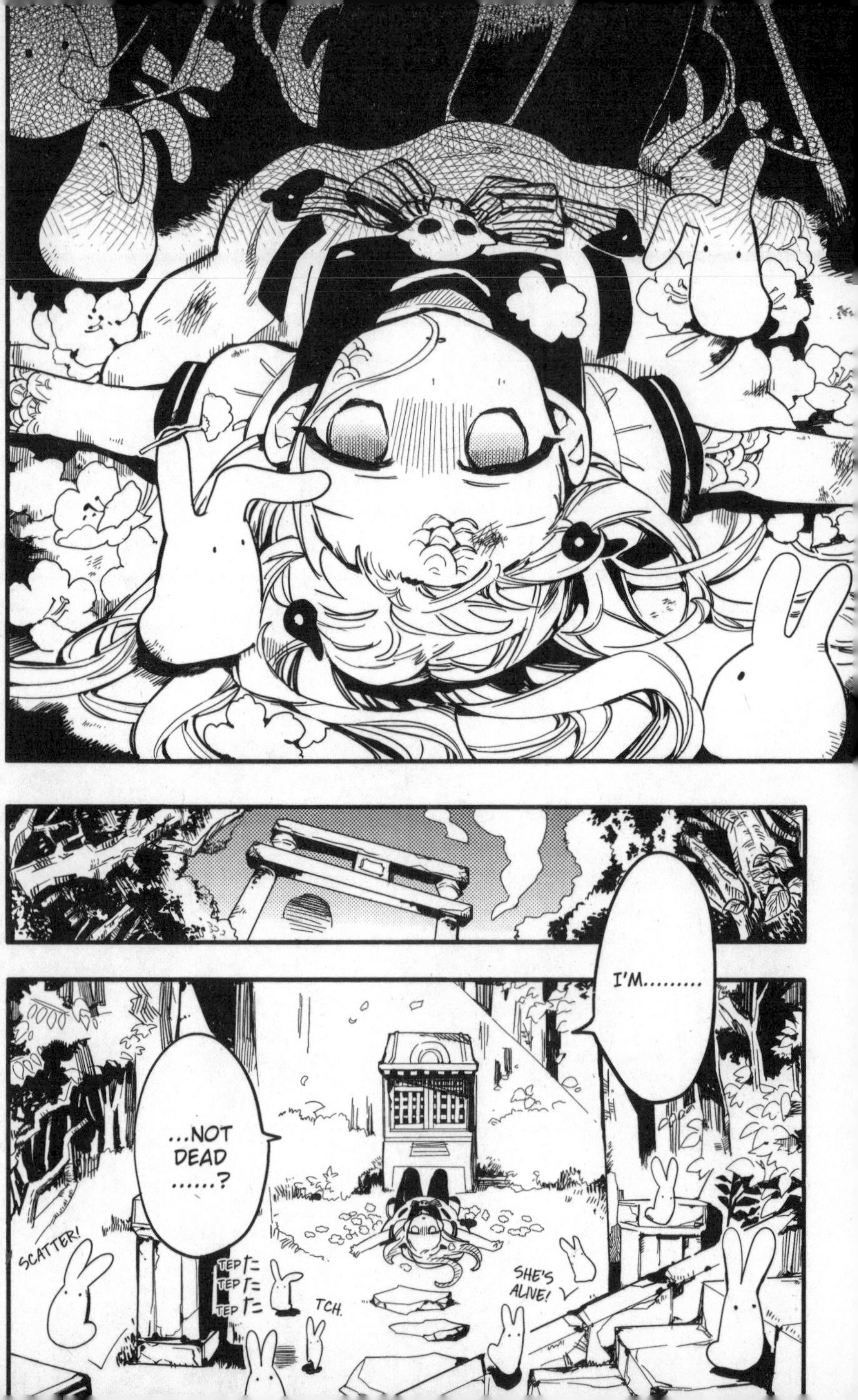
I'M.........
...NOT DEAD ......?
SHE'S ALIVE!
TCH.
TEP
TEP
TEP
SCATTER!

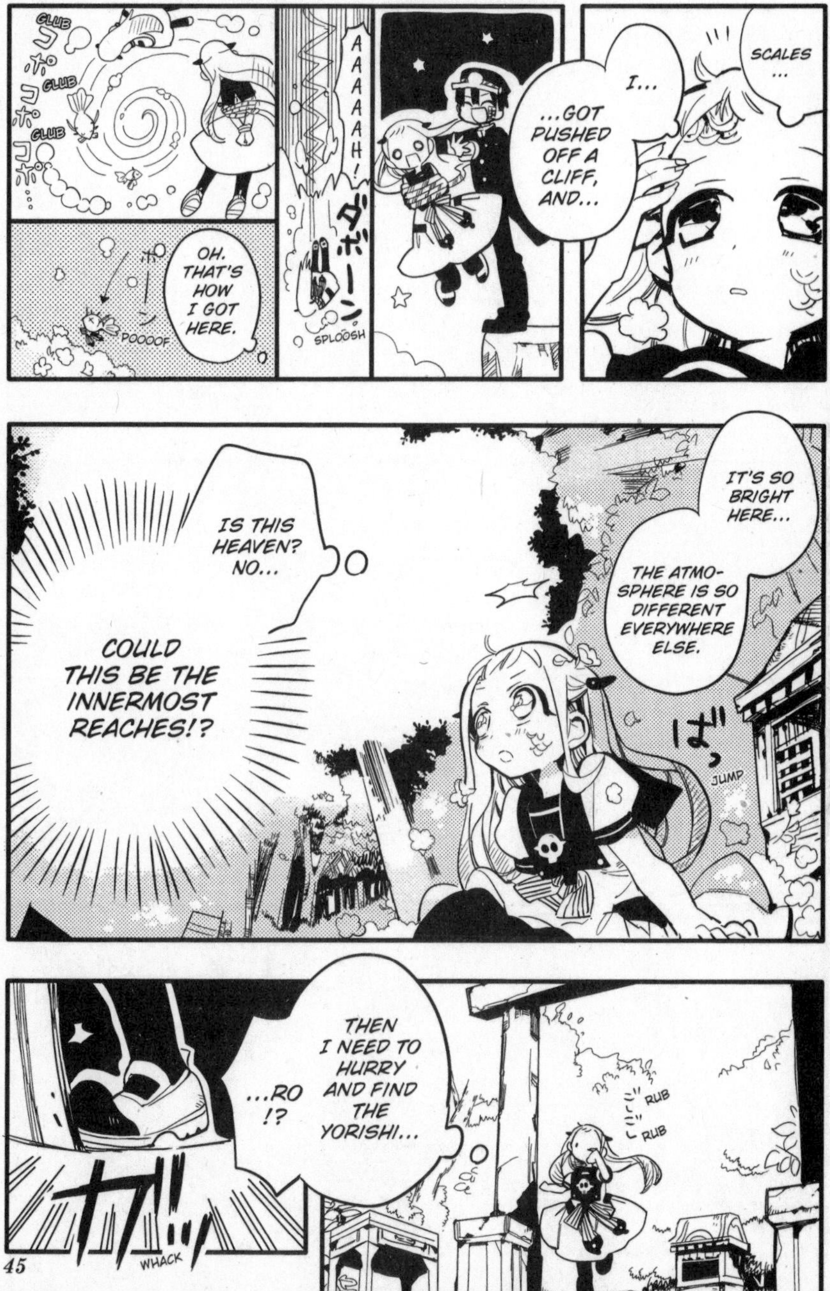
SCALES ...
I...
...GOT PUSHED OFF A CLIFF, AND...
AAAAAAH!
ダボーン
SPLOOSH
GLUB
GLUB
GLUB
コポコポコポ...
OH. THAT'S HOW I GOT HERE.
POOOOF
IT'S SO BRIGHT HERE...
THE ATMO-SPHERE IS SO DIFFERENT EVERYWHERE ELSE.
ぱっ
JUMP
IS THIS HEAVEN? NO...
COULD THIS BE THE INNERMOST REACHES!?
ごしごし
RUB
RUB
THEN I NEED TO HURRY AND FIND THE YORISHI...
...RO !?
ガッ
WHACK

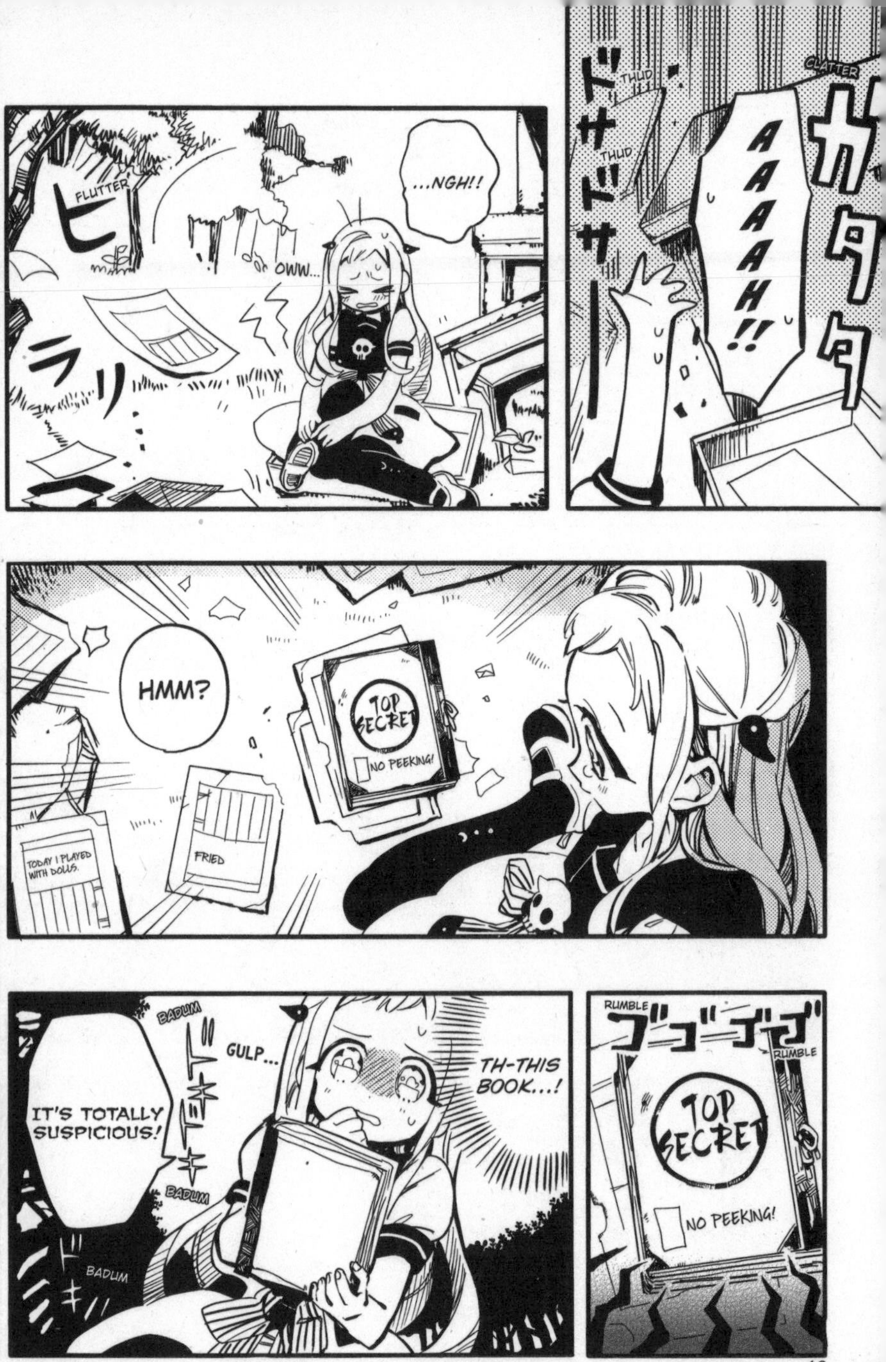
CLATTER
AAAAAAH!!
THUD
THUD
...NGH!!
OWW...
FLUTTER
HMM?
TOP SECRET
NO PEEKING!
TODAY I PLAYED WITH DOLLS.
FRIED
RUMBLE
RUMBLE
TOP SECRET
NO PEEKING!
TH-THIS BOOK...!
GULP...
BADUM
IT'S TOTALLY SUSPICIOUS!
BADUM
BADUM

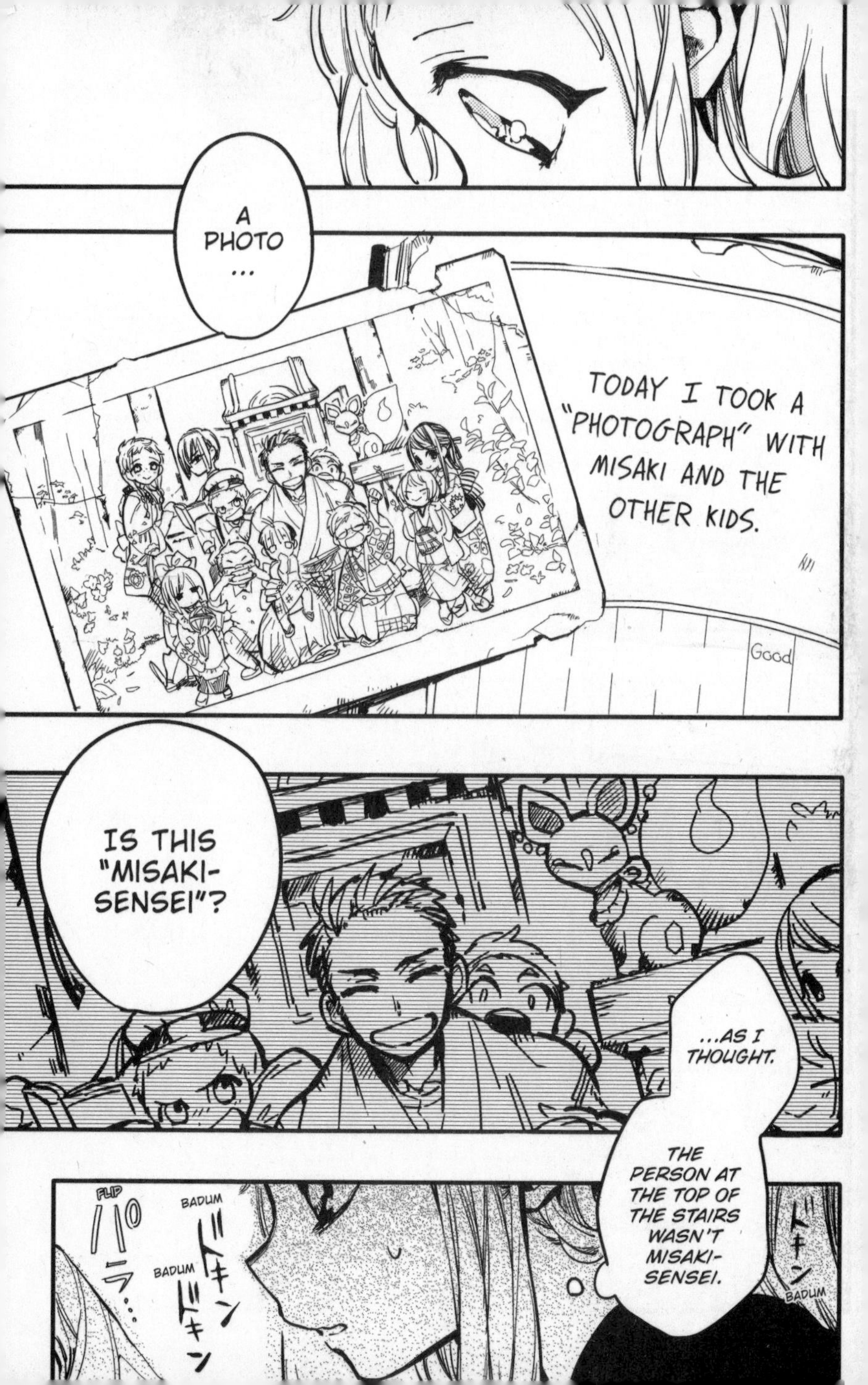
A PHOTO ...
TODAY I TOOK A "PHOTOGRAPH" WITH MISAKI AND THE OTHER KIDS.
Good
IS THIS "MISAKI-SENSEI"?
...AS I THOUGHT.
THE PERSON AT THE TOP OF THE STAIRS WASN'T MISAKI-SENSEI.
ドキン
BADUM
ドキン ドキン
BADUM BADUM
パラ…
FLIP

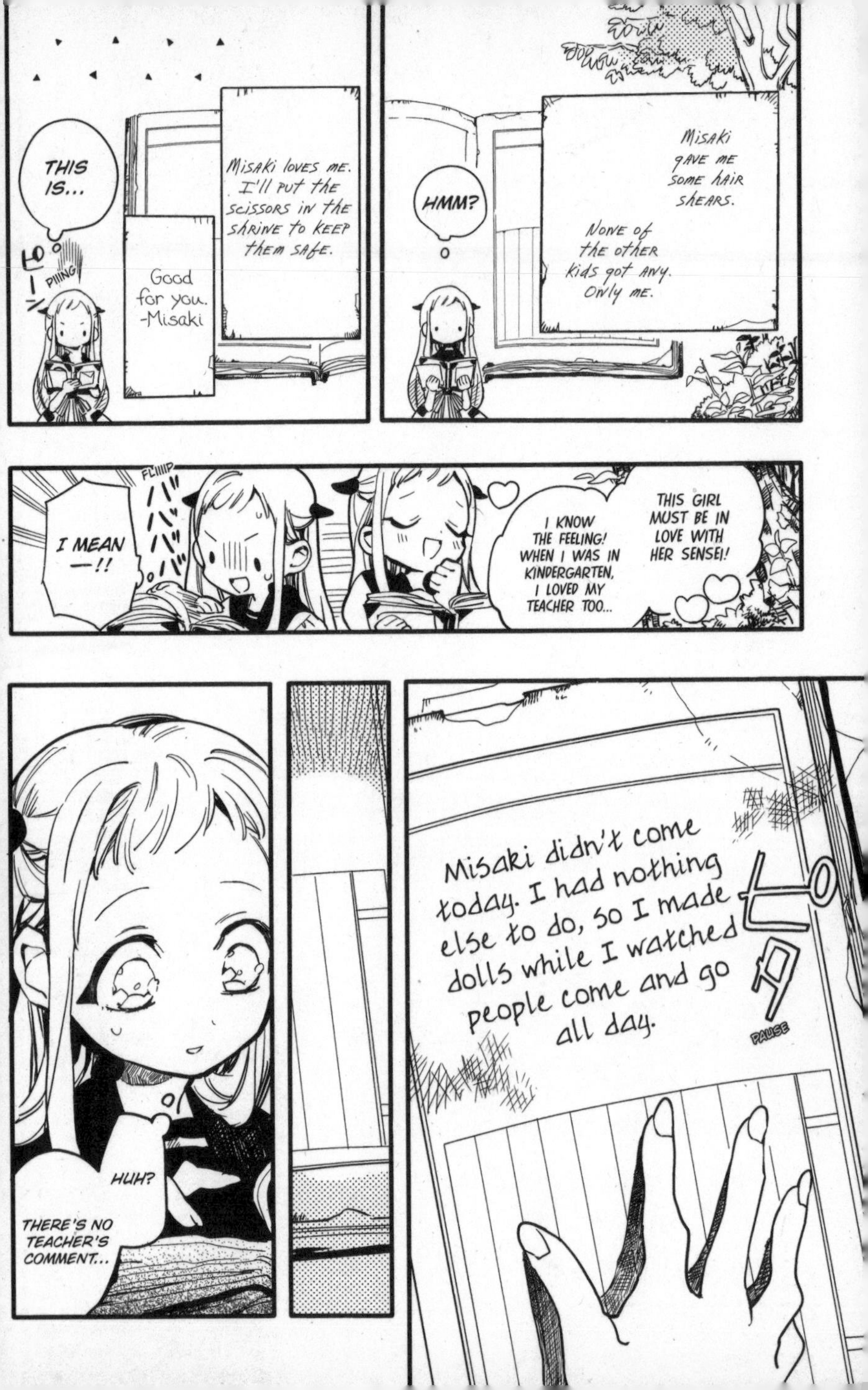
HMM?
Misaki gave me some hair shears.
None of the other kids got any. Only me.
THIS IS...
PIIING
Misaki loves me. I'll put the scissors in the shrine to keep them safe.
Good for you. -Misaki
THIS GIRL MUST BE IN LOVE WITH HER SENSEI!
I KNOW THE FEELING! WHEN I WAS IN KINDERGARTEN, I LOVED MY TEACHER TOO...
FLIIIP
I MEAN—!!
Misaki didn't come today. I had nothing else to do, so I made dolls while I watched people come and go all day.
PAUSE
HUH?
THERE'S NO TEACHER'S COMMENT...

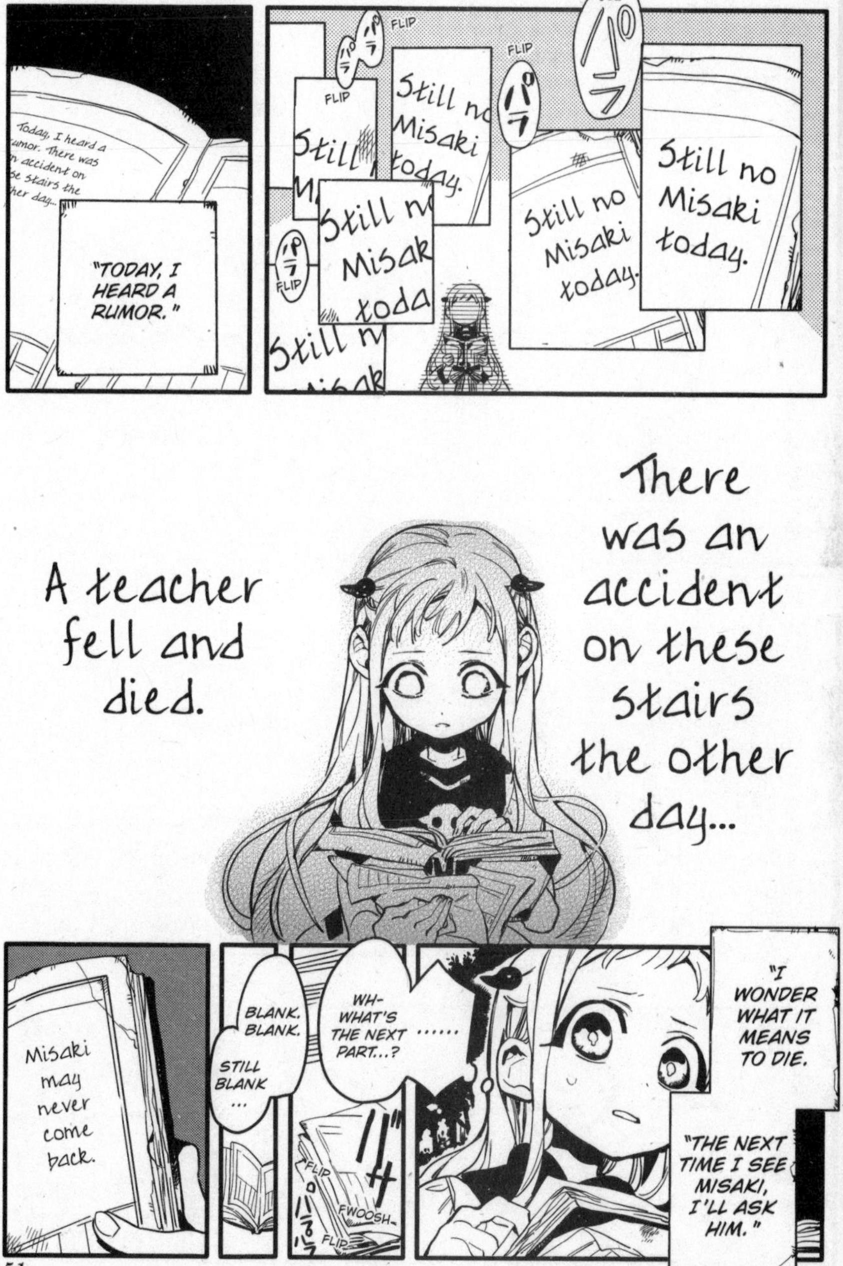
FLIP
FLIP
FLIP
FLIP
Still no Misaki today.
Still no Misaki today.
Still no Misaki today.
Still no Misaki today.
FLIP
Today, I heard a rumor. There was n accident on se stairs the her day...
"TODAY, I HEARD A RUMOR."
There was an accident on these stairs the other day...
A teacher fell and died.
"I WONDER WHAT IT MEANS TO DIE.
"THE NEXT TIME I SEE MISAKI, I'LL ASK HIM."
WH- WHAT'S THE NEXT PART...?
......
FLIP
FWOOSH
FLIP
BLANK. BLANK.
STILL BLANK ...
Misaki may never come back.

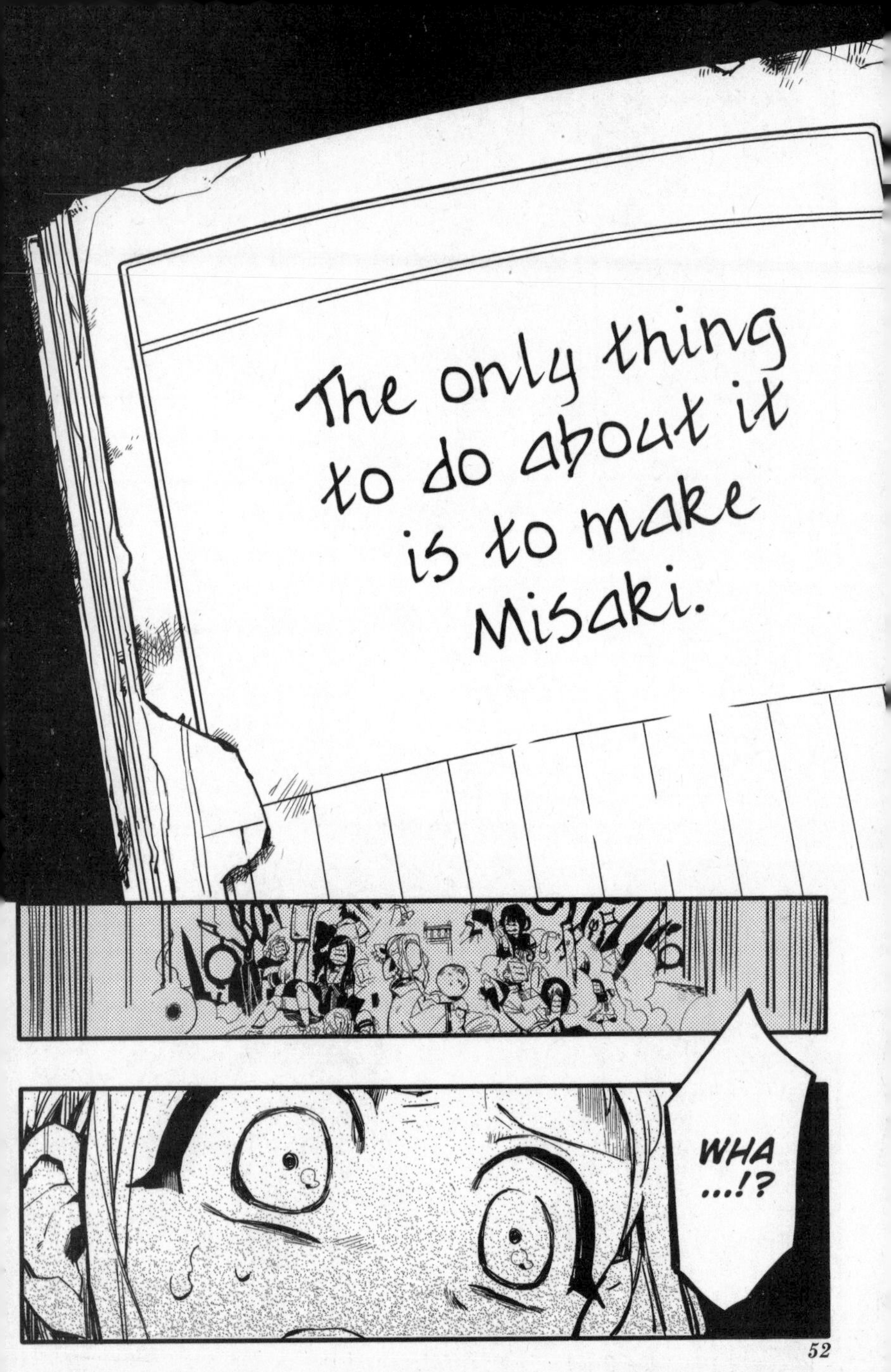
The only thing to do about it is to make Misaki.
WHA ...!?

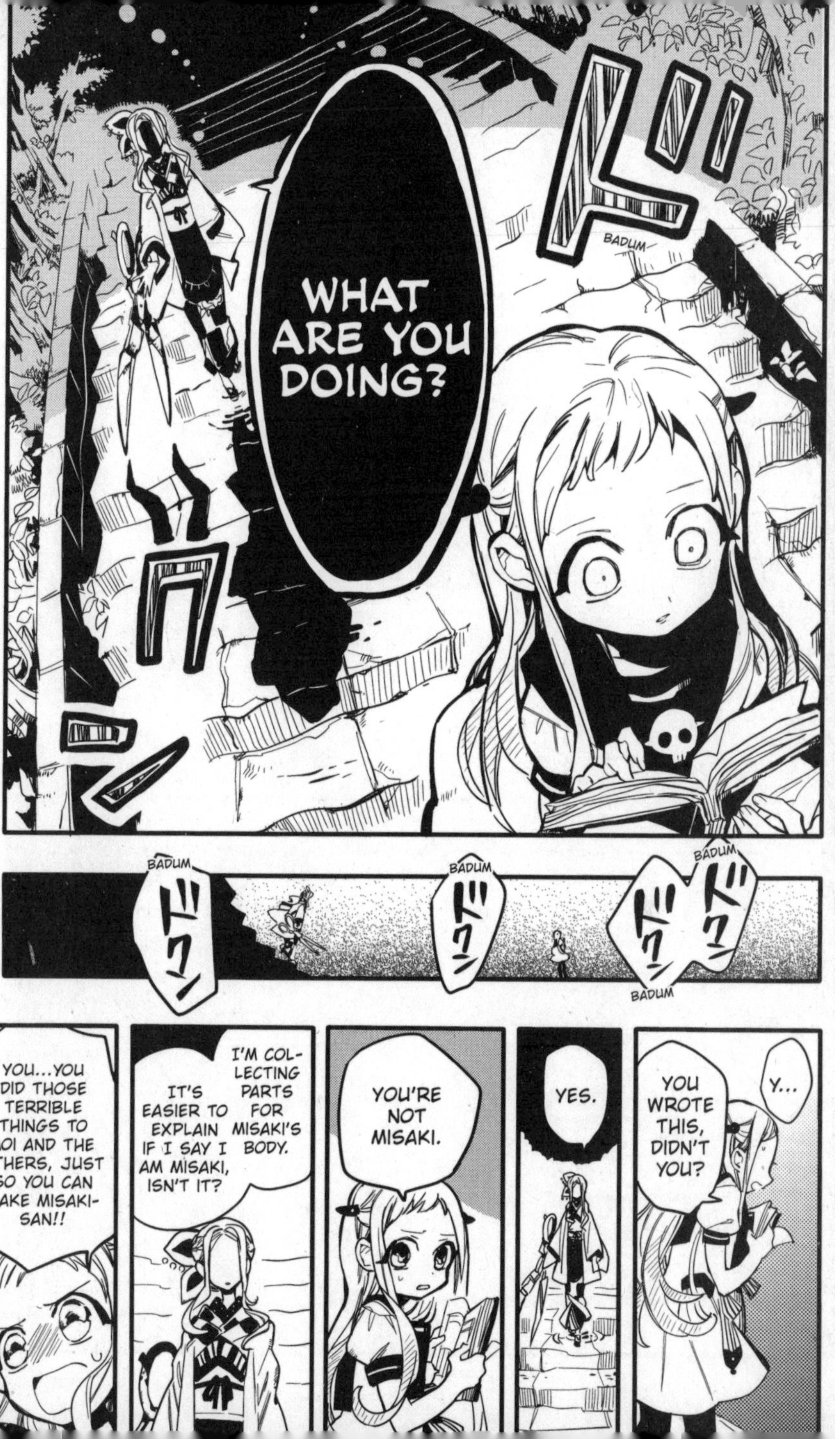
BADUM
WHAT ARE YOU DOING?
BADUM
BADUM
BADUM
BADUM
Y...
YOU WROTE THIS, DIDN'T YOU?
YES.
YOU'RE NOT MISAKI.
I'M COLLECTING PARTS FOR MISAKI'S BODY.
IT'S EASIER TO EXPLAIN IF I SAY I AM MISAKI, ISN'T IT?
YOU...YOU DID THOSE TERRIBLE THINGS TO AOI AND THE OTHERS, JUST SO YOU CAN MAKE MISAKI-SAN!!

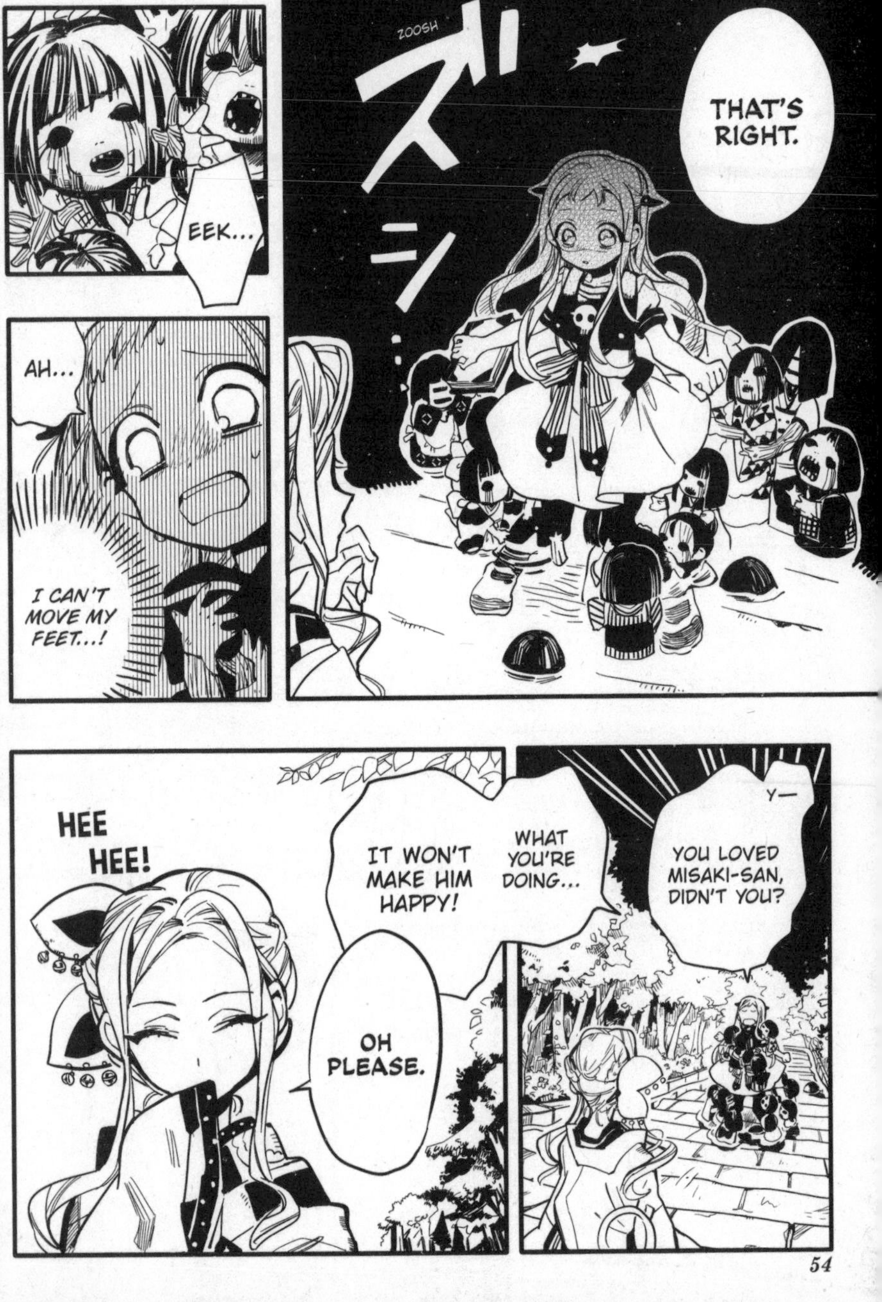
ZOOSH
THAT'S RIGHT.
EEK...
AH...
I CAN'T MOVE MY FEET...!
Y—
YOU LOVED MISAKI-SAN, DIDN'T YOU?
WHAT YOU'RE DOING...
IT WON'T MAKE HIM HAPPY!
OH PLEASE.
HEE HEE!

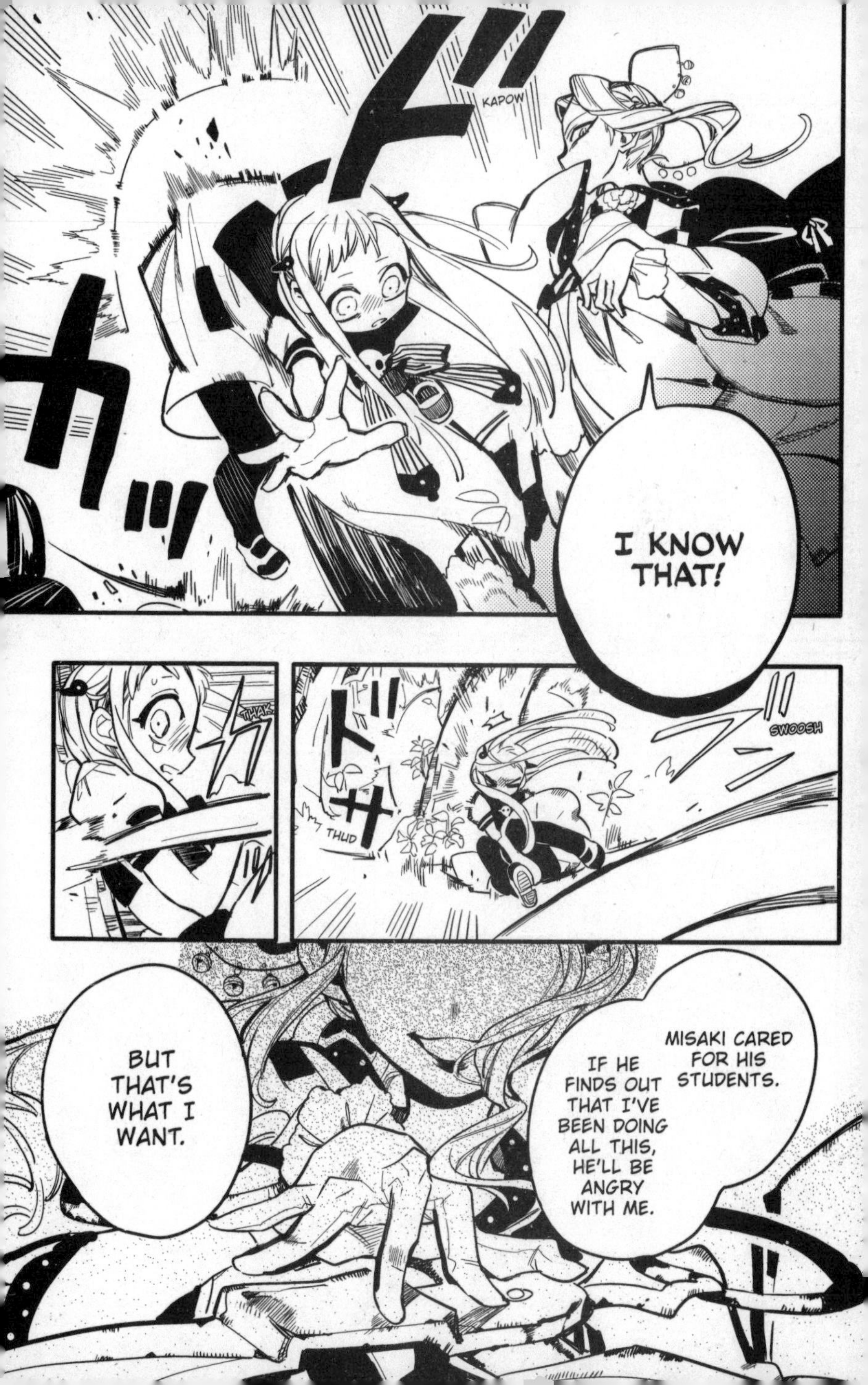
KAPOW
I KNOW THAT!
SWOOSH
THUD
THAK
MISAKI CARED FOR HIS STUDENTS.
IF HE FINDS OUT THAT I'VE BEEN DOING ALL THIS, HE'LL BE ANGRY WITH ME.
BUT THAT'S WHAT I WANT.

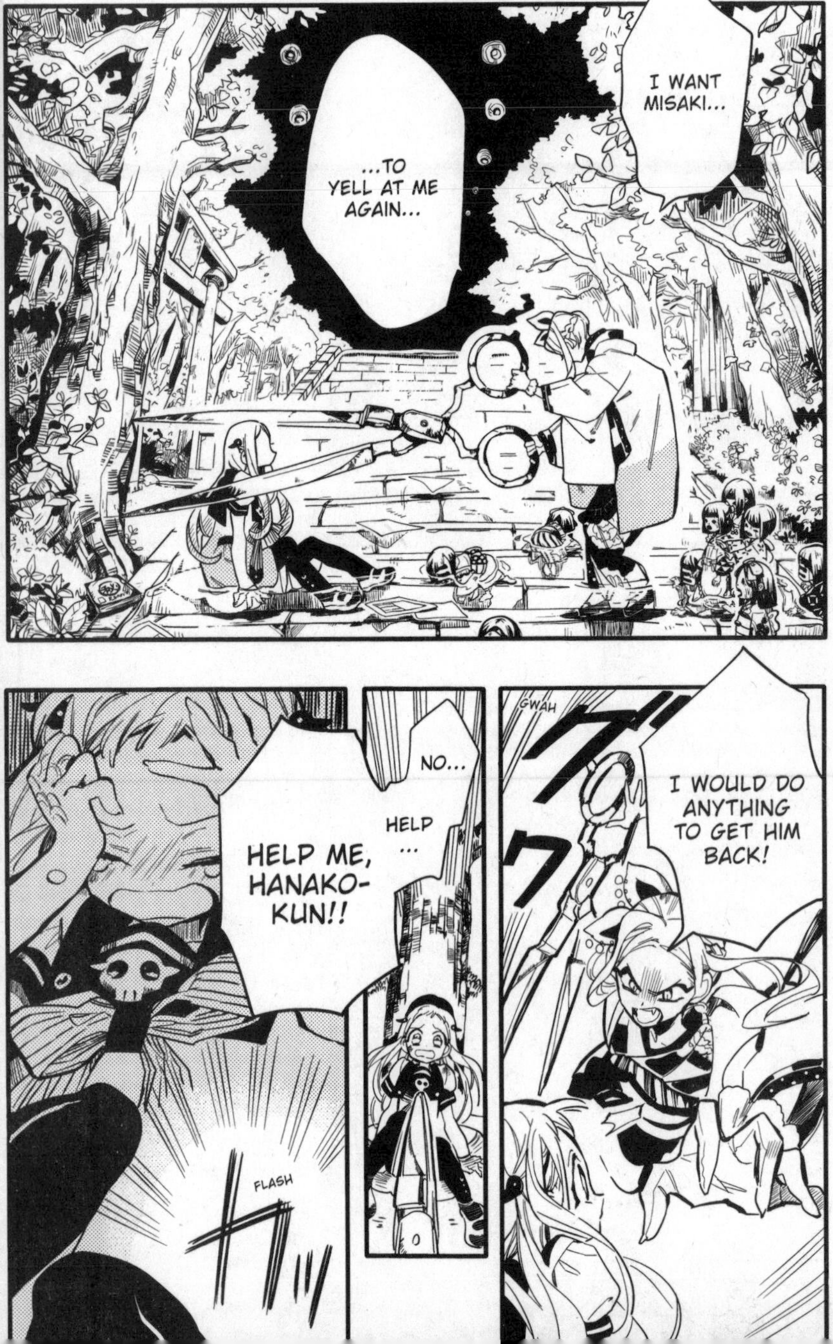
I WANT MISAKI...
...TO YELL AT ME AGAIN...
GWAH
I WOULD DO ANYTHING TO GET HIM BACK!
NO...
HELP ...
HELP ME, HANAKO-KUN!!
FLASH

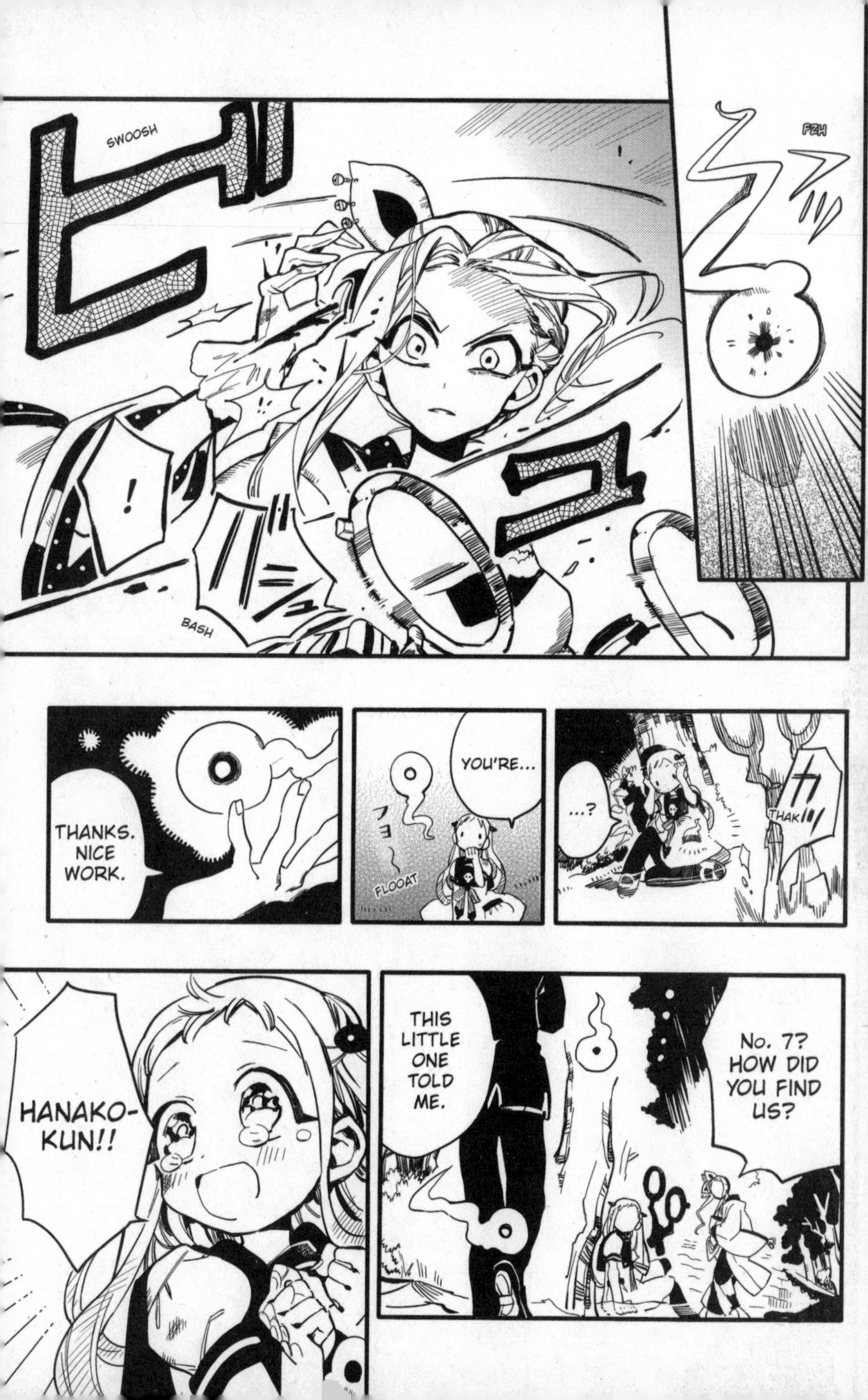
FZH
SWOOSH
BASH
THAK
...?
YOU'RE...
FLOOAT
THANKS. NICE WORK.
No. 7? HOW DID YOU FIND US?
THIS LITTLE ONE TOLD ME.
HANAKO-KUN!!

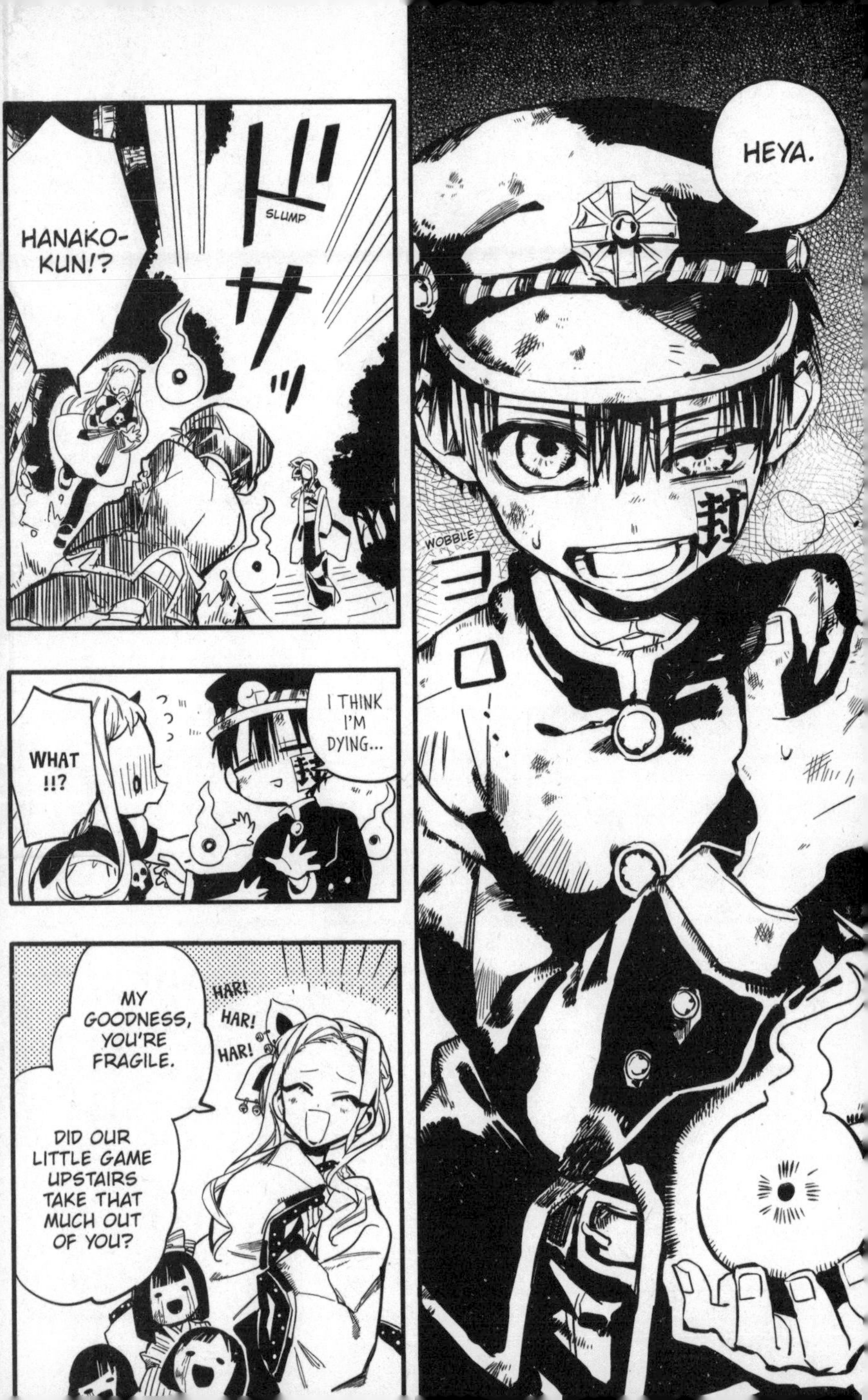
HEYA.
ヨロ
WOBBLE
ドサッ
SLUMP
HANAKO-KUN!?
I THINK I'M DYING...
WHAT !!?
MY GOODNESS, YOU'RE FRAGILE.
HAR! HAR! HAR!
DID OUR LITTLE GAME UPSTAIRS TAKE THAT MUCH OUT OF YOU?

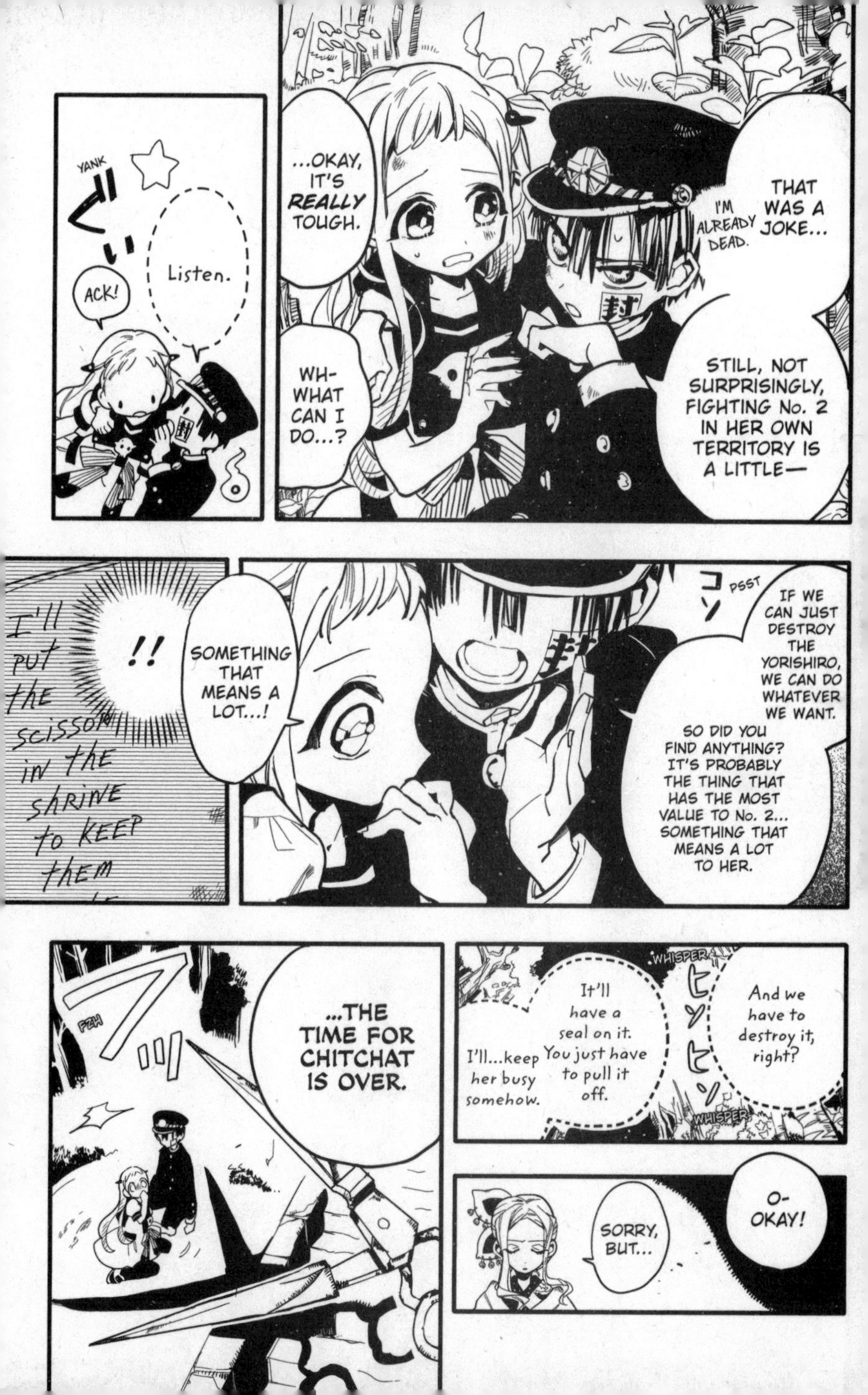
THAT WAS A JOKE...
I'M ALREADY DEAD.
...OKAY, IT'S *REALLY* TOUGH.
STILL, NOT SURPRISINGLY, FIGHTING No. 2 IN HER OWN TERRITORY IS A LITTLE—
WH-WHAT CAN I DO...?
Listen.
YANK
ACK!
PSST
IF WE CAN JUST DESTROY THE YORISHIRO, WE CAN DO WHATEVER WE WANT.
SO DID YOU FIND ANYTHING? IT'S PROBABLY THE THING THAT HAS THE MOST VALUE TO No. 2... SOMETHING THAT MEANS A LOT TO HER.
SOMETHING THAT MEANS A LOT...!
!!
I'll put the scisso in the shrine to keep them
WHISPER
And we have to destroy it, right?
It'll have a seal on it. You just have to pull it off.
I'll...keep her busy somehow.
WHISPER
O-OKAY!
SORRY, BUT...
...THE TIME FOR CHITCHAT IS OVER.
FZH

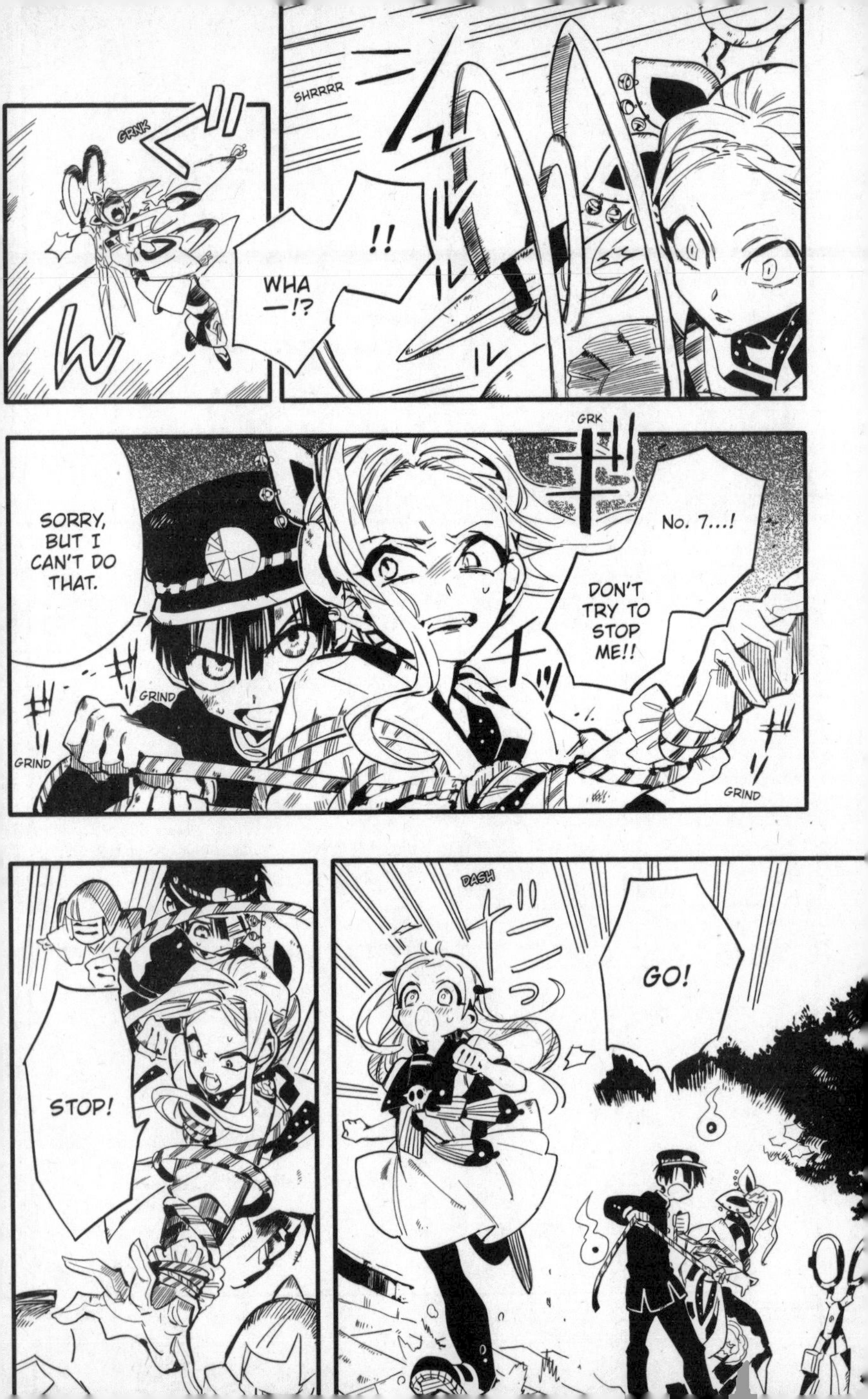
SHRRRR
!!
WHA—!?
GRNK
GRK
No. 7...!
DON'T TRY TO STOP ME!!
SORRY, BUT I CAN'T DO THAT.
GRIND
GRIND
GRIND
DASH
GO!
STOP!

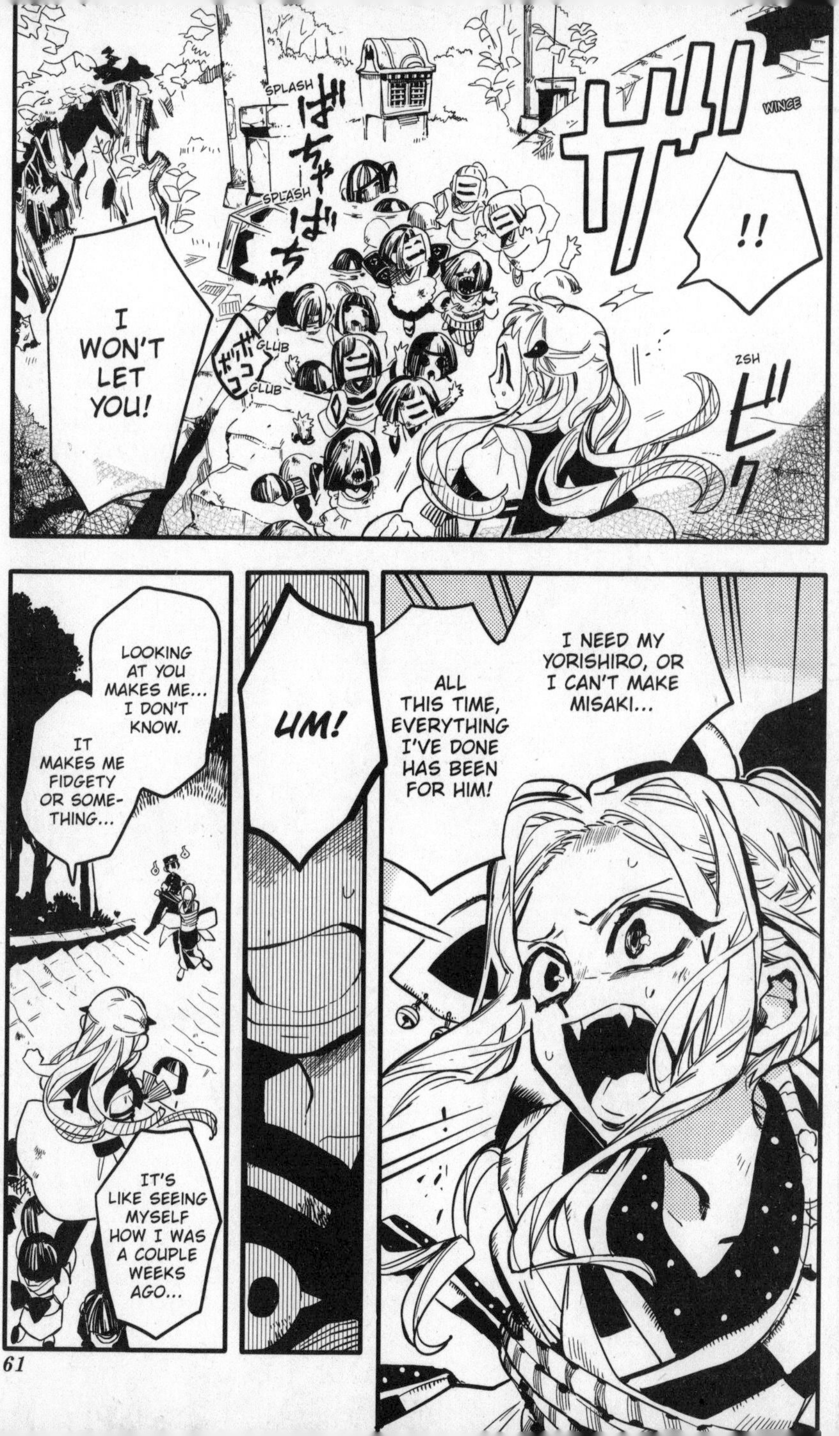
WINCE
!!
ZSH
SPLASH
SPLASH
I WON'T LET YOU!
GLUB
GLUB
I NEED MY YORISHIRO, OR I CAN'T MAKE MISAKI...
ALL THIS TIME, EVERYTHING I'VE DONE HAS BEEN FOR HIM!
UM!
LOOKING AT YOU MAKES ME... I DON'T KNOW.
IT MAKES ME FIDGETY OR SOMETHING...
IT'S LIKE SEEING MYSELF HOW I WAS A COUPLE WEEKS AGO...

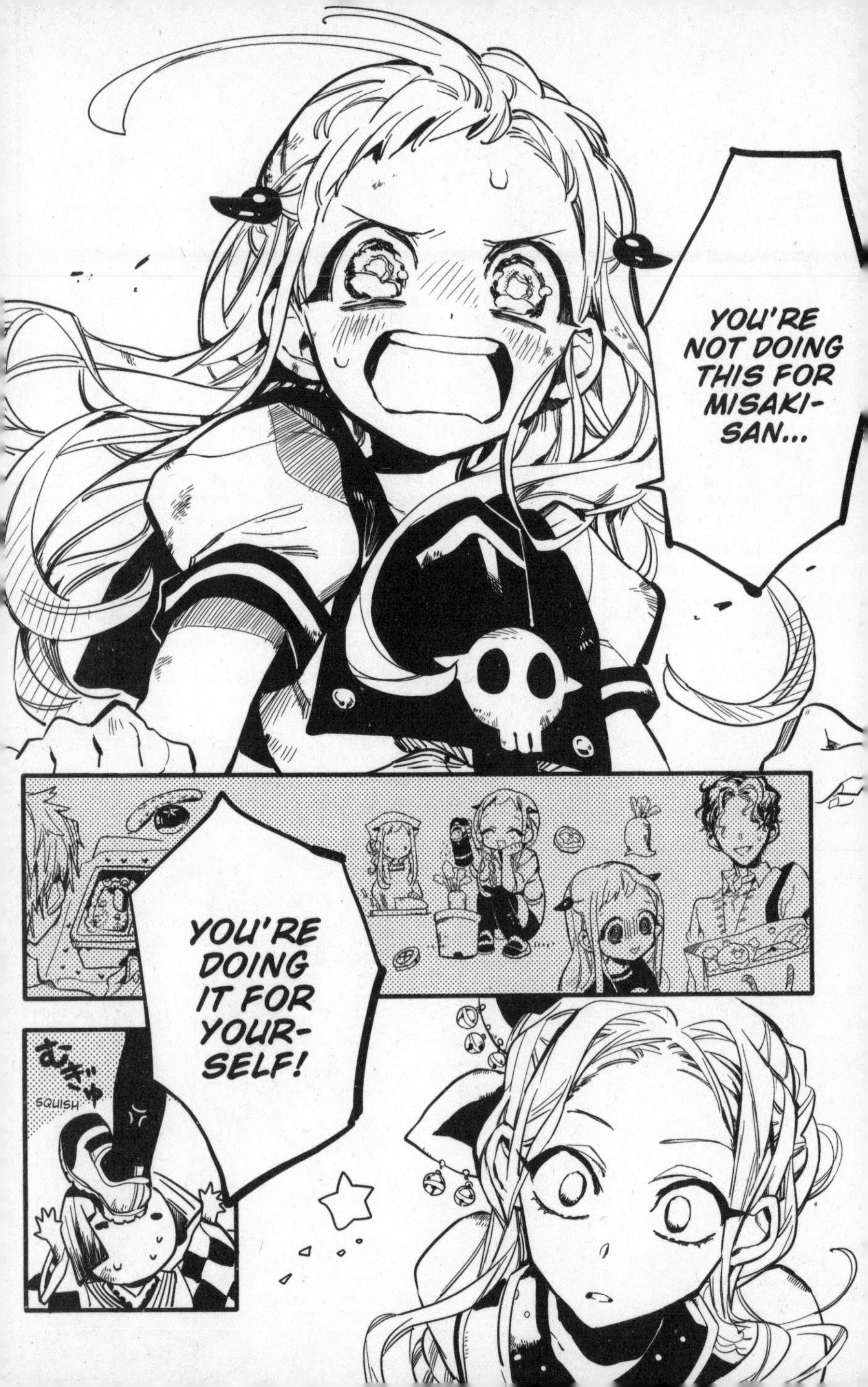
YOU'RE NOT DOING THIS FOR MISAKI-SAN...
YOU'RE DOING IT FOR YOUR-SELF!
むぎゅ
SQUISH

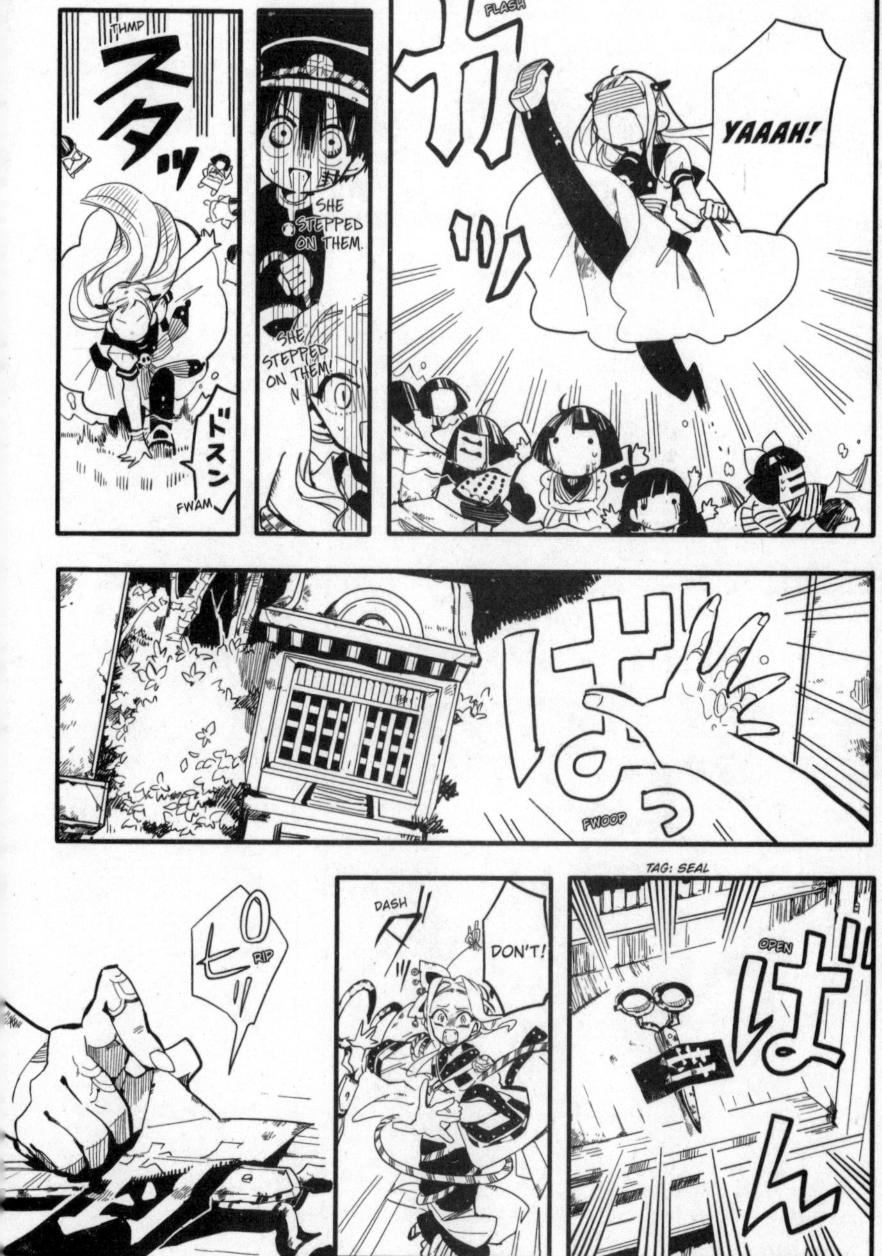
FLASH
カッ
YAAAH!
SHE STEPPED ON THEM.
SHE STEPPED ON THEM!
THMP
スタッ
ドスン
FWAM
ばっ
FWOOP
TAG: SEAL
OPEN
ばん
DASH
ダッ
DON'T!
RIP

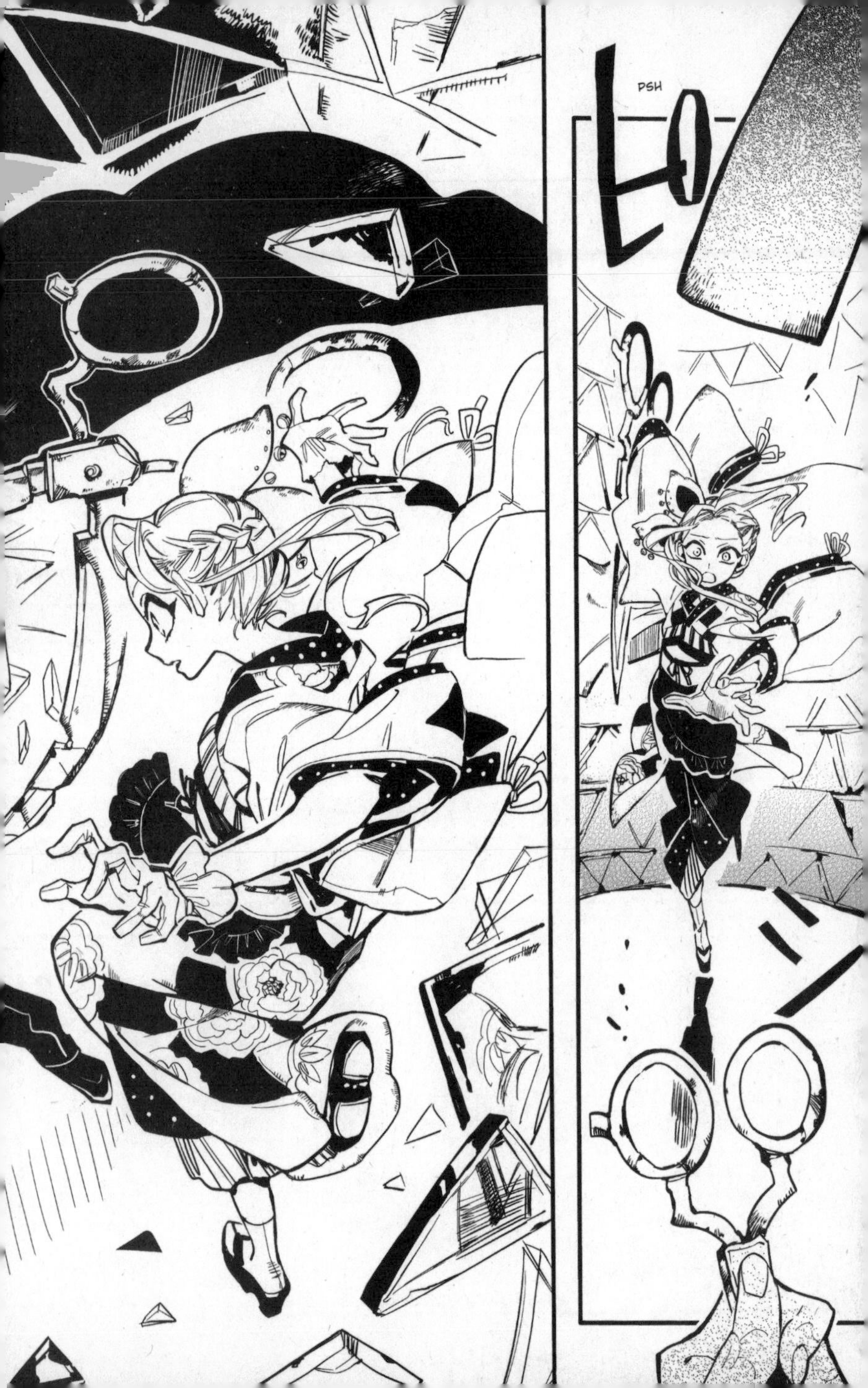
PSH

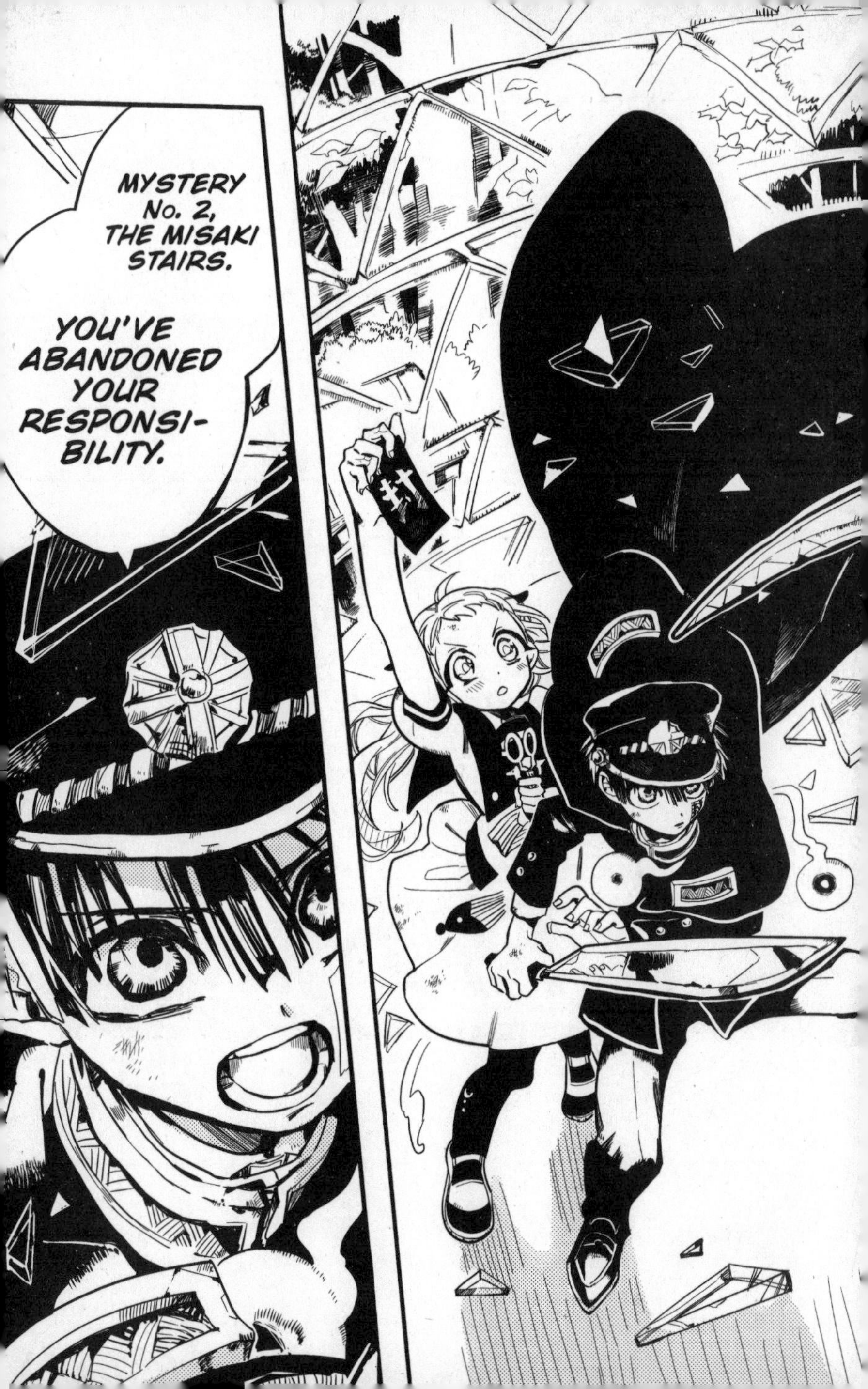
封
MYSTERY No. 2, THE MISAKI STAIRS.
YOU'VE ABANDONED YOUR RESPONSI-BILITY.

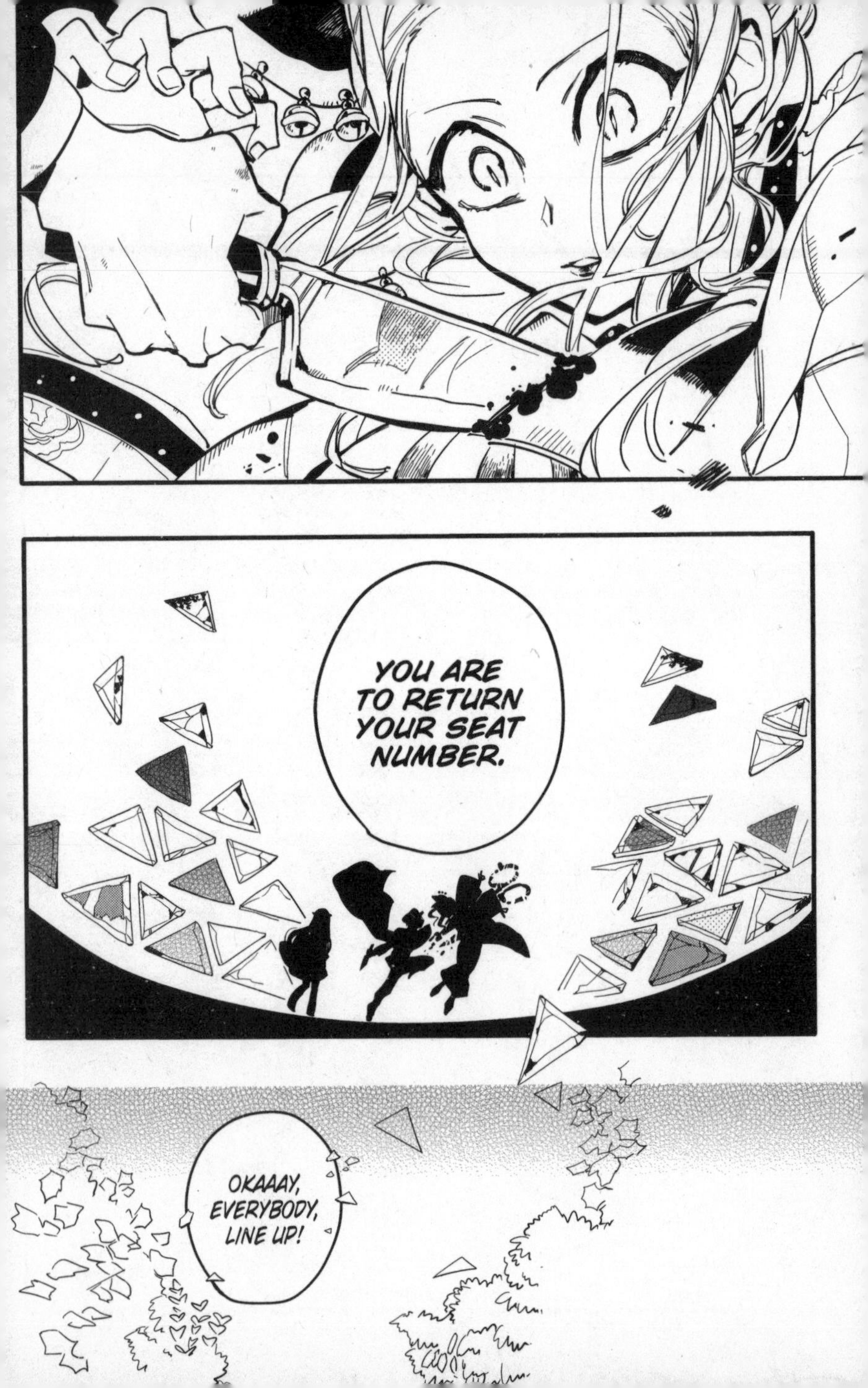
YOU ARE TO RETURN YOUR SEAT NUMBER.
OKAAAY, EVERYBODY, LINE UP!

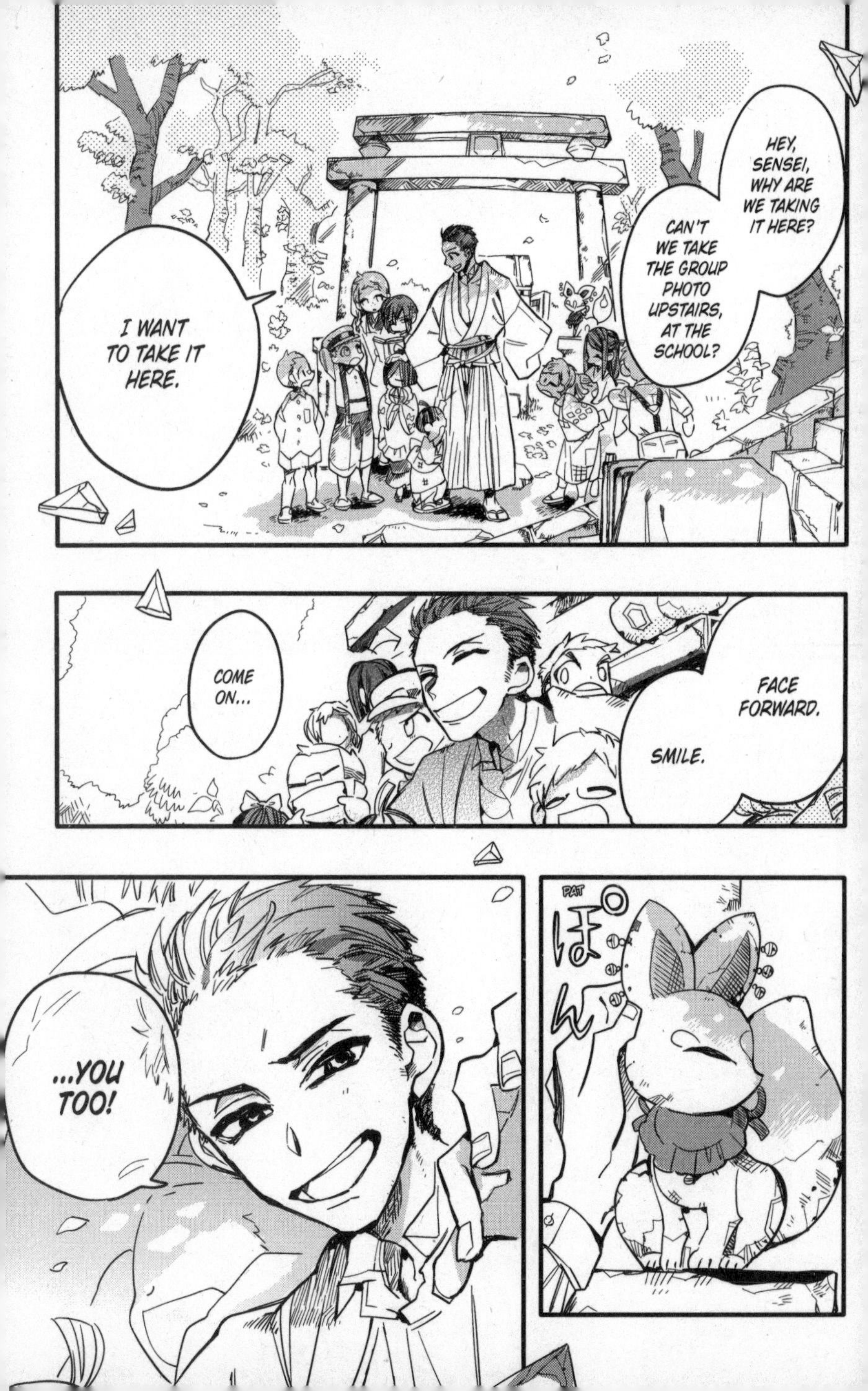
HEY, SENSEI, WHY ARE WE TAKING IT HERE?
CAN'T WE TAKE THE GROUP PHOTO UPSTAIRS, AT THE SCHOOL?
I WANT TO TAKE IT HERE.
FACE FORWARD.
SMILE.
COME ON...
PAT
ぽん
...YOU TOO!

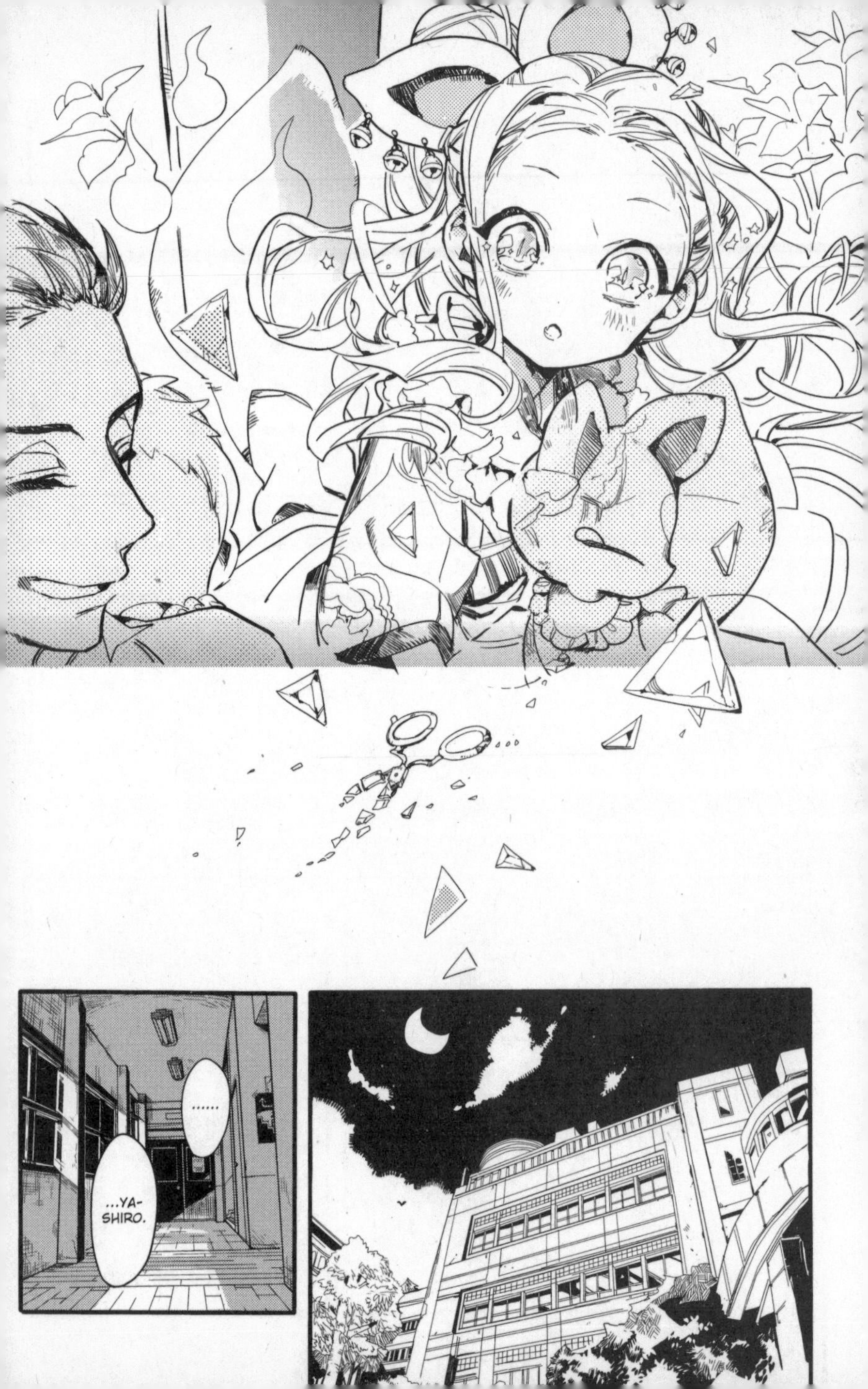
......
...YA-SHIRO.

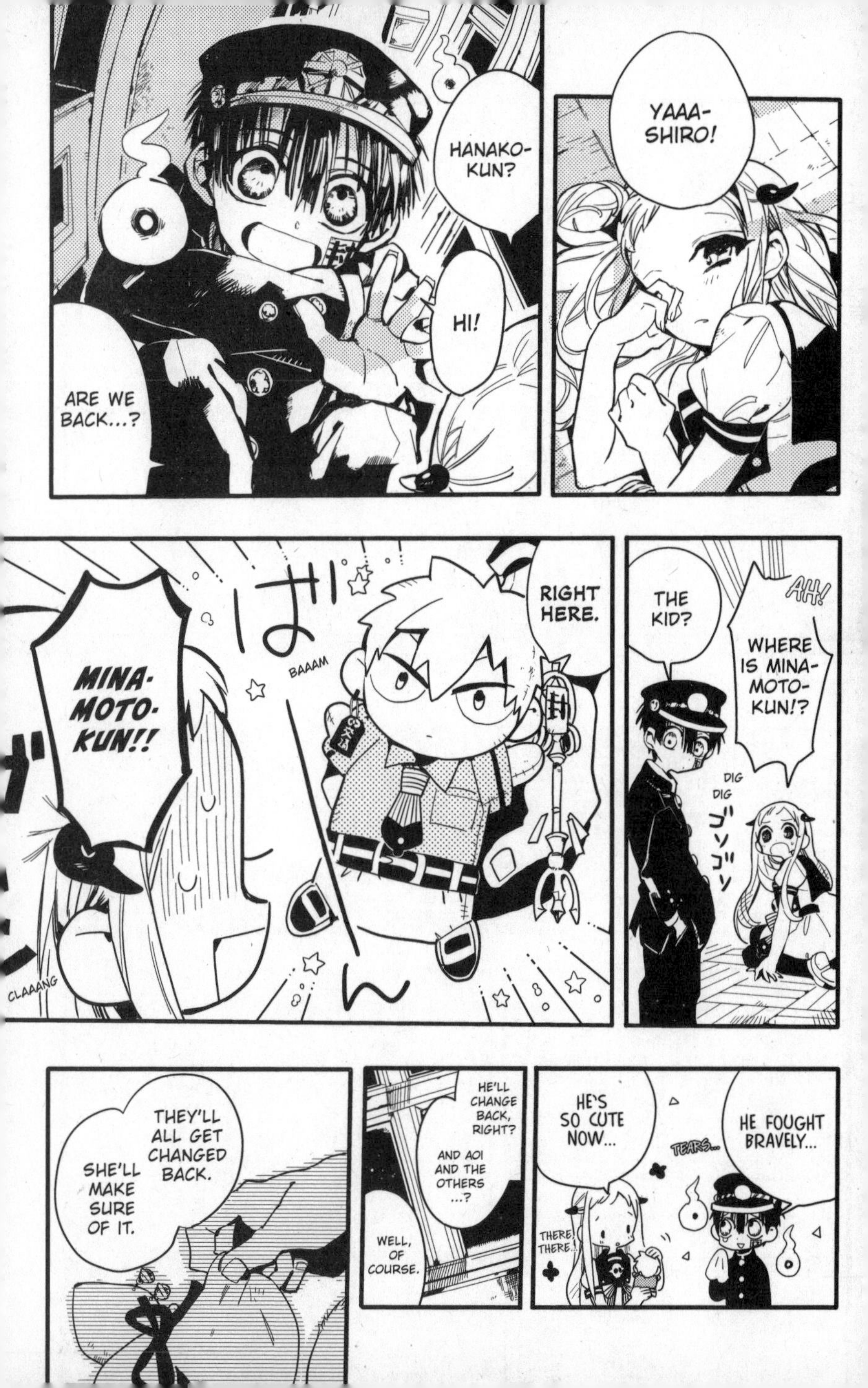
YAAA-SHIRO!
HANAKO-KUN?
HI!
ARE WE BACK...?
AH!
WHERE IS MINA-MOTO-KUN!?
THE KID?
DIG DIG
ゴソゴソ
RIGHT HERE.
ぱん
BAAAM
MINA-MOTO-KUN!!
CLAAANG
HE FOUGHT BRAVELY...
TEARS...
HE'S SO CUTE NOW...
THERE THERE...
HE'LL CHANGE BACK, RIGHT?
AND AOI AND THE OTHERS ...?
WELL, OF COURSE.
THEY'LL ALL GET CHANGED BACK.
SHE'LL MAKE SURE OF IT.

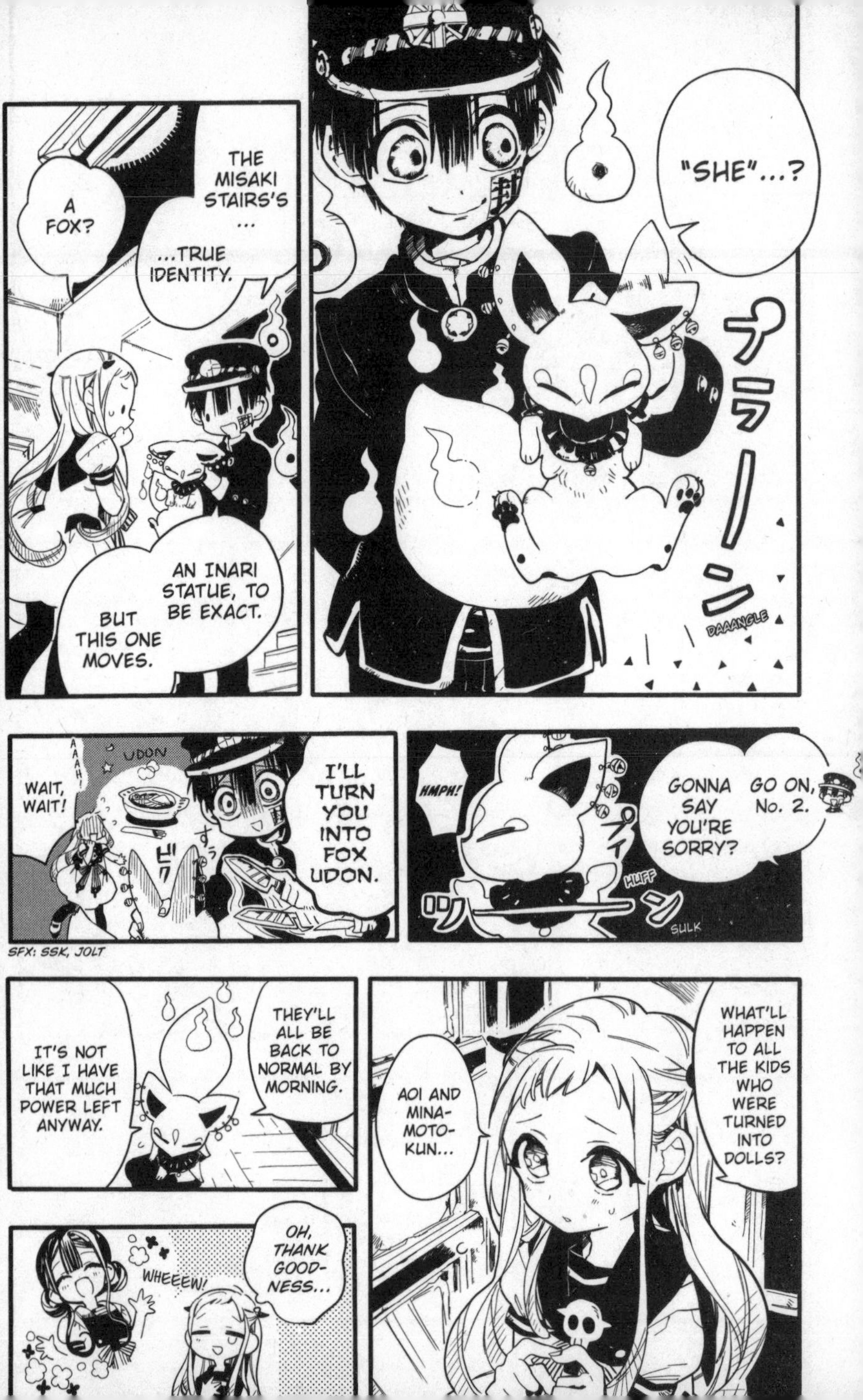
"SHE"...?
DAAANGLE
THE MISAKI STAIRS'S ...
...TRUE IDENTITY.
A FOX?
AN INARI STATUE, TO BE EXACT.
BUT THIS ONE MOVES.
GO ON, No. 2.
GONNA SAY YOU'RE SORRY?
HMPH!
HUFF
SULK
I'LL TURN YOU INTO FOX UDON.
UDON
AAAH!
WAIT, WAIT!
SFX: SSK, JOLT
WHAT'LL HAPPEN TO ALL THE KIDS WHO WERE TURNED INTO DOLLS?
AOI AND MINA-MOTO-KUN...
THEY'LL ALL BE BACK TO NORMAL BY MORNING.
IT'S NOT LIKE I HAVE THAT MUCH POWER LEFT ANYWAY.
OH, THANK GOOD-NESS...
WHEEEW!

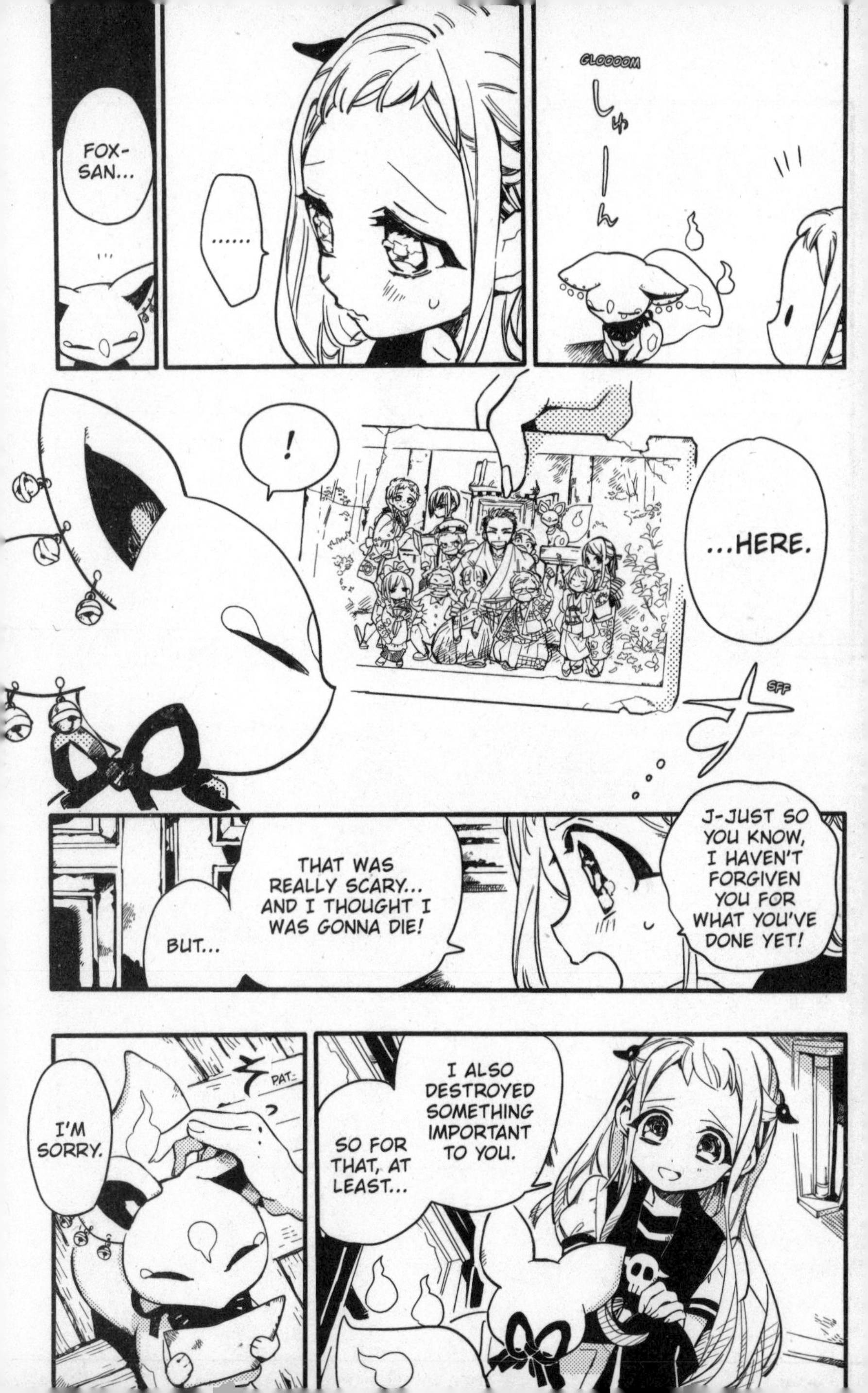
GLOOOOM
しゅーん
......
FOX-SAN...
...HERE.
SFF
!
J-JUST SO YOU KNOW, I HAVEN'T FORGIVEN YOU FOR WHAT YOU'VE DONE YET!
THAT WAS REALLY SCARY... AND I THOUGHT I WAS GONNA DIE!
BUT...
I ALSO DESTROYED SOMETHING IMPORTANT TO YOU.
SO FOR THAT, AT LEAST...
PAT
I'M SORRY.

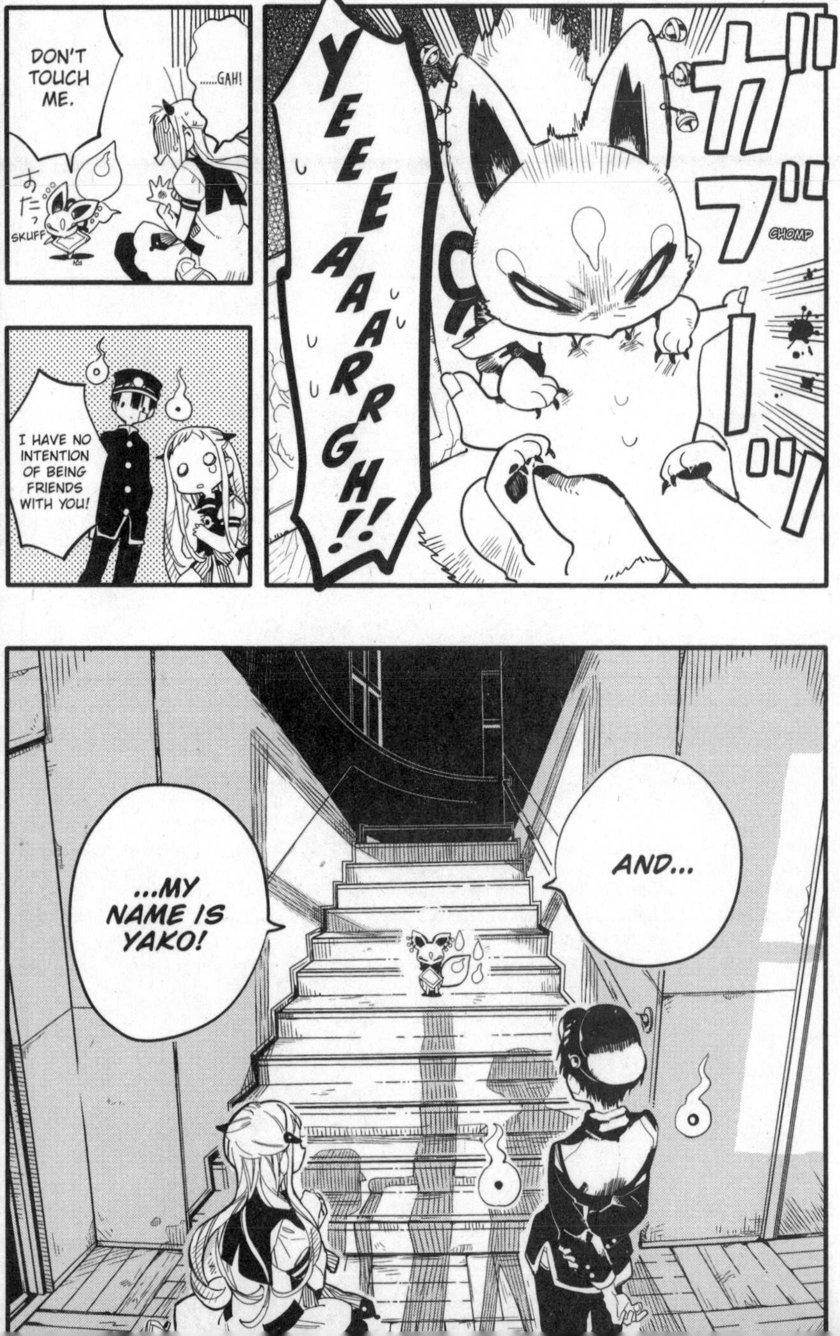
ガブーッ
CHOMP
YEEEAAARRGH!!
......GAH!
DON'T TOUCH ME.
あだっ
SKUFF
I HAVE NO INTENTION OF BEING FRIENDS WITH YOU!
AND...
...MY NAME IS YAKO!

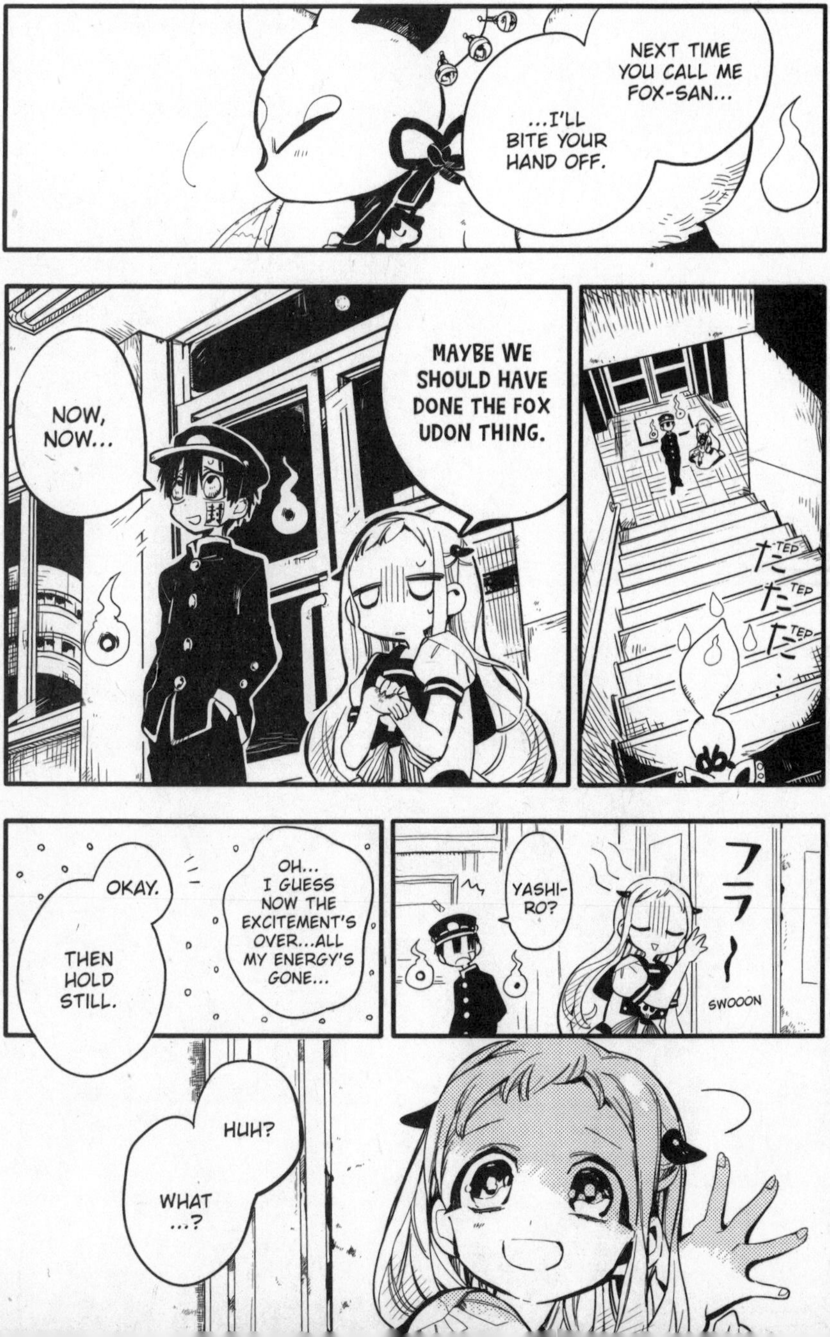
NEXT TIME YOU CALL ME FOX-SAN...
...I'LL BITE YOUR HAND OFF.
たたた
TEP TEP TEP
MAYBE WE SHOULD HAVE DONE THE FOX UDON THING.
NOW, NOW...
フラ〜
SWOOON
YASHIRO?
OH... I GUESS NOW THE EXCITEMENT'S OVER...ALL MY ENERGY'S GONE...
OKAY.
THEN HOLD STILL.
HUH?
WHAT ...?

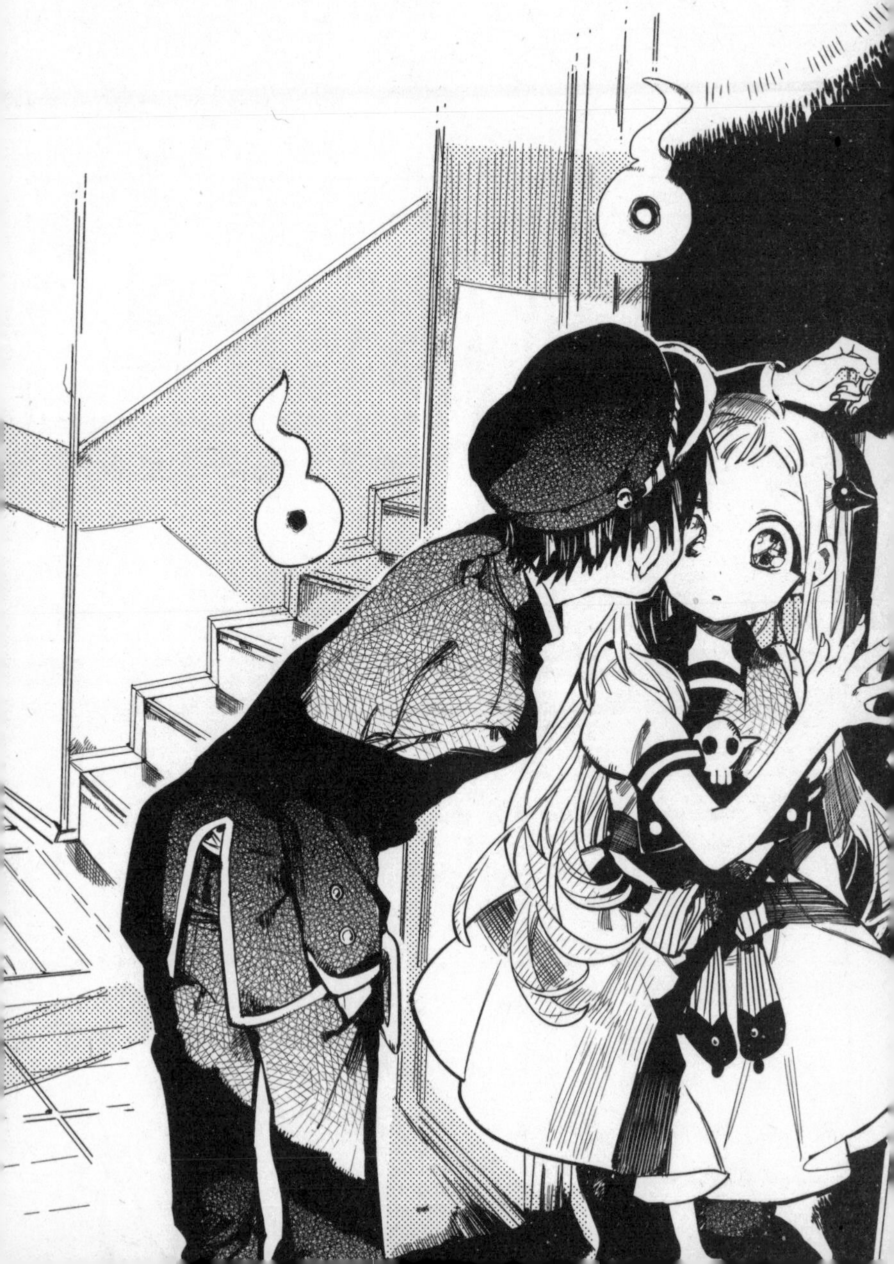

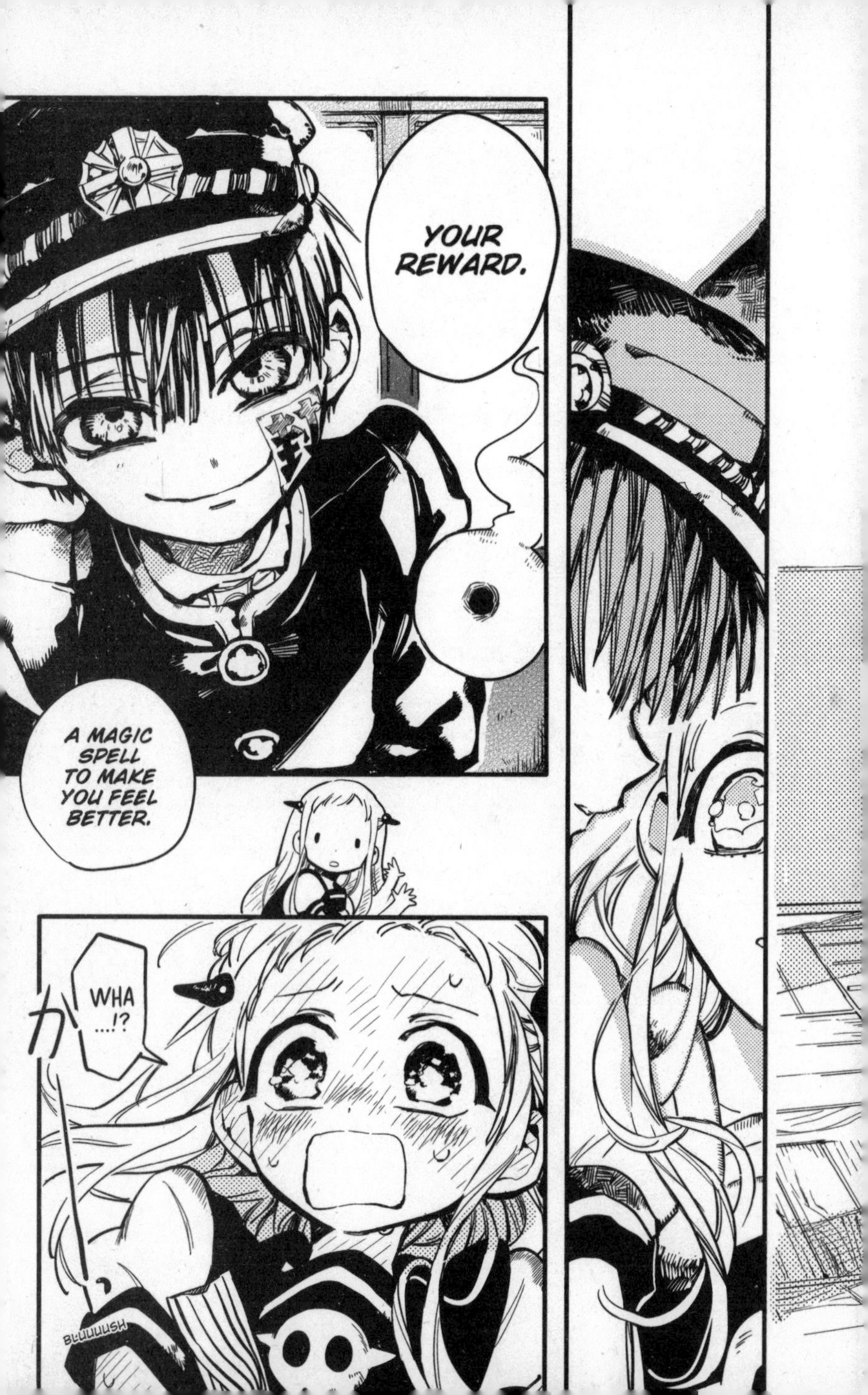
YOUR REWARD.
A MAGIC SPELL TO MAKE YOU FEEL BETTER.
WHA ...!?
カ
BLUUUUSH

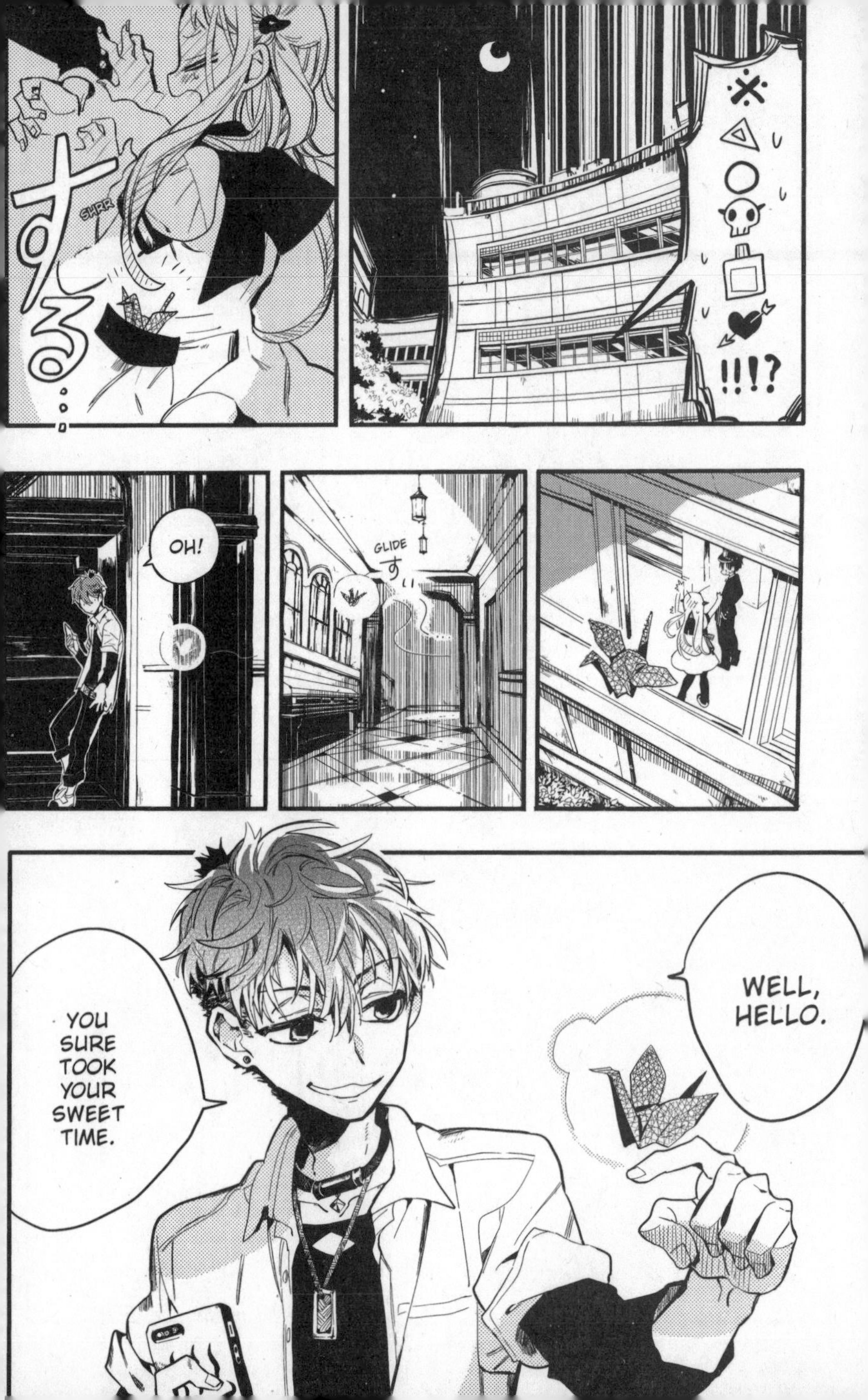
!!!?
する…
SHRR
GLIDE
すい
OH!
WELL, HELLO.
YOU SURE TOOK YOUR SWEET TIME.

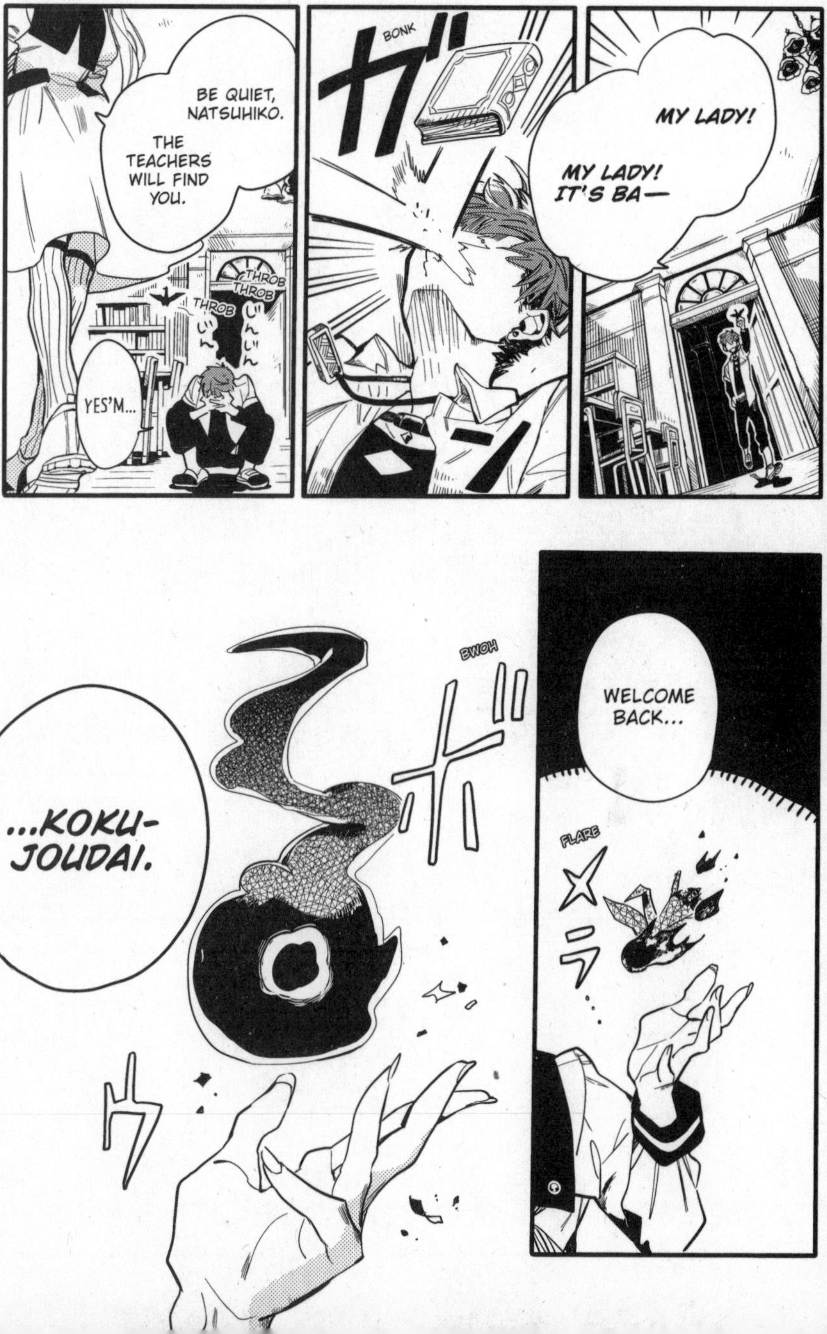

MY LADY!
MY LADY! IT'S BA—
BONK
BE QUIET, NATSUHIKO.
THE TEACHERS WILL FIND YOU.
THROB THROB
THROB
YES'M...
WELCOME BACK...
FLARE
BWOH
...KOKU-JOUDAI.

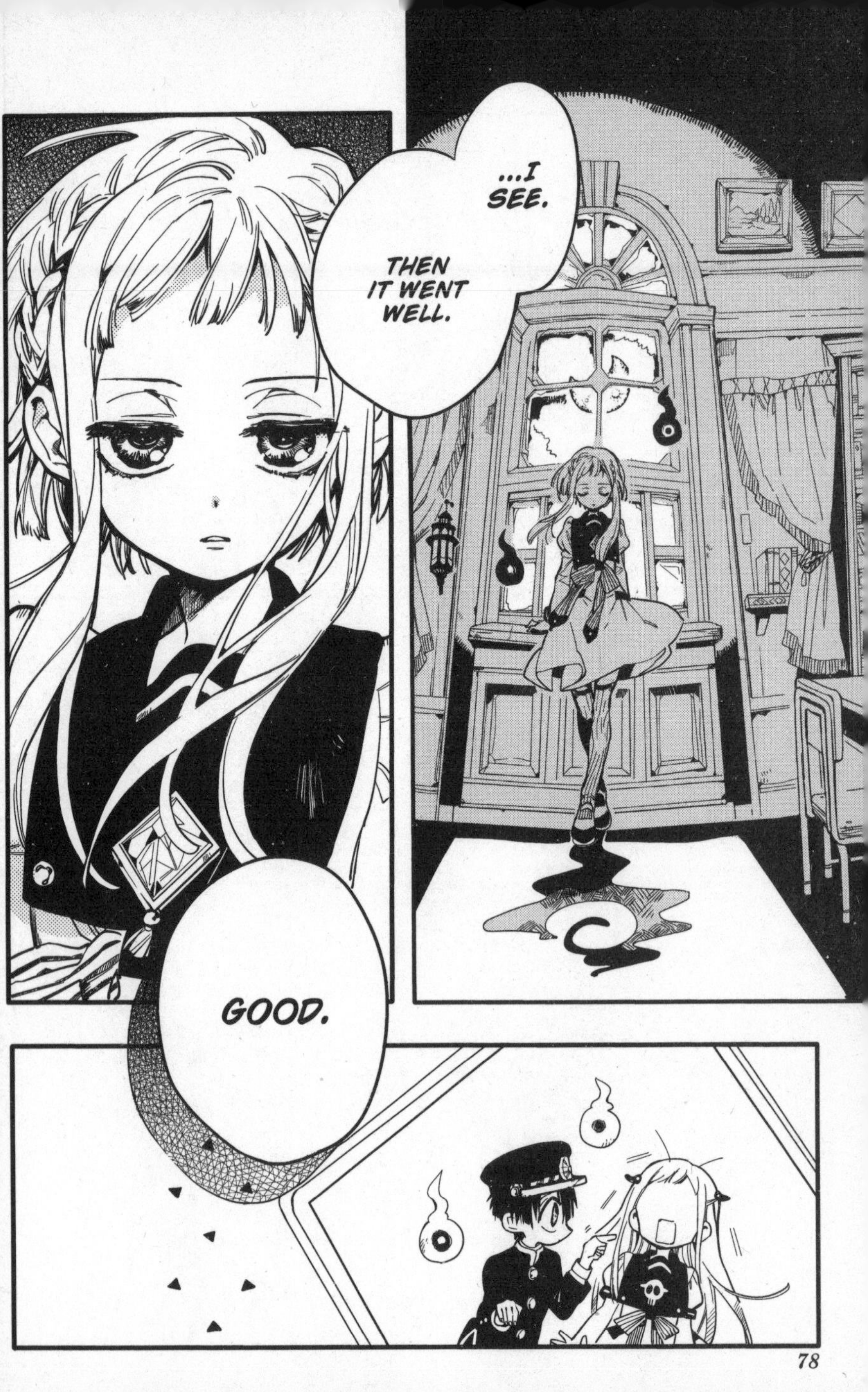
...I SEE.
THEN IT WENT WELL.
GOOD.

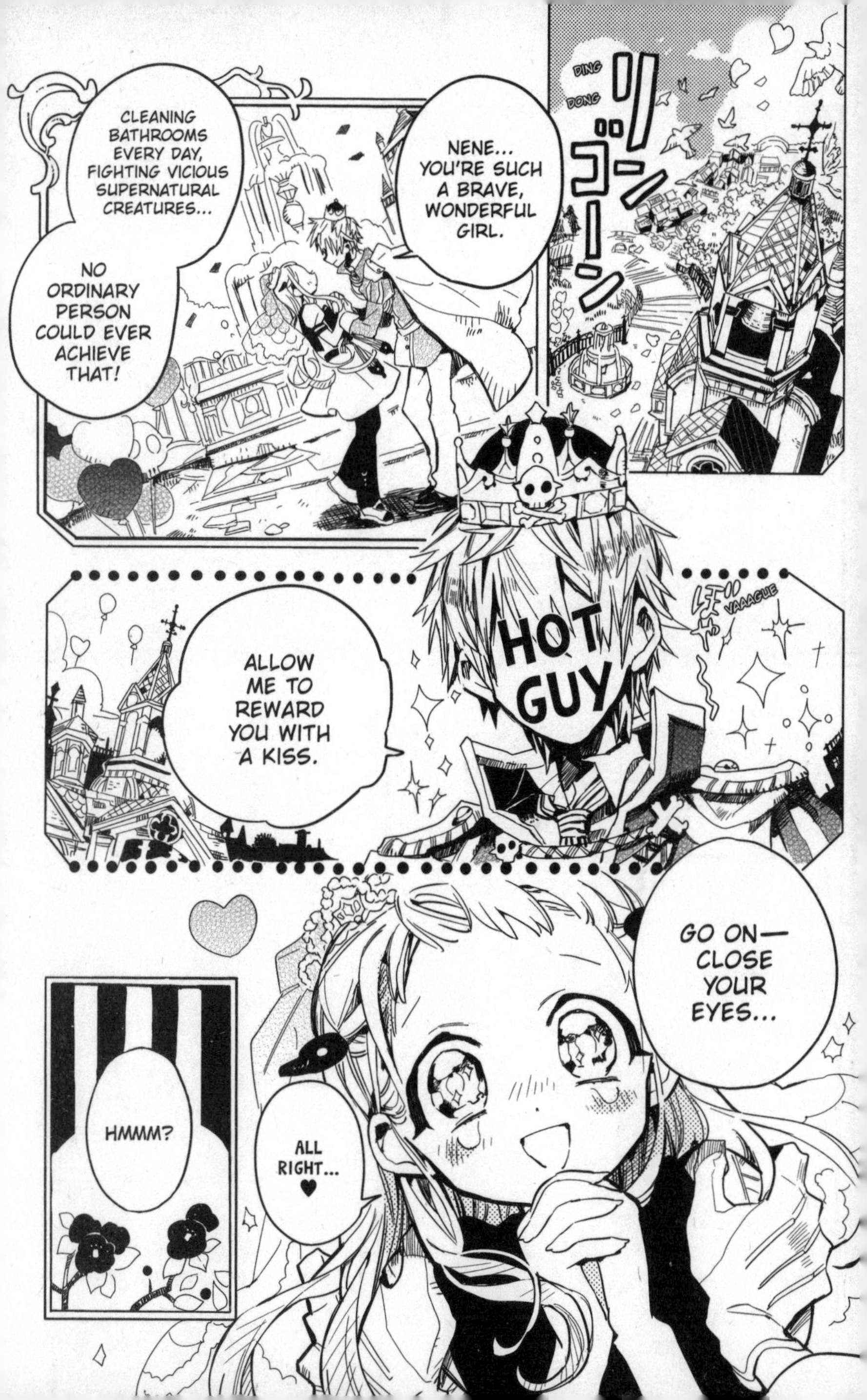
DING DONG
NENE... YOU'RE SUCH A BRAVE, WONDERFUL GIRL.
CLEANING BATHROOMS EVERY DAY, FIGHTING VICIOUS SUPERNATURAL CREATURES...
NO ORDINARY PERSON COULD EVER ACHIEVE THAT!
VAAAGUE
HOT GUY
ALLOW ME TO REWARD YOU WITH A KISS.
GO ON—CLOSE YOUR EYES...
ALL RIGHT... ♥
HMMM?

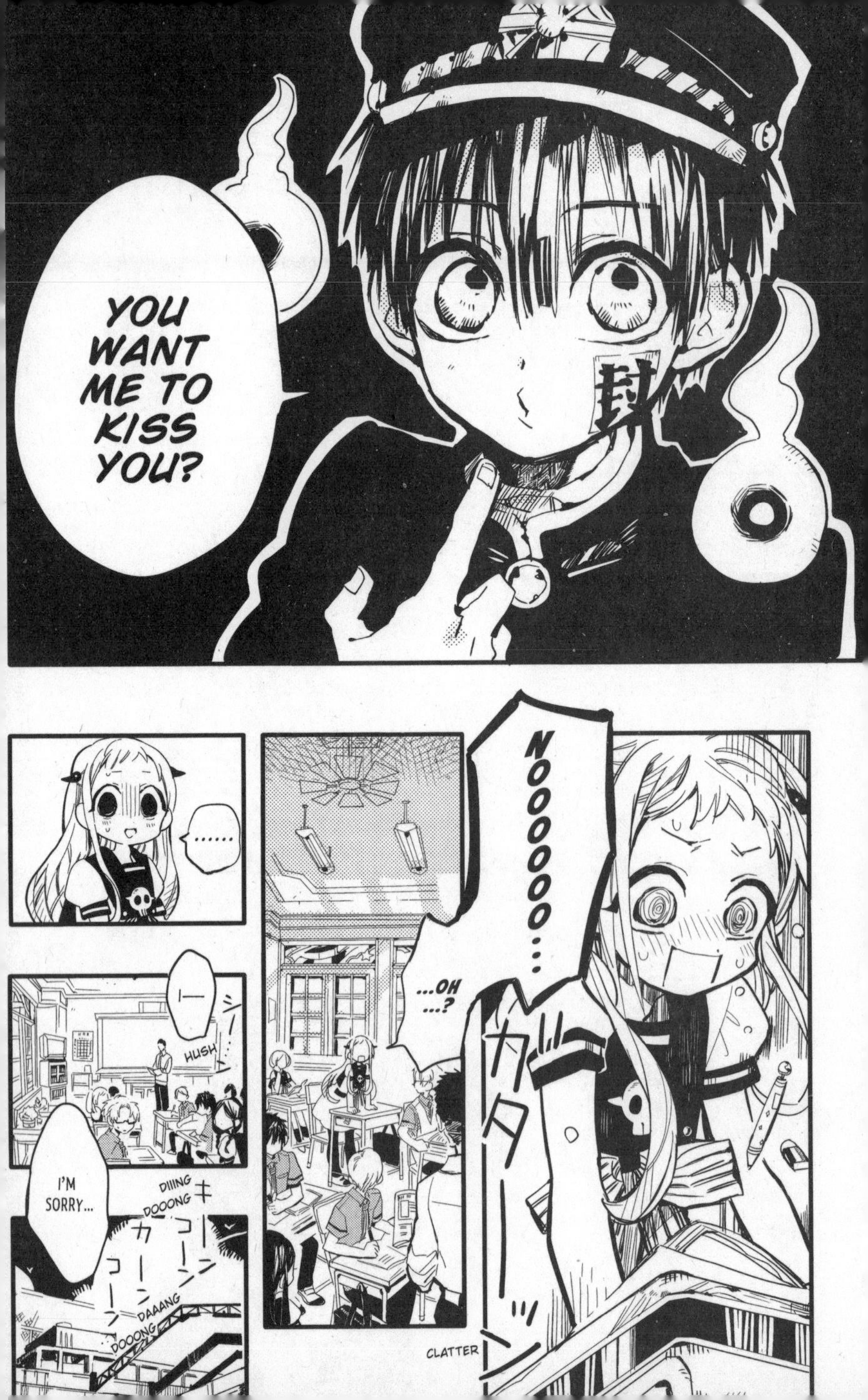

YOU WANT ME TO KISS YOU?
NOOOOOOOO...
カタッ
CLATTER
...OH ...?
....
I—
シーン
HUSH
I'M SORRY...
キーンコーンカーンコーン
DIIING DOOONG DAAANG DOOONG

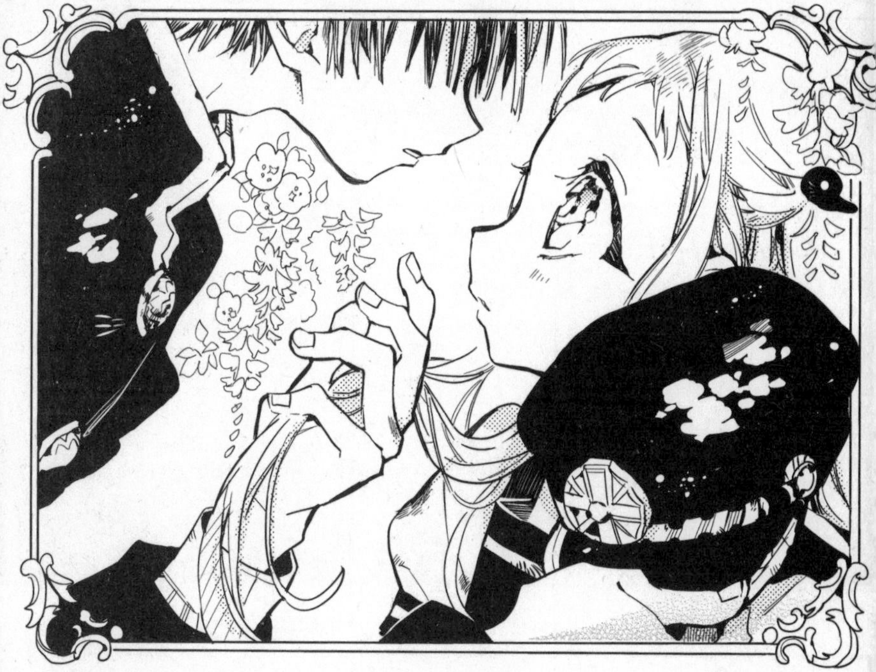

SPOOK 8 THE CONFESSION TREE

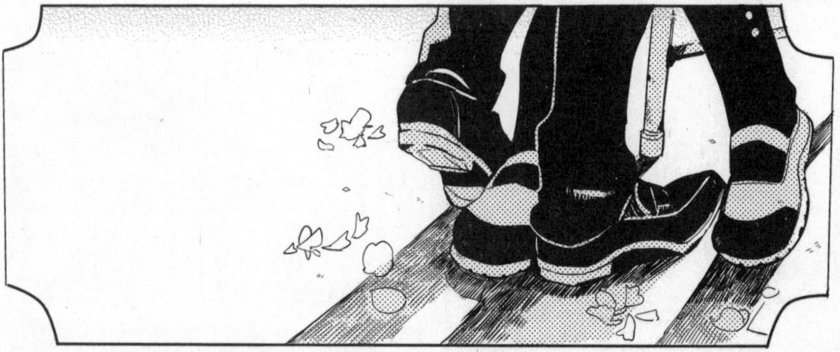

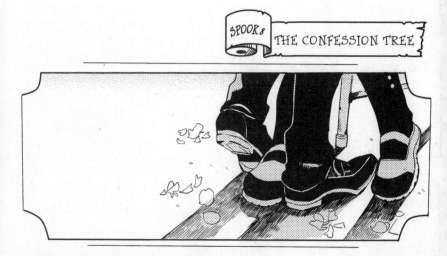

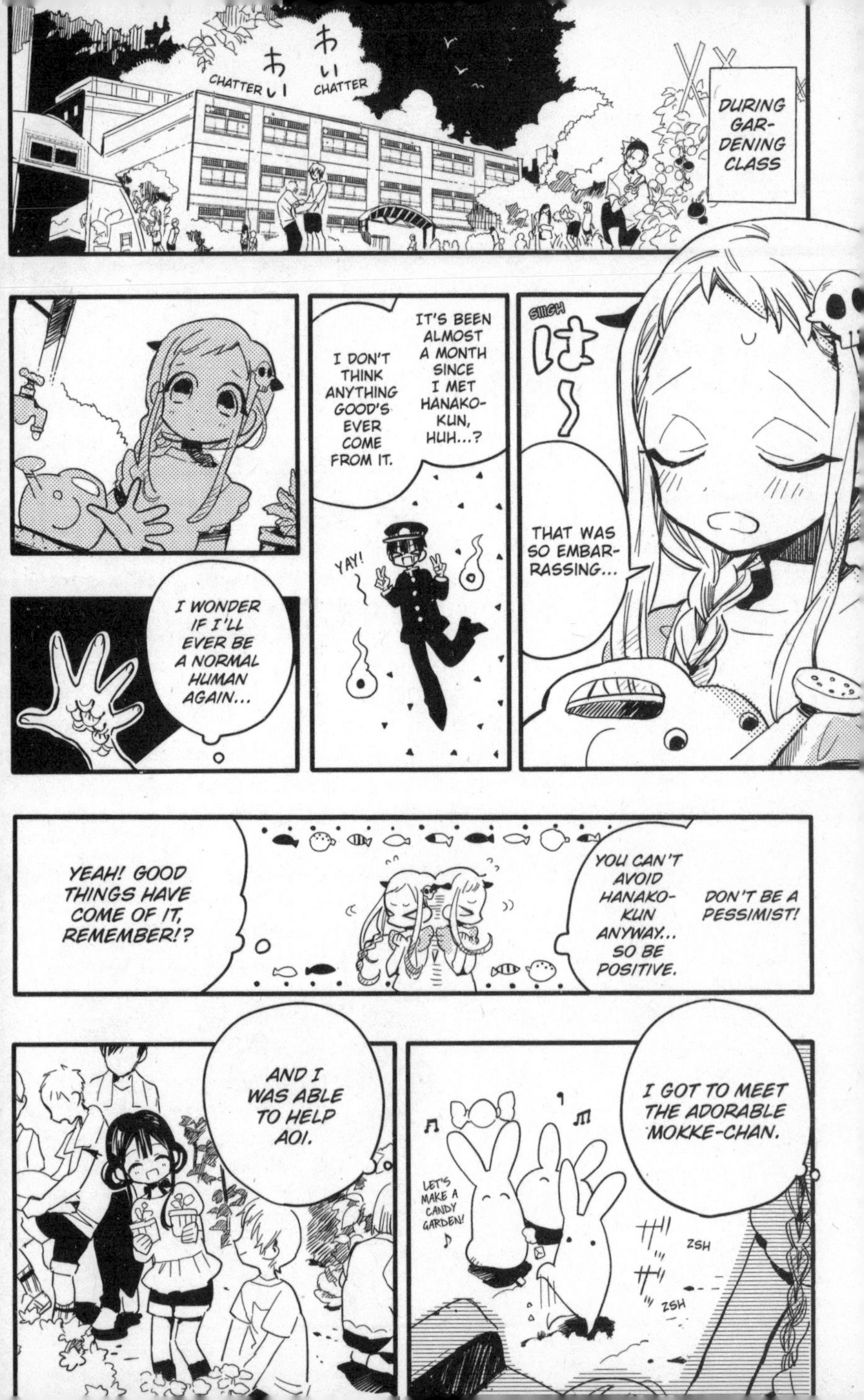
DURING GARDENING CLASS
CHATTER
CHATTER
SIIGH
THAT WAS SO EMBARRASSING...
IT'S BEEN ALMOST A MONTH SINCE I MET HANAKO-KUN, HUH...?
I DON'T THINK ANYTHING GOOD'S EVER COME FROM IT.
YAY!
I WONDER IF I'LL EVER BE A NORMAL HUMAN AGAIN...
DON'T BE A PESSIMIST!
YOU CAN'T AVOID HANAKO-KUN ANYWAY... SO BE POSITIVE.
YEAH! GOOD THINGS HAVE COME OF IT, REMEMBER!?
I GOT TO MEET THE ADORABLE MOKKE-CHAN.
LET'S MAKE A CANDY GARDEN!
ZSH
ZSH
AND I WAS ABLE TO HELP AOI.

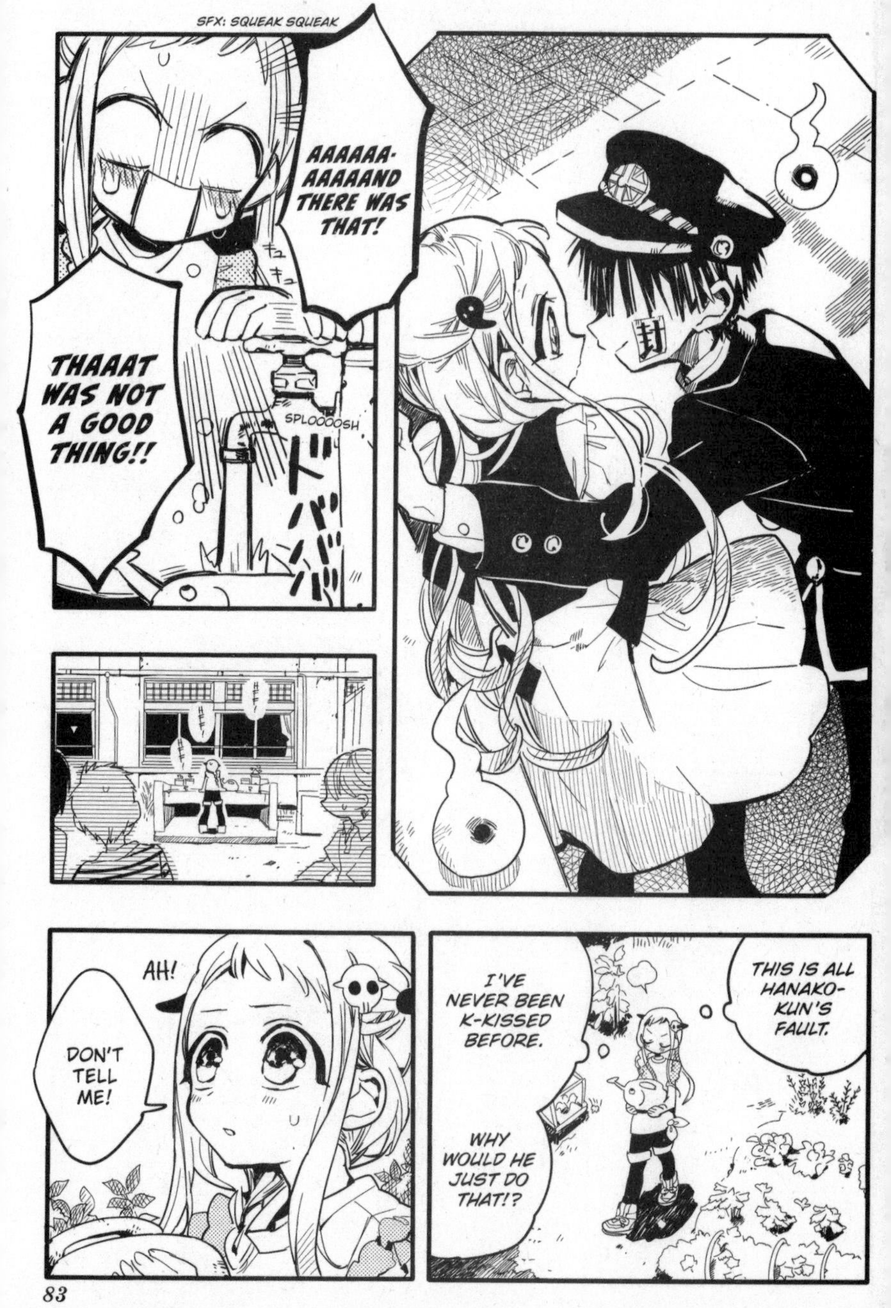
SFX: SQUEAK SQUEAK
AAAAAA-AAAAAND THERE WAS THAT!
THAAAT WAS NOT A GOOD THING!!
SPLOOOOSH
THIS IS ALL HANAKO-KUN'S FAULT.
I'VE NEVER BEEN K-KISSED BEFORE.
WHY WOULD HE JUST DO THAT!?
AH!
DON'T TELL ME!

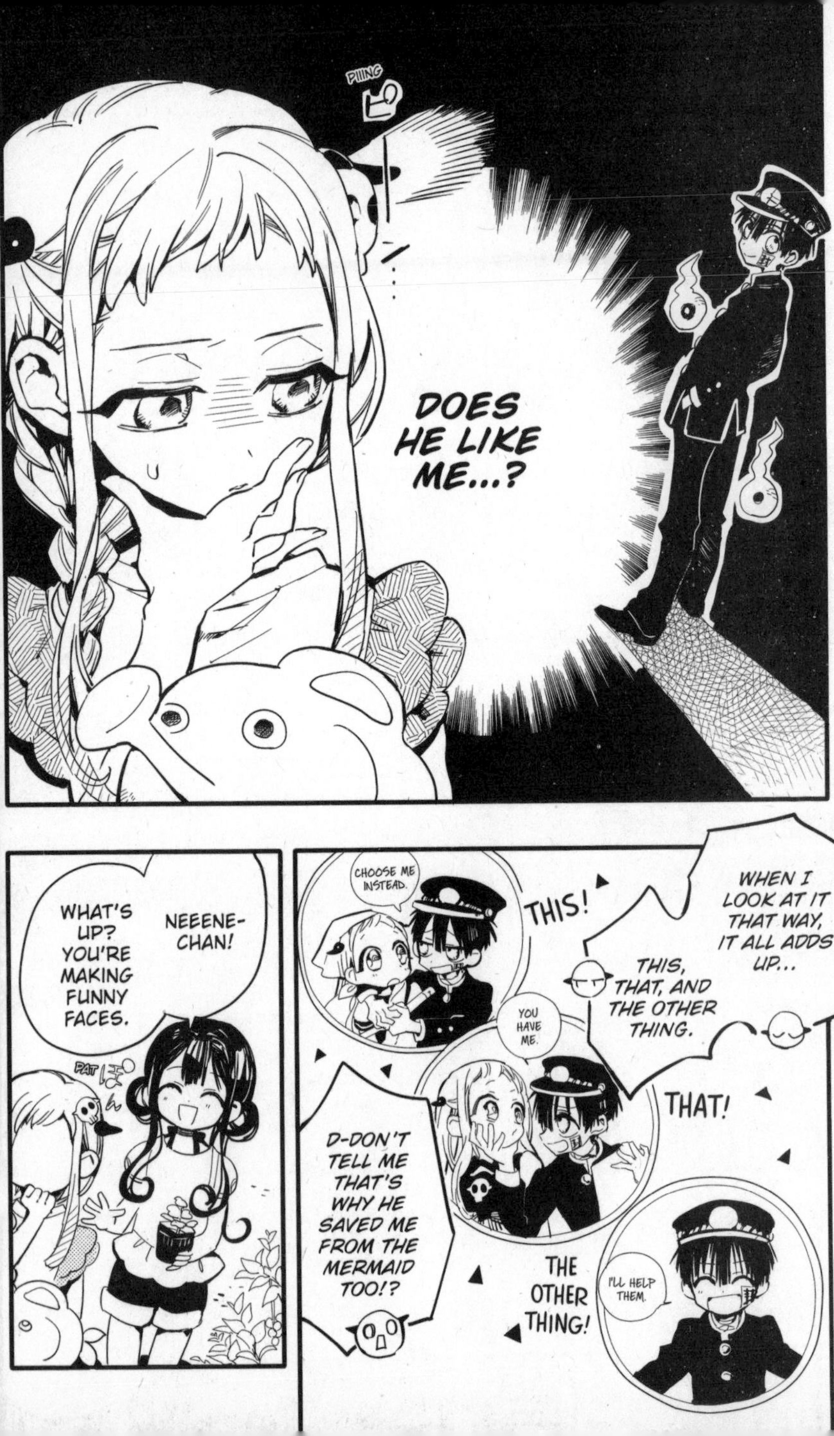
PIIING
DOES HE LIKE ME...?
WHEN I LOOK AT IT THAT WAY, IT ALL ADDS UP...
THIS, THAT, AND THE OTHER THING.
THIS!
CHOOSE ME INSTEAD.
THAT!
YOU HAVE ME.
THE OTHER THING!
I'LL HELP THEM.
D-DON'T TELL ME THAT'S WHY HE SAVED ME FROM THE MERMAID TOO!?
NEEENE-CHAN!
WHAT'S UP? YOU'RE MAKING FUNNY FACES.
PAT

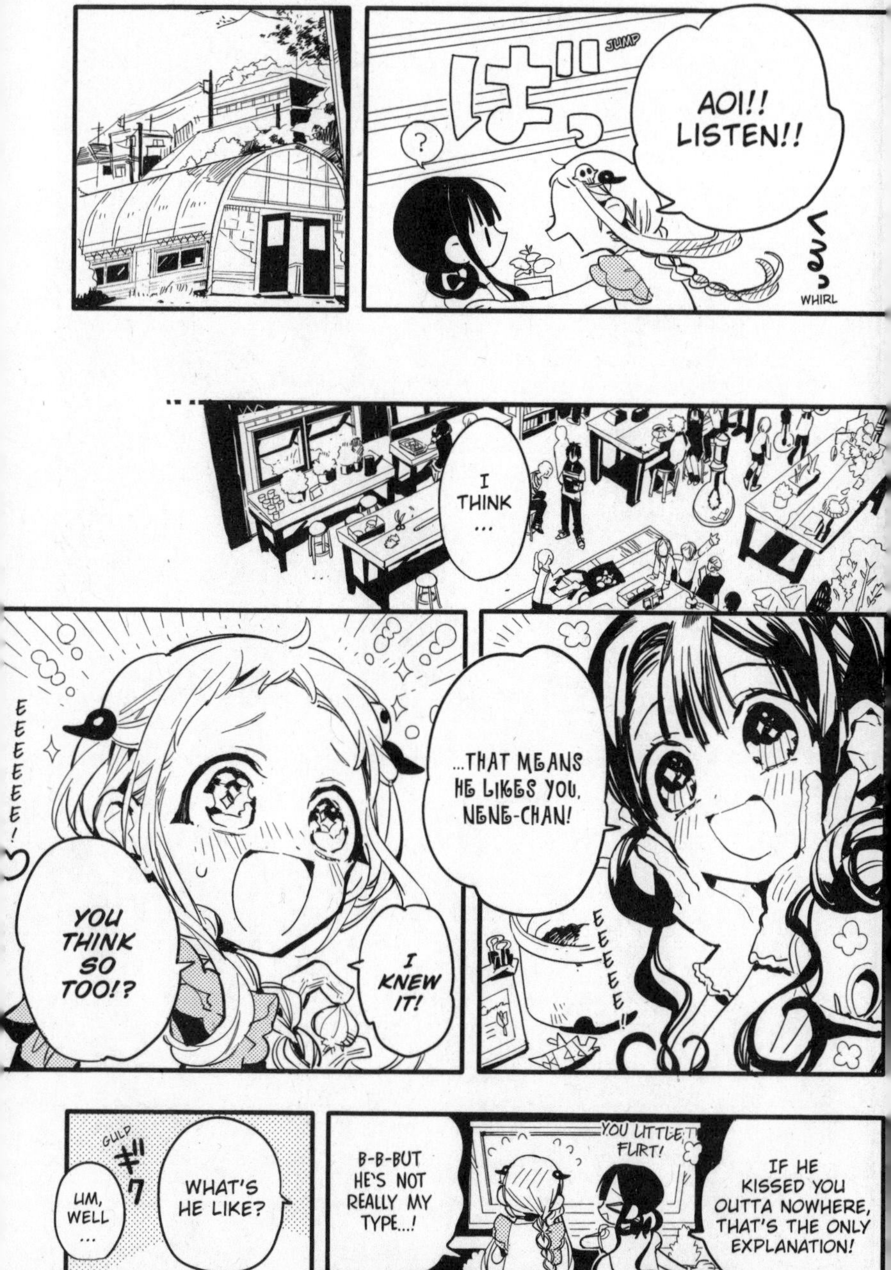
AOI!! LISTEN!!
JUMP
?
WHIRL
I THINK ...
...THAT MEANS HE LIKES YOU, NENE-CHAN!
EEEEEE!!
I KNEW IT!
YOU THINK SO TOO!?
EEEEEEEE!
IF HE KISSED YOU OUTTA NOWHERE, THAT'S THE ONLY EXPLANATION!
YOU LITTLE FLIRT!
B-B-BUT HE'S NOT REALLY MY TYPE...!
WHAT'S HE LIKE?
GULP
UM, WELL ...

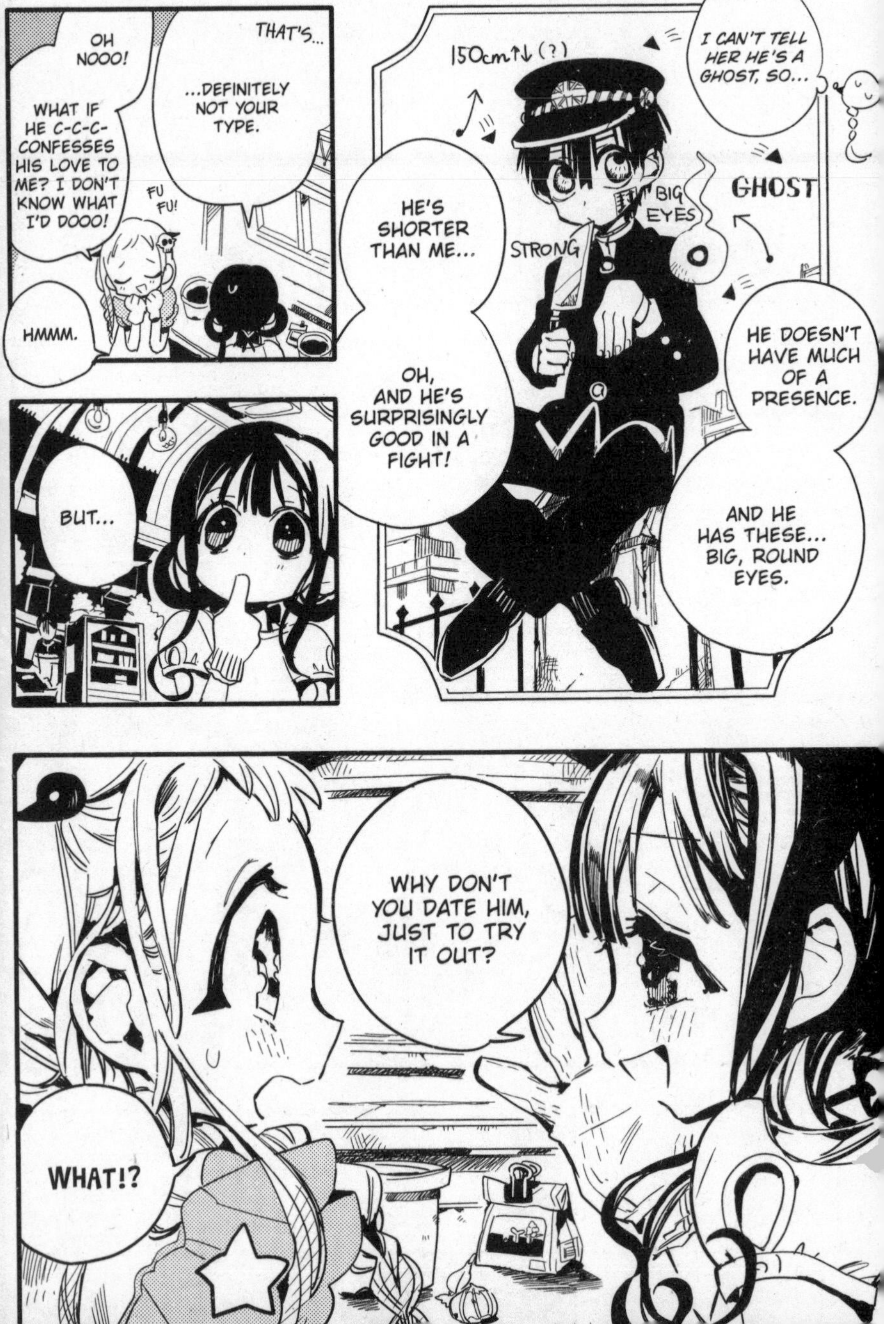

I CAN'T TELL HER HE'S A GHOST, SO...
150cm↑↓(?)
GHOST
BIG EYES
HE DOESN'T HAVE MUCH OF A PRESENCE.
HE'S SHORTER THAN ME...
STRONG
AND HE HAS THESE... BIG, ROUND EYES.
OH, AND HE'S SURPRISINGLY GOOD IN A FIGHT!
THAT'S...
...DEFINITELY NOT YOUR TYPE.
OH NOOO!
WHAT IF HE C-C-C-CONFESSES HIS LOVE TO ME? I DON'T KNOW WHAT I'D DOOO!
FU FU!
HMMM.
BUT...
WHY DON'T YOU DATE HIM, JUST TO TRY IT OUT?
WHAT!?

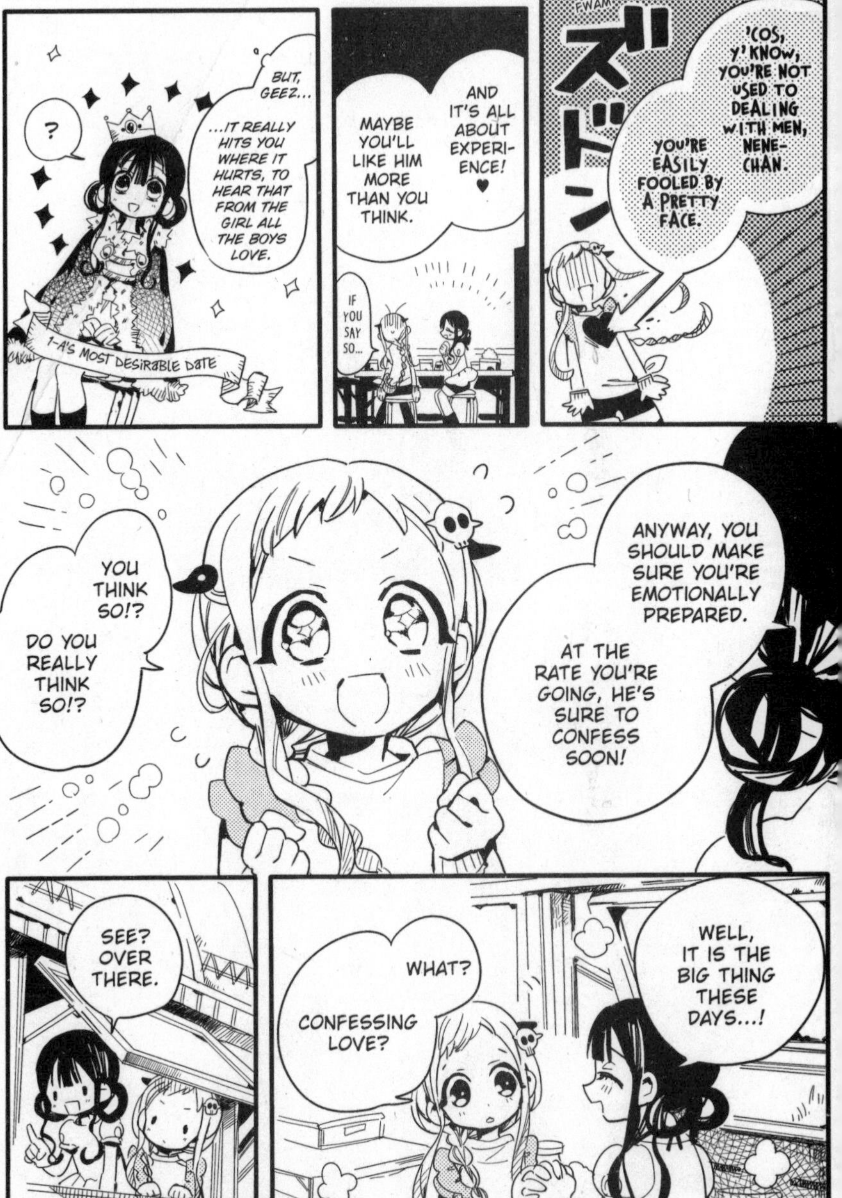
FWAM
'COS, Y'KNOW, YOU'RE NOT USED TO DEALING WITH MEN, NENE-CHAN.
YOU'RE EASILY FOOLED BY A PRETTY FACE.
AND IT'S ALL ABOUT EXPERIENCE! ♥
MAYBE YOU'LL LIKE HIM MORE THAN YOU THINK.
IF YOU SAY SO...
BUT, GEEZ...
...IT REALLY HITS YOU WHERE IT HURTS, TO HEAR THAT FROM THE GIRL ALL THE BOYS LOVE.
?
1-A'S MOST DESIRABLE DATE
ANYWAY, YOU SHOULD MAKE SURE YOU'RE EMOTIONALLY PREPARED.
AT THE RATE YOU'RE GOING, HE'S SURE TO CONFESS SOON!
YOU THINK SO!?
DO YOU REALLY THINK SO!?
WELL, IT IS THE BIG THING THESE DAYS...!
WHAT?
CONFESSING LOVE?
SEE? OVER THERE.

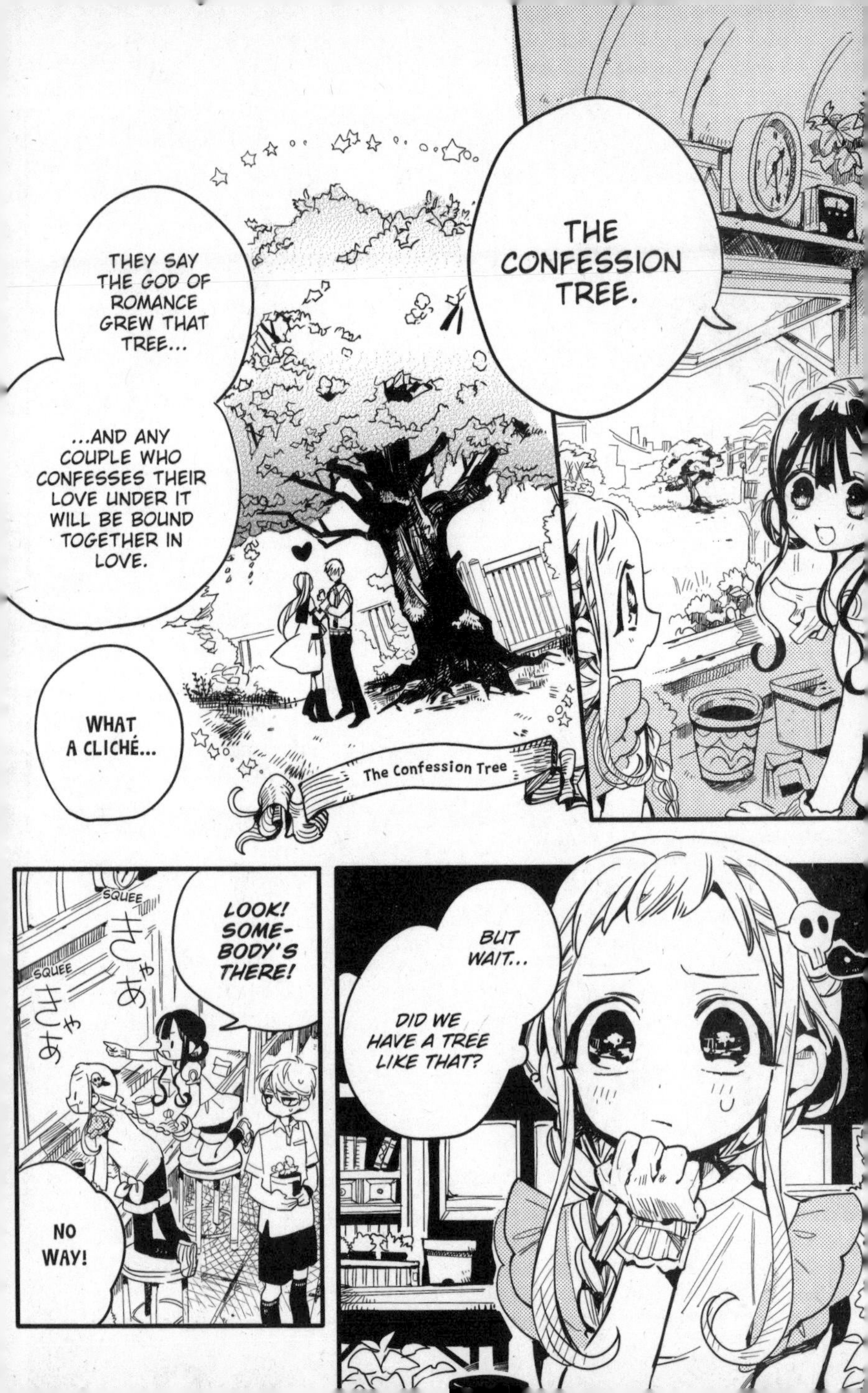
THE CONFESSION TREE.
THEY SAY THE GOD OF ROMANCE GREW THAT TREE...
...AND ANY COUPLE WHO CONFESSES THEIR LOVE UNDER IT WILL BE BOUND TOGETHER IN LOVE.
WHAT A CLICHÉ...
The Confession Tree
BUT WAIT...
DID WE HAVE A TREE LIKE THAT?
LOOK! SOME-BODY'S THERE!
SQUEE
きゃあ
SQUEE
きゃあ
NO WAY!

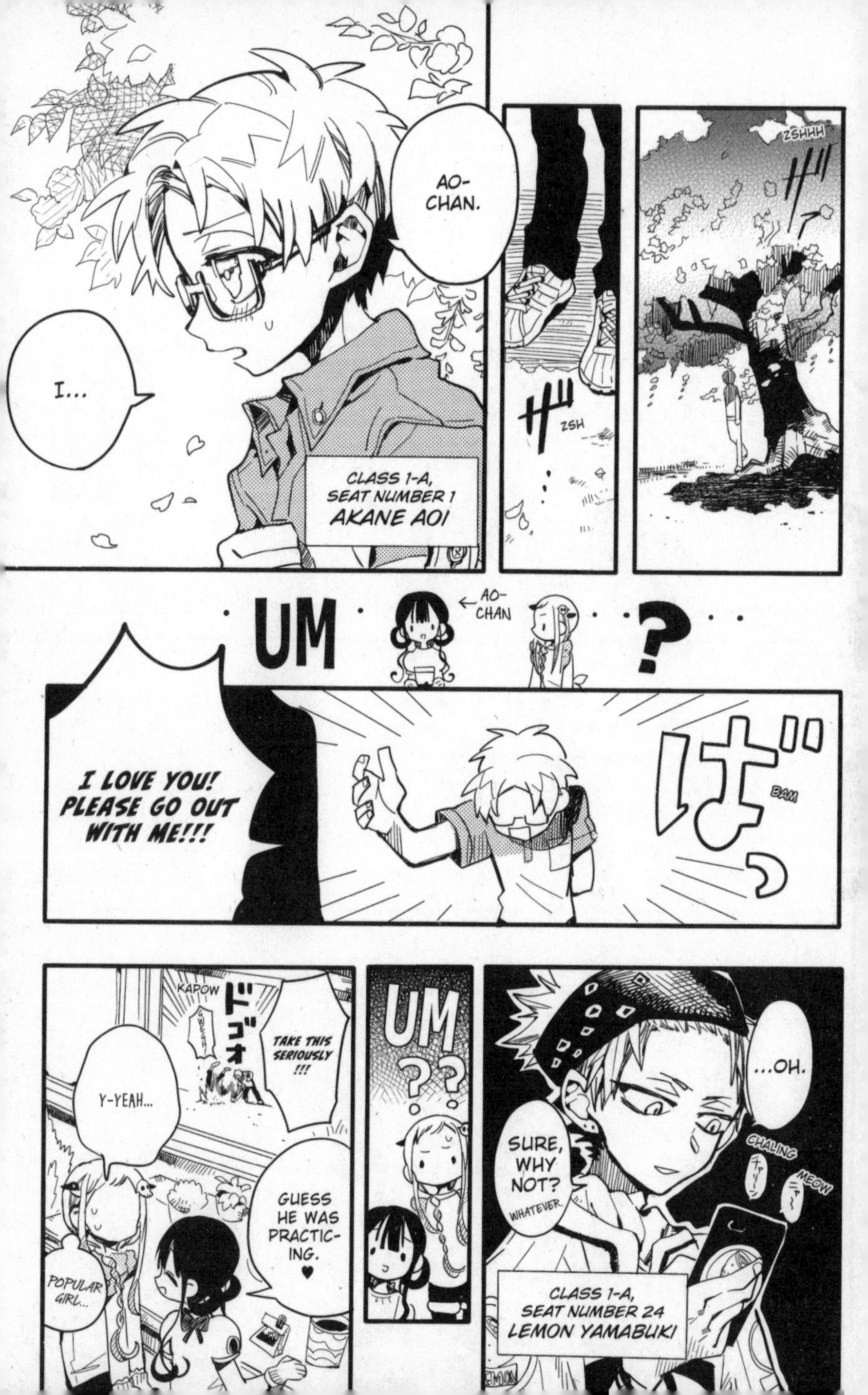
ZSHHH
ザッ
ザッ
ZSH
AO-CHAN.
I...
CLASS 1-A, SEAT NUMBER 1 AKANE AOI
UM
AO-CHAN
?
I LOVE YOU! PLEASE GO OUT WITH ME!!!
ばっ
BAM
...OH.
SURE, WHY NOT?
WHATEVER.
CHALING
チャリーン
MEOW
ニャ~
CLASS 1-A, SEAT NUMBER 24 LEMON YAMABUKI
UM
??
TAKE THIS SERIOUSLY!!!
ドゴォ
KAPOW
GWESH!
Y-YEAH...
GUESS HE WAS PRACTICING. ♥
POPULAR GIRL...

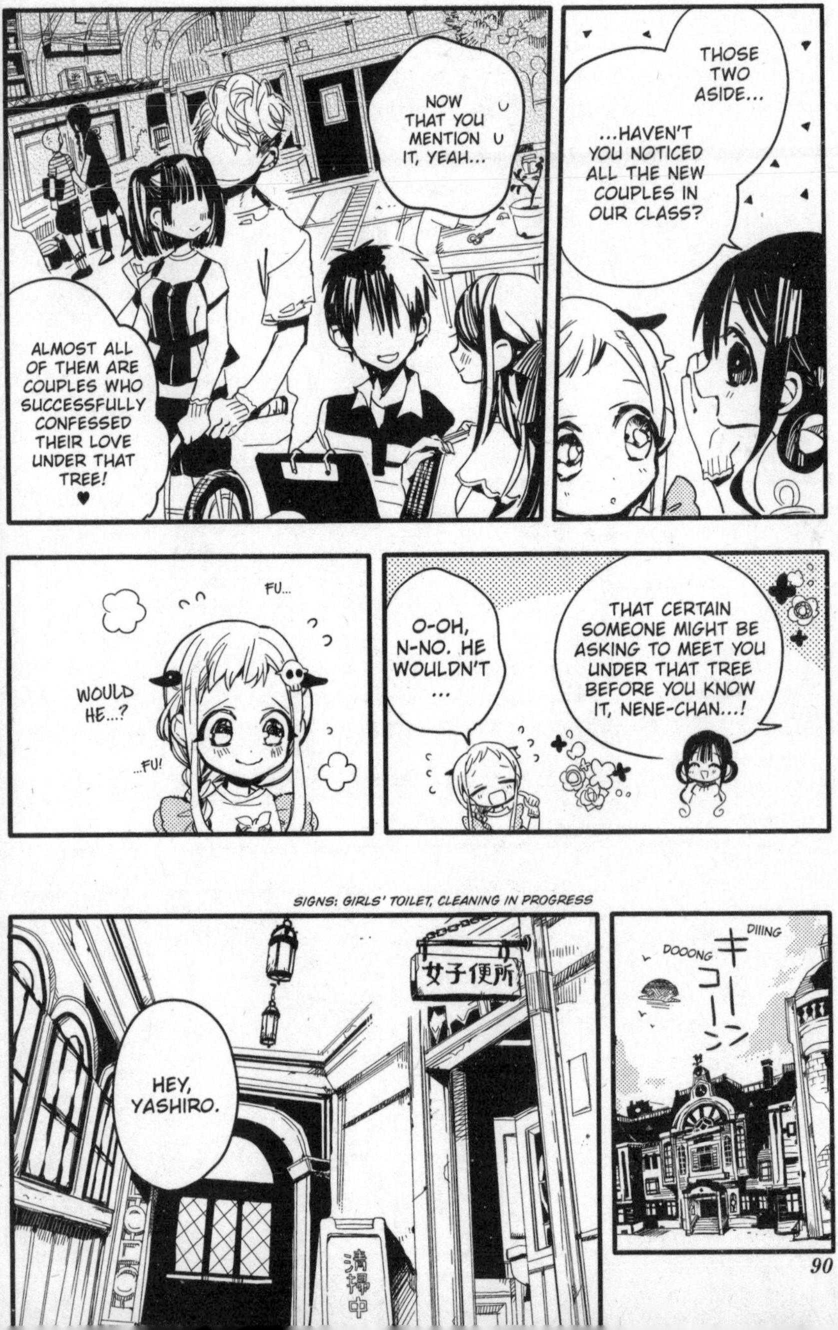
THOSE TWO ASIDE...
...HAVEN'T YOU NOTICED ALL THE NEW COUPLES IN OUR CLASS?
NOW THAT YOU MENTION IT, YEAH...
ALMOST ALL OF THEM ARE COUPLES WHO SUCCESSFULLY CONFESSED THEIR LOVE UNDER THAT TREE! ♥
THAT CERTAIN SOMEONE MIGHT BE ASKING TO MEET YOU UNDER THAT TREE BEFORE YOU KNOW IT, NENE-CHAN...!
O-OH, N-NO. HE WOULDN'T ...
FU...
WOULD HE...?
...FU!
DIIING
DOOONG
SIGNS: GIRLS' TOILET, CLEANING IN PROGRESS
女子便所
HEY, YASHIRO.
清掃中

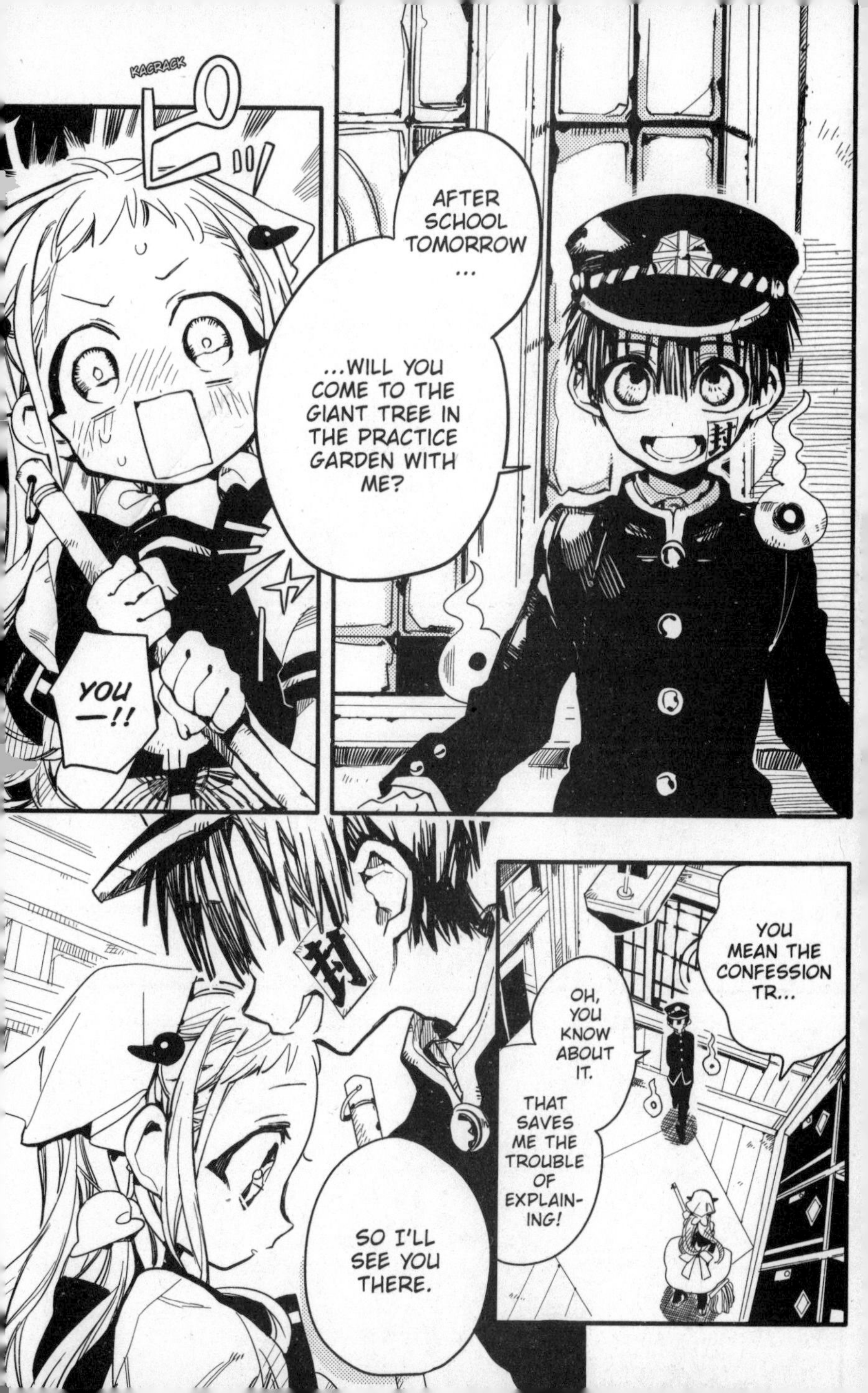
AFTER SCHOOL TOMORROW ...
...WILL YOU COME TO THE GIANT TREE IN THE PRACTICE GARDEN WITH ME?
KACRACK
DO
YOU—!!
YOU MEAN THE CONFESSION TR...
OH, YOU KNOW ABOUT IT.
THAT SAVES ME THE TROUBLE OF EXPLAIN-ING!
SO I'LL SEE YOU THERE.

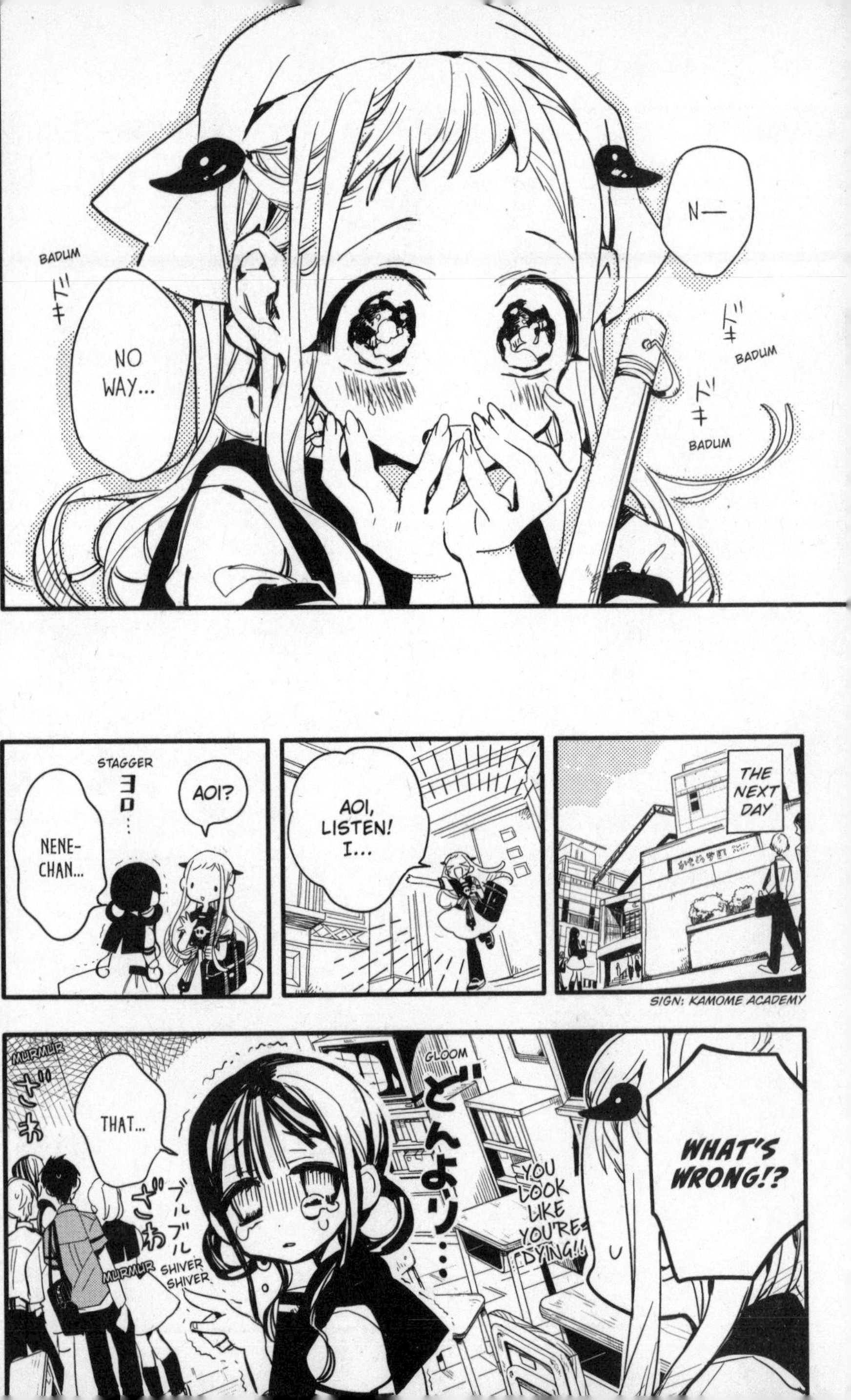
N—
ドキ
BADUM
ドキ
BADUM
NO WAY...
ドキ
BADUM
THE NEXT DAY
SIGN: KAMOME ACADEMY
AOI, LISTEN! I...
AOI?
ヨロ…
STAGGER
NENE-CHAN...
WHAT'S WRONG!?
YOU LOOK LIKE YOU'RE DYING!!
どんより…
GLOOM
THAT...
ざわ
MURMUR
ブルブル
SHIVER SHIVER
ざわ
MURMUR

ARMBAND: STUDENT COUNCIL

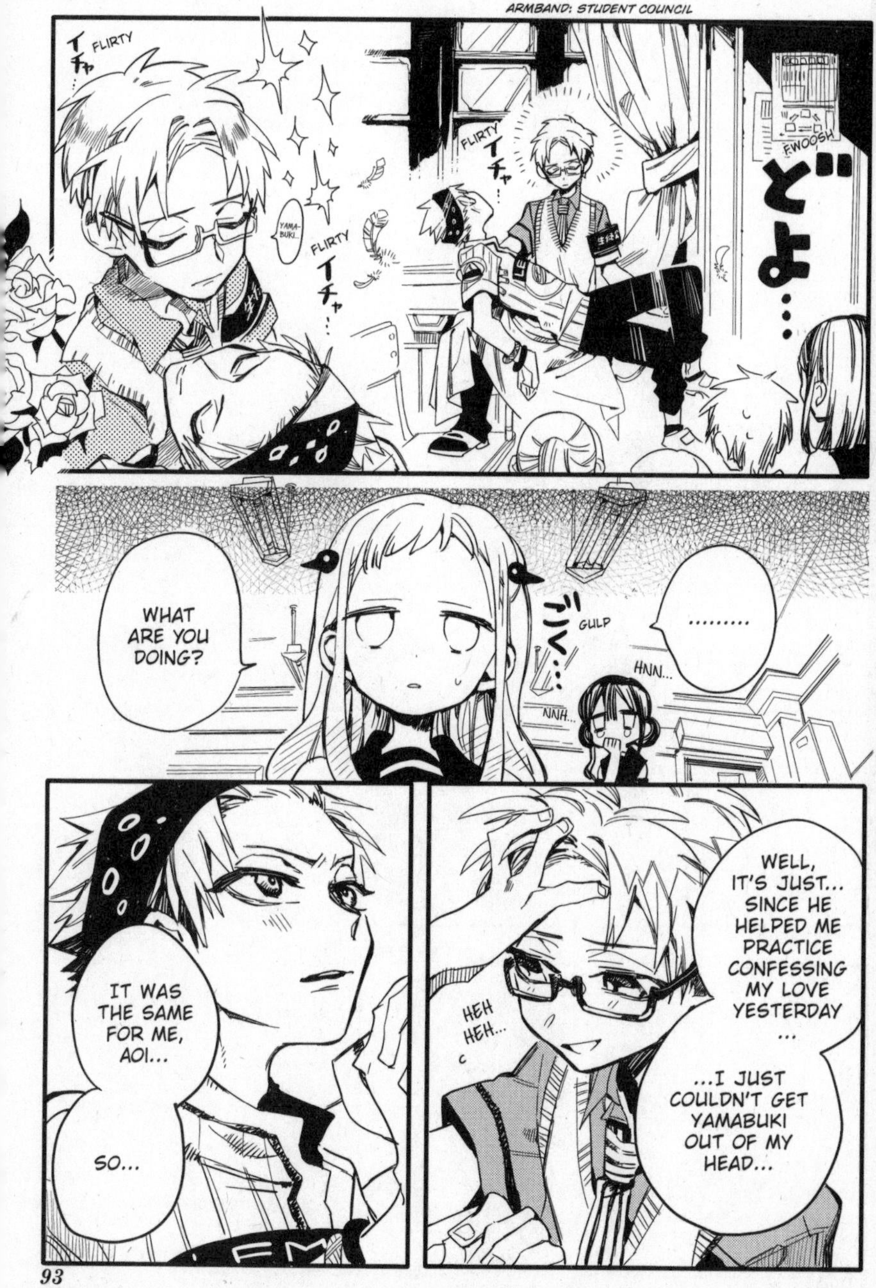

FWOOSH
どよ…
FLIRTY
イチャ…
YAMA-BUKI…
FLIRTY
イチャ…
FLIRTY
イチャ…
………
HNN…
ごく…
GULP
NNH…
WHAT ARE YOU DOING?
WELL, IT'S JUST… SINCE HE HELPED ME PRACTICE CONFESSING MY LOVE YESTERDAY …
…I JUST COULDN'T GET YAMABUKI OUT OF MY HEAD…
HEH HEH…
IT WAS THE SAME FOR ME, AOI…
SO…

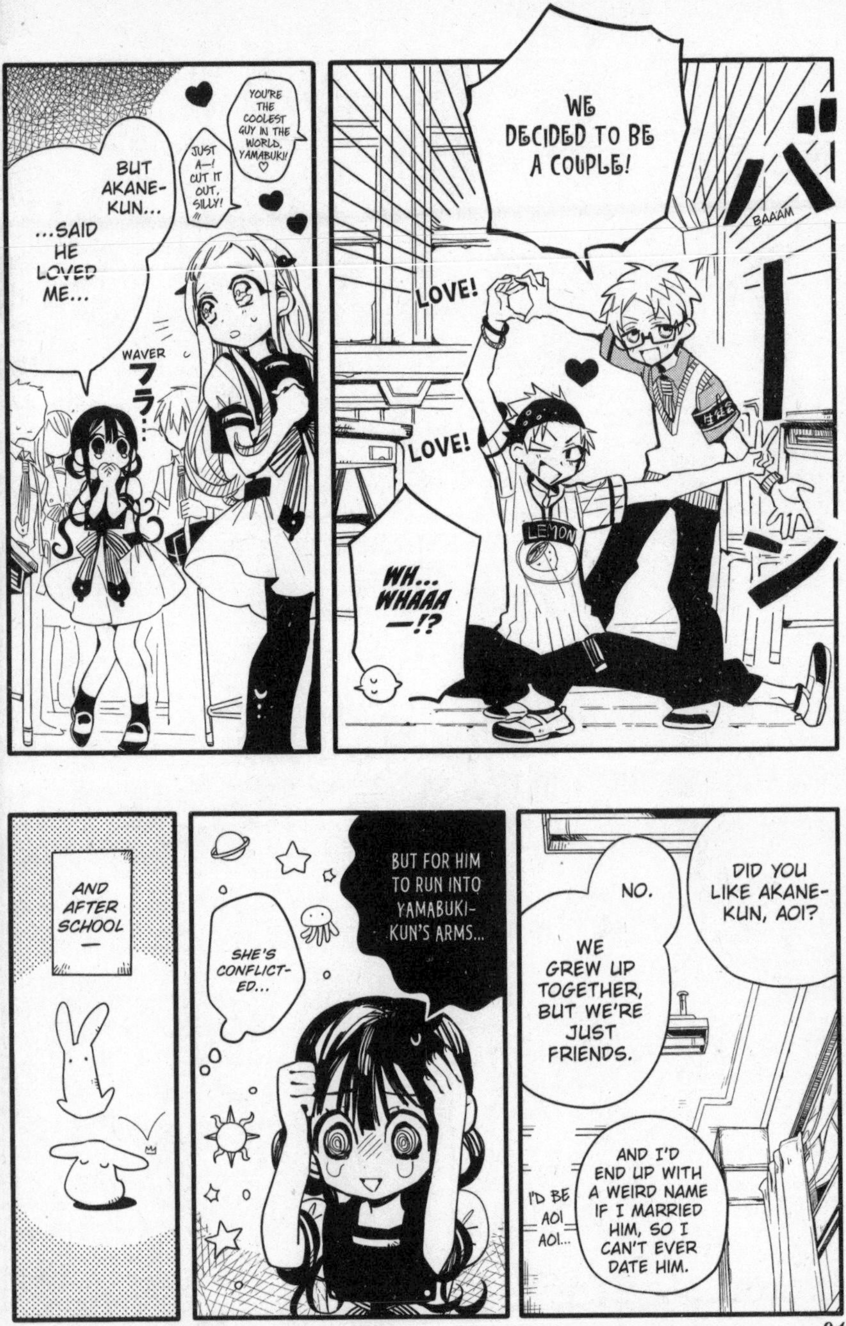
WE DECIDED TO BE A COUPLE!
バーン
BAAAM
LOVE!
LOVE!
WH... WHAAA—!?
YOU'RE THE COOLEST GUY IN THE WORLD, YAMABUKI! ♡
JUST A—! CUT IT OUT, SILLY!
BUT AKANE-KUN...
...SAID HE LOVED ME...
フラ…
WAVER
DID YOU LIKE AKANE-KUN, AOI?
NO.
WE GREW UP TOGETHER, BUT WE'RE JUST FRIENDS.
AND I'D END UP WITH A WEIRD NAME IF I MARRIED HIM, SO I CAN'T EVER DATE HIM.
I'D BE AOI AOI...
BUT FOR HIM TO RUN INTO YAMABUKI-KUN'S ARMS...
SHE'S CONFLICTED...
AND AFTER SCHOOL—

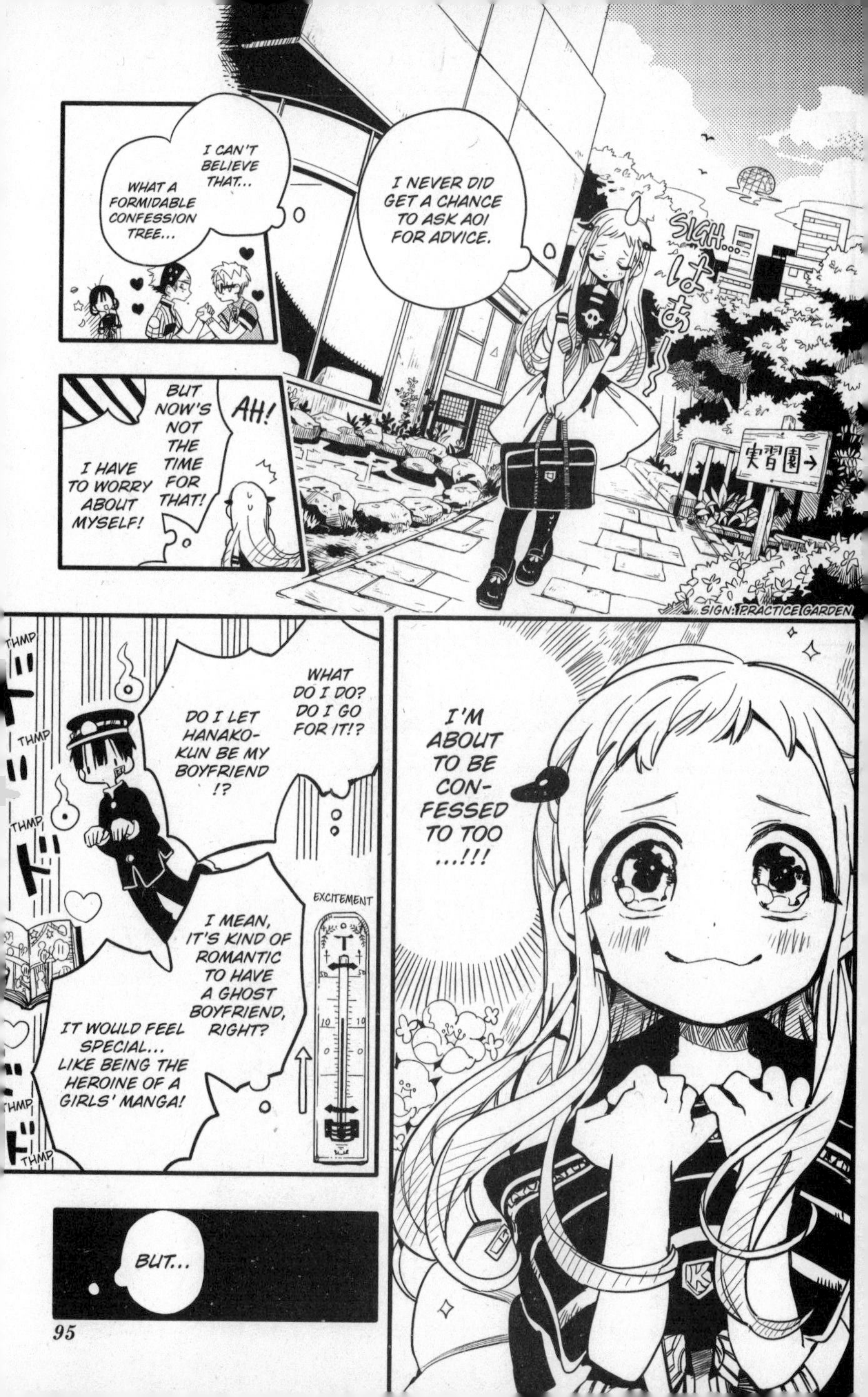

I NEVER DID GET A CHANCE TO ASK AOI FOR ADVICE.
SIGH... はぁ~
実習園→
SIGN: PRACTICE GARDEN
I CAN'T BELIEVE THAT...
WHAT A FORMIDABLE CONFESSION TREE...
AH!
BUT NOW'S NOT THE TIME FOR THAT!
I HAVE TO WORRY ABOUT MYSELF!
I'M ABOUT TO BE CON-FESSED TO TOO ...!!!
WHAT DO I DO? DO I GO FOR IT!?
DO I LET HANAKO-KUN BE MY BOYFRIEND !?
THMP
THMP
THMP
EXCITEMENT
I MEAN, IT'S KIND OF ROMANTIC TO HAVE A GHOST BOYFRIEND, RIGHT?
IT WOULD FEEL SPECIAL... LIKE BEING THE HEROINE OF A GIRLS' MANGA!
THMP
THMP
BUT...

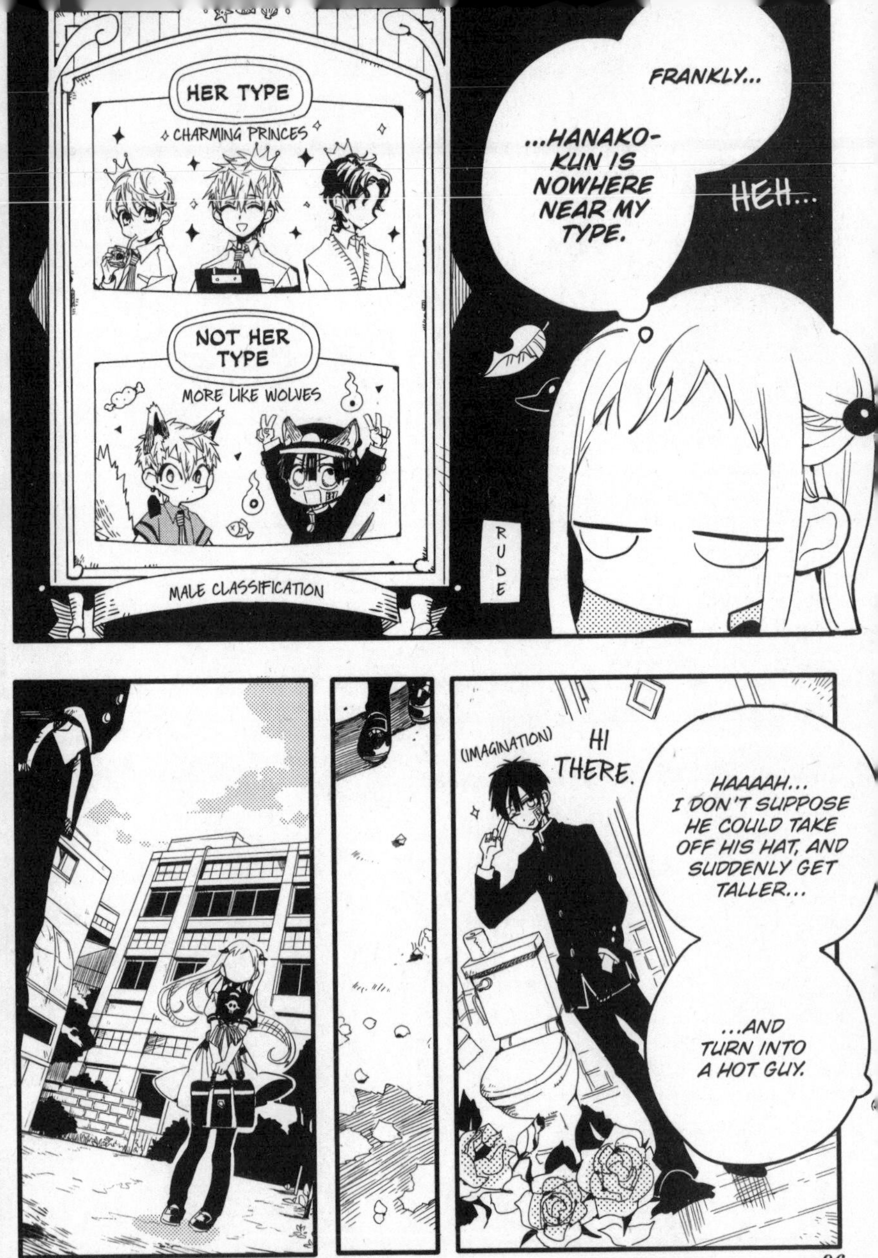
FRANKLY...
...HANAKO-KUN IS NOWHERE NEAR MY TYPE.
HEH...
RUDE
HER TYPE
CHARMING PRINCES
NOT HER TYPE
MORE LIKE WOLVES
MALE CLASSIFICATION
(IMAGINATION)
HI THERE.
HAAAAH... I DON'T SUPPOSE HE COULD TAKE OFF HIS HAT, AND SUDDENLY GET TALLER...
...AND TURN INTO A HOT GUY.

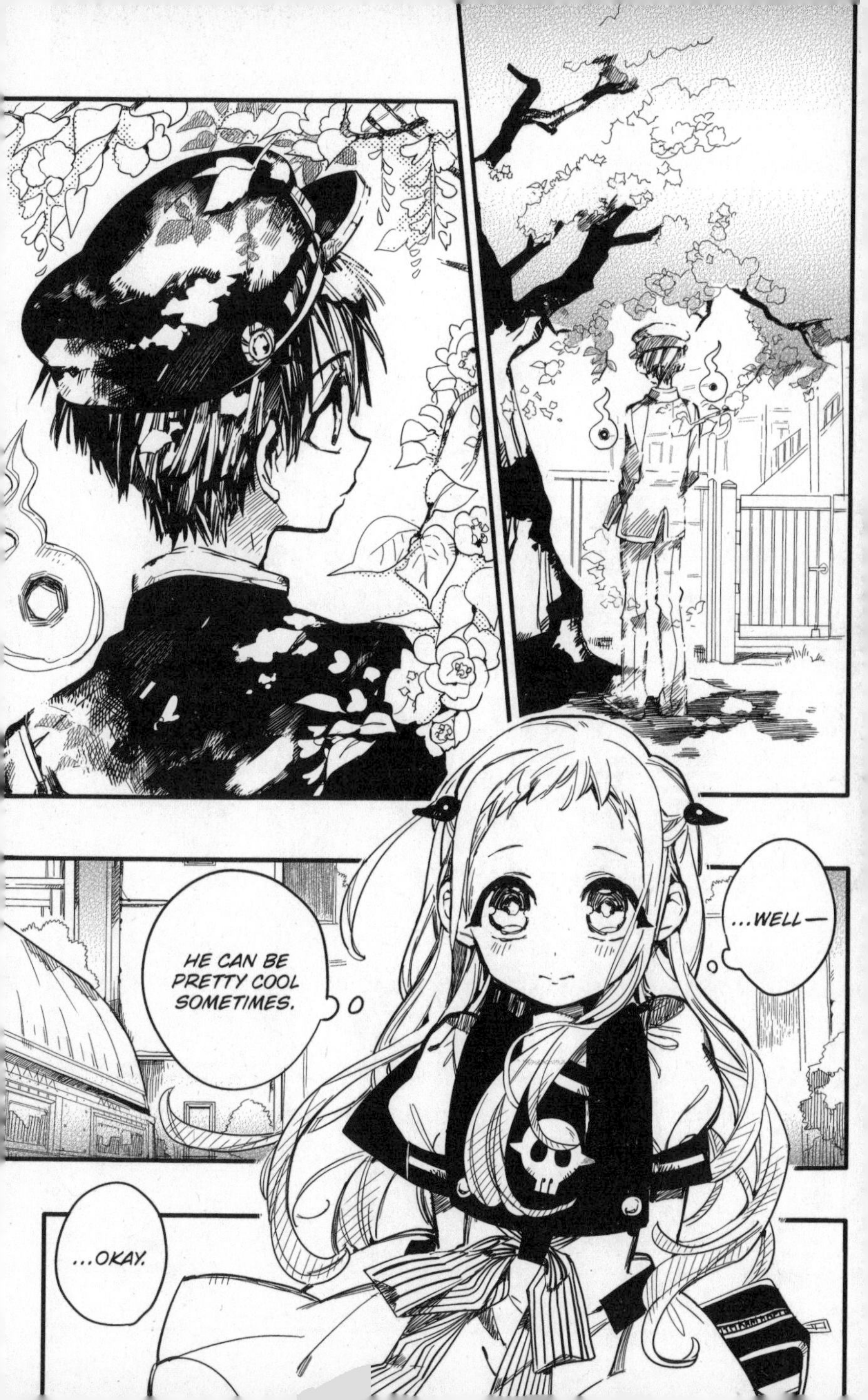
...WELL—
HE CAN BE PRETTY COOL SOMETIMES.
...OKAY.

SIGN: FESTIVAL

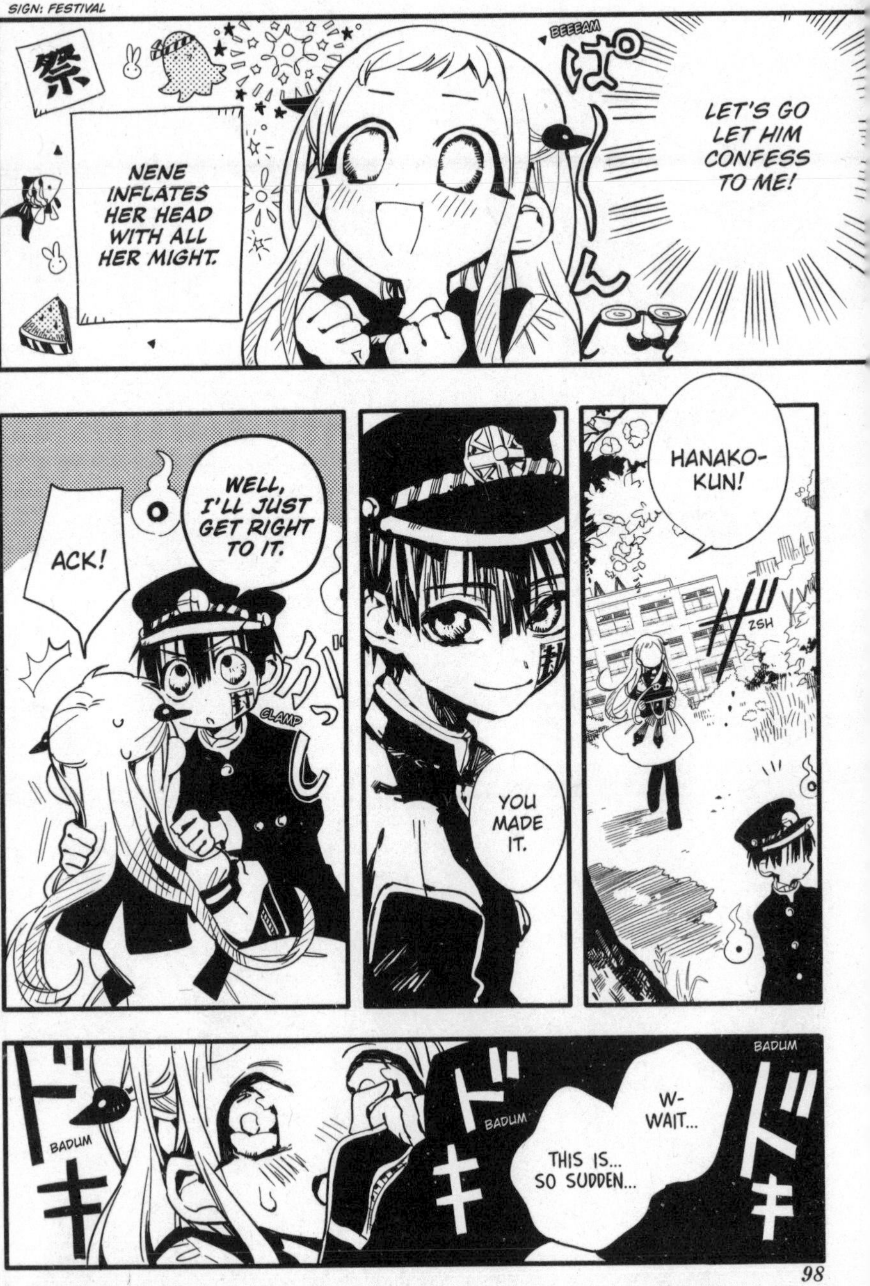
BEEEAM
LET'S GO LET HIM CONFESS TO ME!
NENE INFLATES HER HEAD WITH ALL HER MIGHT.
HANAKO-KUN!
ZSH
YOU MADE IT.
WELL, I'LL JUST GET RIGHT TO IT.
ACK!
CLAMP
BADUM
W-WAIT...
THIS IS... SO SUDDEN...
BADUM
BADUM

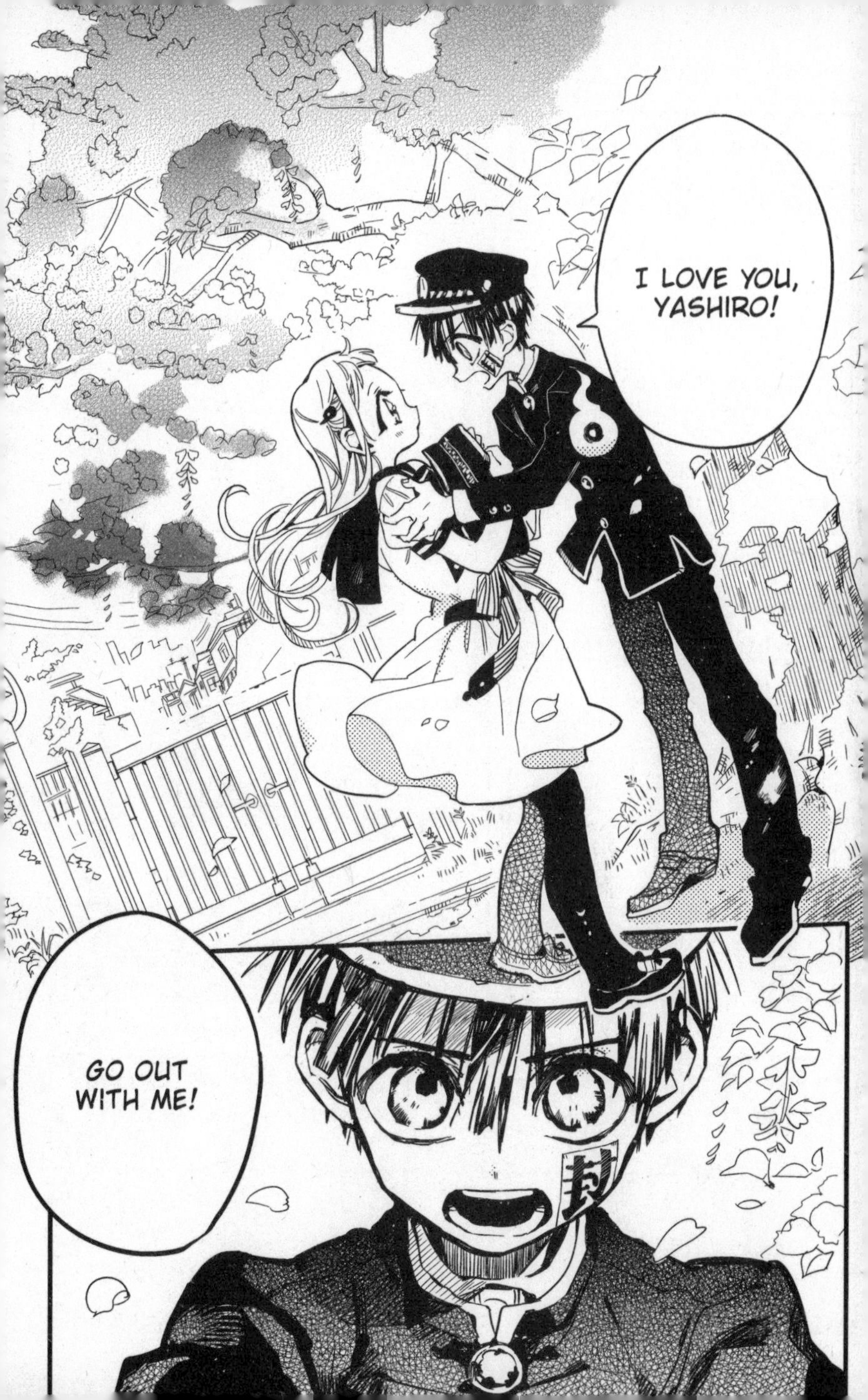
I LOVE YOU, YASHIRO!
GO OUT WITH ME!

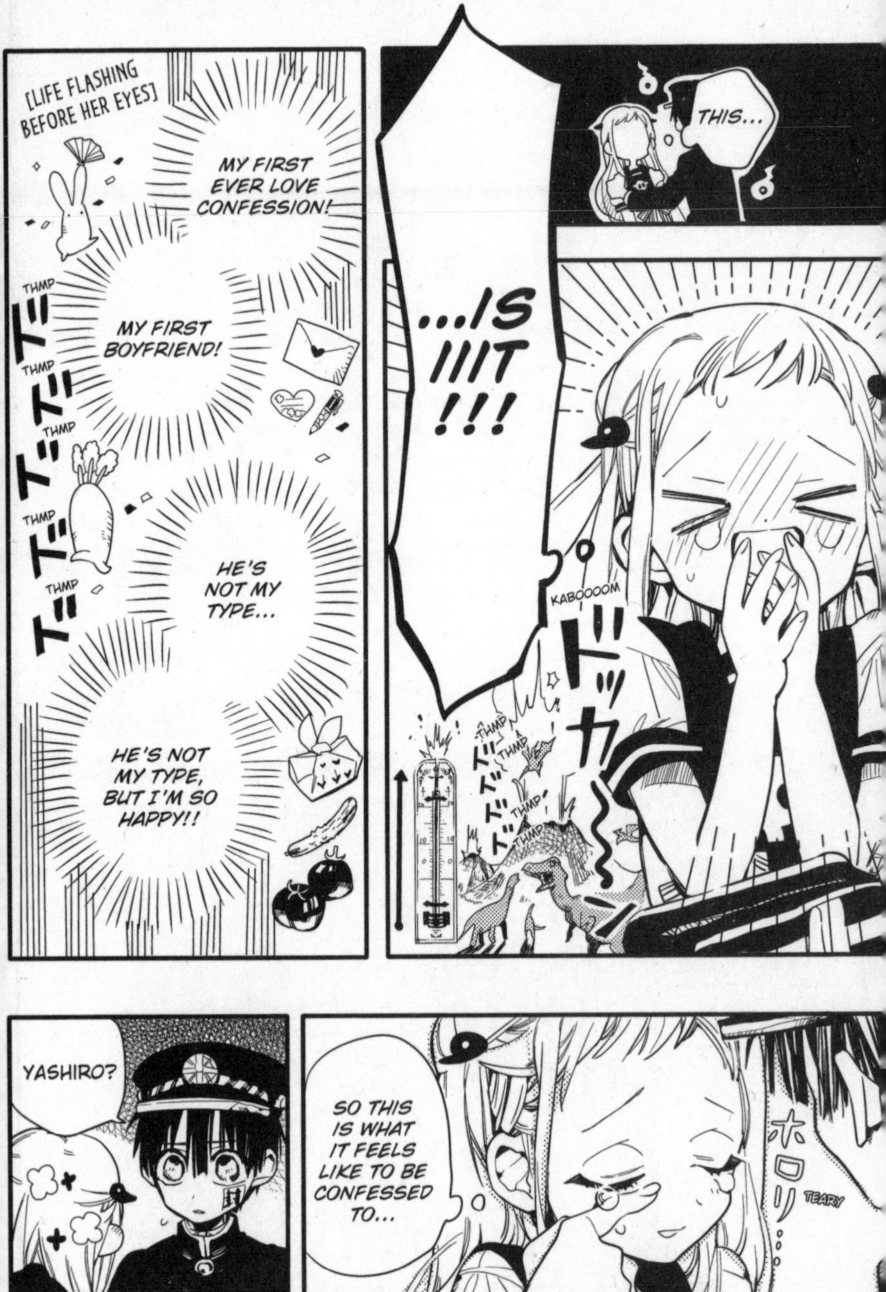
THIS...
...IS IIIT!!!
KABOOOOM
THMP
THMP
THMP
THMP
[LIFE FLASHING BEFORE HER EYES]
MY FIRST EVER LOVE CONFESSION!
THMP
MY FIRST BOYFRIEND!
THMP
THMP
THMP
HE'S NOT MY TYPE...
THMP
HE'S NOT MY TYPE, BUT I'M SO HAPPY!!
SO THIS IS WHAT IT FEELS LIKE TO BE CONFESSED TO...
TEARY
YASHIRO?

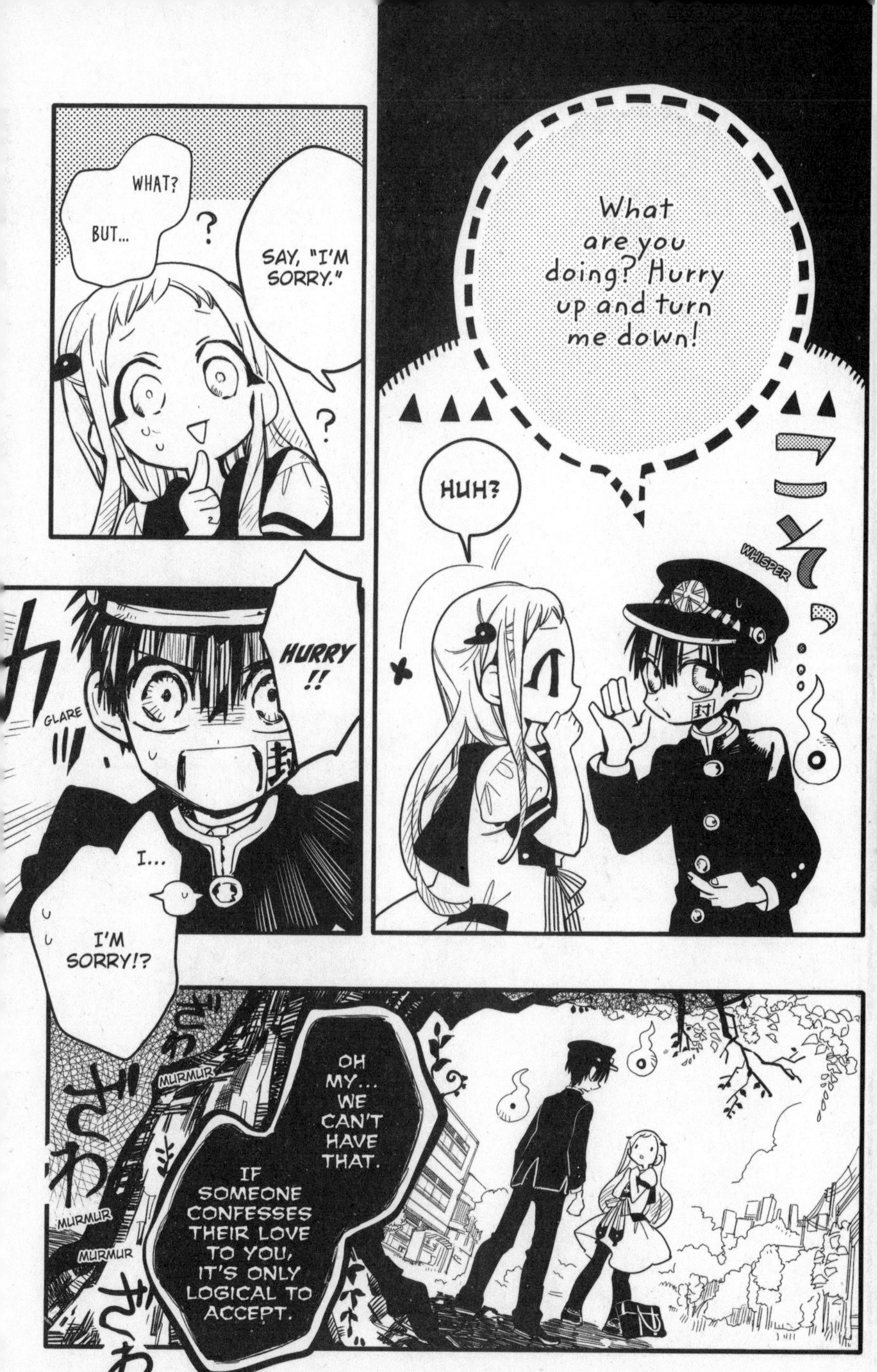
What are you doing? Hurry up and turn me down!
WHISPER
HUH?
SAY, "I'M SORRY."
WHAT?
BUT...
HURRY!!
GLARE
I...
I'M SORRY!?
MURMUR
OH MY... WE CAN'T HAVE THAT.
IF SOMEONE CONFESSES THEIR LOVE TO YOU, IT'S ONLY LOGICAL TO ACCEPT.
MURMUR
MURMUR

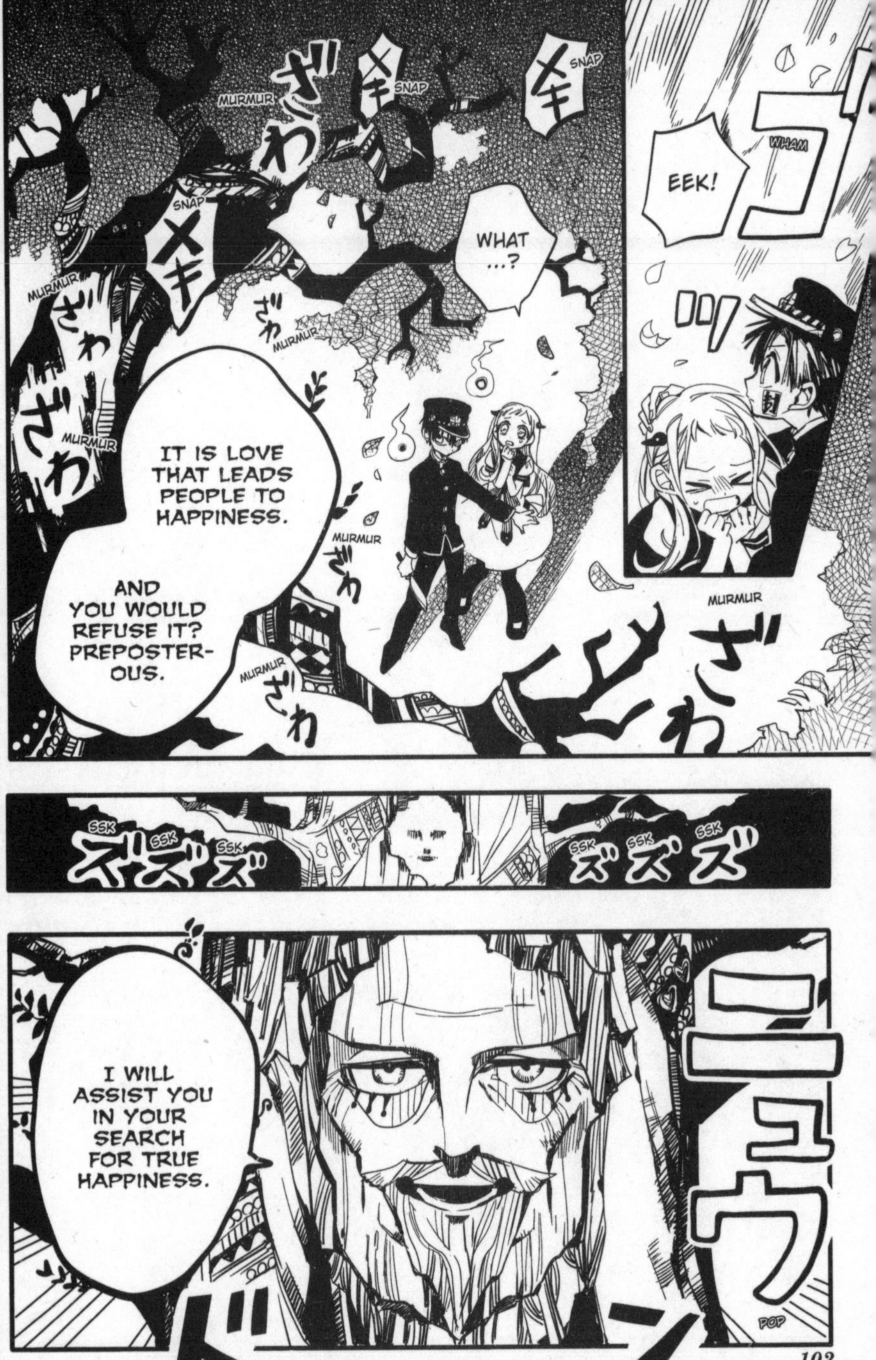

ゴッ
WHAM
EEK!
ざわ
MURMUR
メキ
SNAP
メキ
SNAP
メキ
SNAP
ざわ
MURMUR
WHAT ...?
ざわ
MURMUR
ざわ
MURMUR
IT IS LOVE THAT LEADS PEOPLE TO HAPPINESS.
AND YOU WOULD REFUSE IT? PREPOSTER-OUS.
ざわ
MURMUR
ざわ
MURMUR
ざわ
MURMUR
ズズズ
SSK SSK SSK
ズズズ
SSK SSK SSK
ニュウ
POP
I WILL ASSIST YOU IN YOUR SEARCH FOR TRUE HAPPINESS.
ドーン
BOOM

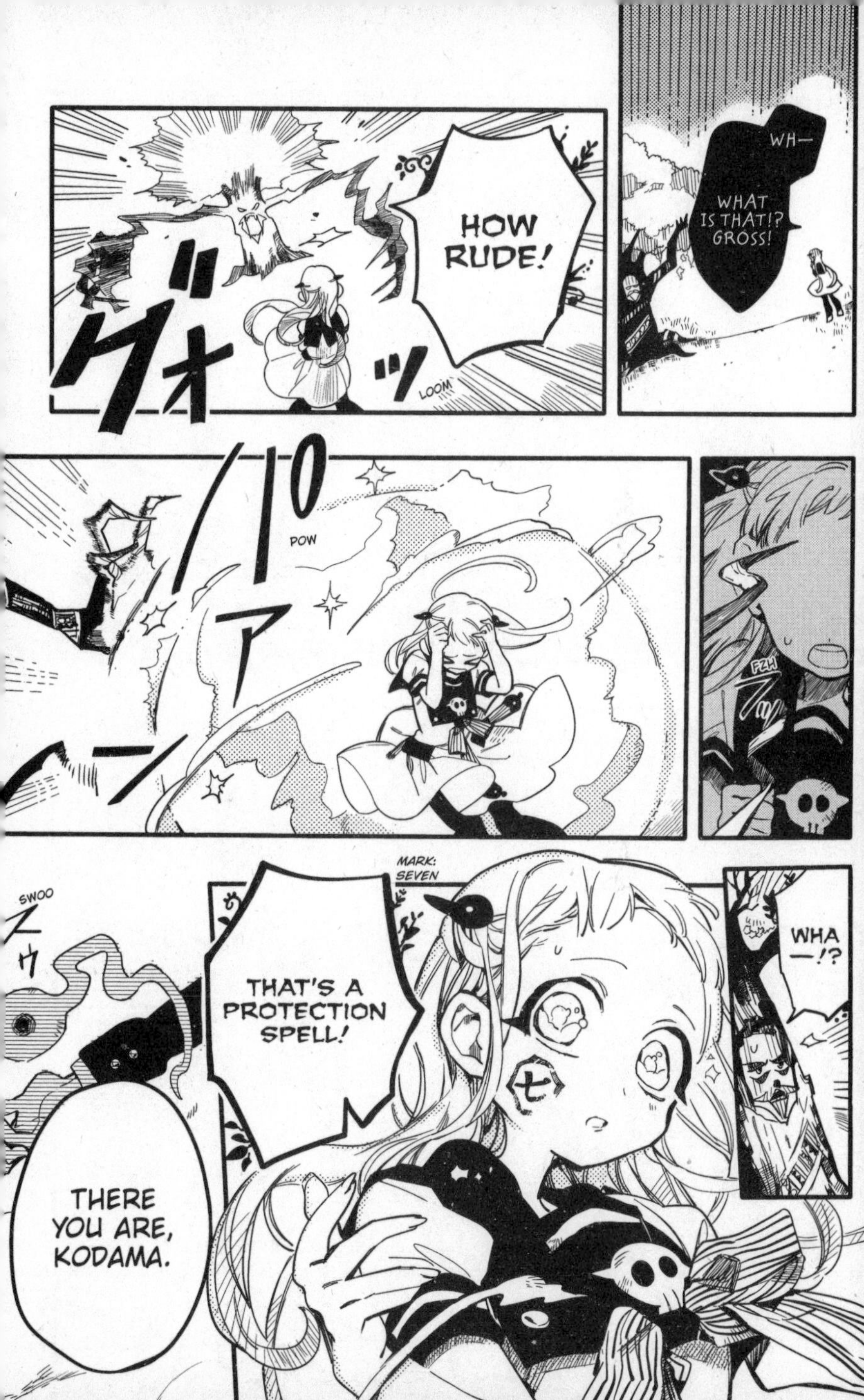
WH—
WHAT IS THAT!? GROSS!
HOW RUDE!
グオッ
LOOM
FZH
パァーン
POW
WHA—!?
MARK: SEVEN
THAT'S A PROTECTION SPELL!
SWOO
スゥ
THERE YOU ARE, KODAMA.

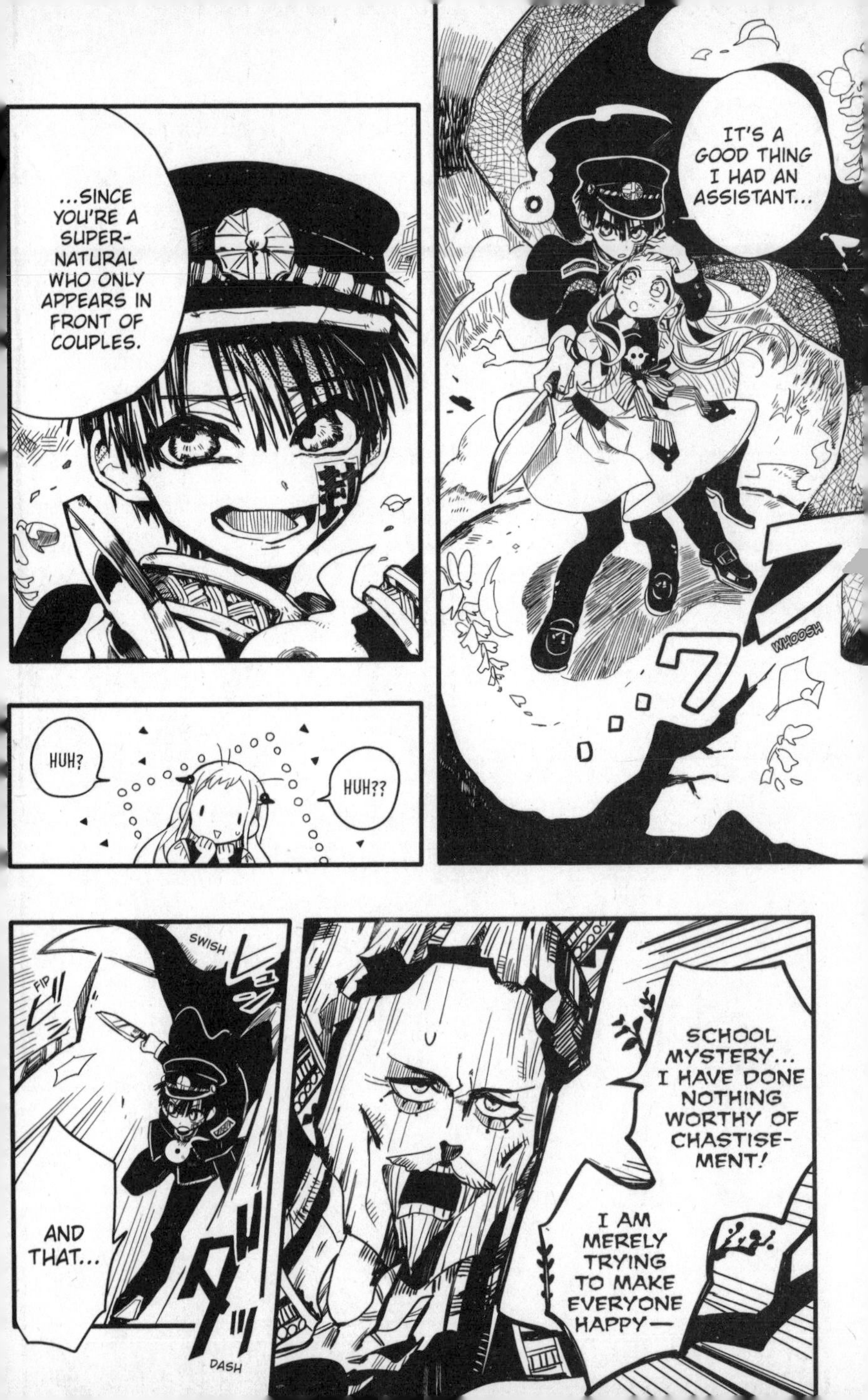
IT'S A GOOD THING I HAD AN ASSISTANT...
WHOOSH
...SINCE YOU'RE A SUPER-NATURAL WHO ONLY APPEARS IN FRONT OF COUPLES.
HUH??
HUH?
SCHOOL MYSTERY... I HAVE DONE NOTHING WORTHY OF CHASTISE-MENT!
I AM MERELY TRYING TO MAKE EVERYONE HAPPY—
SWISH
FIP
AND THAT...
DASH

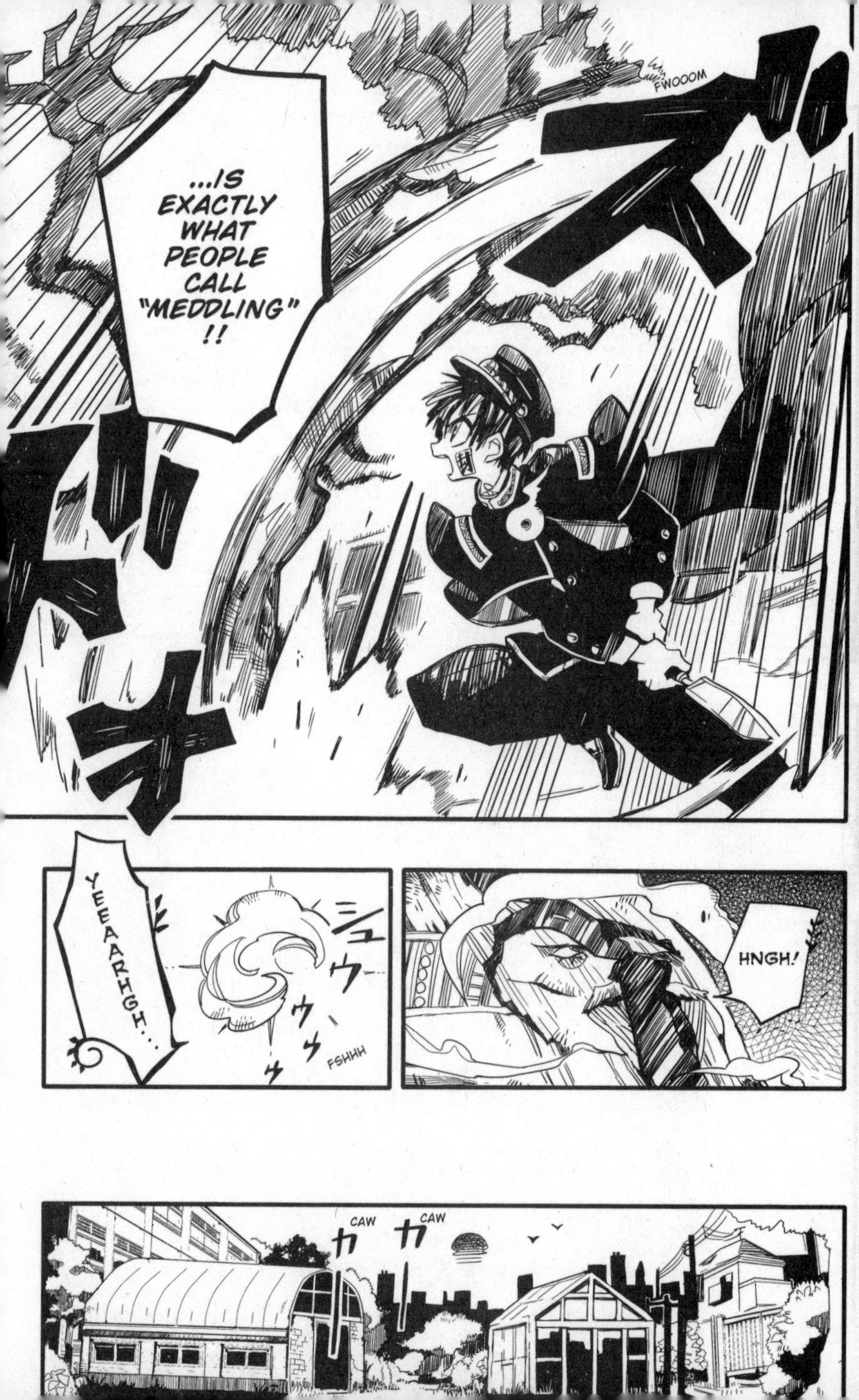
FWOOOM
...IS EXACTLY WHAT PEOPLE CALL "MEDDLING" !!
HNGH!
YEEAARGH...
FSHHH
CAW
CAW

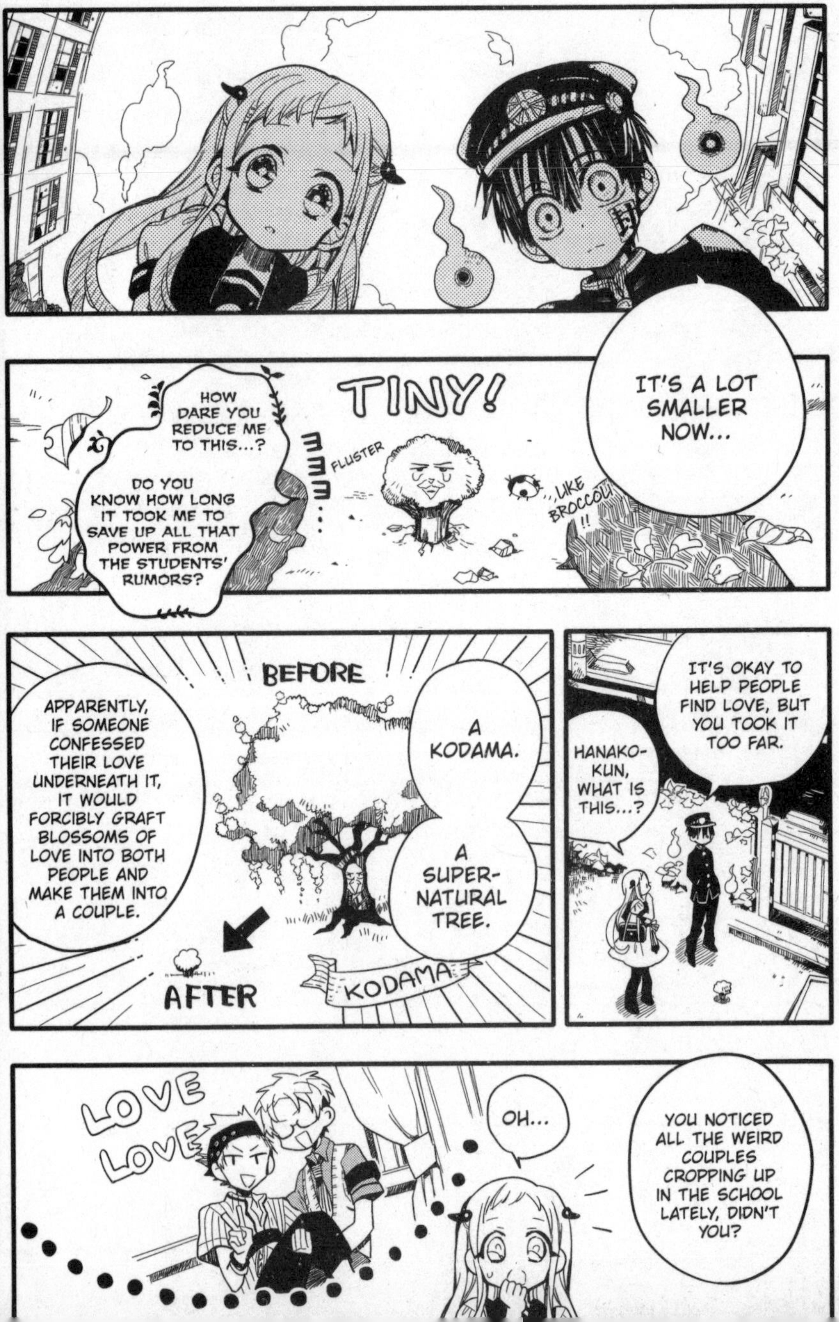
IT'S A LOT SMALLER NOW...
...LIKE BROCCOLI!!
TINY!
FLUSTER
HOW DARE YOU REDUCE ME TO THIS...?
DO YOU KNOW HOW LONG IT TOOK ME TO SAVE UP ALL THAT POWER FROM THE STUDENTS' RUMORS?
IT'S OKAY TO HELP PEOPLE FIND LOVE, BUT YOU TOOK IT TOO FAR.
HANAKO-KUN, WHAT IS THIS...?
BEFORE
A KODAMA.
A SUPER-NATURAL TREE.
APPARENTLY, IF SOMEONE CONFESSED THEIR LOVE UNDERNEATH IT, IT WOULD FORCIBLY GRAFT BLOSSOMS OF LOVE INTO BOTH PEOPLE AND MAKE THEM INTO A COUPLE.
KODAMA
AFTER
YOU NOTICED ALL THE WEIRD COUPLES CROPPING UP IN THE SCHOOL LATELY, DIDN'T YOU?
OH...
LOVE
LOVE

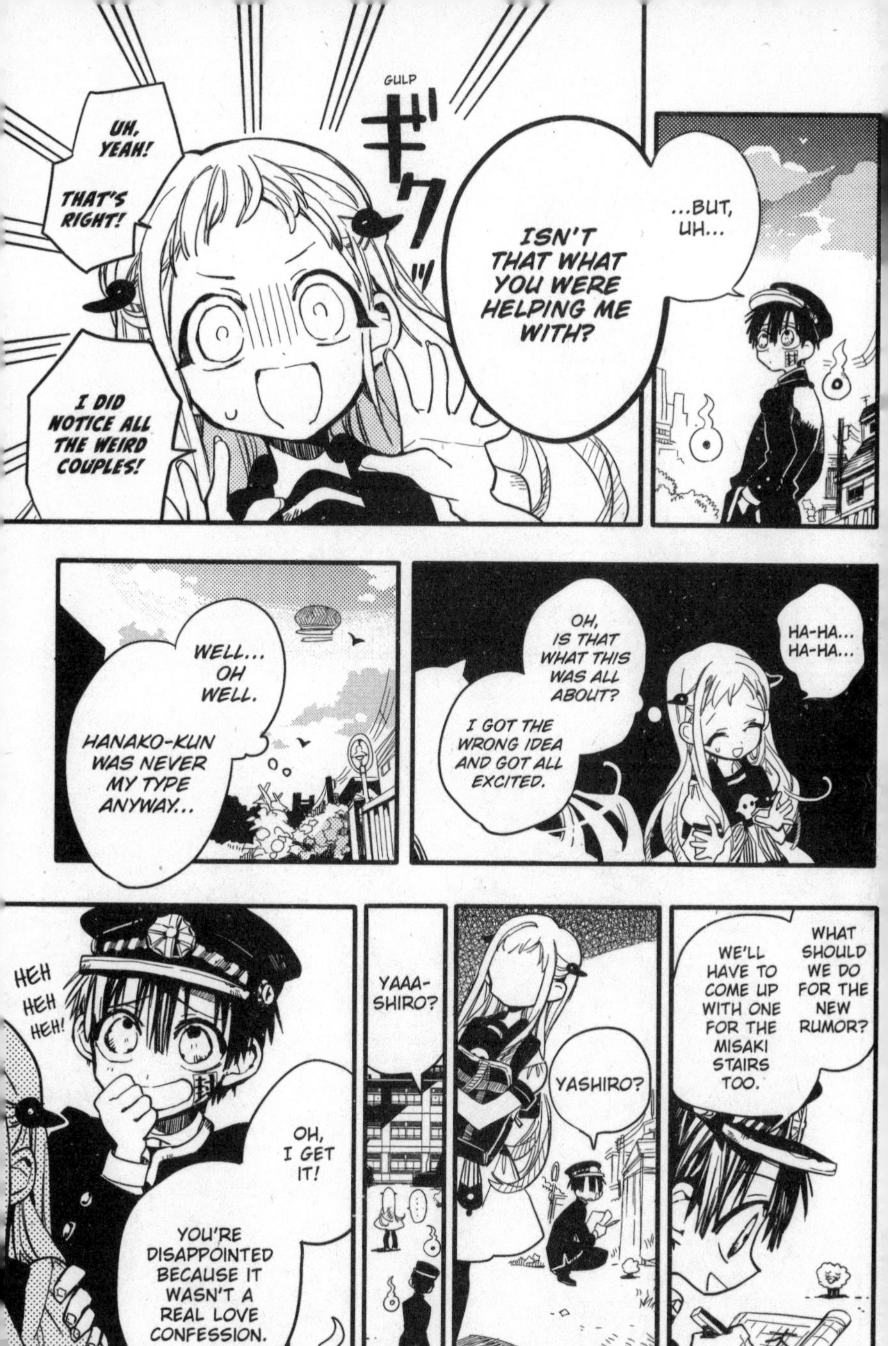
...BUT, UH...
ISN'T THAT WHAT YOU WERE HELPING ME WITH?
GULP
ギクッ
UH, YEAH!
THAT'S RIGHT!
I DID NOTICE ALL THE WEIRD COUPLES!
HA-HA... HA-HA...
OH, IS THAT WHAT THIS WAS ALL ABOUT?
I GOT THE WRONG IDEA AND GOT ALL EXCITED.
WELL... OH WELL.
HANAKO-KUN WAS NEVER MY TYPE ANYWAY...
WHAT SHOULD WE DO FOR THE NEW RUMOR?
WE'LL HAVE TO COME UP WITH ONE FOR THE MISAKI STAIRS TOO.
YASHIRO?
YAAA-SHIRO?
HEH HEH HEH!
OH, I GET IT!
YOU'RE DISAPPOINTED BECAUSE IT WASN'T A REAL LOVE CONFESSION.
BOOK: TREE

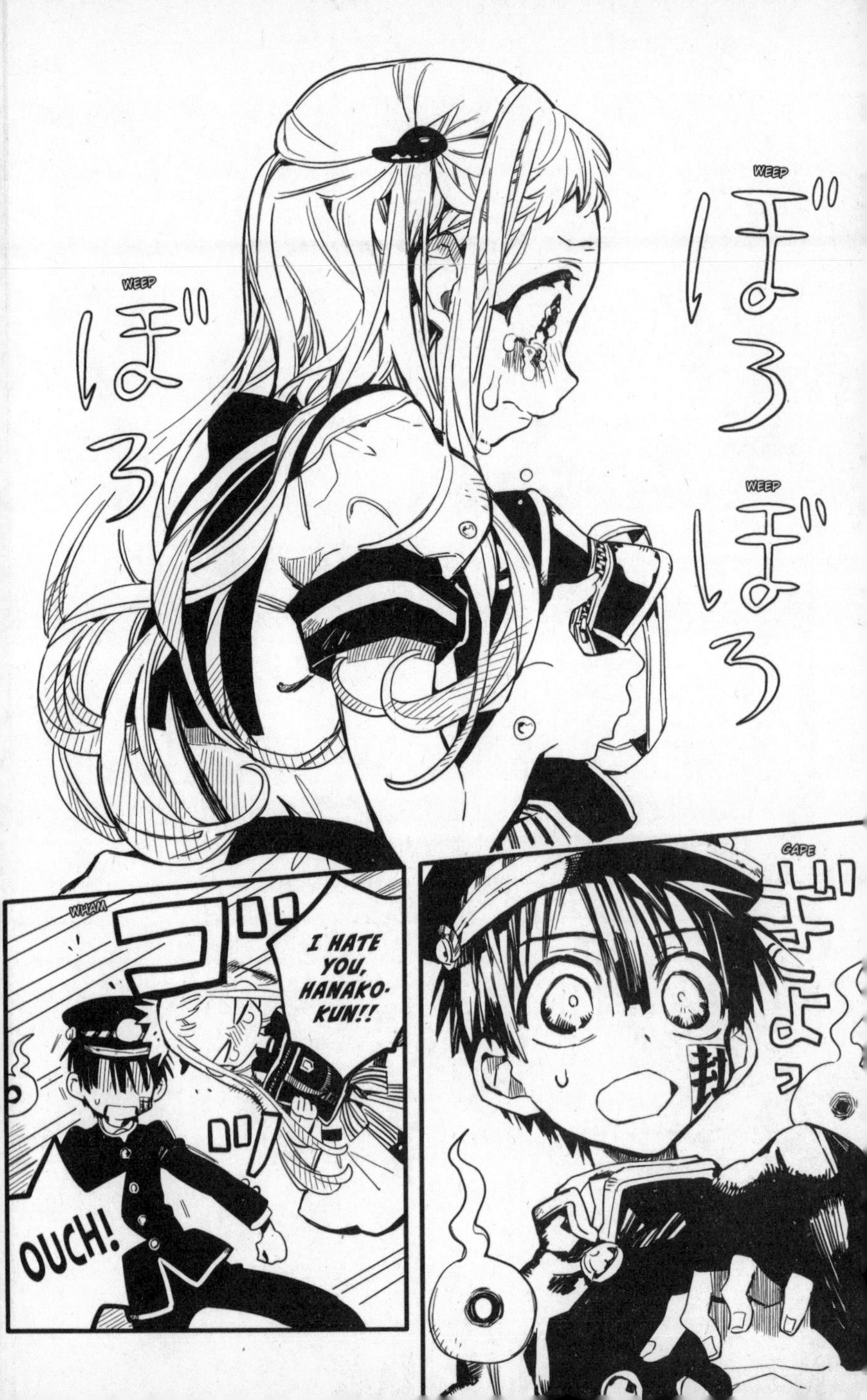
WEEP
ぼろ
WEEP
ぼろ
WEEP
ぼろ
GAPE
ぎょっ
WHAM
ゴッ
I HATE YOU, HANAKO-KUN!!
OUCH!

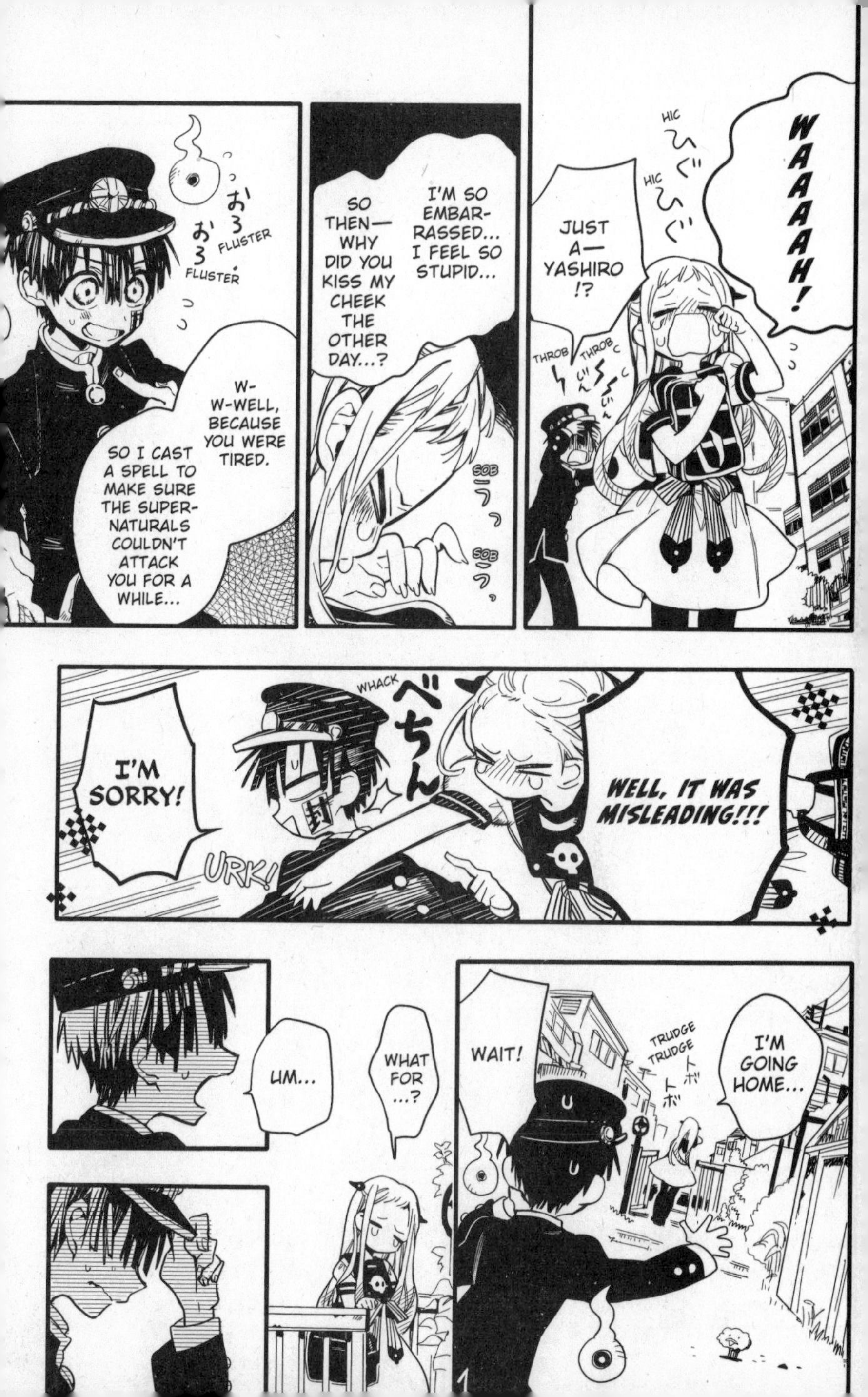
WAAAAAH!
HIC ひぐ
HIC ひぐ
JUST A— YASHIRO!?
THROB じん
THROB じん
I'M SO EMBARRASSED... I FEEL SO STUPID...
SO THEN—WHY DID YOU KISS MY CHEEK THE OTHER DAY...?
SOB
SOB
おろ FLUSTER
おろ FLUSTER
W-W-WELL, BECAUSE YOU WERE TIRED.
SO I CAST A SPELL TO MAKE SURE THE SUPERNATURALS COULDN'T ATTACK YOU FOR A WHILE...
WELL, IT WAS MISLEADING!!!
WHACK べちん
URK!
I'M SORRY!
I'M GOING HOME...
TRUDGE トボ
TRUDGE トボ
WAIT!
WHAT FOR...?
UM...

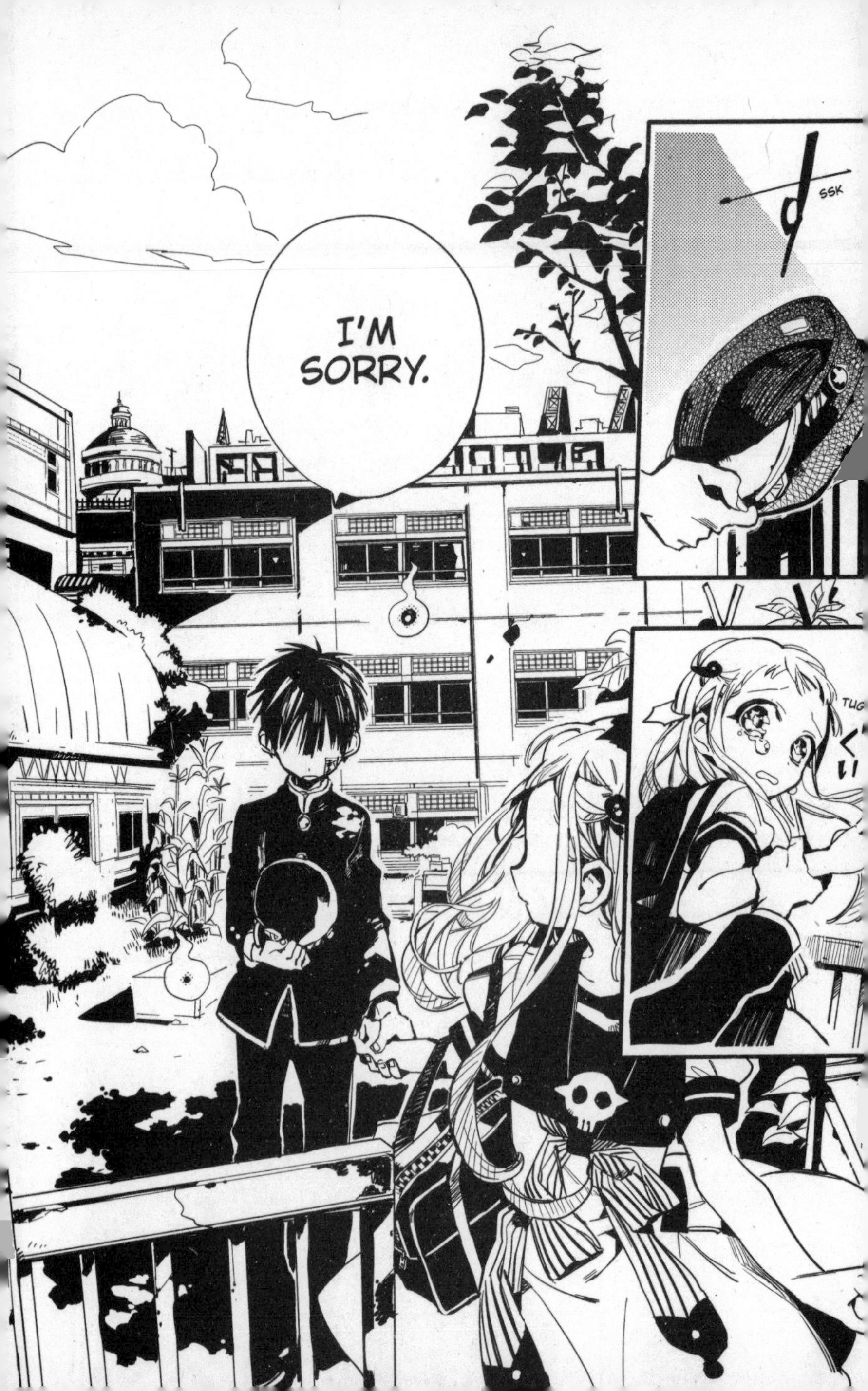
SSK
TUG
I'M SORRY.

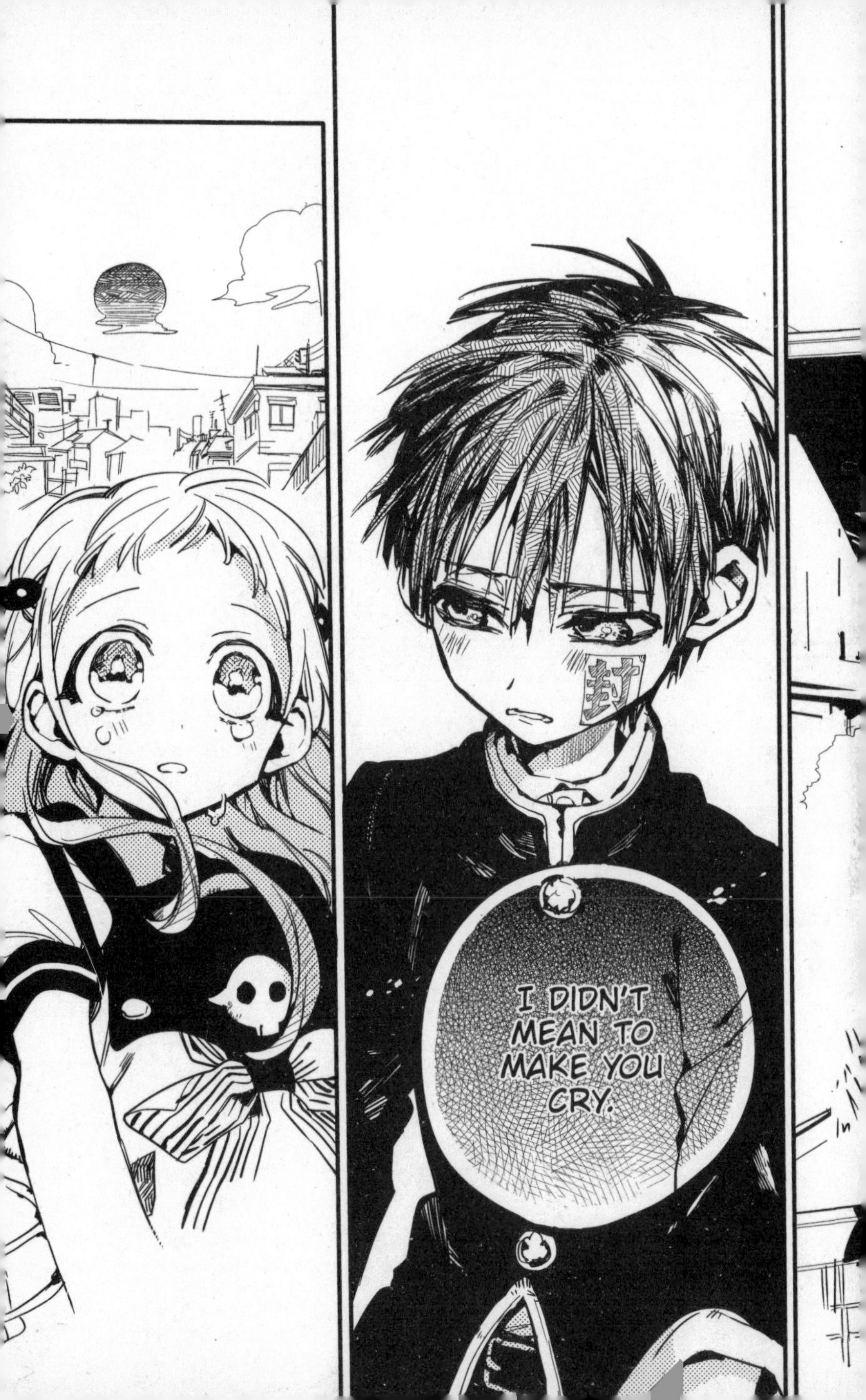
I DIDN'T MEAN TO MAKE YOU CRY.

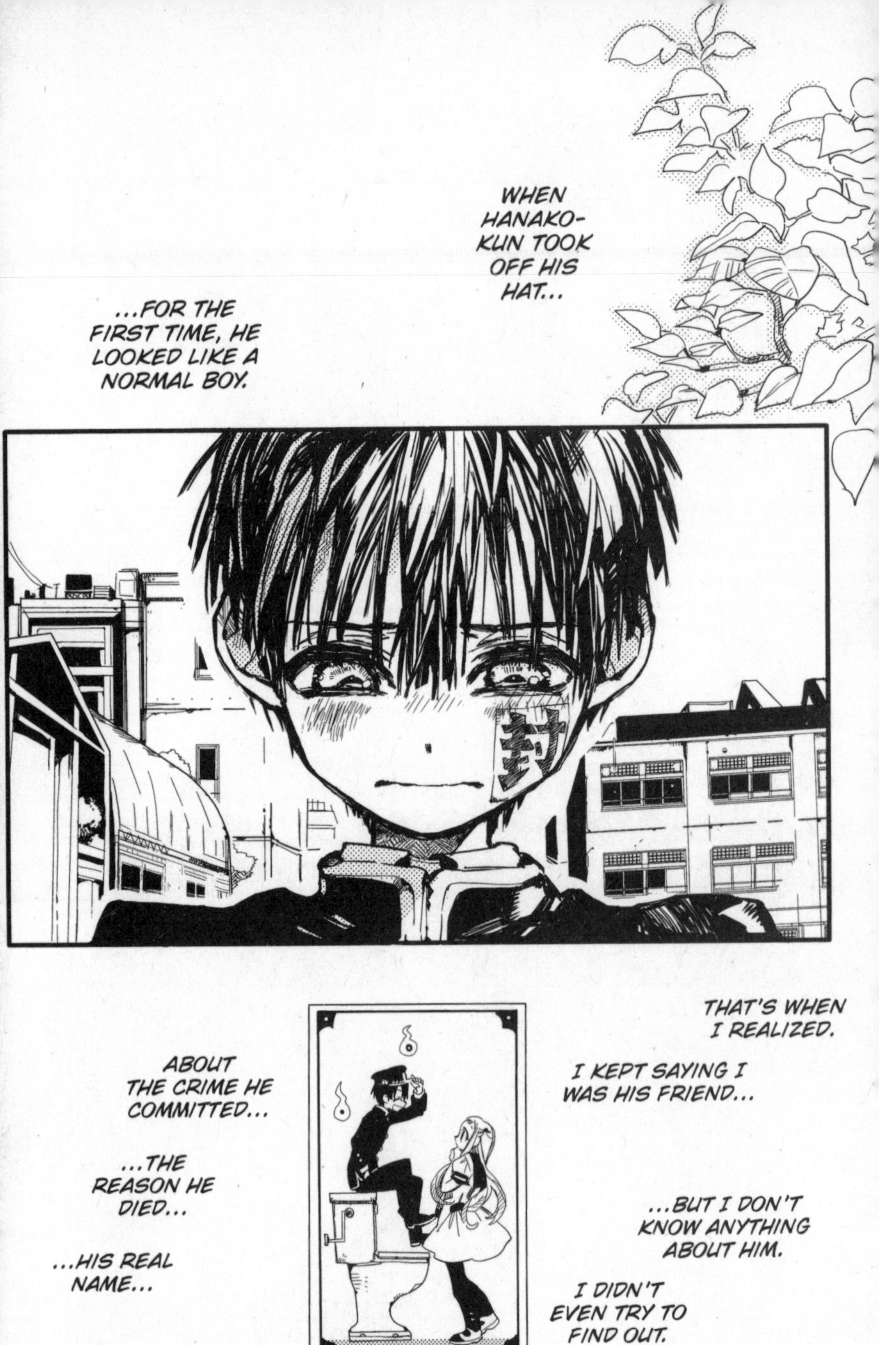
WHEN HANAKO-KUN TOOK OFF HIS HAT...
...FOR THE FIRST TIME, HE LOOKED LIKE A NORMAL BOY.
THAT'S WHEN I REALIZED.
I KEPT SAYING I WAS HIS FRIEND...
ABOUT THE CRIME HE COMMITTED...
...THE REASON HE DIED...
...HIS REAL NAME...
...BUT I DON'T KNOW ANYTHING ABOUT HIM.
I DIDN'T EVEN TRY TO FIND OUT.

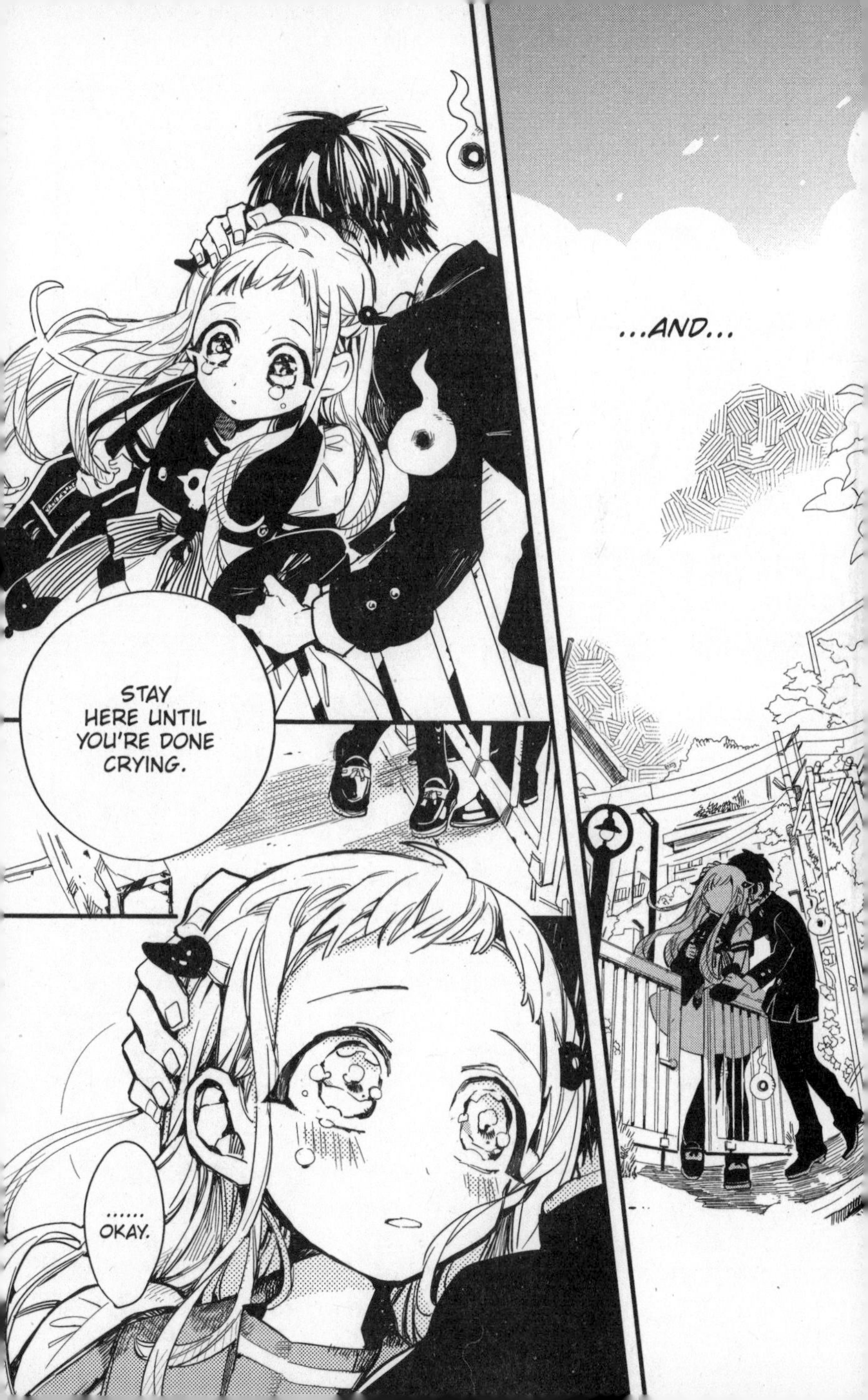
...AND...
STAY HERE UNTIL YOU'RE DONE CRYING.
...... OKAY.

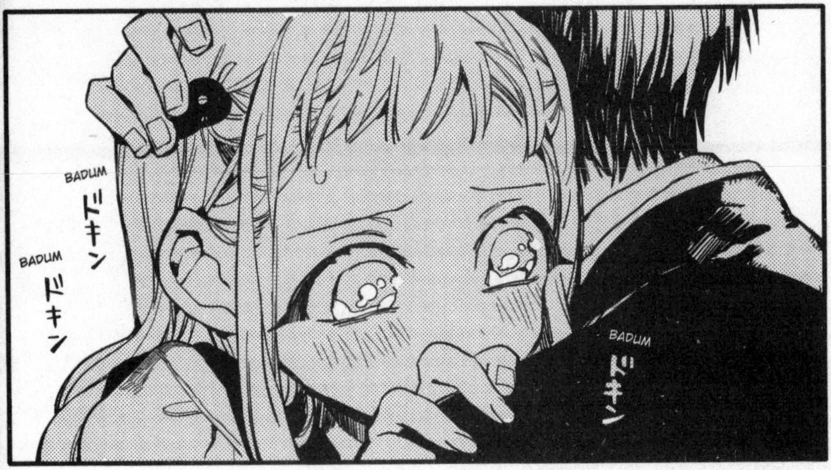
BADUM
ドキン
BADUM
ドキン
BADUM
ドキン

AT THIS MOMENT, FOR THE FIRST TIME...

...I FELT LIKE I WANTED TO KNOW MORE ABOUT HIM.

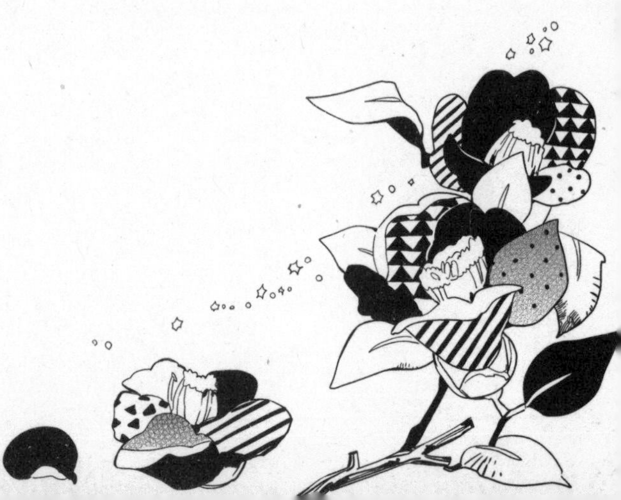

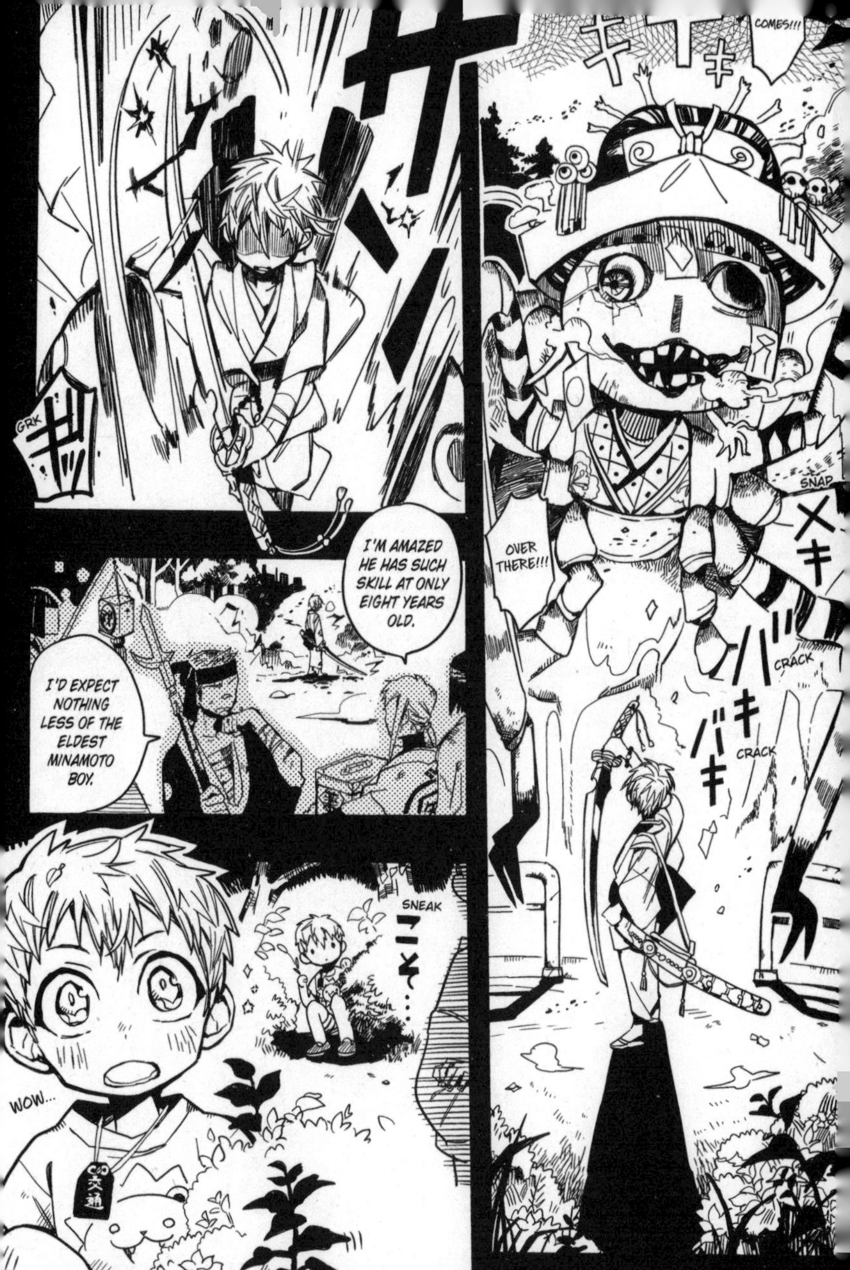
COMES!!!
OVER THERE!!!
SNAP
CRACK
CRACK
GRK
I'M AMAZED HE HAS SUCH SKILL AT ONLY EIGHT YEARS OLD.
I'D EXPECT NOTHING LESS OF THE ELDEST MINAMOTO BOY.
SNEAK
WOW...

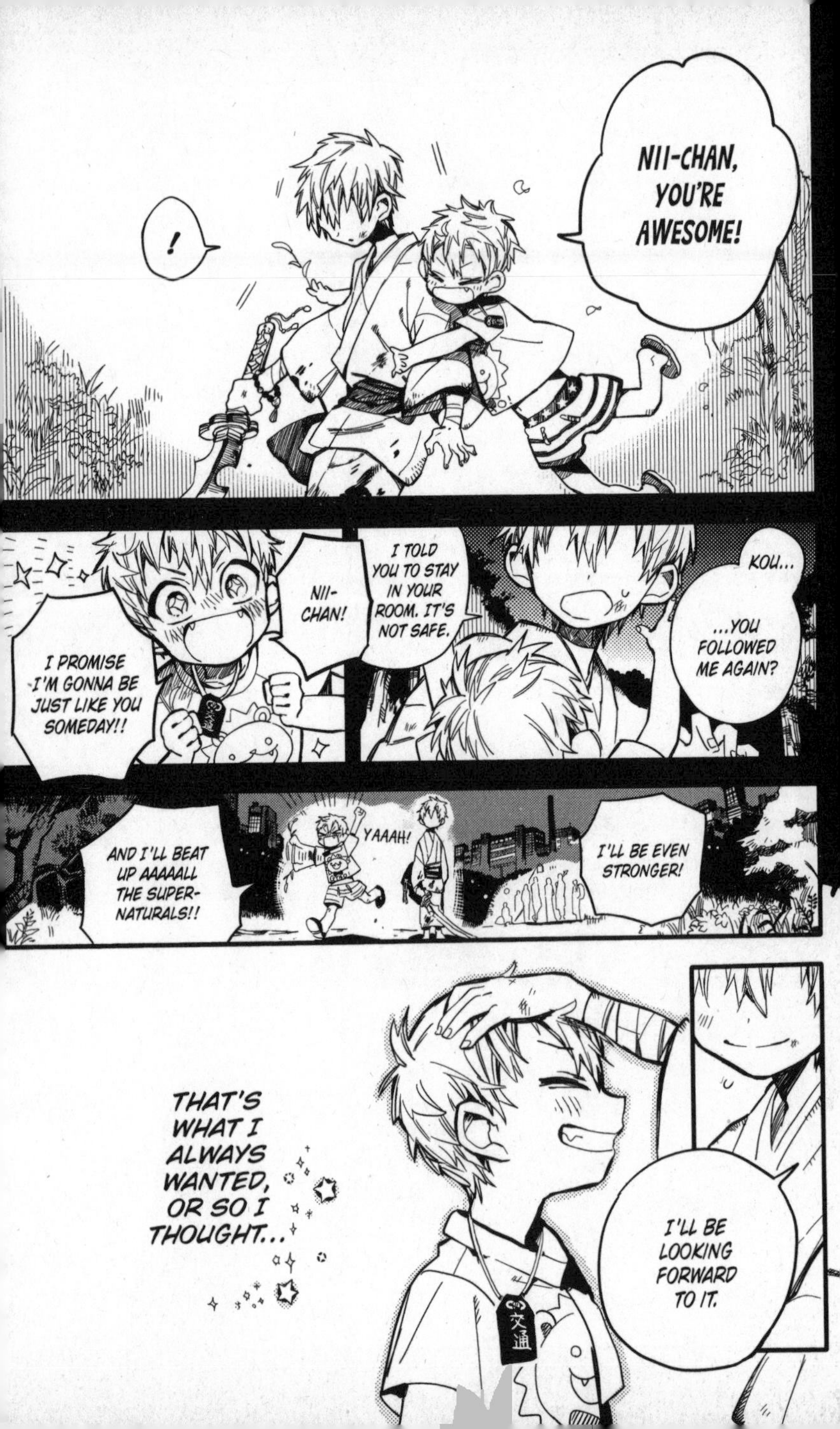
NII-CHAN, YOU'RE AWESOME!
!
KOU...
...YOU FOLLOWED ME AGAIN?
I TOLD YOU TO STAY IN YOUR ROOM. IT'S NOT SAFE.
NII-CHAN!
I PROMISE I'M GONNA BE JUST LIKE YOU SOMEDAY!!
I'LL BE EVEN STRONGER!
YAAAH!
AND I'LL BEAT UP AAAAALL THE SUPER-NATURALS!!
I'LL BE LOOKING FORWARD TO IT.
THAT'S WHAT I ALWAYS WANTED, OR SO I THOUGHT...

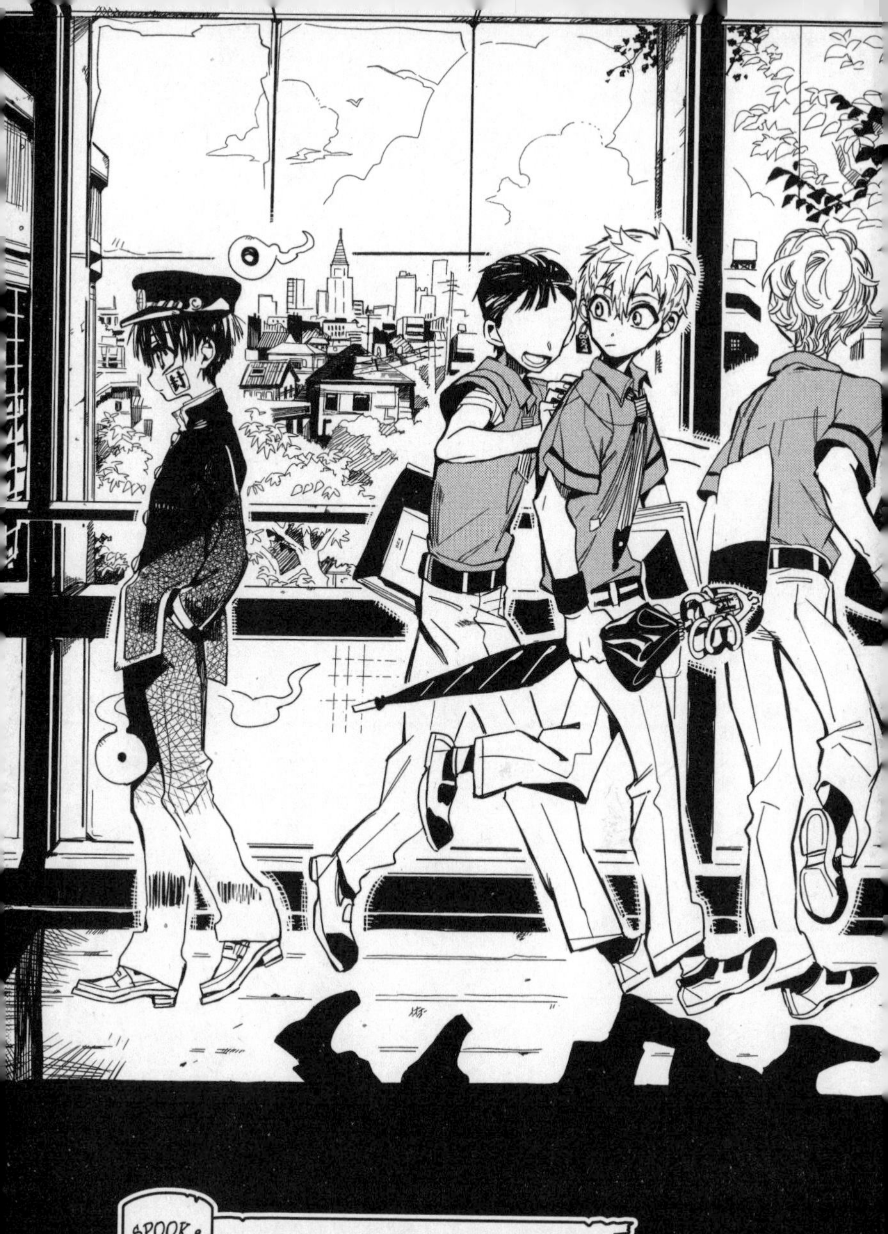

SPOOK 9 THE YOUNG EXORCIST (PART 1)

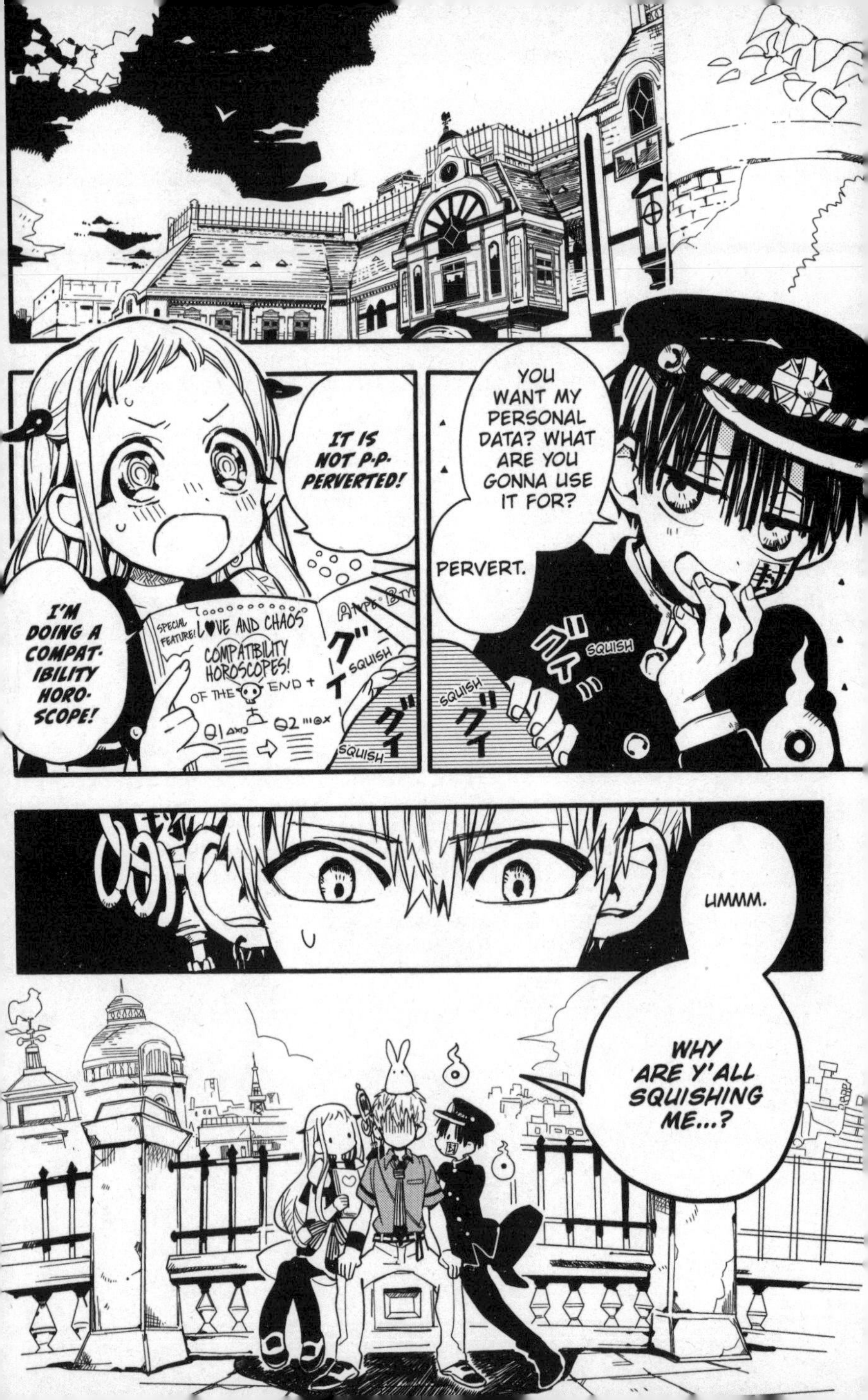

YOU WANT MY PERSONAL DATA? WHAT ARE YOU GONNA USE IT FOR?
PERVERT.
SQUISH
SQUISH
IT IS NOT P-P-PERVERTED!
I'M DOING A COMPATIBILITY HOROSCOPE!
SPECIAL FEATURE! LOVE AND CHAOS COMPATIBILITY HOROSCOPES! OF THE END
SQUISH
SQUISH
UMMM.
WHY ARE Y'ALL SQUISHING ME...?

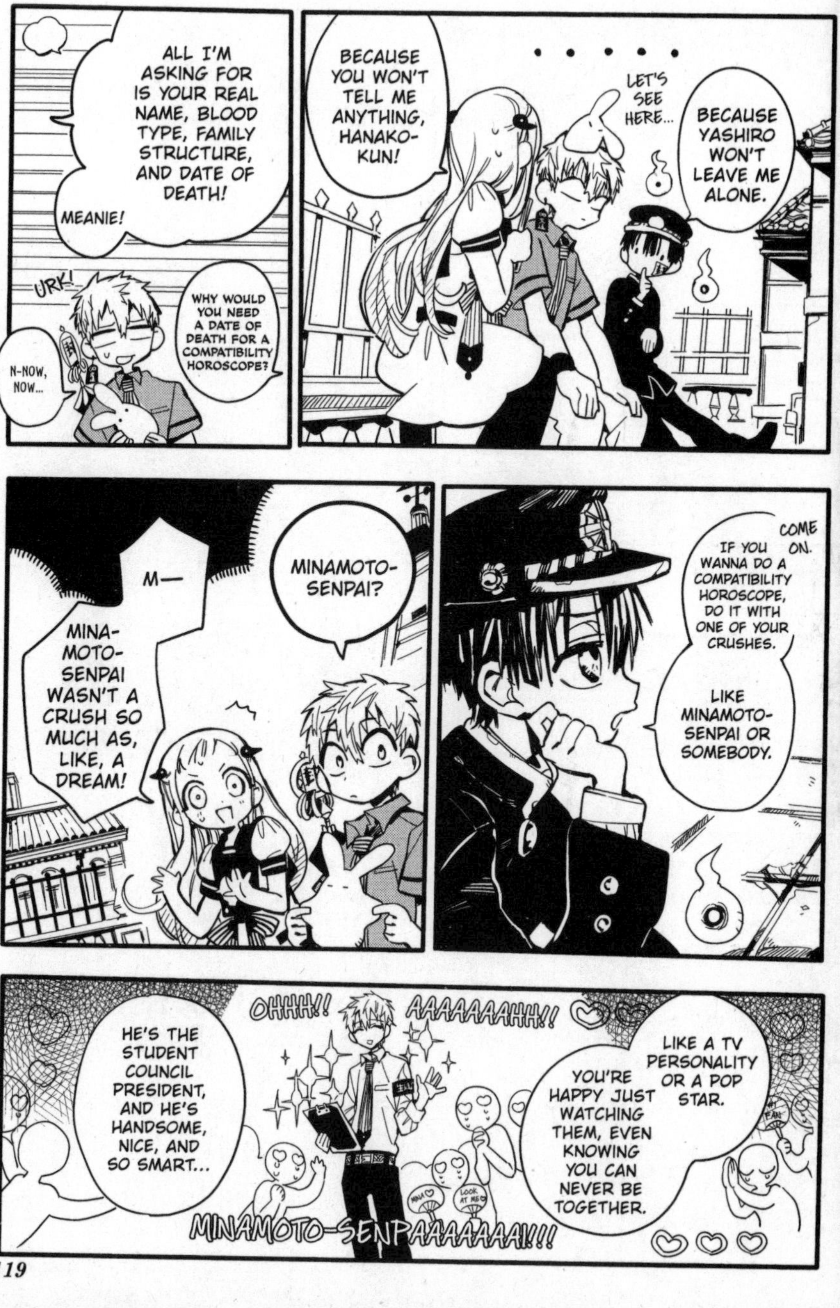

• • • • •
LET'S SEE HERE...
BECAUSE YASHIRO WON'T LEAVE ME ALONE.
BECAUSE YOU WON'T TELL ME ANYTHING, HANAKO-KUN!
ALL I'M ASKING FOR IS YOUR REAL NAME, BLOOD TYPE, FAMILY STRUCTURE, AND DATE OF DEATH!
MEANIE!
URK!
WHY WOULD YOU NEED A DATE OF DEATH FOR A COMPATIBILITY HOROSCOPE?
N-NOW, NOW...
COME ON.
IF YOU WANNA DO A COMPATIBILITY HOROSCOPE, DO IT WITH ONE OF YOUR CRUSHES.
LIKE MINAMOTO-SENPAI OR SOMEBODY.
MINAMOTO-SENPAI?
M—
MINA-MOTO-SENPAI WASN'T A CRUSH SO MUCH AS, LIKE, A DREAM!
LIKE A TV PERSONALITY OR A POP STAR.
YOU'RE HAPPY JUST WATCHING THEM, EVEN KNOWING YOU CAN NEVER BE TOGETHER.
AAAAAAAHH!!
OHHHH!!
HE'S THE STUDENT COUNCIL PRESIDENT, AND HE'S HANDSOME, NICE, AND SO SMART...
LOOK AT ME
MINAMOTO-SENPAAAAAAAI!!!

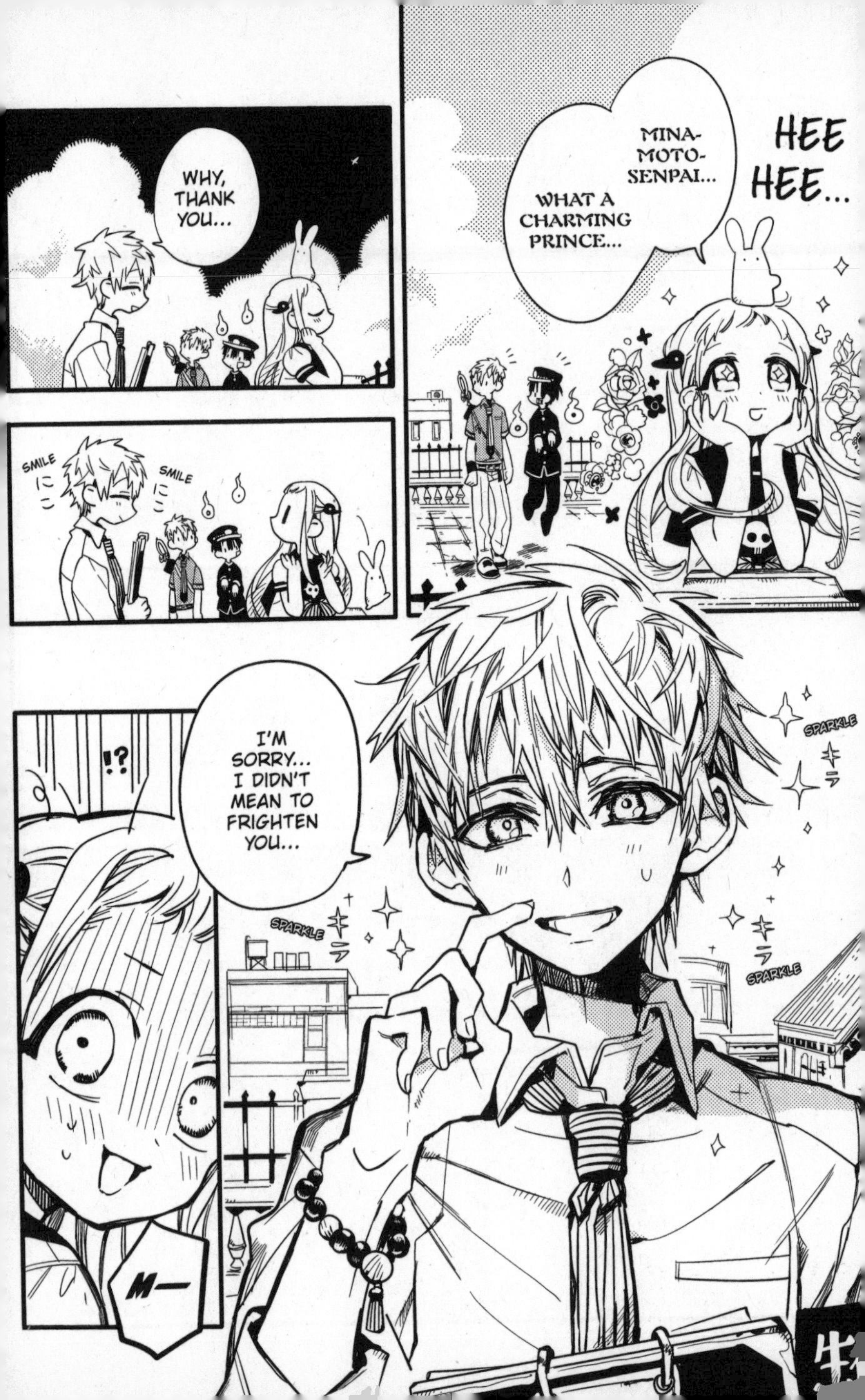
MINA-MOTO-SENPAI... WHAT A CHARMING PRINCE...
HEE HEE...
WHY, THANK YOU...
SMILE
SMILE
I'M SORRY... I DIDN'T MEAN TO FRIGHTEN YOU...
SPARKLE
SPARKLE
SPARKLE
!?
M—

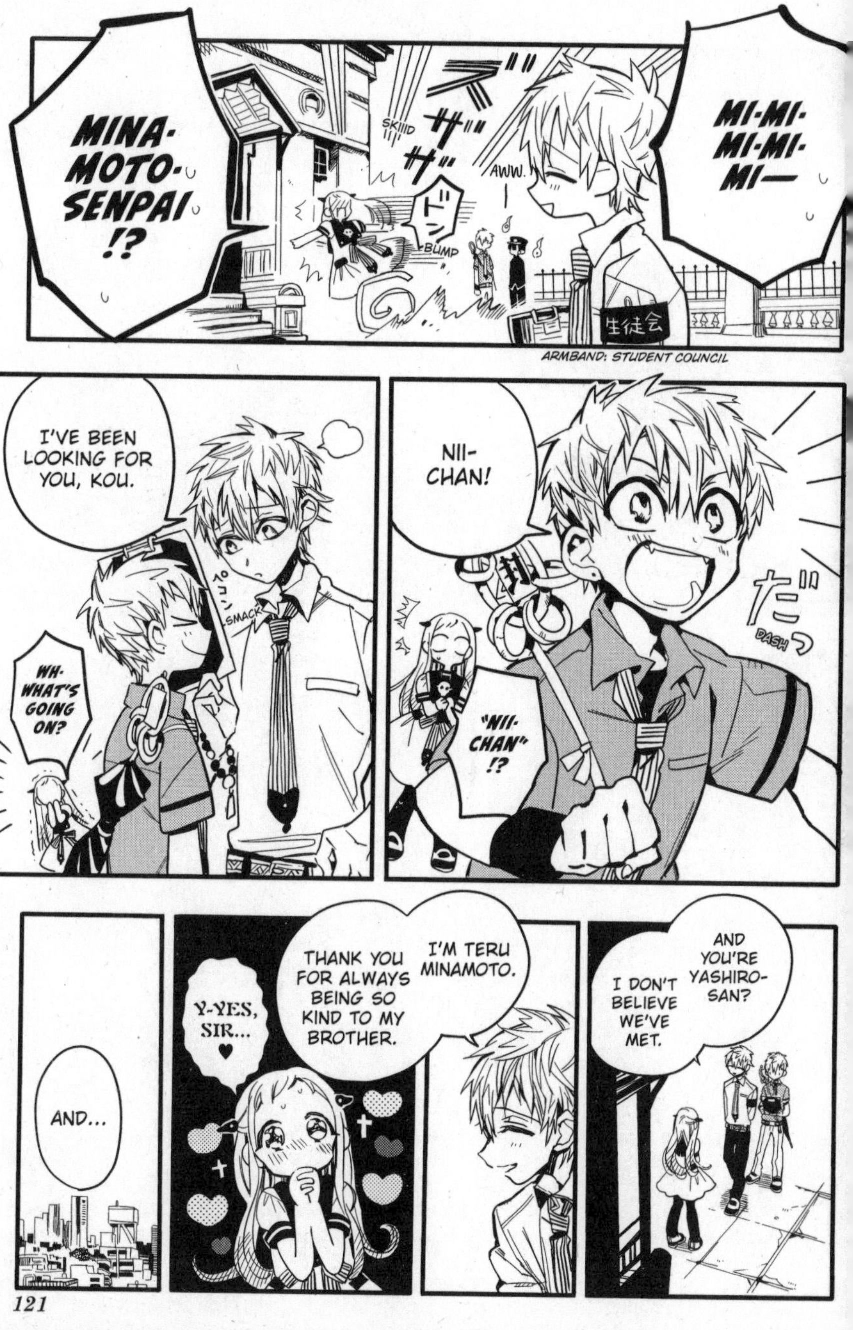
MI-MI-MI-MI-MI—
AWW.
ズザザ
SKIIID
ドン
BUMP
MINA-MOTO-SENPAI!?
生徒会
ARMBAND: STUDENT COUNCIL
NII-CHAN!
だっ
DASH
"NII-CHAN"!?
I'VE BEEN LOOKING FOR YOU, KOU.
ペコン
SMACK
WH-WHAT'S GOING ON?
AND YOU'RE YASHIRO-SAN?
I DON'T BELIEVE WE'VE MET.
I'M TERU MINAMOTO.
THANK YOU FOR ALWAYS BEING SO KIND TO MY BROTHER.
Y-YES, SIR... ♥
AND...

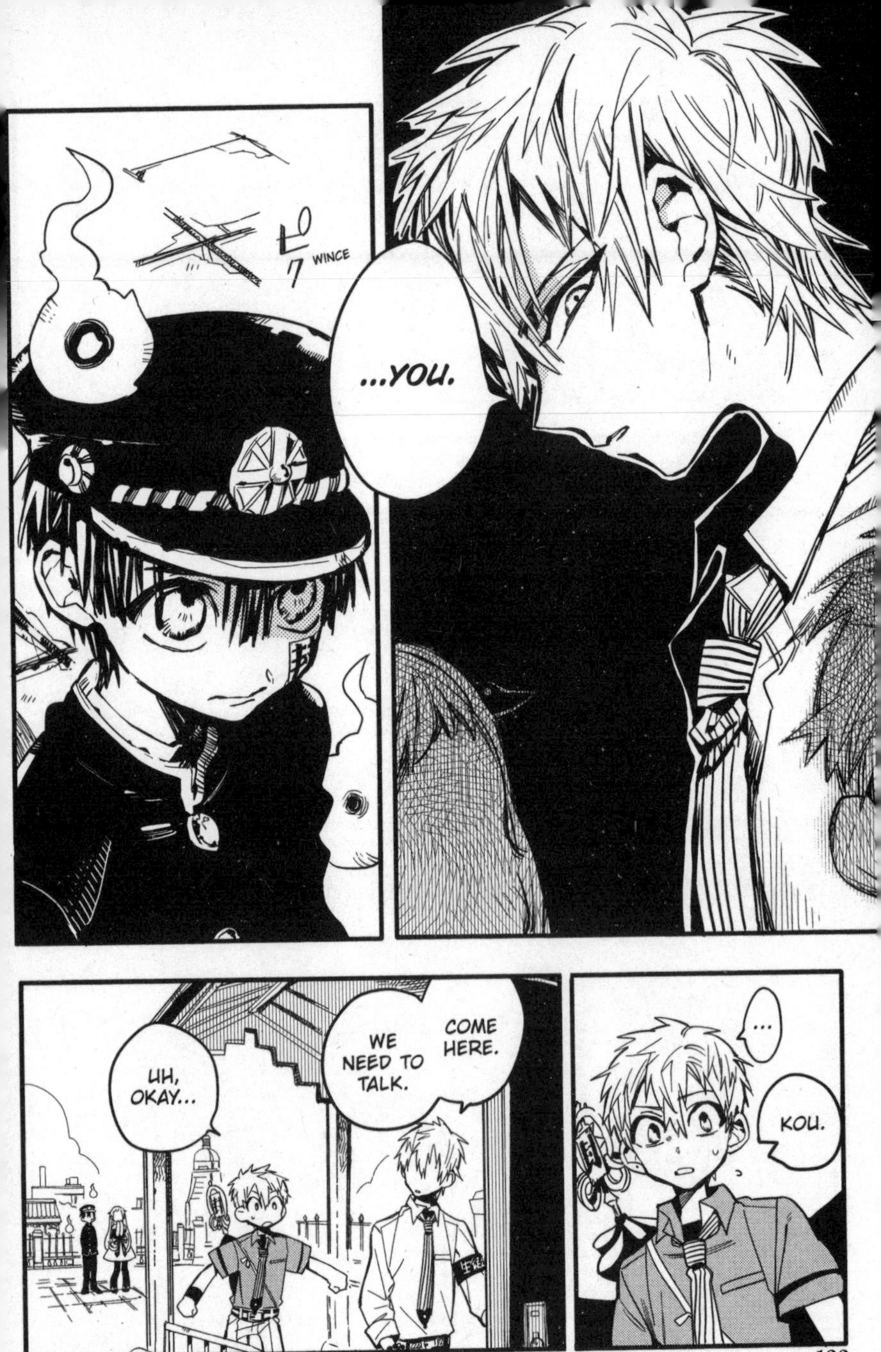
...YOU.
ピク
WINCE
...
KOU.
COME HERE.
WE NEED TO TALK.
UH, OKAY...

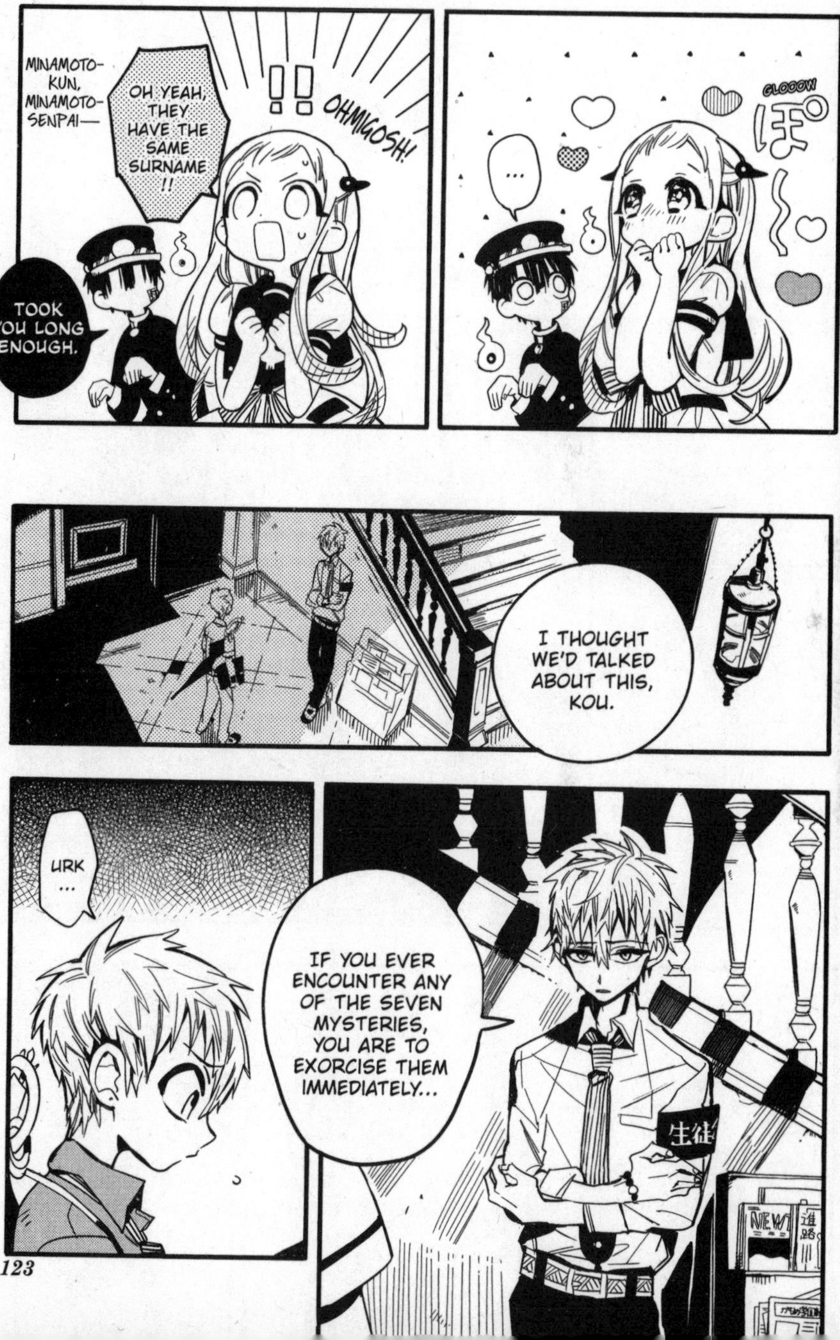
GLOOOW
ぽ〜
...
OHMIGOSH!
!!
OH YEAH, THEY HAVE THE SAME SURNAME!!
MINAMOTO-KUN, MINAMOTO-SENPAI—
TOOK YOU LONG ENOUGH.
I THOUGHT WE'D TALKED ABOUT THIS, KOU.
IF YOU EVER ENCOUNTER ANY OF THE SEVEN MYSTERIES, YOU ARE TO EXORCISE THEM IMMEDIATELY...
URK...

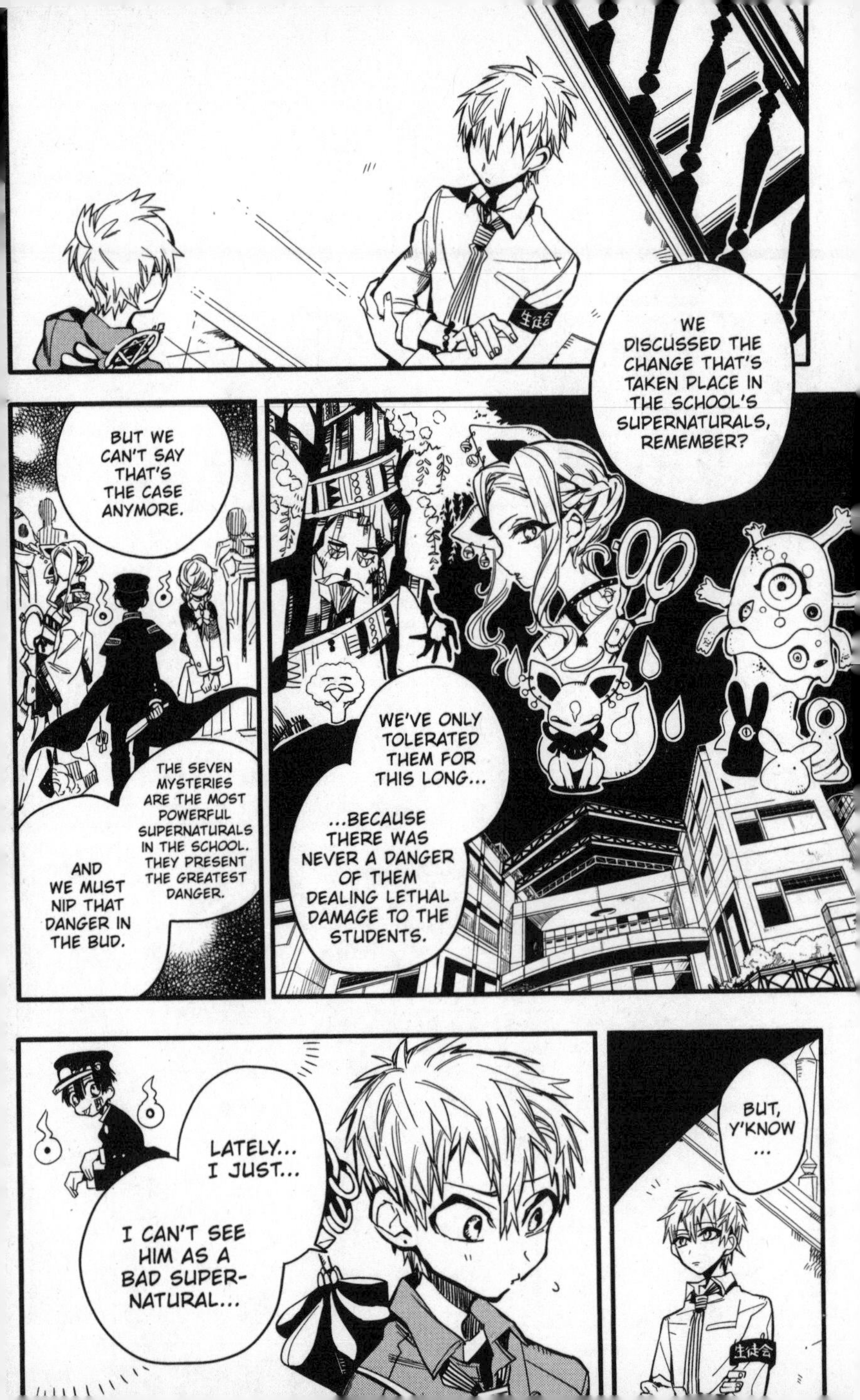
WE DISCUSSED THE CHANGE THAT'S TAKEN PLACE IN THE SCHOOL'S SUPERNATURALS, REMEMBER?
WE'VE ONLY TOLERATED THEM FOR THIS LONG...
...BECAUSE THERE WAS NEVER A DANGER OF THEM DEALING LETHAL DAMAGE TO THE STUDENTS.
BUT WE CAN'T SAY THAT'S THE CASE ANYMORE.
THE SEVEN MYSTERIES ARE THE MOST POWERFUL SUPERNATURALS IN THE SCHOOL. THEY PRESENT THE GREATEST DANGER.
AND WE MUST NIP THAT DANGER IN THE BUD.
BUT, Y'KNOW ...
LATELY... I JUST...
I CAN'T SEE HIM AS A BAD SUPER-NATURAL...

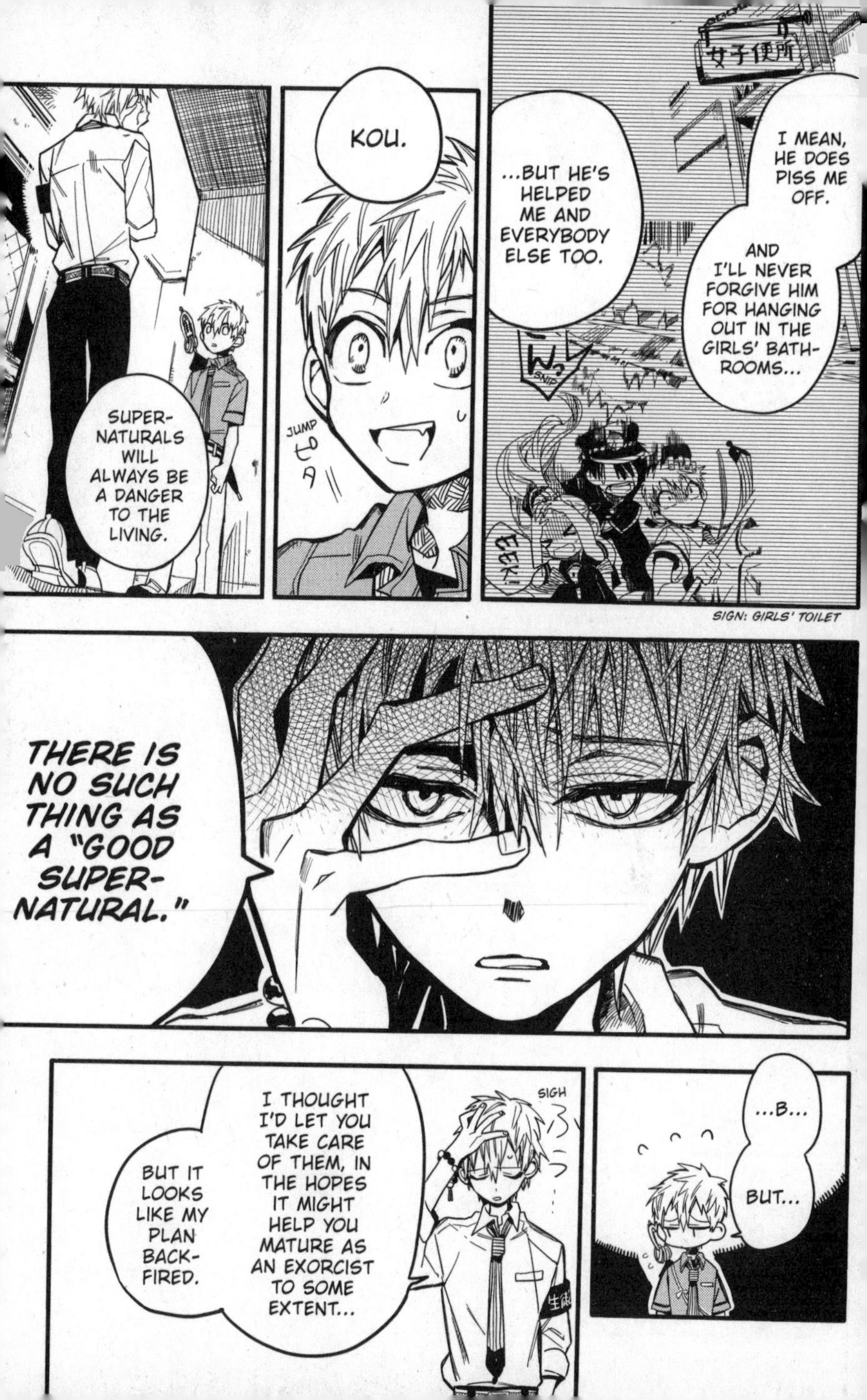
女子便所
I MEAN, HE DOES PISS ME OFF.
AND I'LL NEVER FORGIVE HIM FOR HANGING OUT IN THE GIRLS' BATHROOMS...
SNIP
EEK!
...BUT HE'S HELPED ME AND EVERYBODY ELSE TOO.
SIGN: GIRLS' TOILET
KOU.
JUMP
SUPER-NATURALS WILL ALWAYS BE A DANGER TO THE LIVING.
THERE IS NO SUCH THING AS A "GOOD SUPER-NATURAL."
...B...
BUT...
SIGH
I THOUGHT I'D LET YOU TAKE CARE OF THEM, IN THE HOPES IT MIGHT HELP YOU MATURE AS AN EXORCIST TO SOME EXTENT...
BUT IT LOOKS LIKE MY PLAN BACK-FIRED.

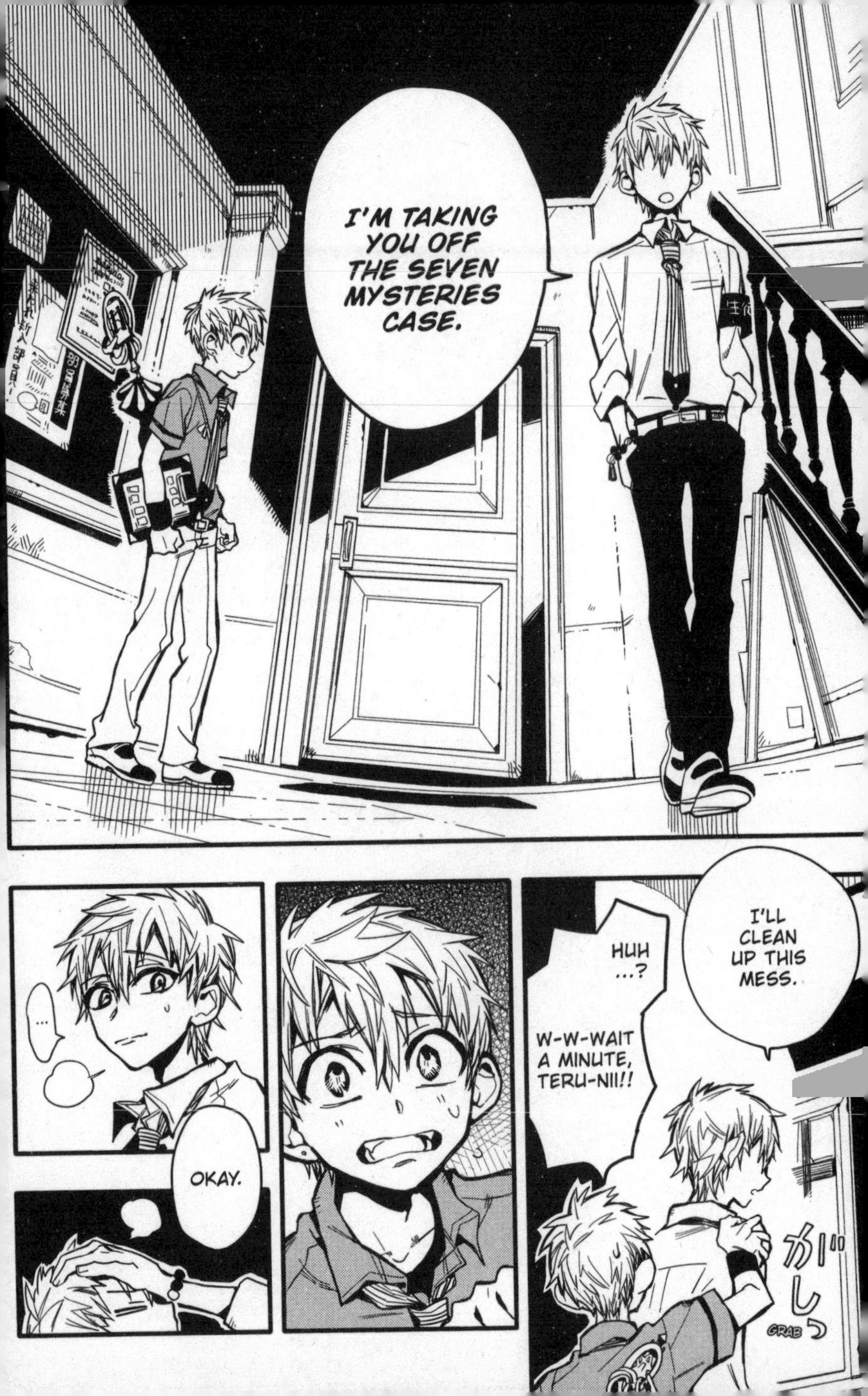
I'M TAKING YOU OFF THE SEVEN MYSTERIES CASE.
I'LL CLEAN UP THIS MESS.
HUH ...?
W-W-WAIT A MINUTE, TERU-NII!!
がしっ
GRAB
...
OKAY.

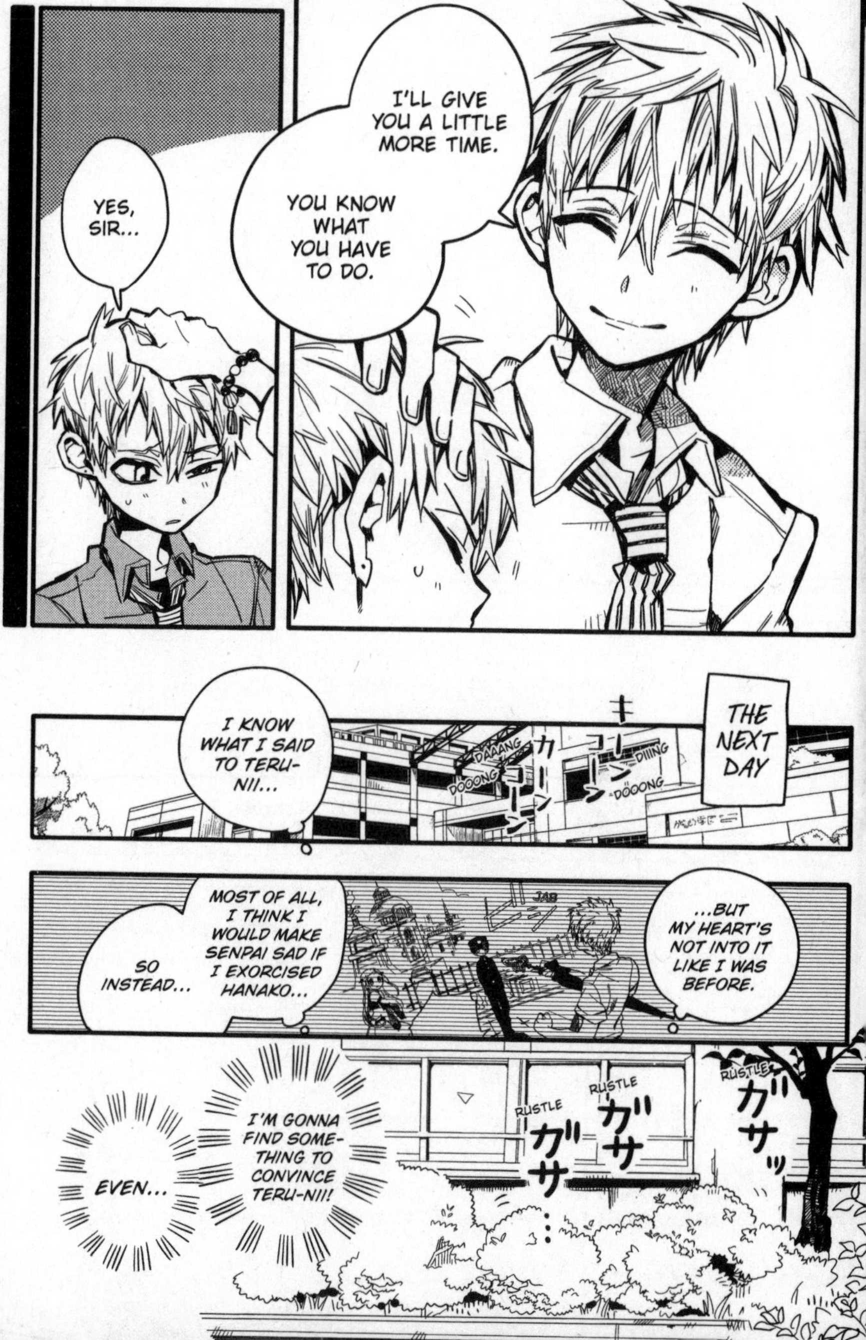

I'LL GIVE YOU A LITTLE MORE TIME.
YOU KNOW WHAT YOU HAVE TO DO.
YES, SIR...
THE NEXT DAY
キーンコーン
DIIING
DOOONG
カーンコーン
DAAANG
DOOONG
I KNOW WHAT I SAID TO TERU-NII...
...BUT MY HEART'S NOT INTO IT LIKE I WAS BEFORE.
JAB
MOST OF ALL, I THINK I WOULD MAKE SENPAI SAD IF I EXORCISED HANAKO...
SO INSTEAD...
RUSTLE
ガサッ
RUSTLE
ガサ
RUSTLE
ガサ
I'M GONNA FIND SOME-THING TO CONVINCE TERU-NII!
EVEN...

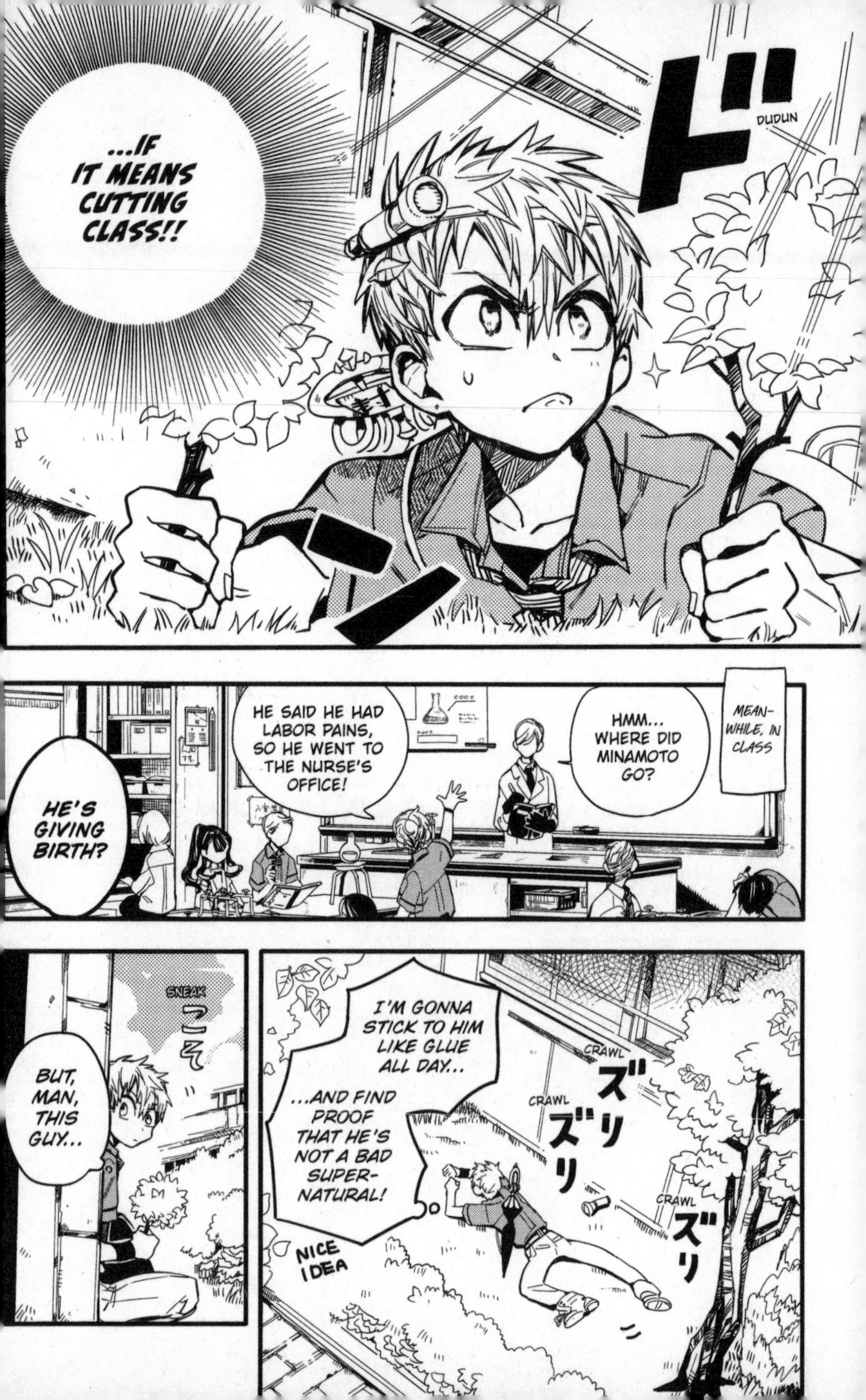
ド
DUDUN
...IF IT MEANS CUTTING CLASS!!
MEAN-WHILE, IN CLASS
HMM... WHERE DID MINAMOTO GO?
HE SAID HE HAD LABOR PAINS, SO HE WENT TO THE NURSE'S OFFICE!
HE'S GIVING BIRTH?
I'M GONNA STICK TO HIM LIKE GLUE ALL DAY...
...AND FIND PROOF THAT HE'S NOT A BAD SUPER-NATURAL!
ズリ
CRAWL
ズリ
CRAWL
ズリ
CRAWL
NICE IDEA
こそ
SNEAK
BUT, MAN, THIS GUY...

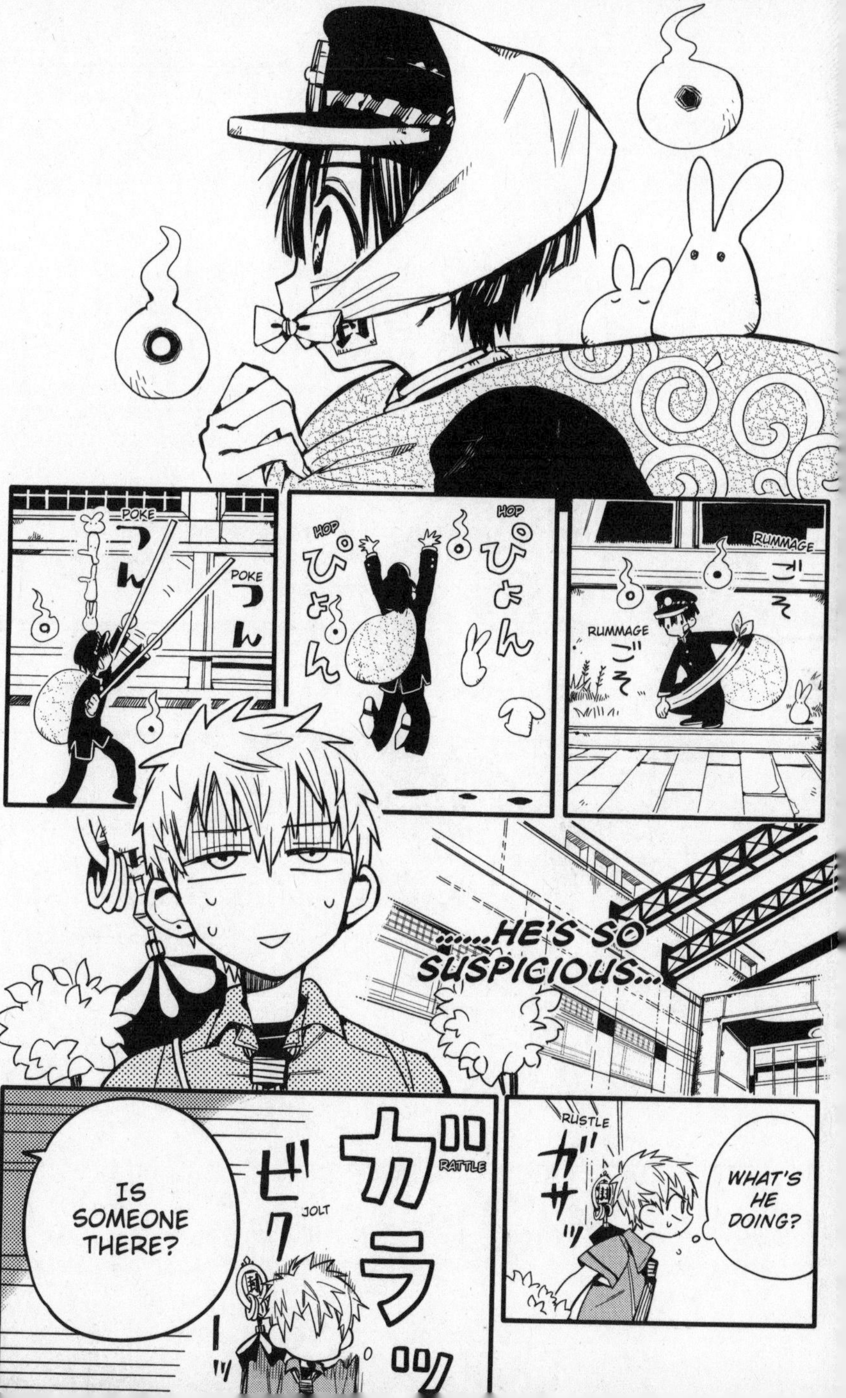
RUMMAGE
ごそ
RUMMAGE
ごそ
HOP
ぴょん
HOP
ぴょん
POKE
つん
POKE
つん
......HE'S SO SUSPICIOUS...
RUSTLE
ガサッ
WHAT'S HE DOING?
カラッ
RATTLE
ビクッ
JOLT
IS SOMEONE THERE?

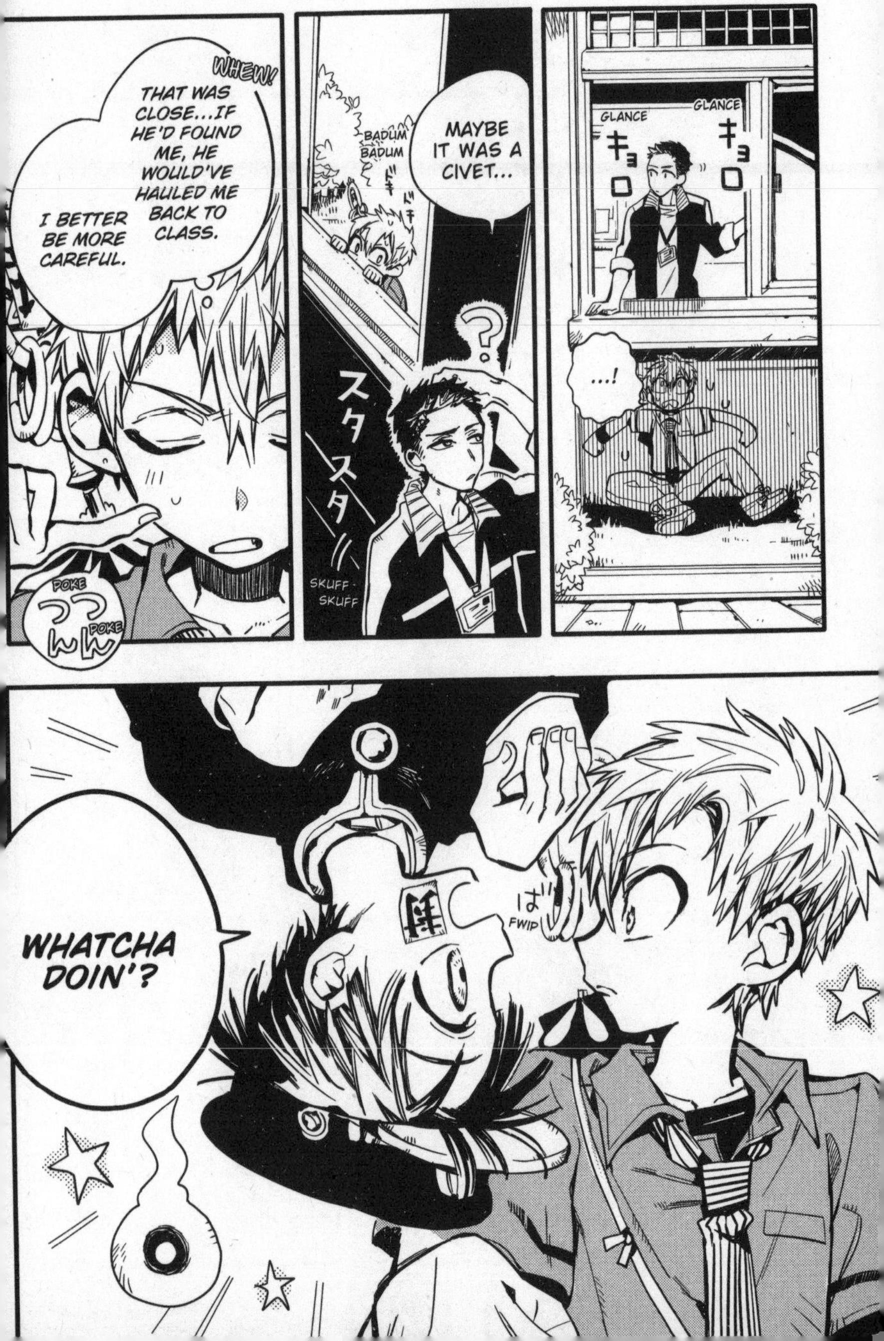
GLANCE
キョロ
GLANCE
キョロ
...!
MAYBE IT WAS A CIVET...
BADUM BADUM
ドキドキ
?
スタスタ
SKUFF SKUFF
WHEW!
THAT WAS CLOSE...IF HE'D FOUND ME, HE WOULD'VE HAULED ME BACK TO CLASS.
I BETTER BE MORE CAREFUL.
POKE
つんつん
POKE
ぱ
FWIP
WHATCHA DOIN'?

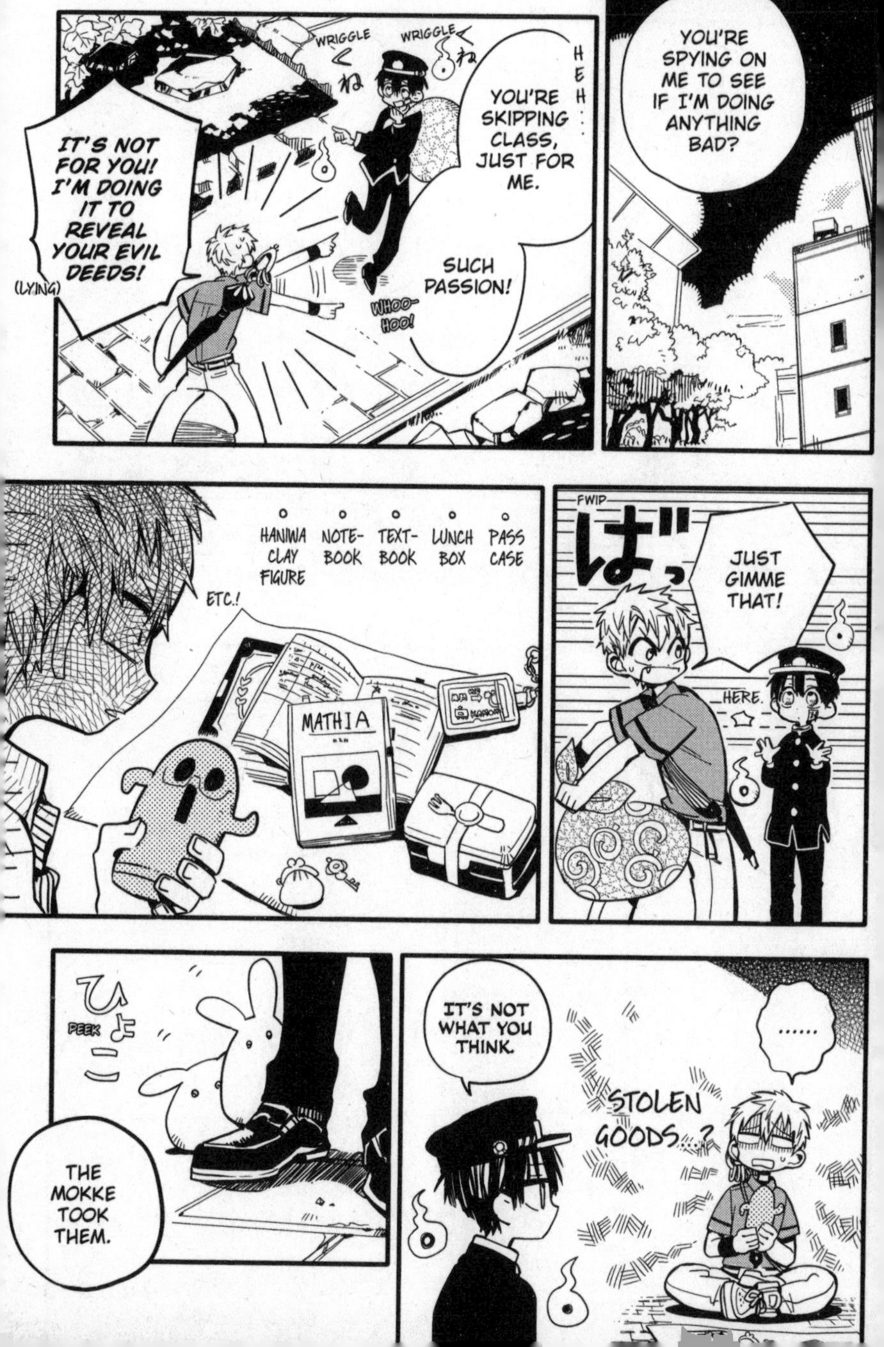
YOU'RE SPYING ON ME TO SEE IF I'M DOING ANYTHING BAD?
HEH...
WRIGGLE
WRIGGLE
YOU'RE SKIPPING CLASS, JUST FOR ME.
SUCH PASSION!
WHOO-HOO!
IT'S NOT FOR YOU! I'M DOING IT TO REVEAL YOUR EVIL DEEDS!
(LYING)
FWIP
JUST GIMME THAT!
HERE.
PASS CASE
LUNCH BOX
TEXT-BOOK
NOTE-BOOK
HANIWA CLAY FIGURE
ETC.!
MATHIA
......
IT'S NOT WHAT YOU THINK.
STOLEN GOODS...?
PEEK
THE MOKKE TOOK THEM.

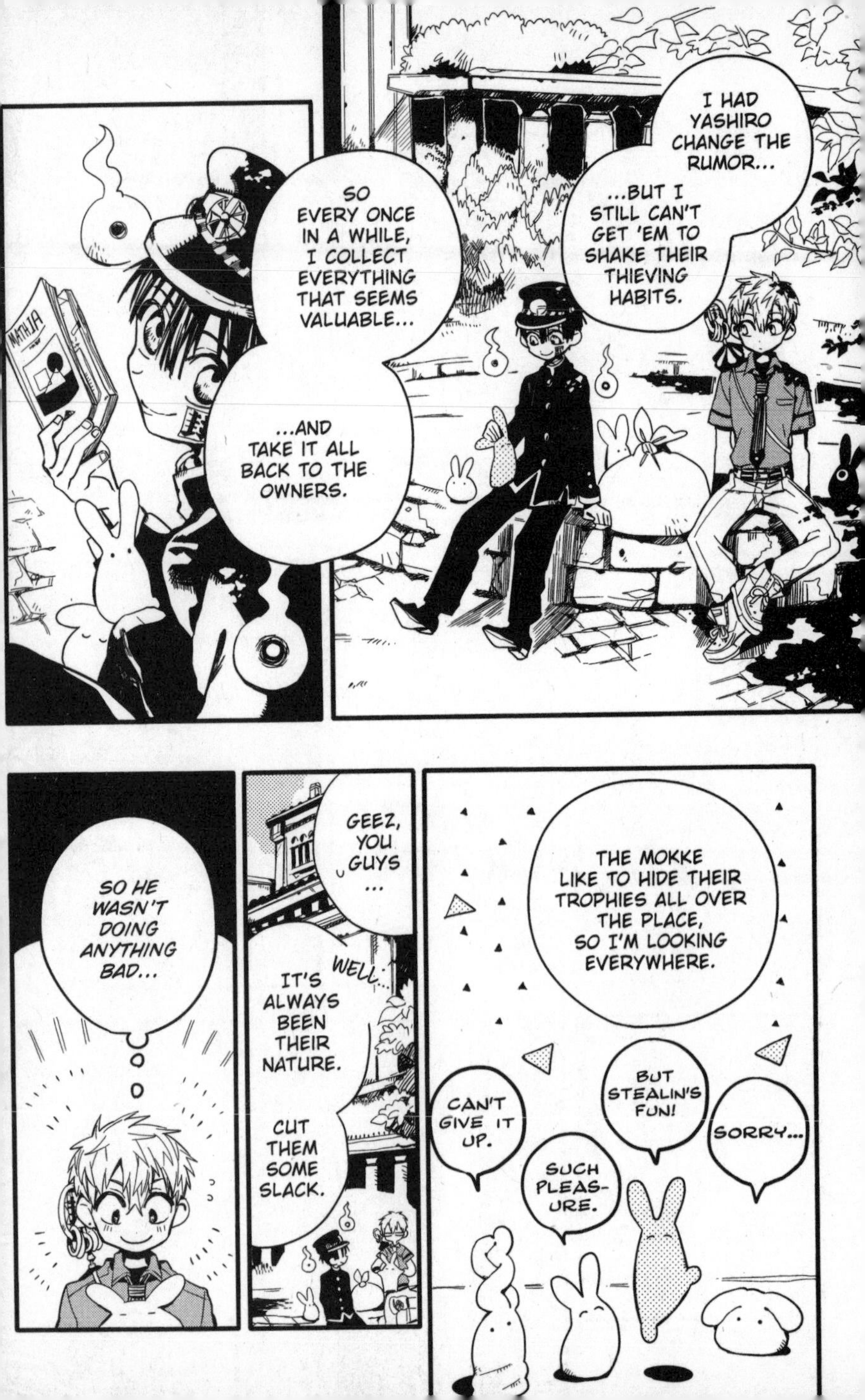
I HAD YASHIRO CHANGE THE RUMOR...
...BUT I STILL CAN'T GET 'EM TO SHAKE THEIR THIEVING HABITS.
SO EVERY ONCE IN A WHILE, I COLLECT EVERYTHING THAT SEEMS VALUABLE...
...AND TAKE IT ALL BACK TO THE OWNERS.
THE MOKKE LIKE TO HIDE THEIR TROPHIES ALL OVER THE PLACE, SO I'M LOOKING EVERYWHERE.
SORRY...
BUT STEALIN'S FUN!
SUCH PLEAS-URE.
CAN'T GIVE IT UP.
GEEZ, YOU GUYS...
WELL...
IT'S ALWAYS BEEN THEIR NATURE.
CUT THEM SOME SLACK.
SO HE WASN'T DOING ANYTHING BAD...

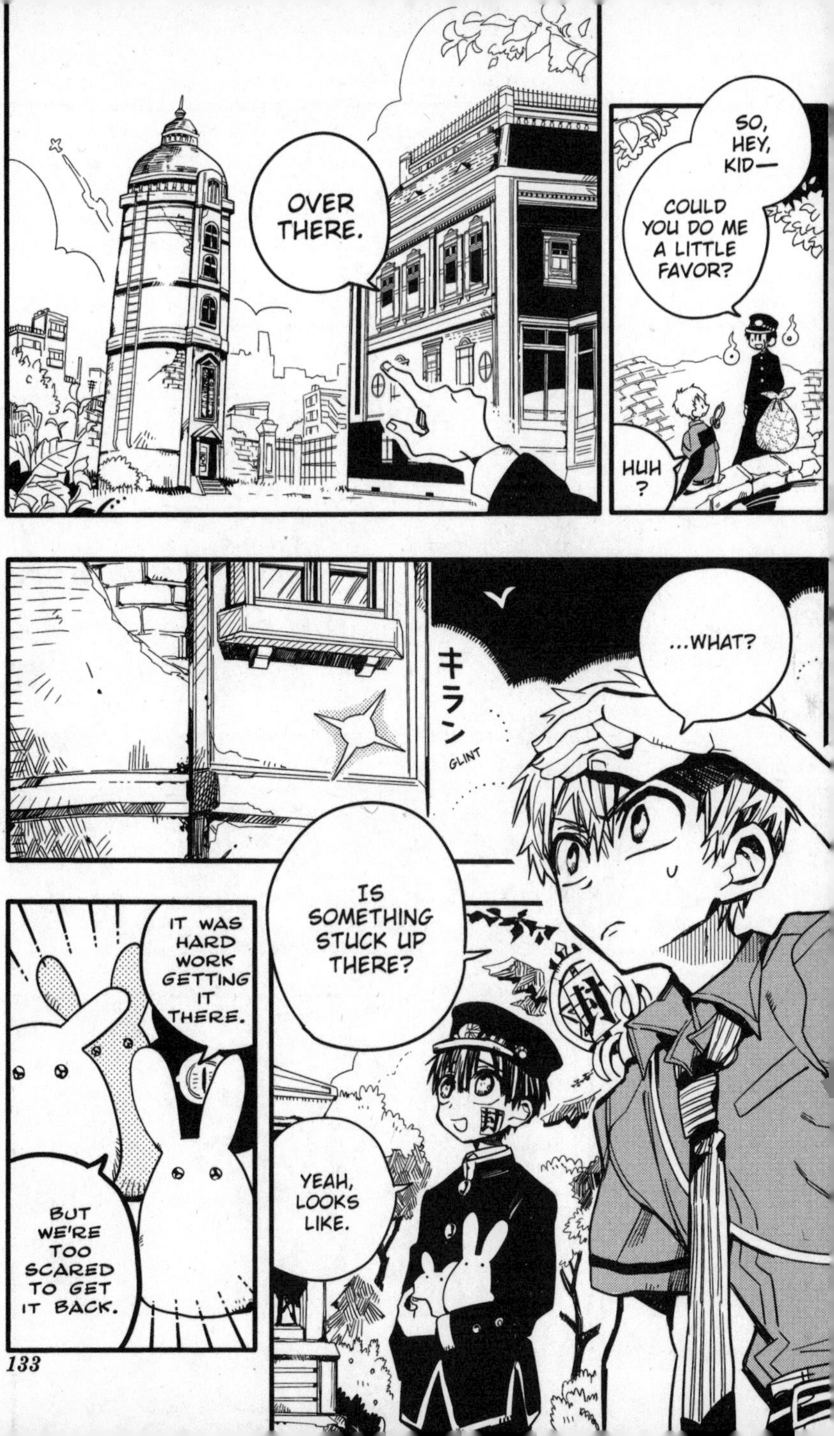
SO, HEY, KID—
COULD YOU DO ME A LITTLE FAVOR?
HUH?
OVER THERE.
...WHAT?
IS SOMETHING STUCK UP THERE?
YEAH, LOOKS LIKE.
キラン
GLINT
IT WAS HARD WORK GETTING IT THERE.
BUT WE'RE TOO SCARED TO GET IT BACK.

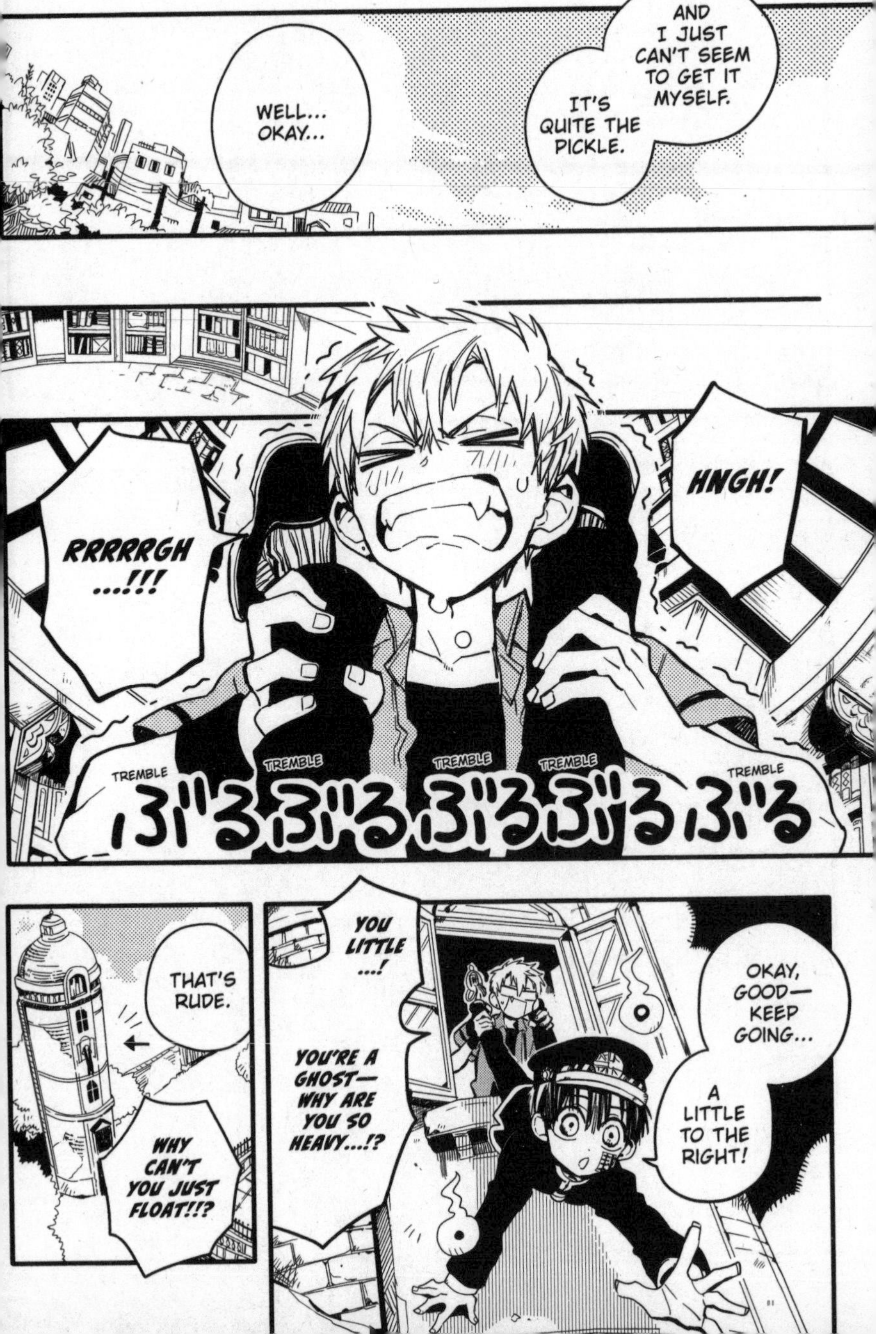
AND I JUST CAN'T SEEM TO GET IT MYSELF.
IT'S QUITE THE PICKLE.
WELL... OKAY...
HNGH!
RRRRRGH ...!!!
TREMBLE TREMBLE TREMBLE TREMBLE TREMBLE
ぶるぶるぶるぶるぶる
OKAY, GOOD— KEEP GOING...
A LITTLE TO THE RIGHT!
YOU LITTLE ...!
YOU'RE A GHOST— WHY ARE YOU SO HEAVY...!?
THAT'S RUDE.
WHY CAN'T YOU JUST FLOAT!!?

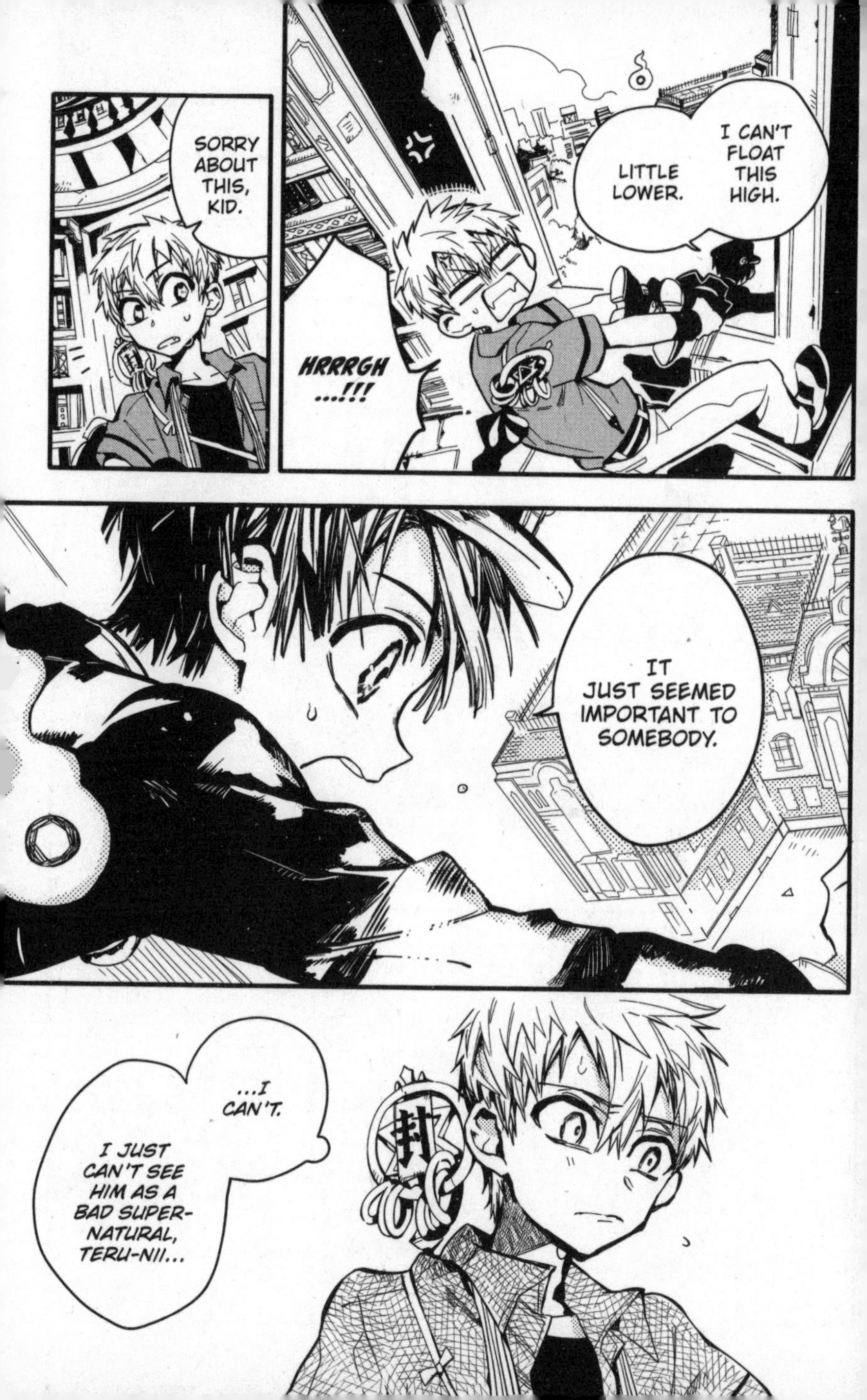
I CAN'T FLOAT THIS HIGH.
LITTLE LOWER.
HRRRGH ......!!!
SORRY ABOUT THIS, KID.
IT JUST SEEMED IMPORTANT TO SOMEBODY.
...I CAN'T.
I JUST CAN'T SEE HIM AS A BAD SUPER-NATURAL, TERU-NII...

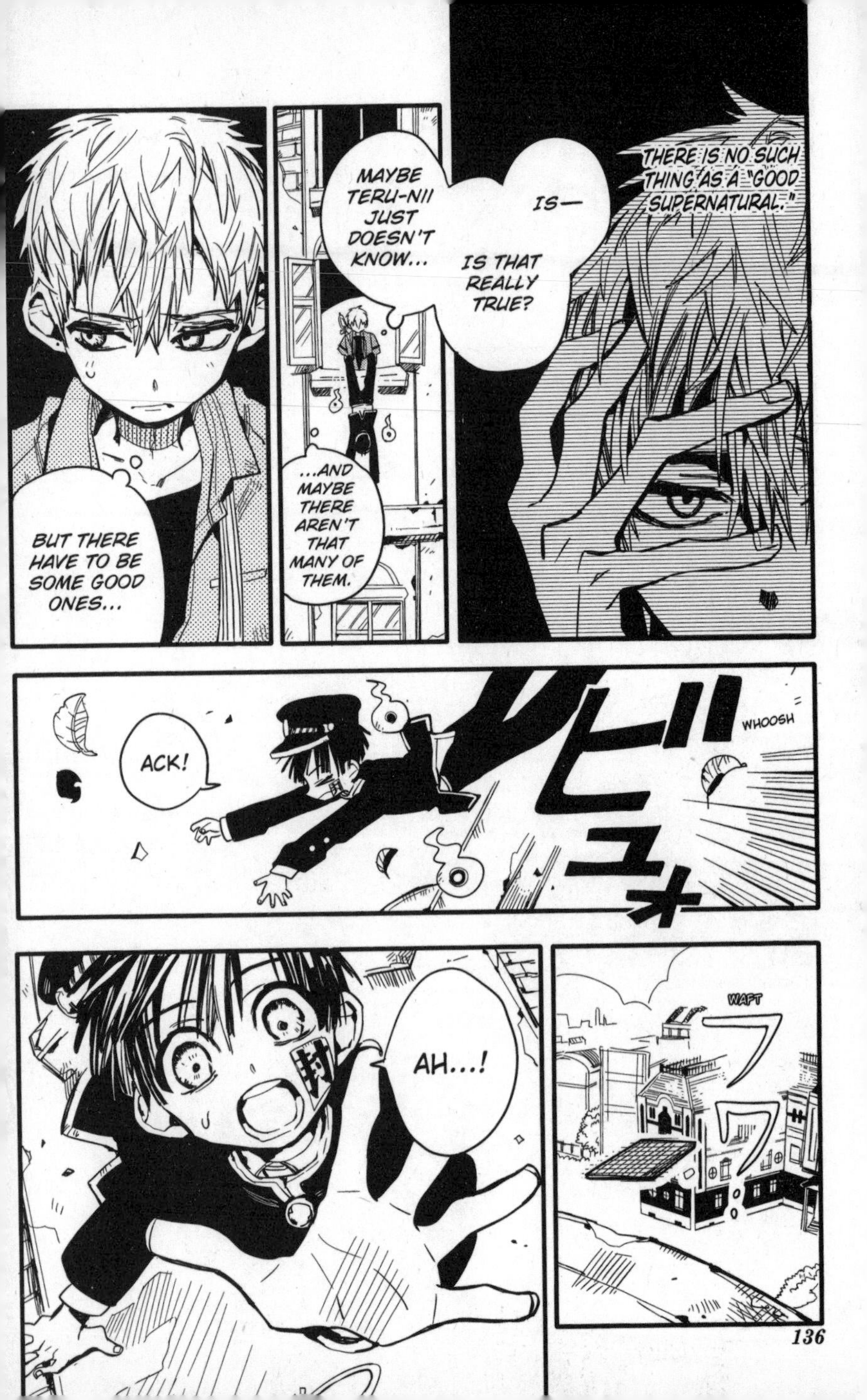
THERE IS NO SUCH THING AS A "GOOD SUPERNATURAL."
IS—
IS THAT REALLY TRUE?
MAYBE TERU-NII JUST DOESN'T KNOW...
...AND MAYBE THERE AREN'T THAT MANY OF THEM.
BUT THERE HAVE TO BE SOME GOOD ONES...
WHOOSH
ACK!
WAFT
AH...!

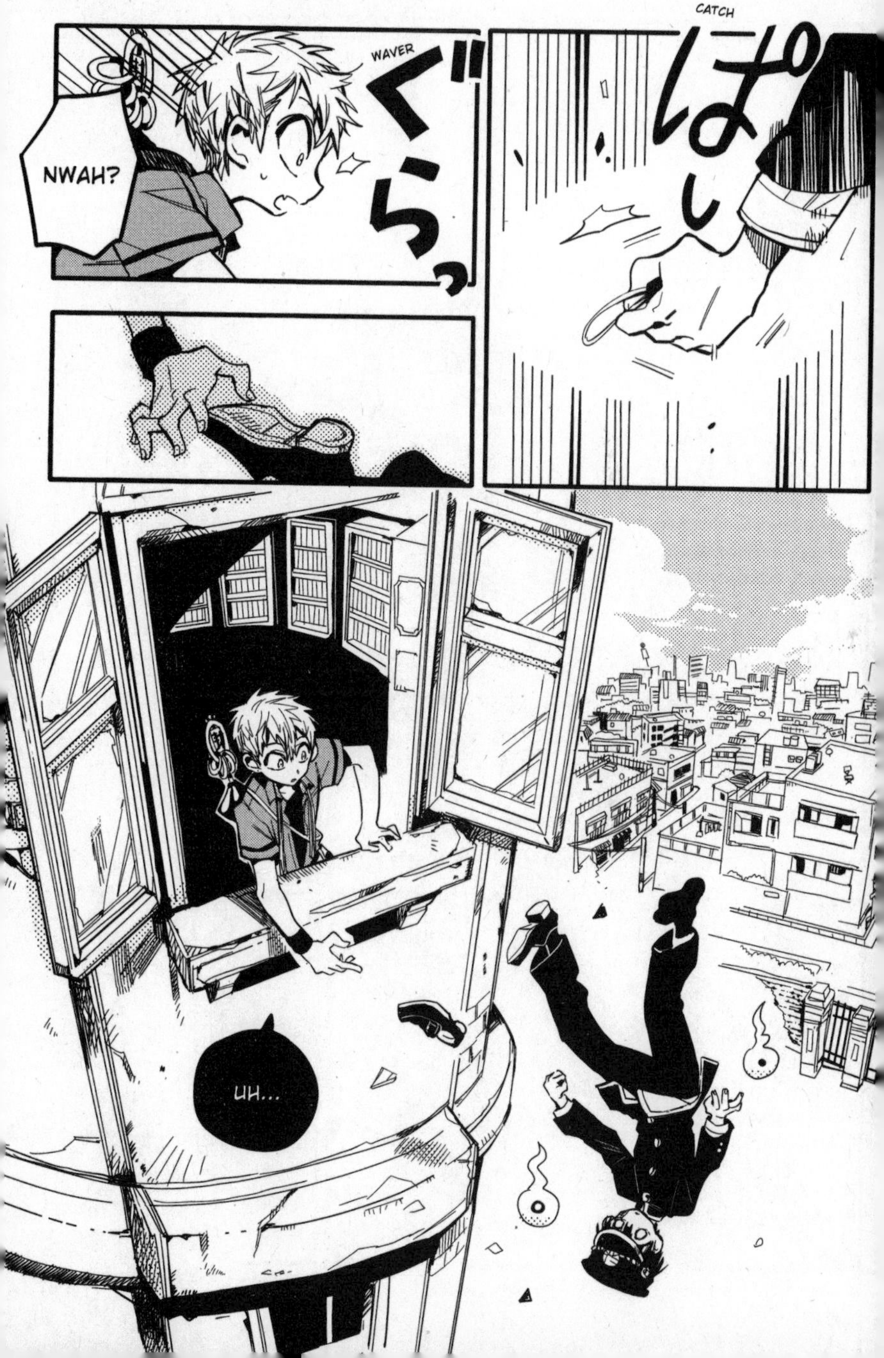
CATCH
ぱしっ
WAVER
ぐらっ
NWAH?
UH...

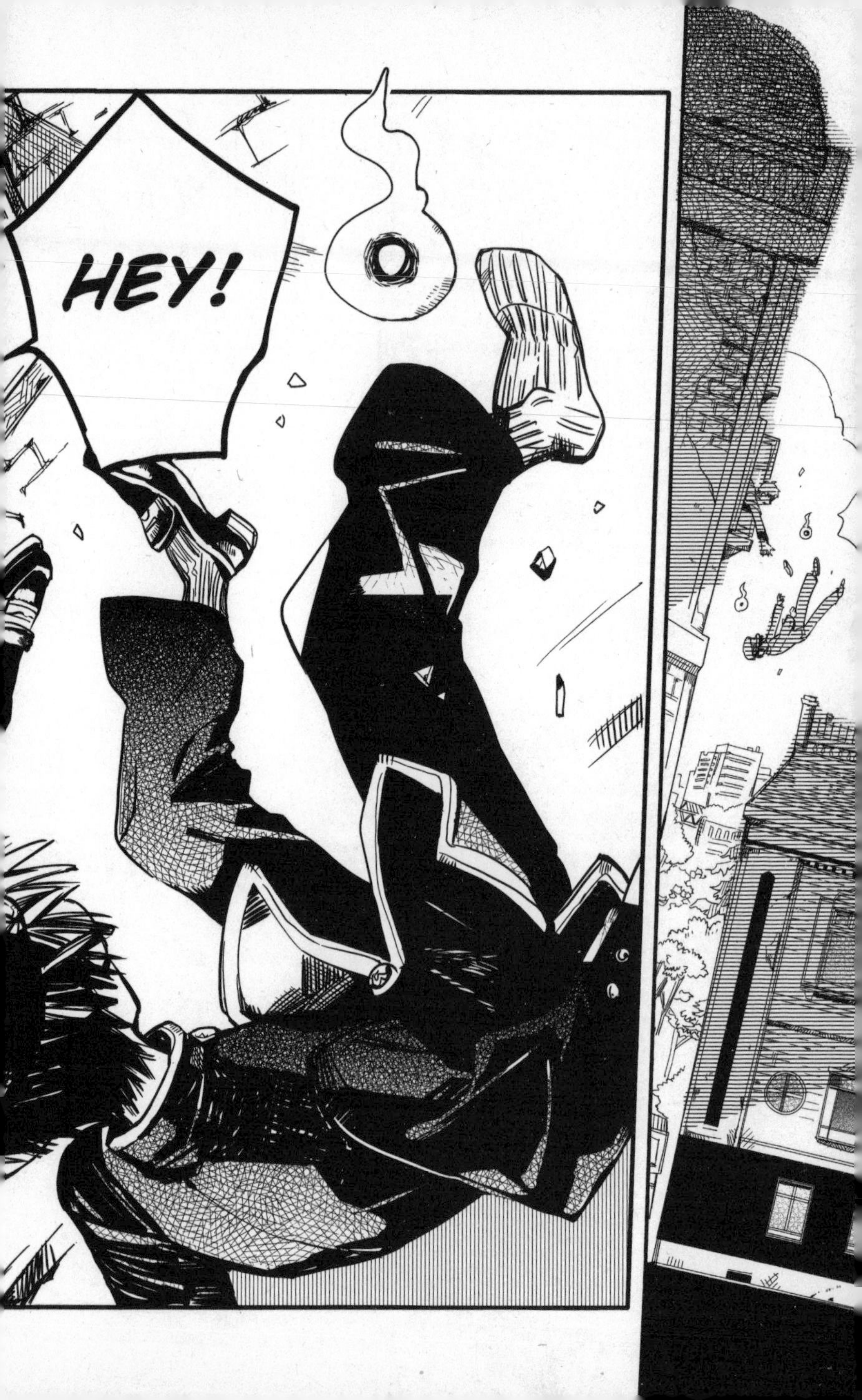
HEY!

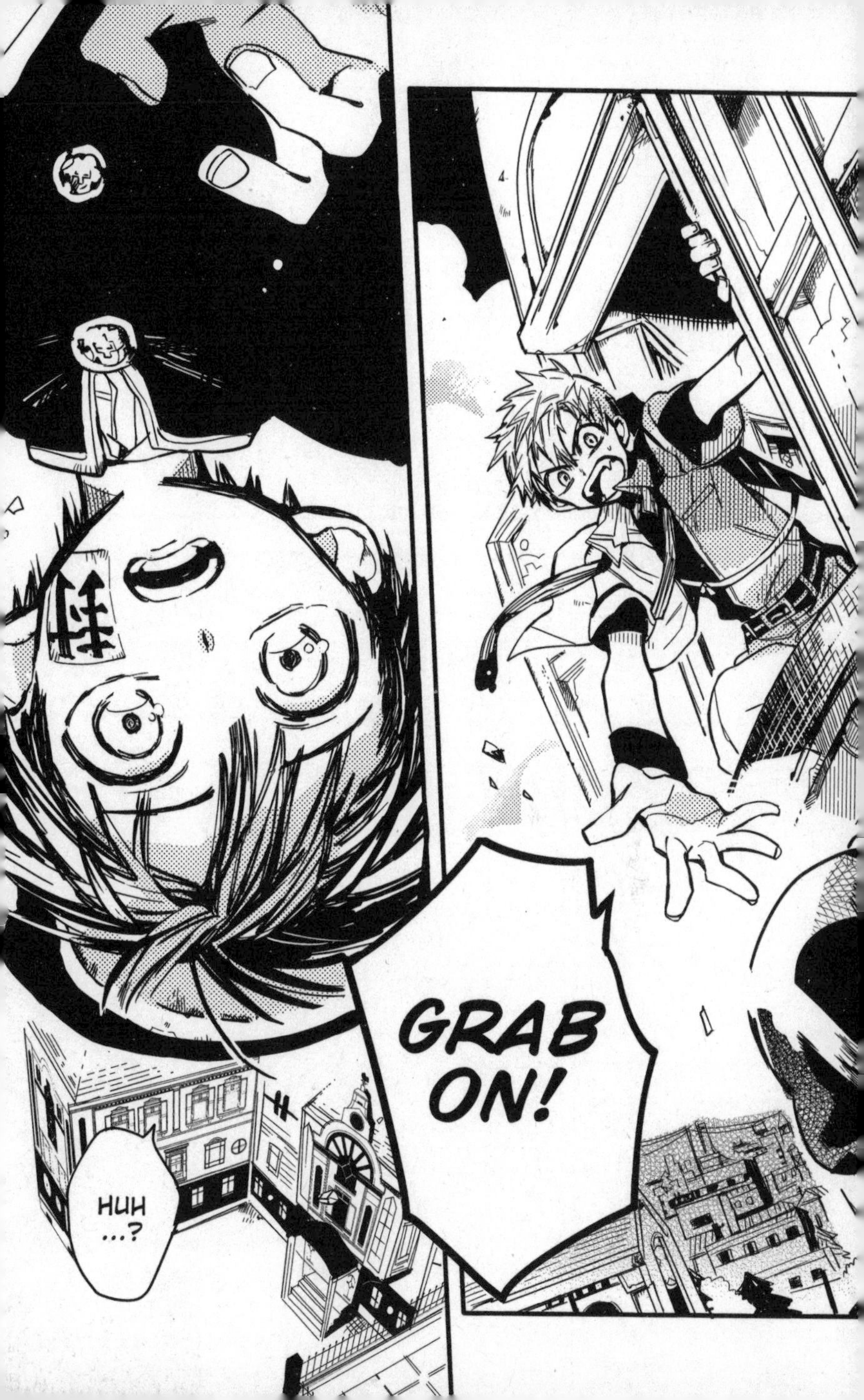
GRAB ON!
HUH ...?

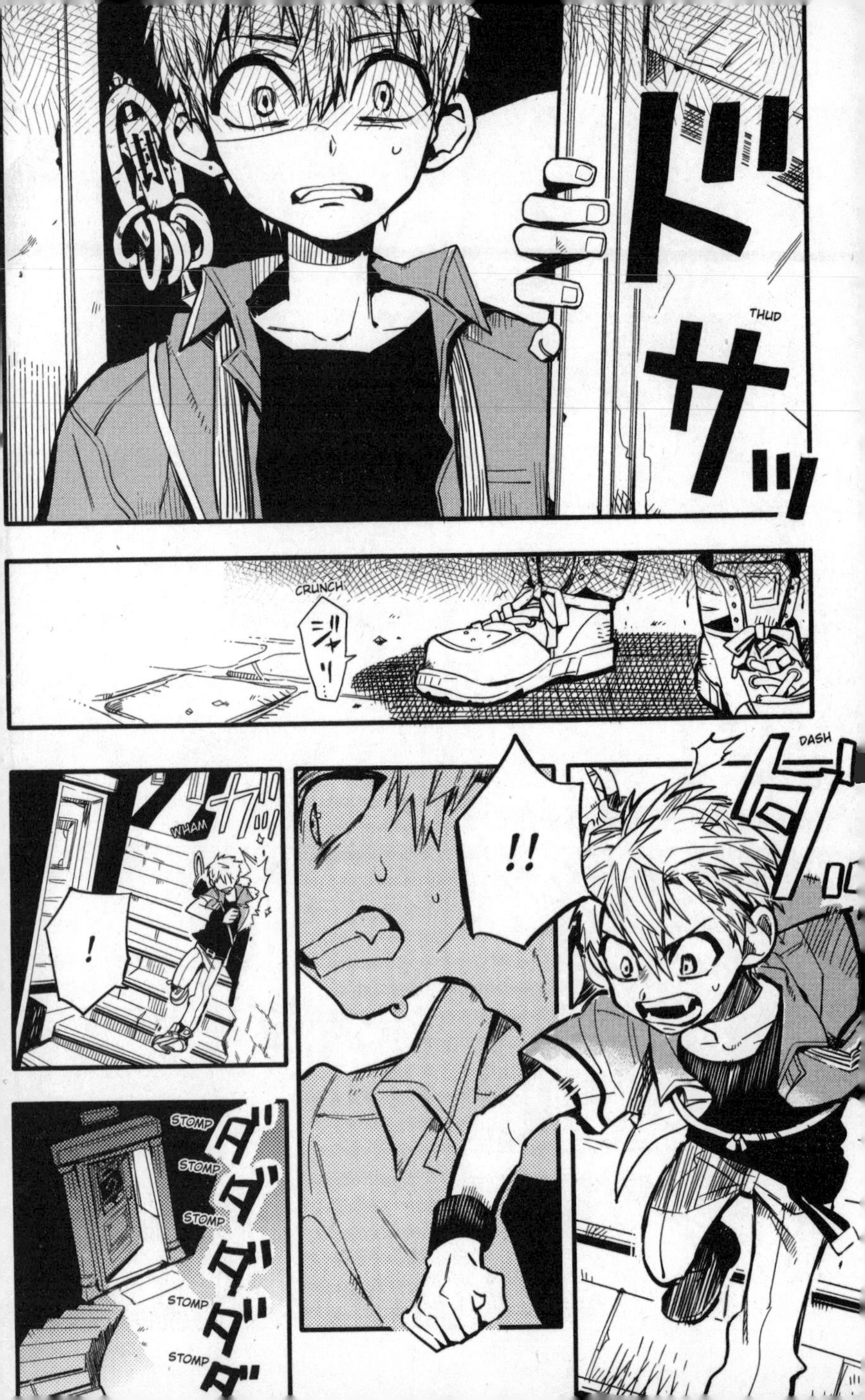
ドサッ
THUD
CRUNCH
ジャリ…
ダッ
DASH
!!
ガッ
WHAM
!
ダダダダダ
STOMP
STOMP
STOMP
STOMP
STOMP

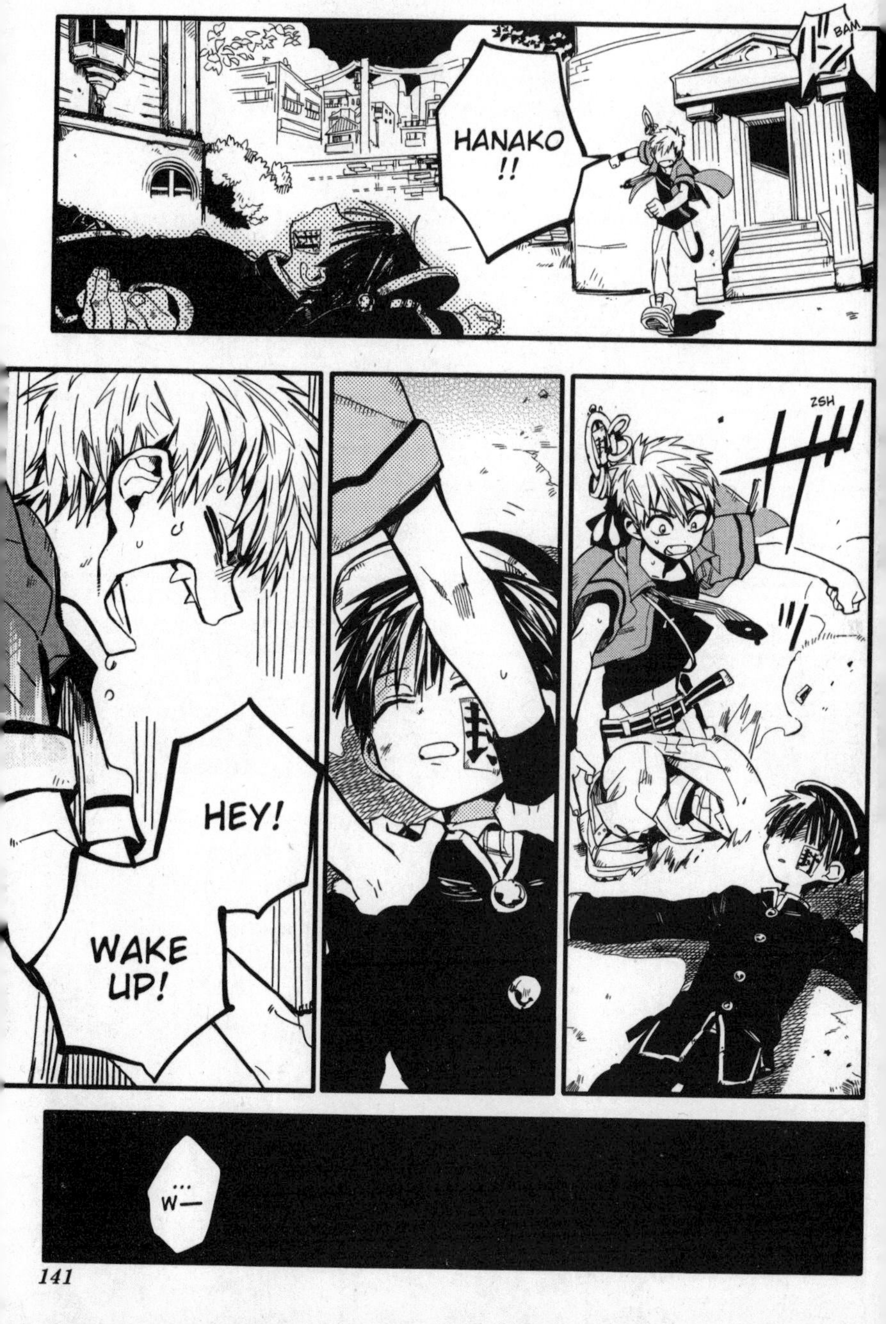
BAM
HANAKO !!
ZSH
HEY!
WAKE UP!
... W—

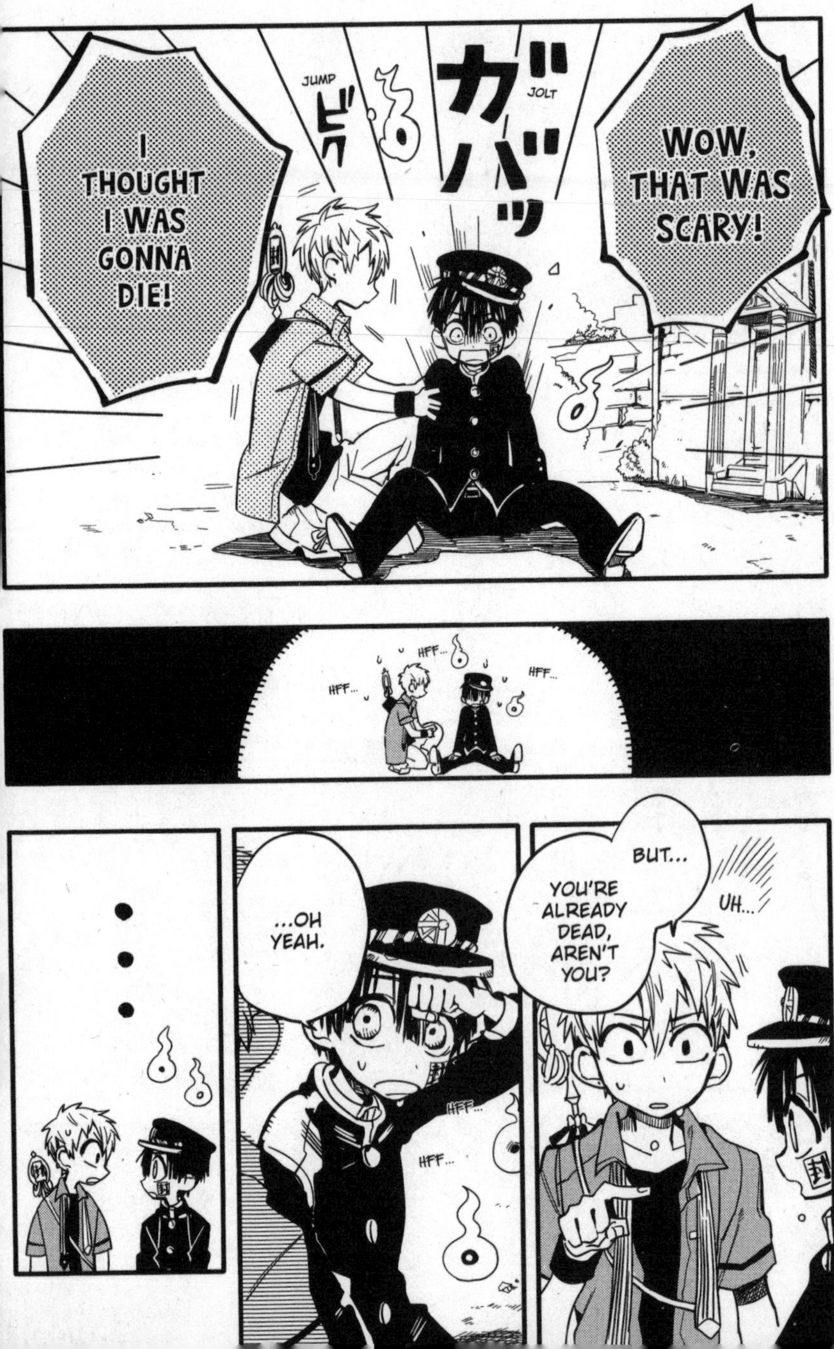
WOW, THAT WAS SCARY!
JOLT
ガバッ
JUMP
ビク
I THOUGHT I WAS GONNA DIE!
HFF...
HFF...
HFF...
BUT... YOU'RE ALREADY DEAD, AREN'T YOU?
UH...
...OH YEAH.
HFF...
HFF...
...

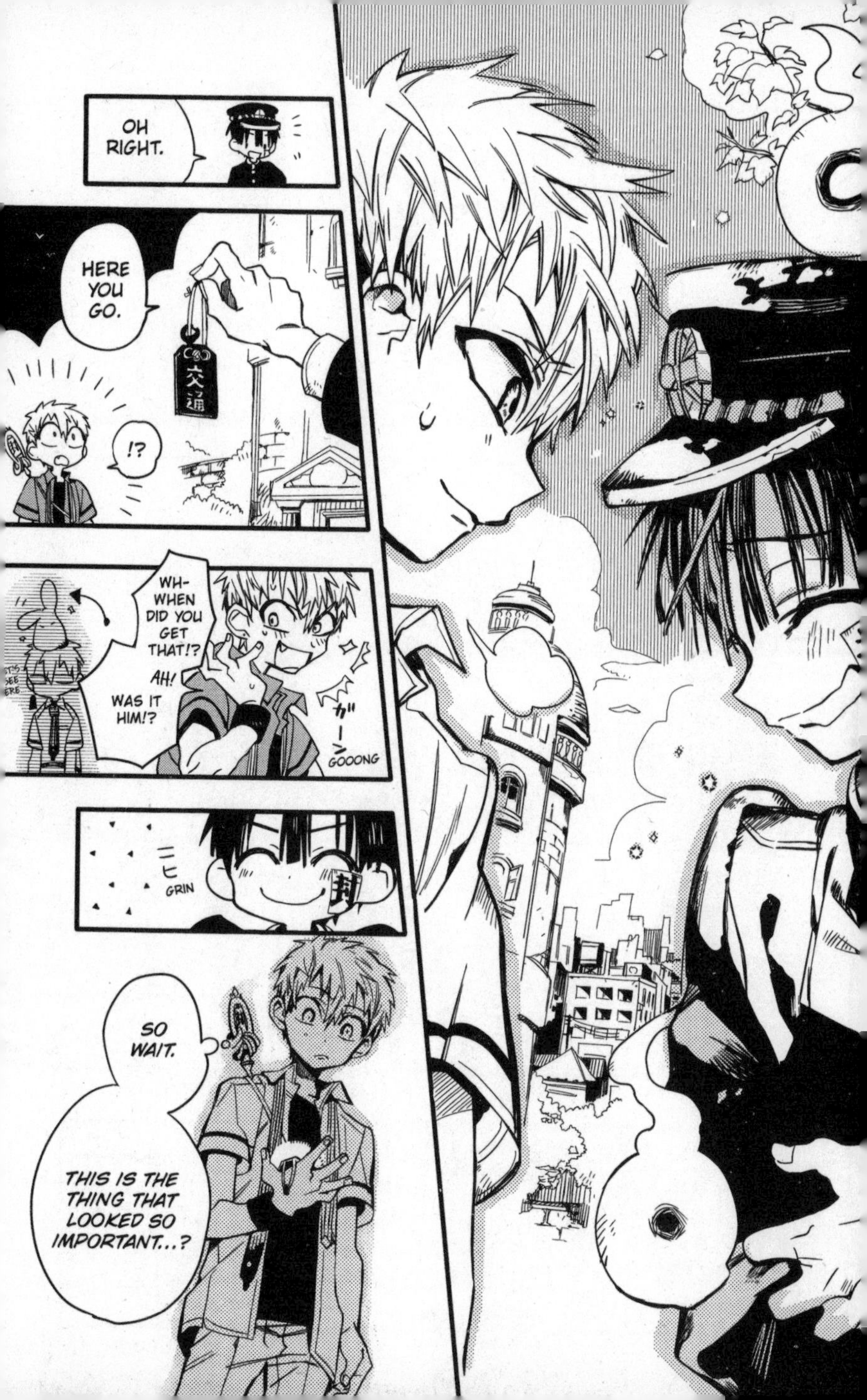
OH RIGHT.
HERE YOU GO.
!?
WH-WHEN DID YOU GET THAT!?
AH! WAS IT HIM!?
GOOONG
GRIN
SO WAIT.
THIS IS THE THING THAT LOOKED SO IMPORTANT...?

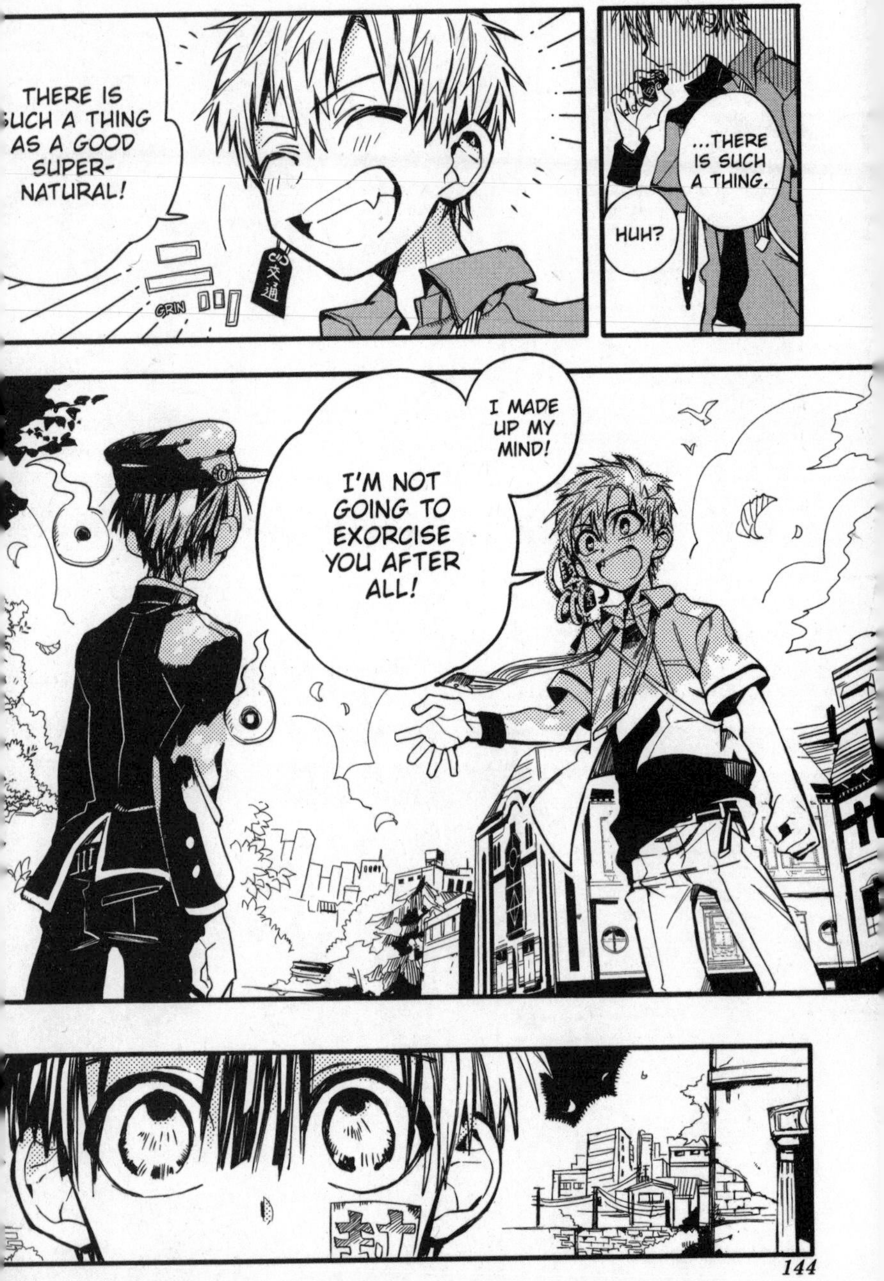
...THERE IS SUCH A THING.
HUH?
THERE IS SUCH A THING AS A GOOD SUPER-NATURAL!
GRIN
I MADE UP MY MIND!
I'M NOT GOING TO EXORCISE YOU AFTER ALL!

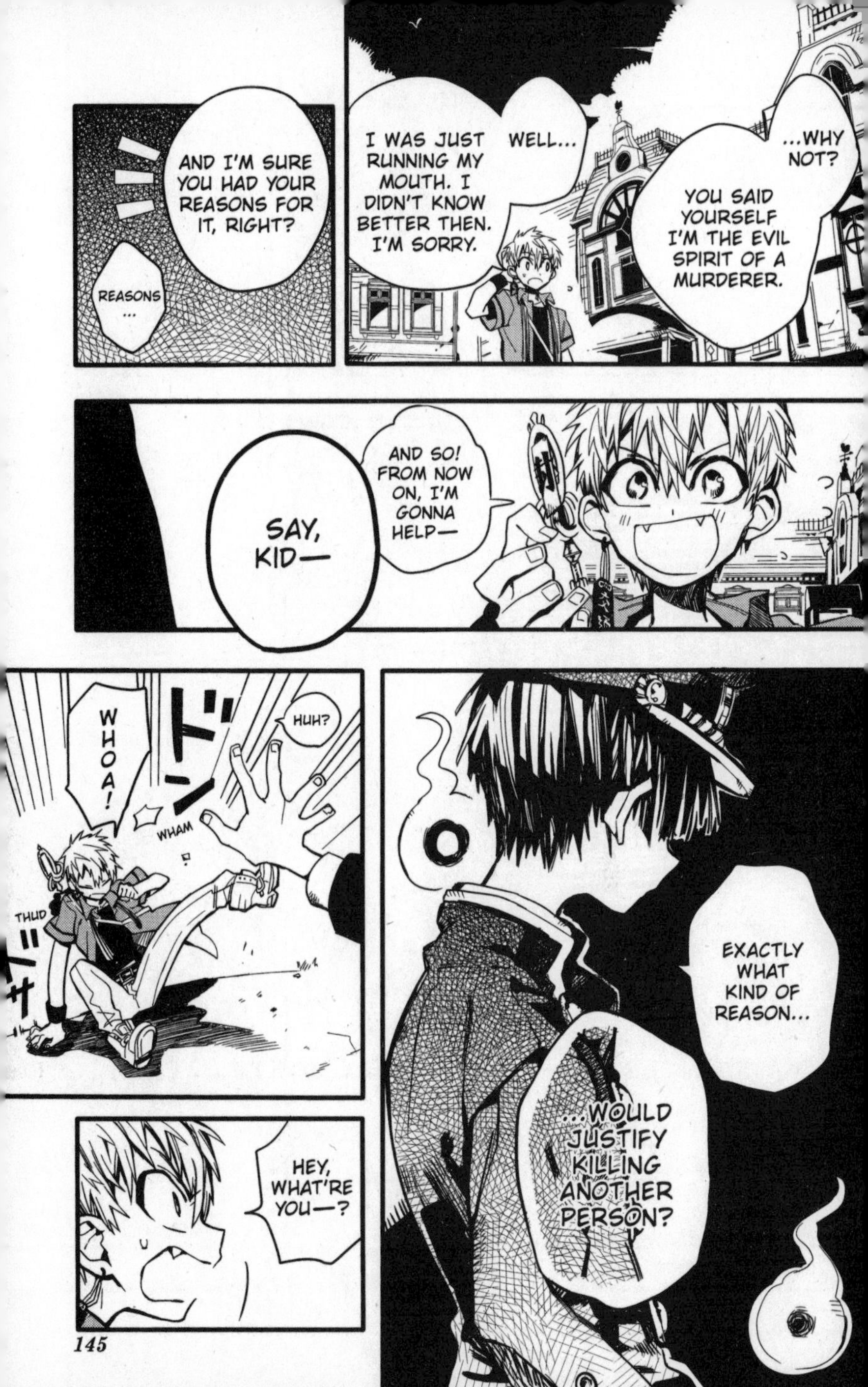
...WHY NOT?
YOU SAID YOURSELF I'M THE EVIL SPIRIT OF A MURDERER.
WELL...
I WAS JUST RUNNING MY MOUTH. I DIDN'T KNOW BETTER THEN. I'M SORRY.
AND I'M SURE YOU HAD YOUR REASONS FOR IT, RIGHT?
REASONS ...
AND SO! FROM NOW ON, I'M GONNA HELP—
SAY, KID—
EXACTLY WHAT KIND OF REASON...
...WOULD JUSTIFY KILLING ANOTHER PERSON?
HUH?
ドン
WHOA!
WHAM
THUD
HEY, WHAT'RE YOU—?

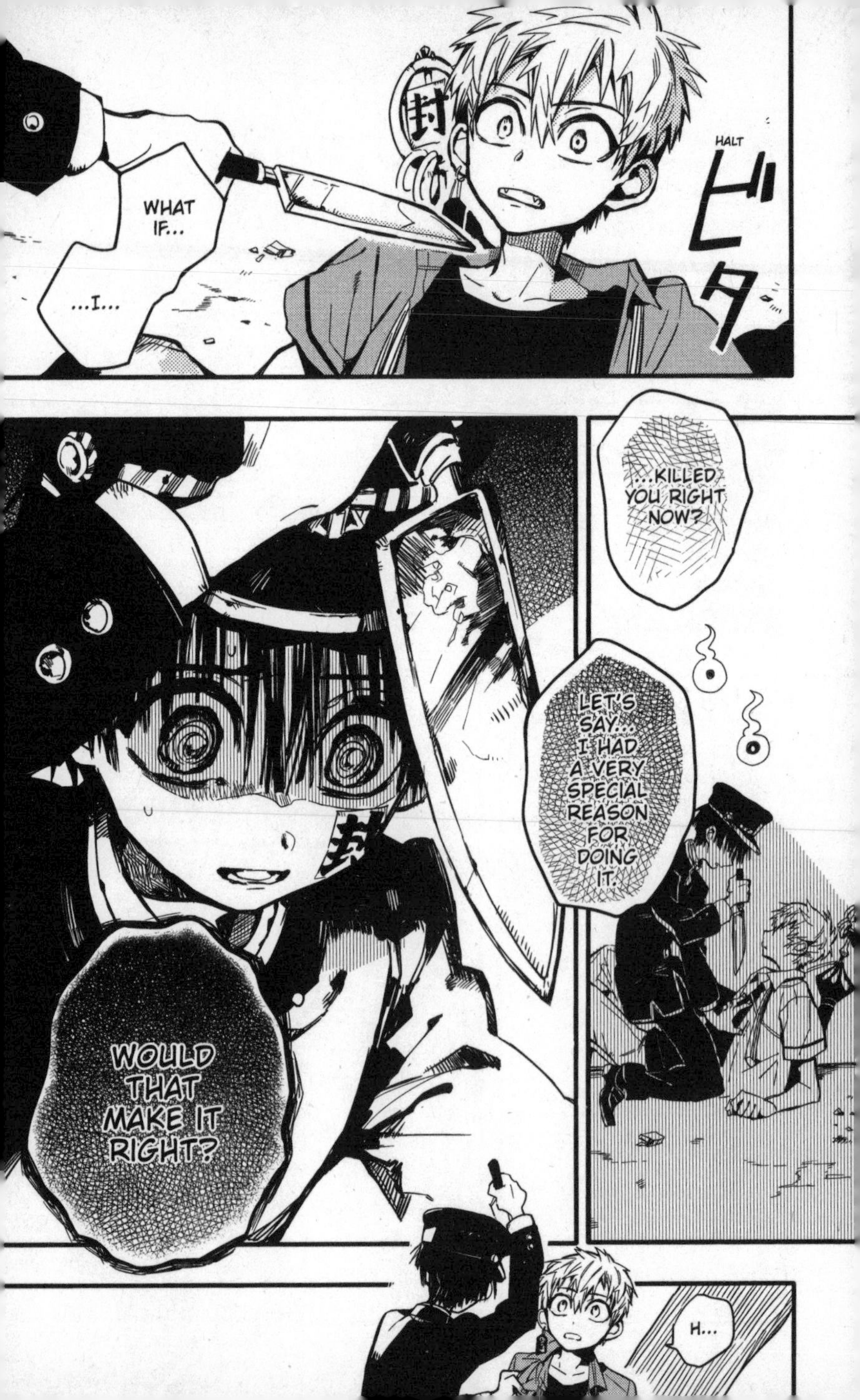
HALT
WHAT IF...
...I...
...KILLED YOU RIGHT NOW?
LET'S SAY... I HAD A VERY SPECIAL REASON FOR DOING IT.
WOULD THAT MAKE IT RIGHT?
H...

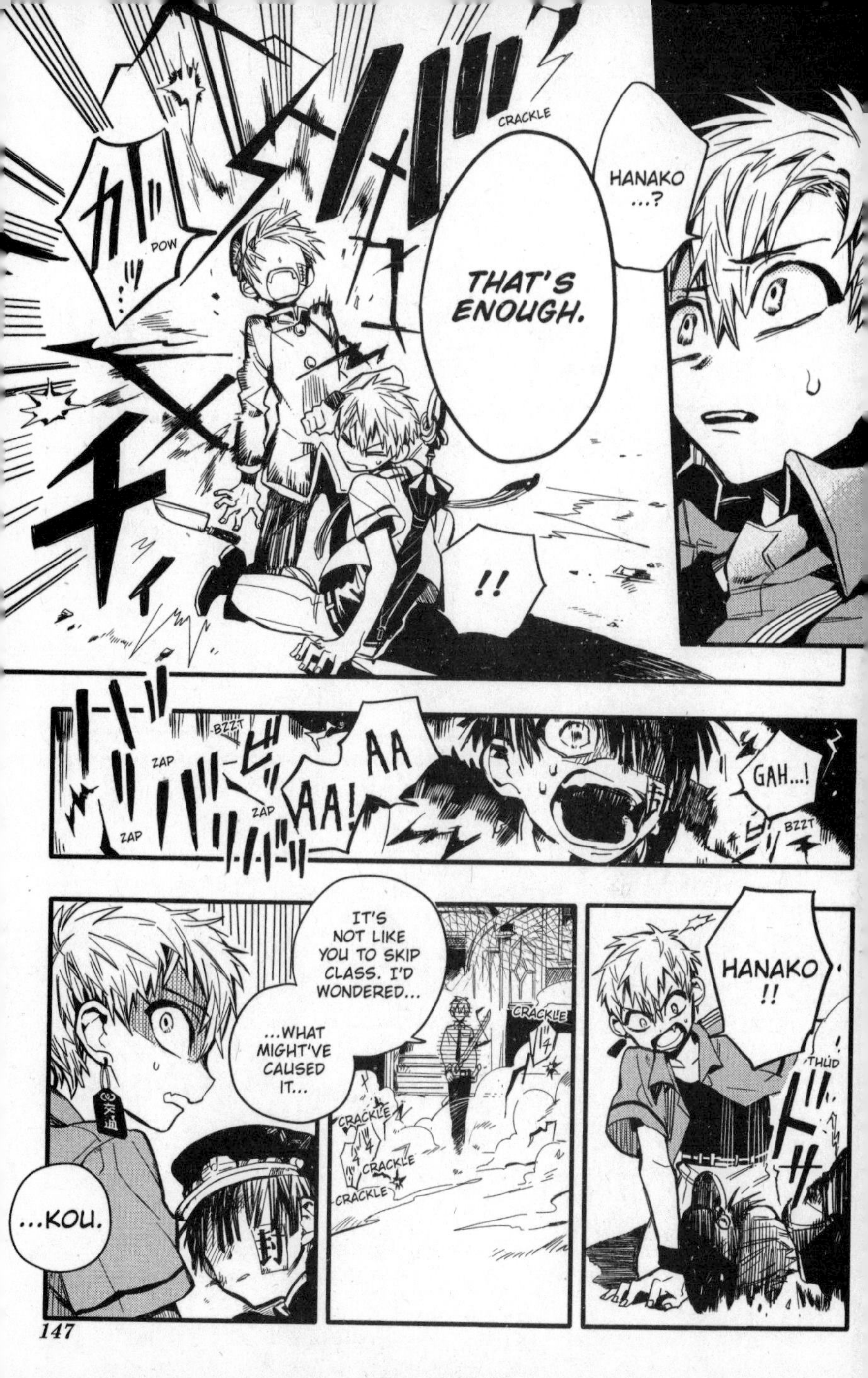
HANAKO ...?
CRACKLE
THAT'S ENOUGH.
POW
!!
GAH...!
BZZT
AA AA!
BZZT
ZAP
ZAP
ZAP
HANAKO !!
THUD
IT'S NOT LIKE YOU TO SKIP CLASS. I'D WONDERED...
...WHAT MIGHT'VE CAUSED IT...
CRACKLE
CRACKLE
CRACKLE
CRACKLE
...KOU.

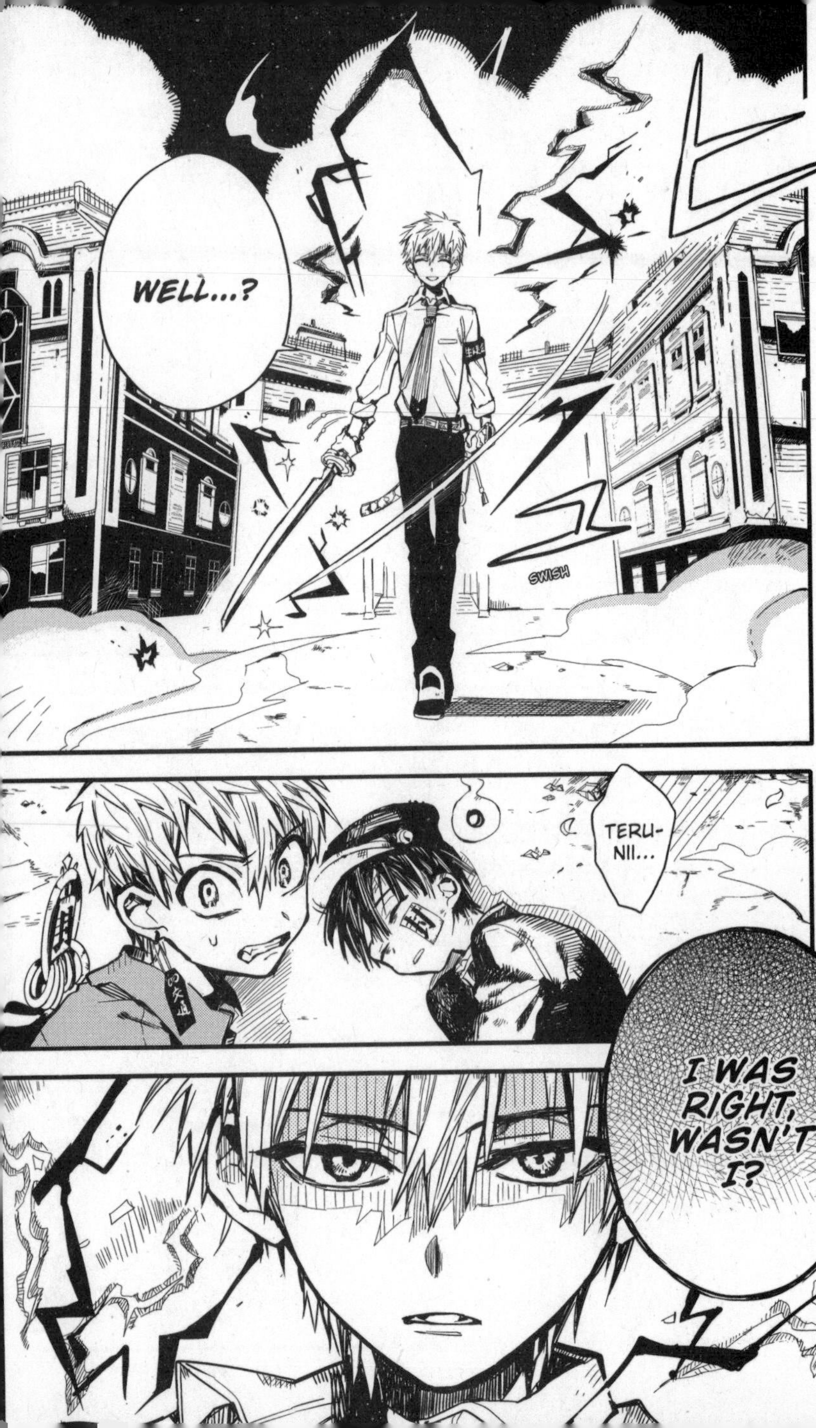
WELL...?
SWISH
TERU-NII...
I WAS RIGHT, WASN'T I?

SPOOK 10 THE YOUNG EXORCIST (PART 2)

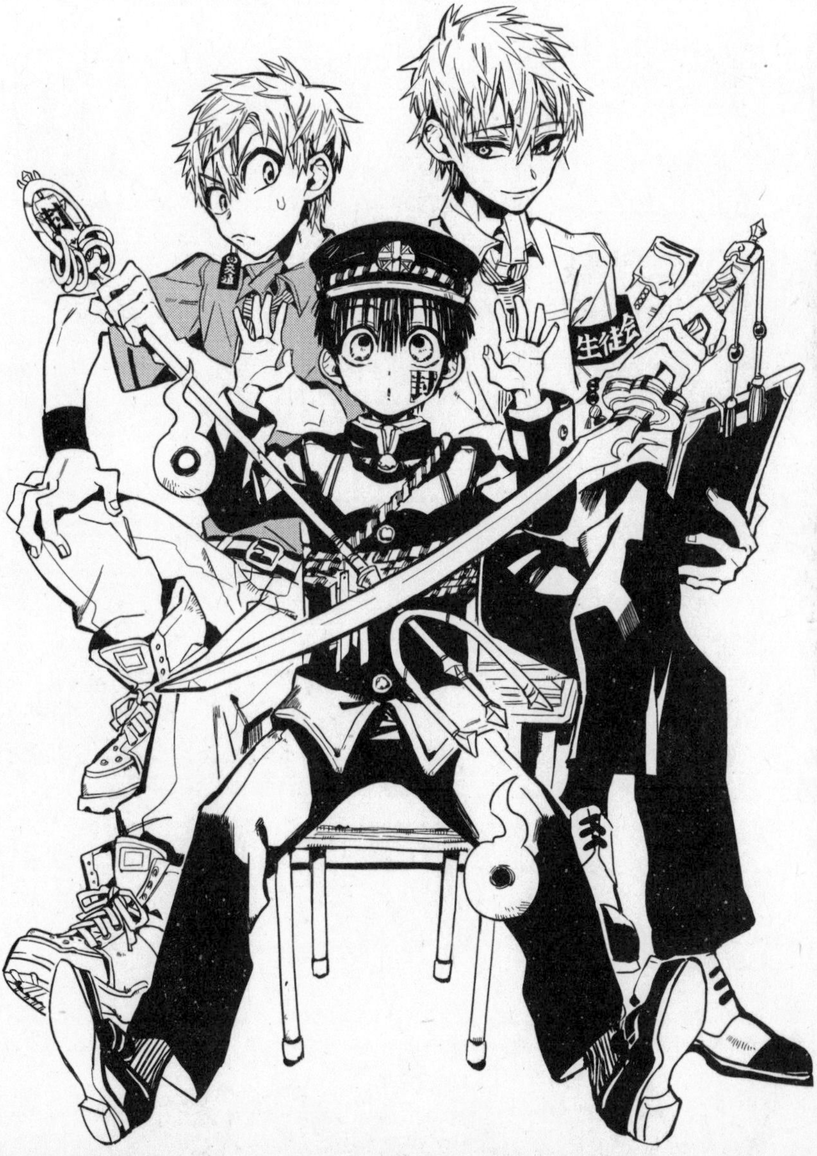
生徒会

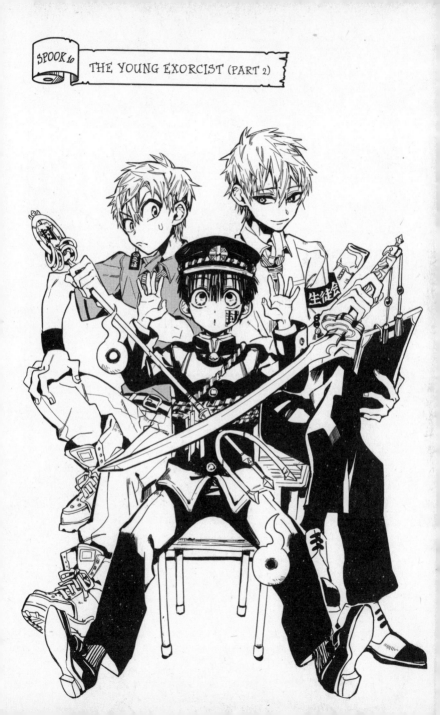

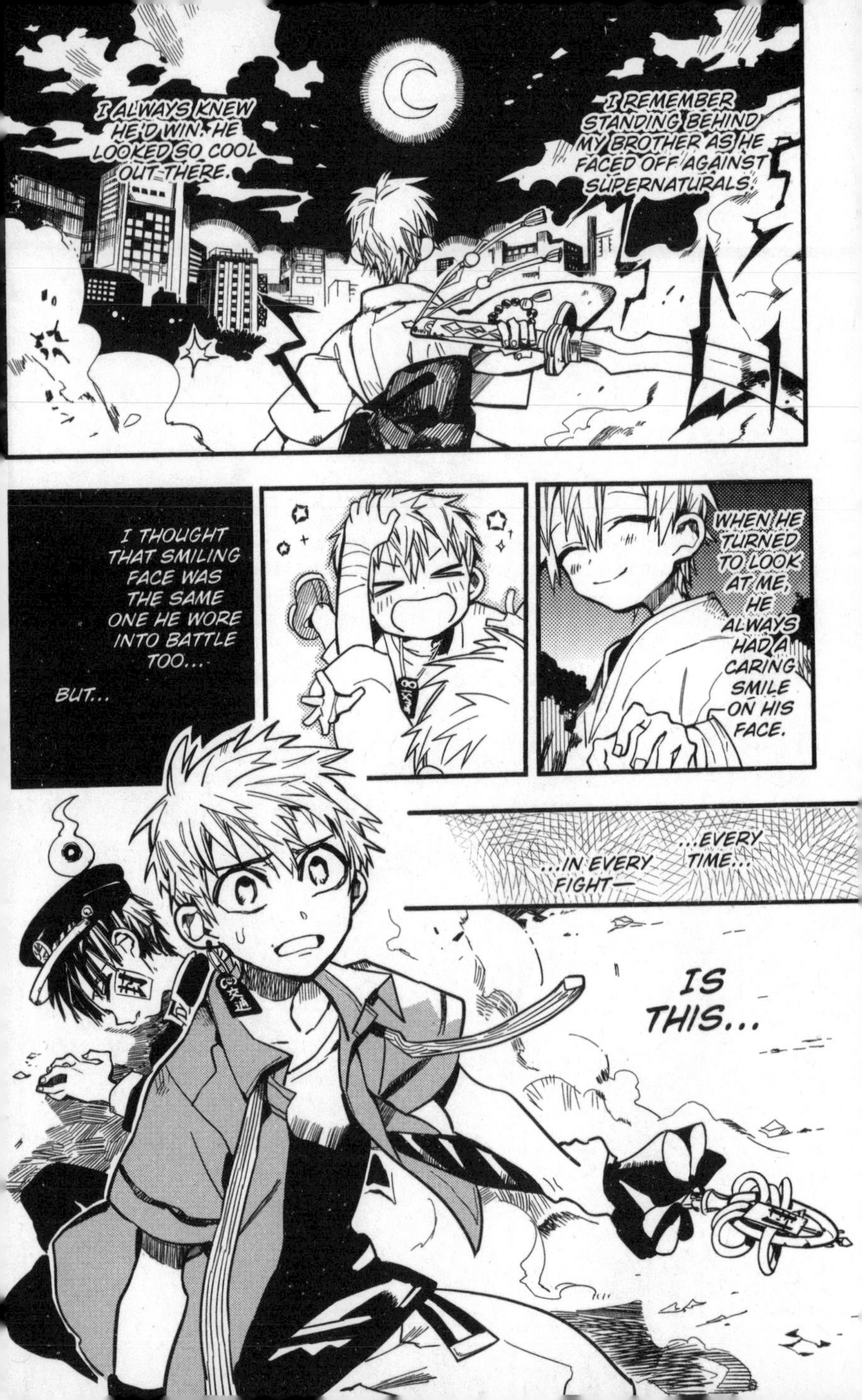
I REMEMBER STANDING BEHIND MY BROTHER AS HE FACED OFF AGAINST SUPERNATURALS.
I ALWAYS KNEW HE'D WIN. HE LOOKED SO COOL OUT THERE.
WHEN HE TURNED TO LOOK AT ME, HE ALWAYS HAD A CARING SMILE ON HIS FACE.
I THOUGHT THAT SMILING FACE WAS THE SAME ONE HE WORE INTO BATTLE TOO...
BUT...
...EVERY TIME...
...IN EVERY FIGHT—
IS THIS...

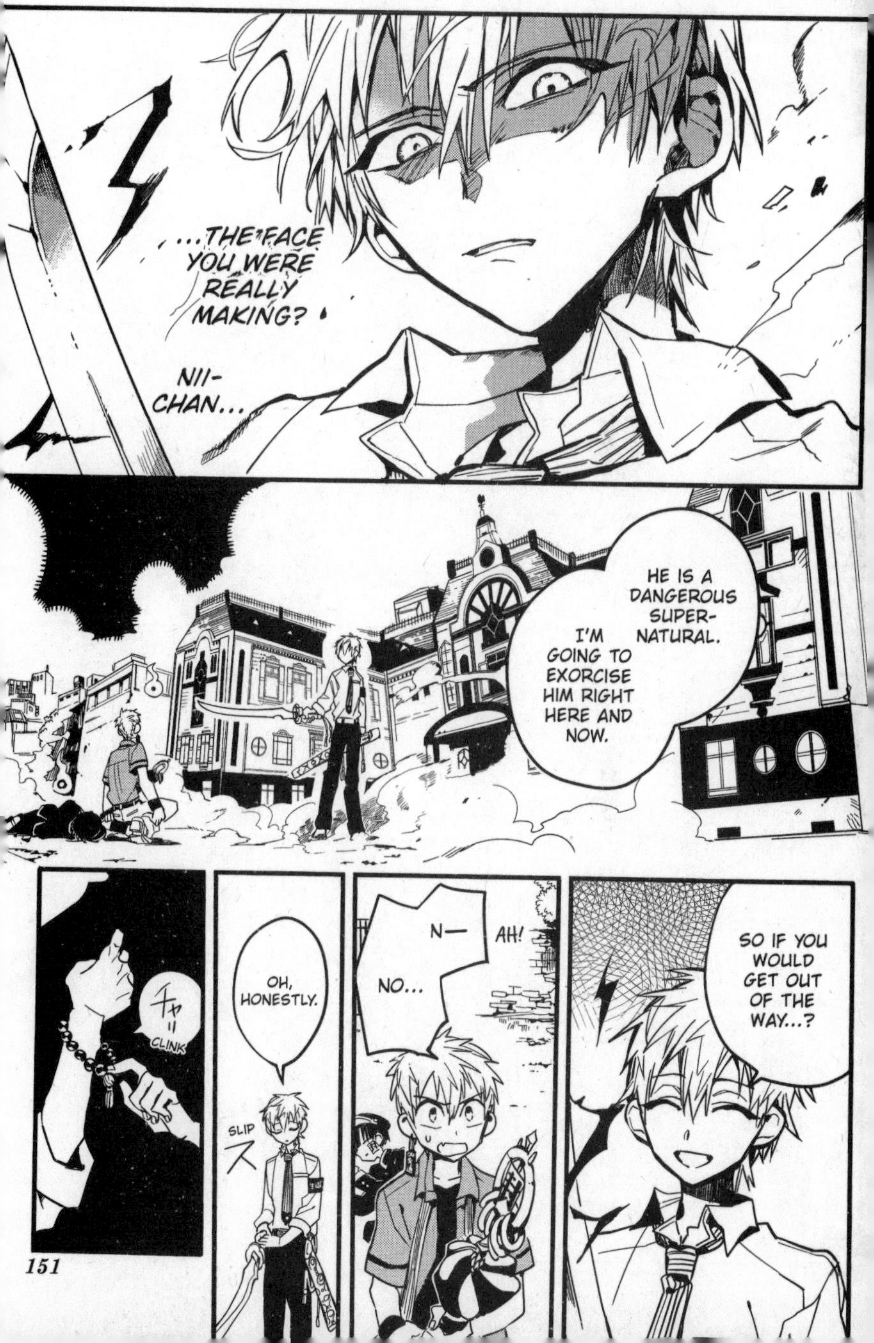
...THE FACE YOU WERE REALLY MAKING?
NII-CHAN...
HE IS A DANGEROUS SUPER-NATURAL.
I'M GOING TO EXORCISE HIM RIGHT HERE AND NOW.
SO IF YOU WOULD GET OUT OF THE WAY...?
AH!
N—
NO...
OH, HONESTLY.
ス
SLIP
チャリ
CLINK

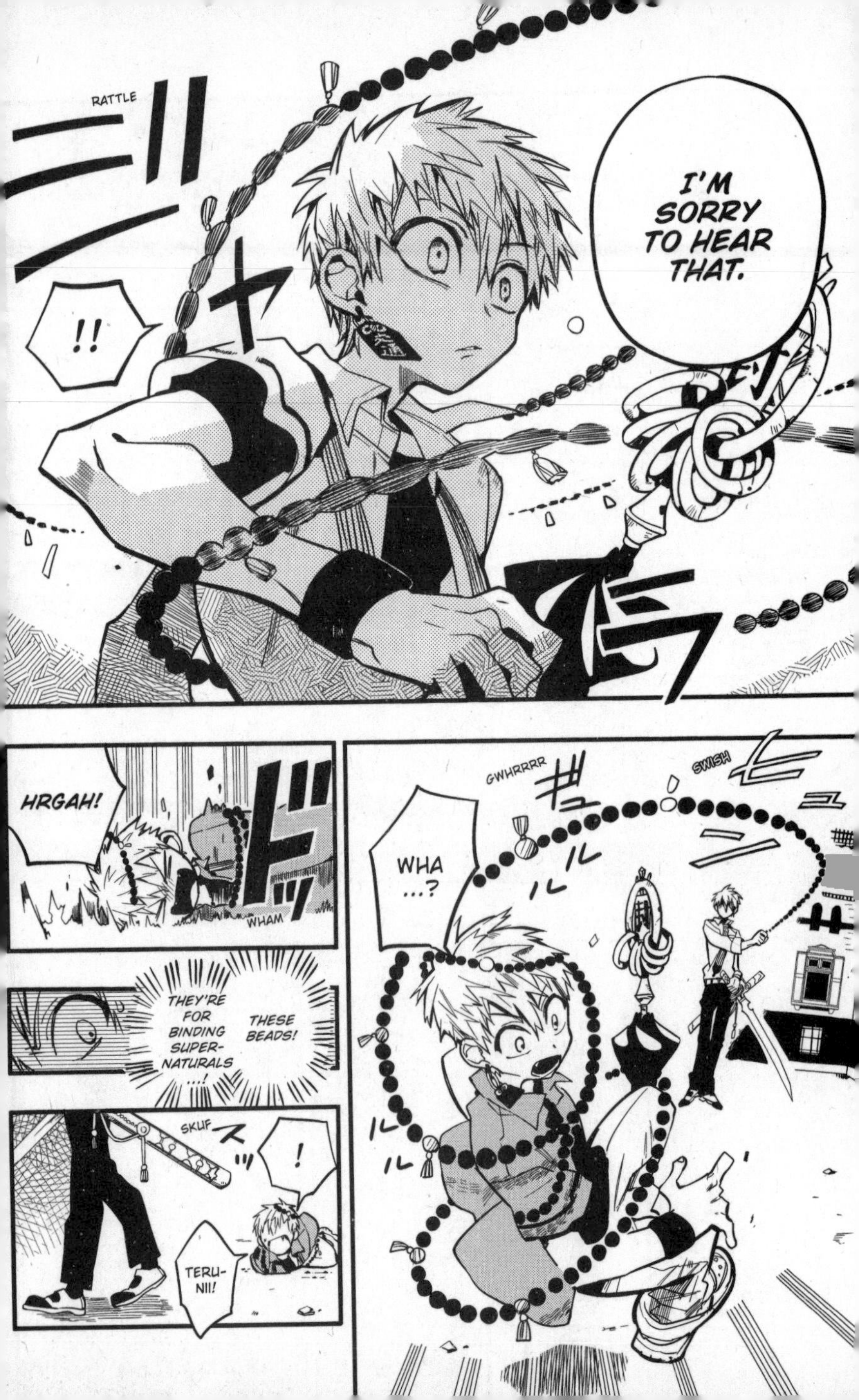
I'M SORRY TO HEAR THAT.
RATTLE
!!
SWISH
GWHRRRR
WHA ...?
HRGAH!
WHAM
THESE BEADS!
THEY'RE FOR BINDING SUPER-NATURALS ...!
SKUF
!
TERU-NII!

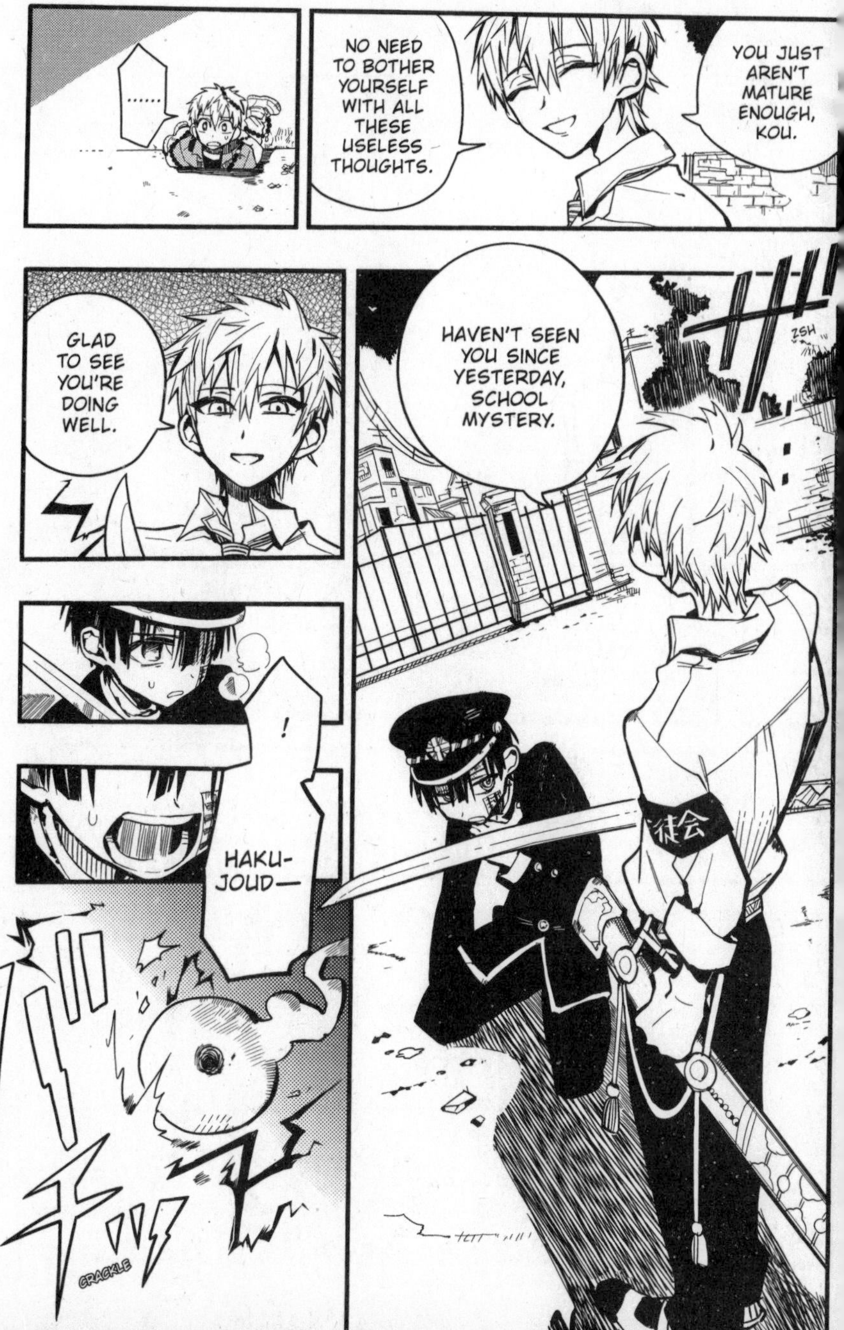
YOU JUST AREN'T MATURE ENOUGH, KOU.
NO NEED TO BOTHER YOURSELF WITH ALL THESE USELESS THOUGHTS.
......
HAVEN'T SEEN YOU SINCE YESTERDAY, SCHOOL MYSTERY.
ZSH
GLAD TO SEE YOU'RE DOING WELL.
!
HAKU-JOUD—
CRACKLE

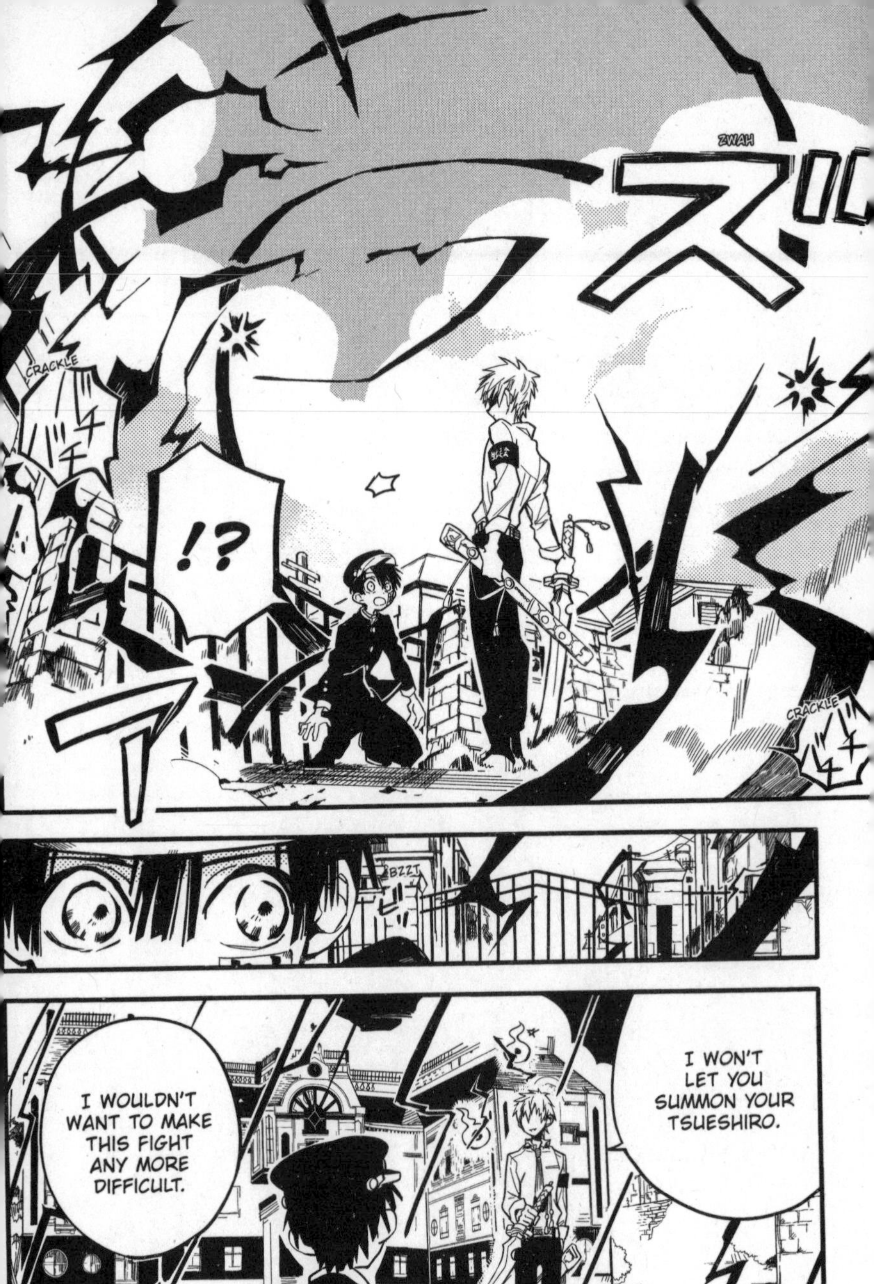
ZWAH
CRACKLE
!?
CRACKLE
BZZT
I WON'T LET YOU SUMMON YOUR TSUESHIRO.
I WOULDN'T WANT TO MAKE THIS FIGHT ANY MORE DIFFICULT.

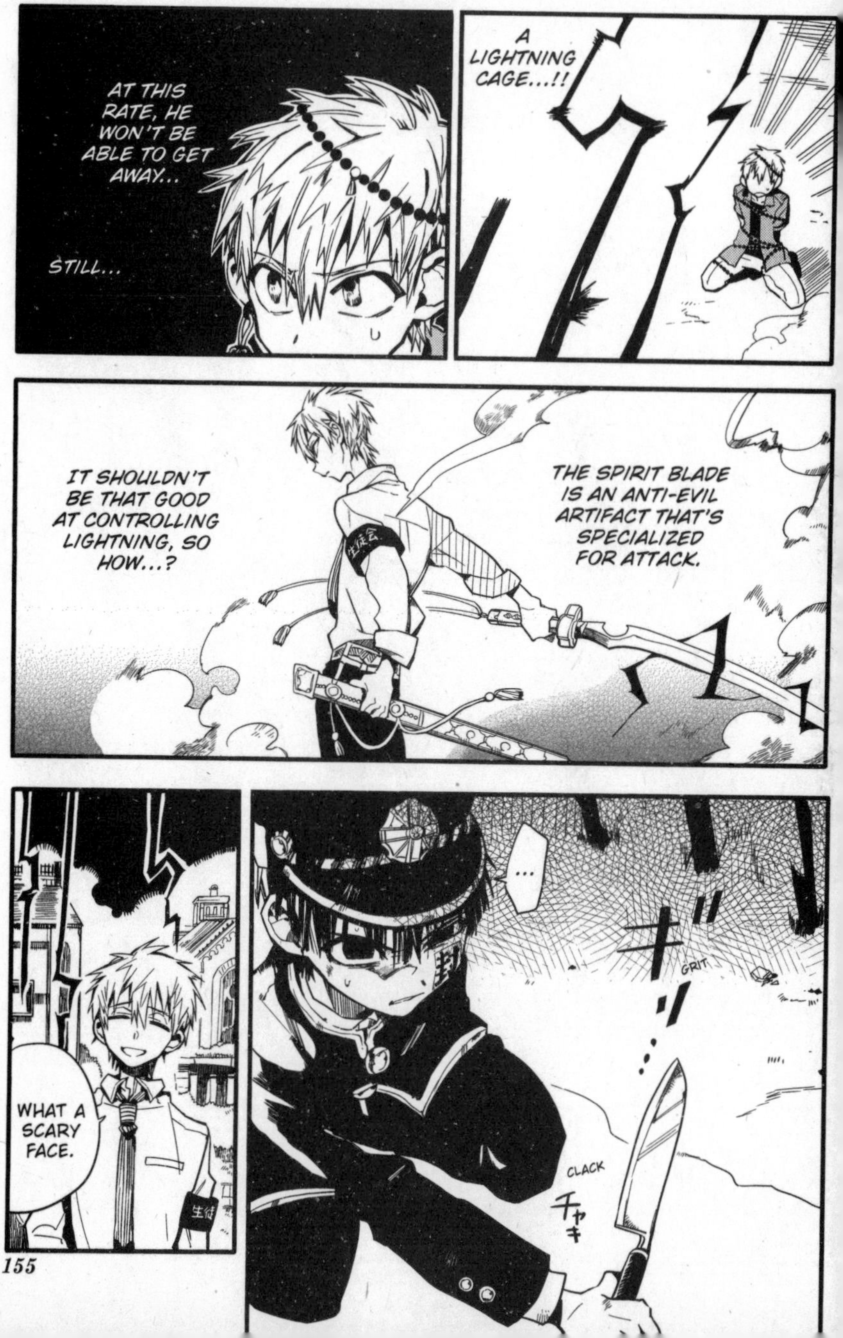
A LIGHTNING CAGE...!!
AT THIS RATE, HE WON'T BE ABLE TO GET AWAY...
STILL...
THE SPIRIT BLADE IS AN ANTI-EVIL ARTIFACT THAT'S SPECIALIZED FOR ATTACK.
IT SHOULDN'T BE THAT GOOD AT CONTROLLING LIGHTNING, SO HOW...?
...
ギリ
GRIT
CLACK
チャキ
WHAT A SCARY FACE.

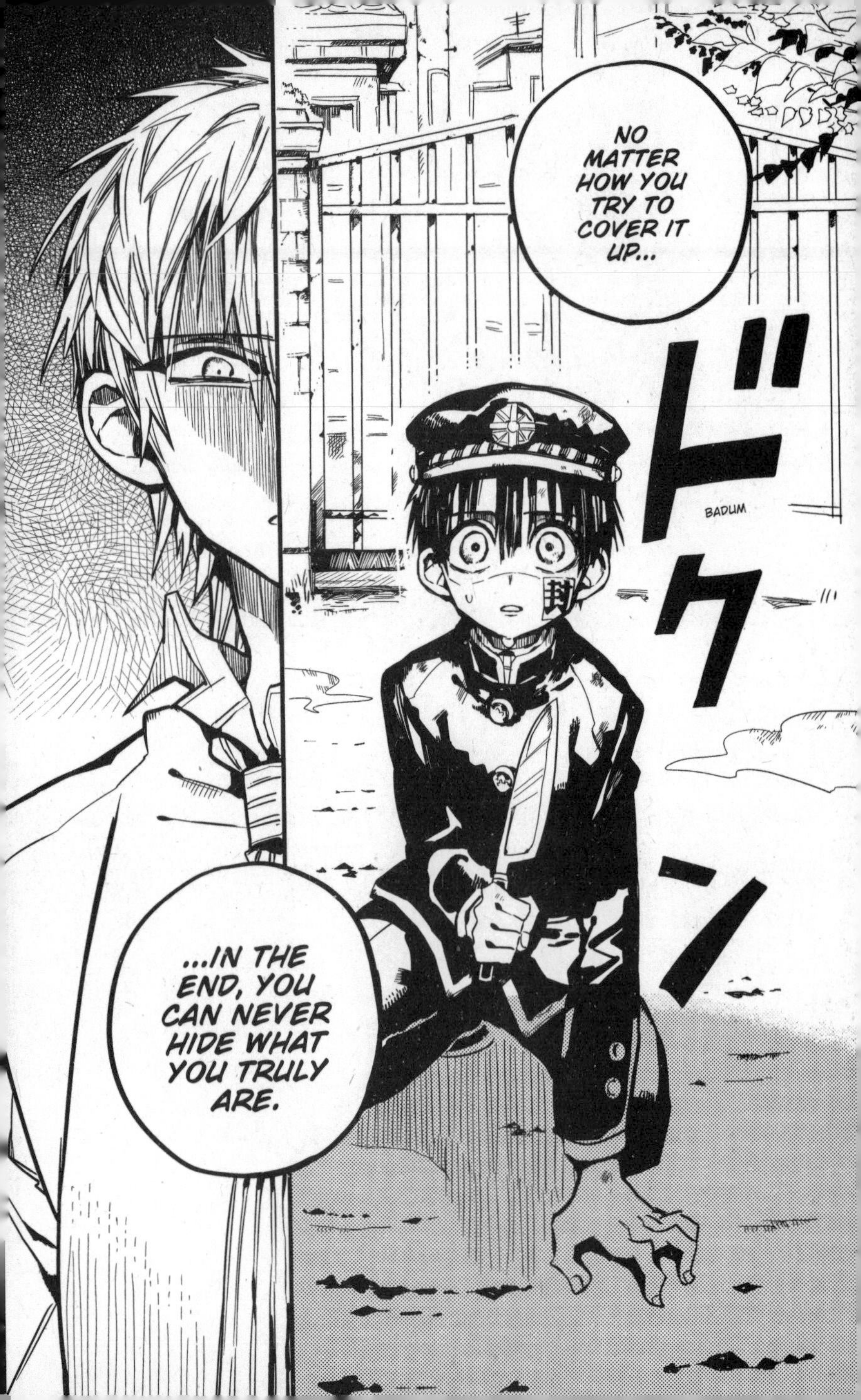
NO MATTER HOW YOU TRY TO COVER IT UP...
ドクン
BADUM
...IN THE END, YOU CAN NEVER HIDE WHAT YOU TRULY ARE.

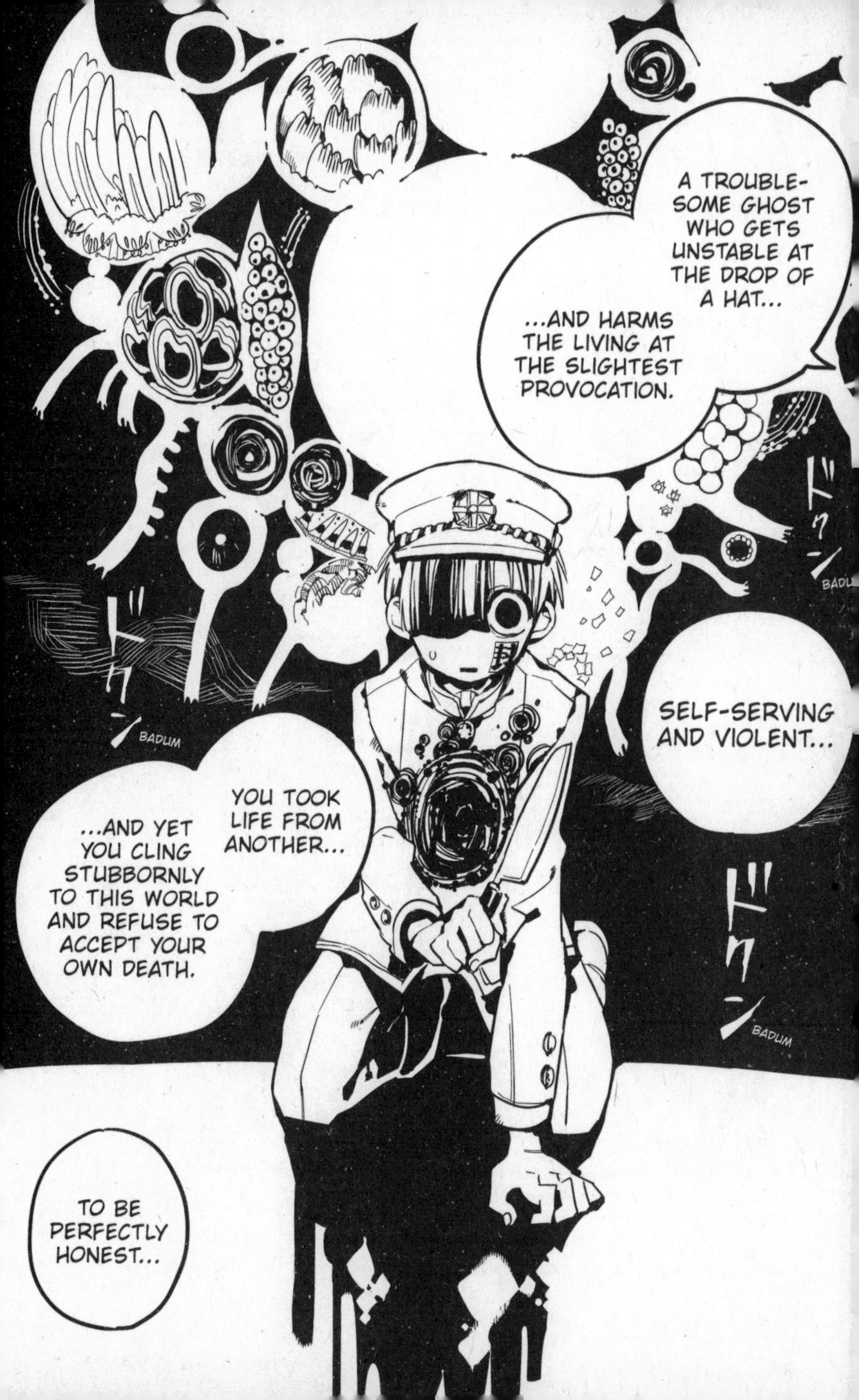
A TROUBLE-SOME GHOST WHO GETS UNSTABLE AT THE DROP OF A HAT...
...AND HARMS THE LIVING AT THE SLIGHTEST PROVOCATION.
BADU
BADUM
SELF-SERVING AND VIOLENT...
BADUM
YOU TOOK LIFE FROM ANOTHER...
...AND YET YOU CLING STUBBORNLY TO THIS WORLD AND REFUSE TO ACCEPT YOUR OWN DEATH.
TO BE PERFECTLY HONEST...

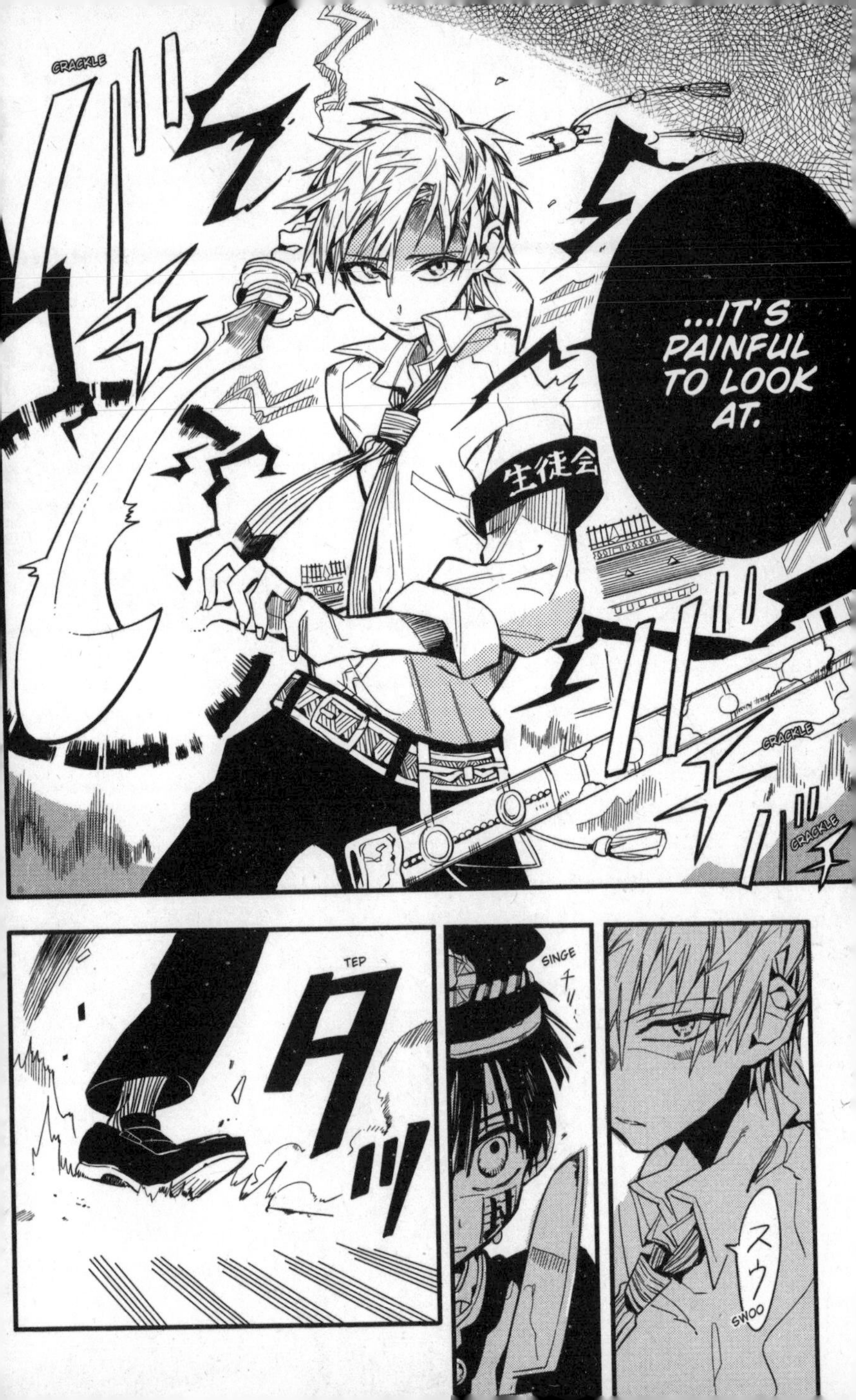
...IT'S PAINFUL TO LOOK AT.
CRACKLE
生徒会
CRACKLE
CRACKLE
スウ
SWOO
チリ
SINGE
タッ
TEP

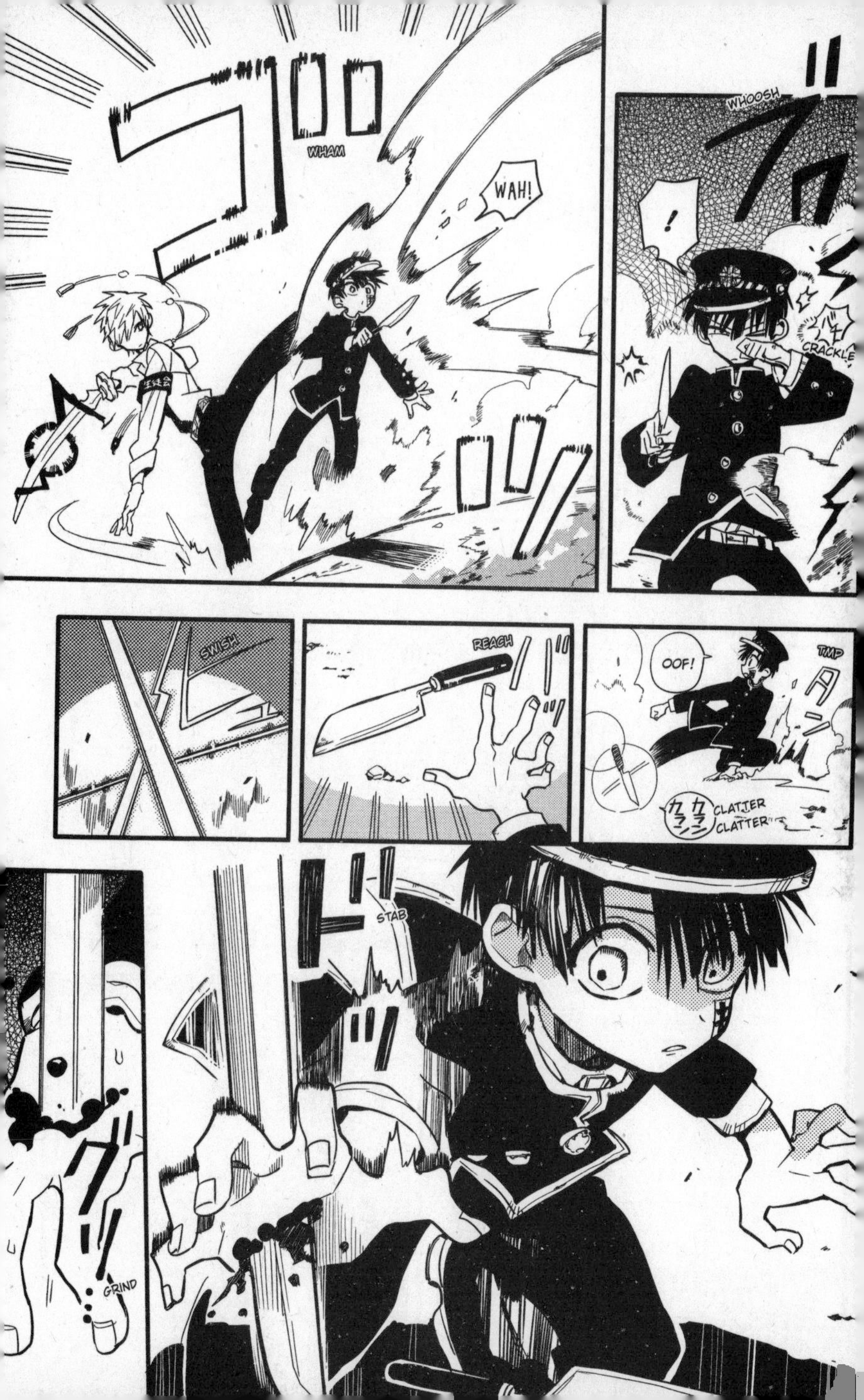
WHOOSH
!
CRACKLE
WHAM
WAH!
!
OOF!
TMP
CLATTER
CLATTER
REACH
SWISH
STAB
GRIND

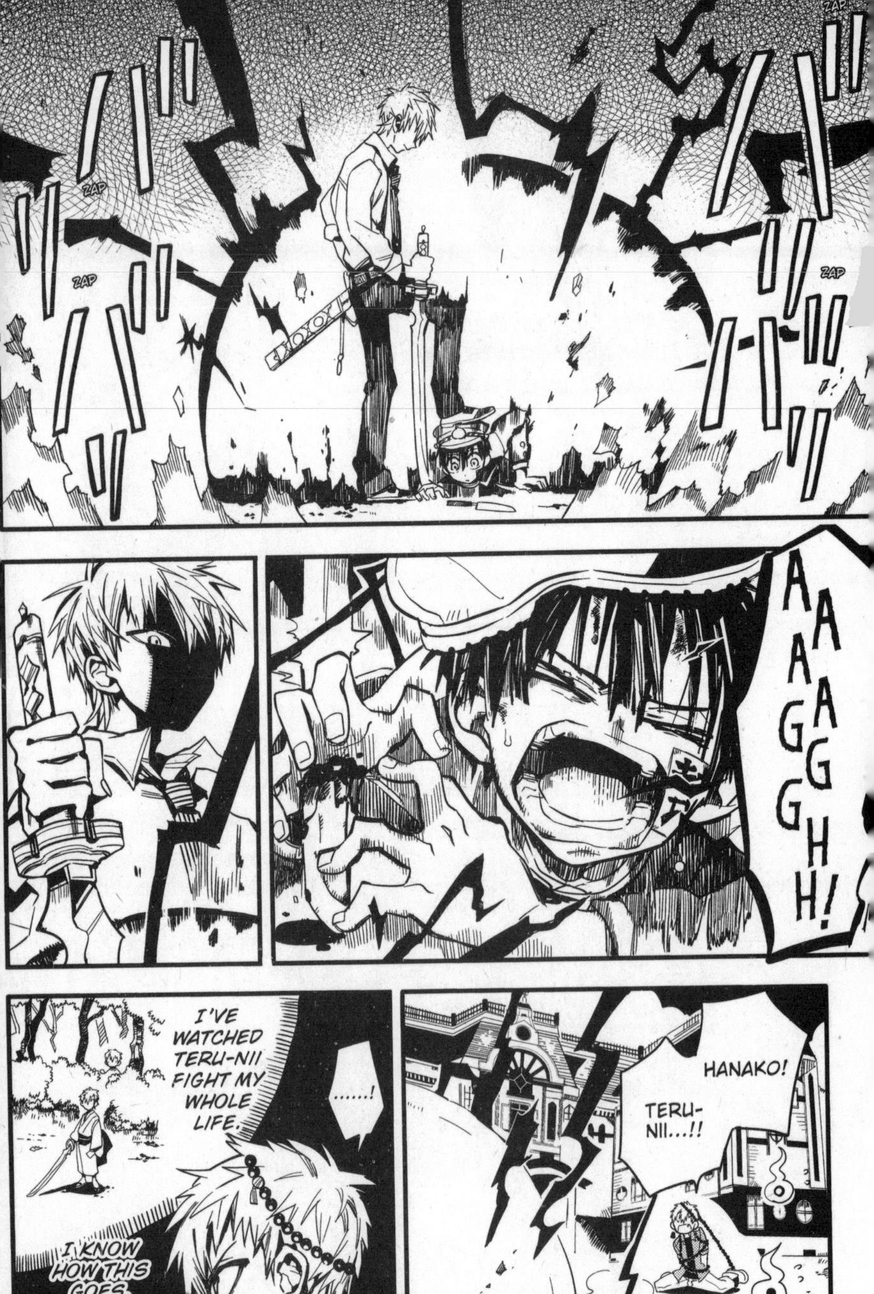
ZAP
ZAP
ZAP
ZAP
AAAAGGGHH!
HANAKO!
TERU-NII...!!
......!
I'VE WATCHED TERU-NII FIGHT MY WHOLE LIFE.
I KNOW HOW THIS GOES.

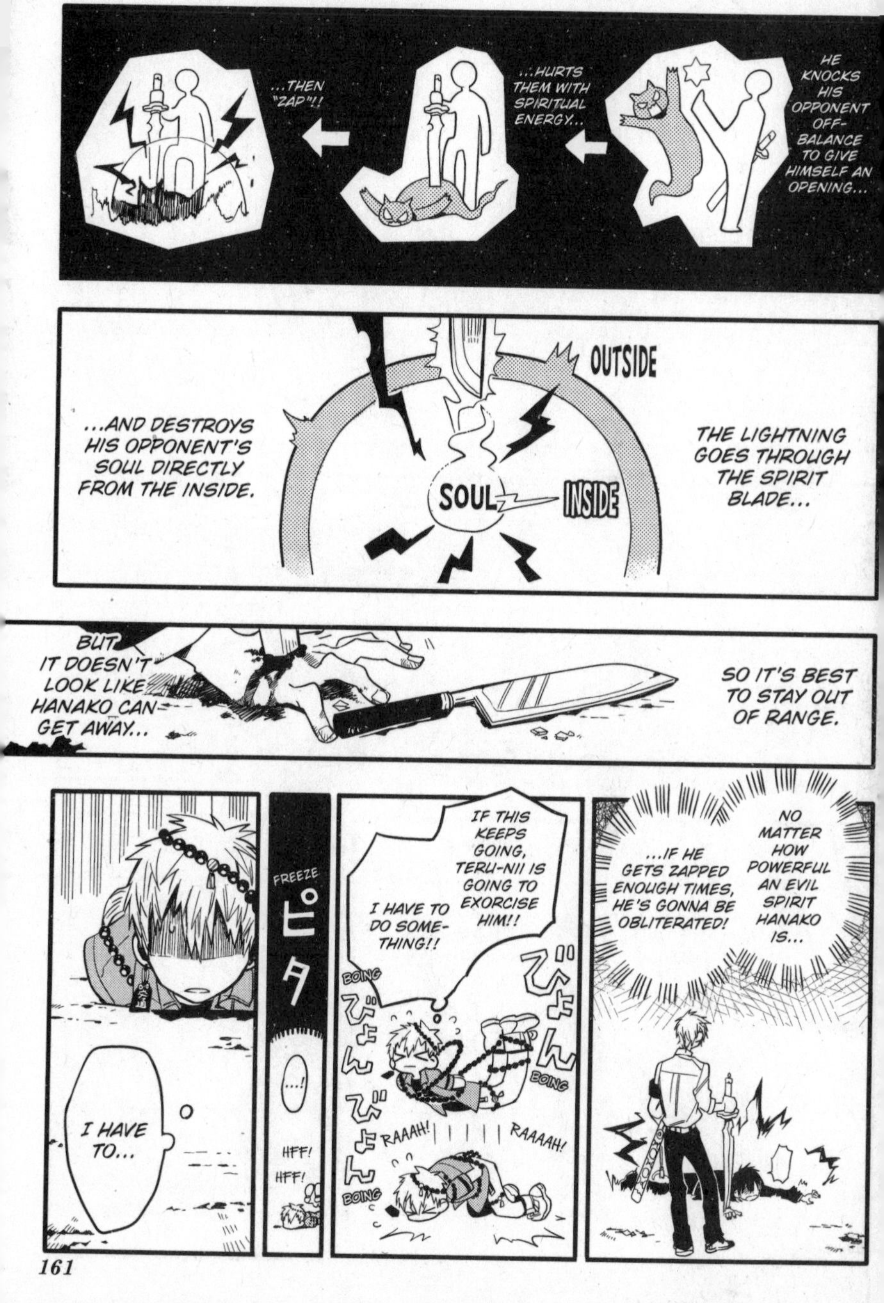
HE KNOCKS HIS OPPONENT OFF-BALANCE TO GIVE HIMSELF AN OPENING...
...HURTS THEM WITH SPIRITUAL ENERGY...
...THEN "ZAP"!!
THE LIGHTNING GOES THROUGH THE SPIRIT BLADE...
OUTSIDE
SOUL
INSIDE
...AND DESTROYS HIS OPPONENT'S SOUL DIRECTLY FROM THE INSIDE.
SO IT'S BEST TO STAY OUT OF RANGE.
BUT IT DOESN'T LOOK LIKE HANAKO CAN GET AWAY...
NO MATTER HOW POWERFUL AN EVIL SPIRIT HANAKO IS...
...IF HE GETS ZAPPED ENOUGH TIMES, HE'S GONNA BE OBLITERATED!
!
IF THIS KEEPS GOING, TERU-NII IS GOING TO EXORCISE HIM!!
I HAVE TO DO SOME-THING!!
BOING びょん
BOING びょん
RAAAAH!
RAAAH!
BOING びょん
BOING びょん
FREEZE ピタ
...!
HFF! HFF!
I HAVE TO...

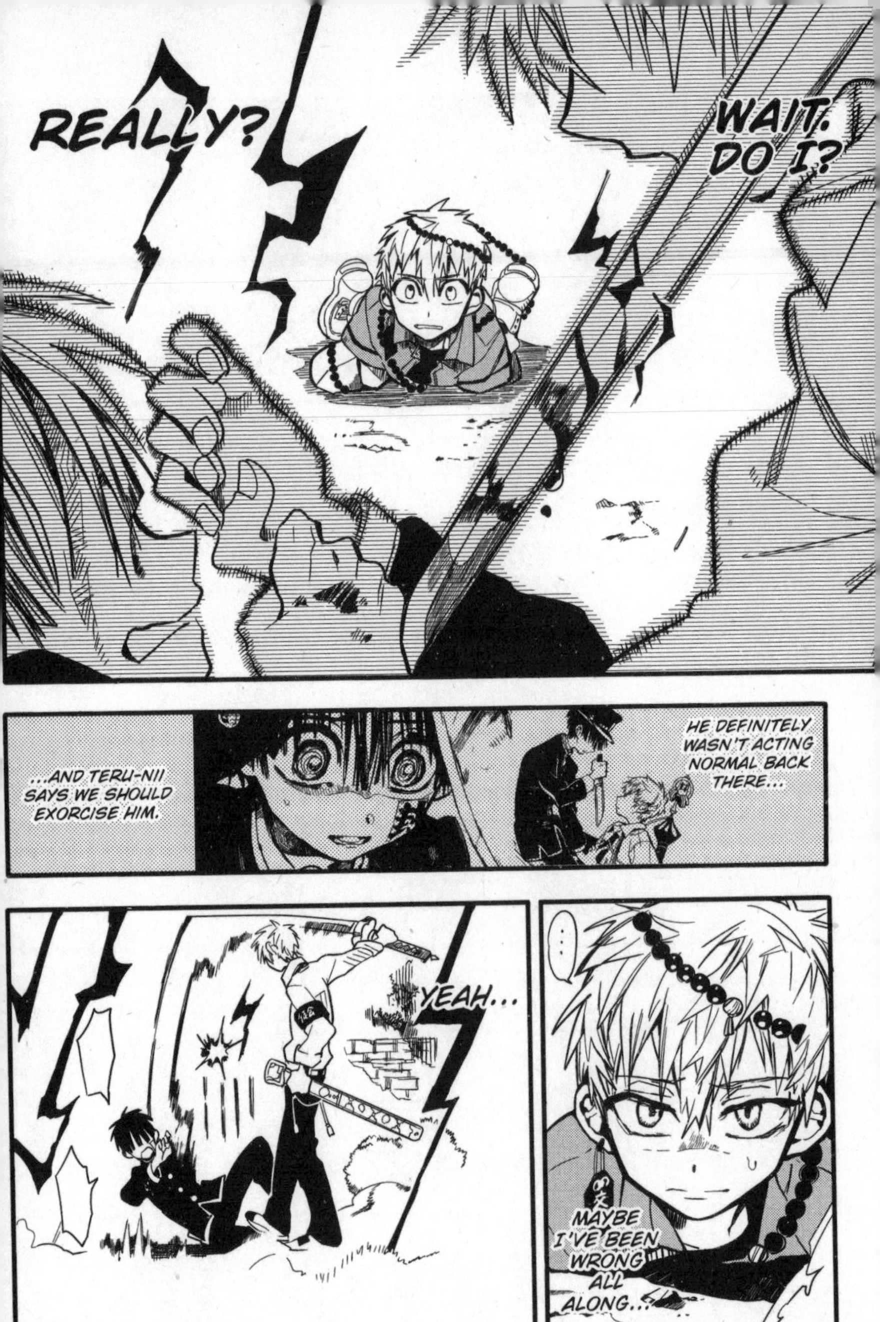
WAIT. DO I?
REALLY?
HE DEFINITELY WASN'T ACTING NORMAL BACK THERE...
...AND TERU-NII SAYS WE SHOULD EXORCISE HIM.
...
MAYBE I'VE BEEN WRONG ALL ALONG...
YEAH...

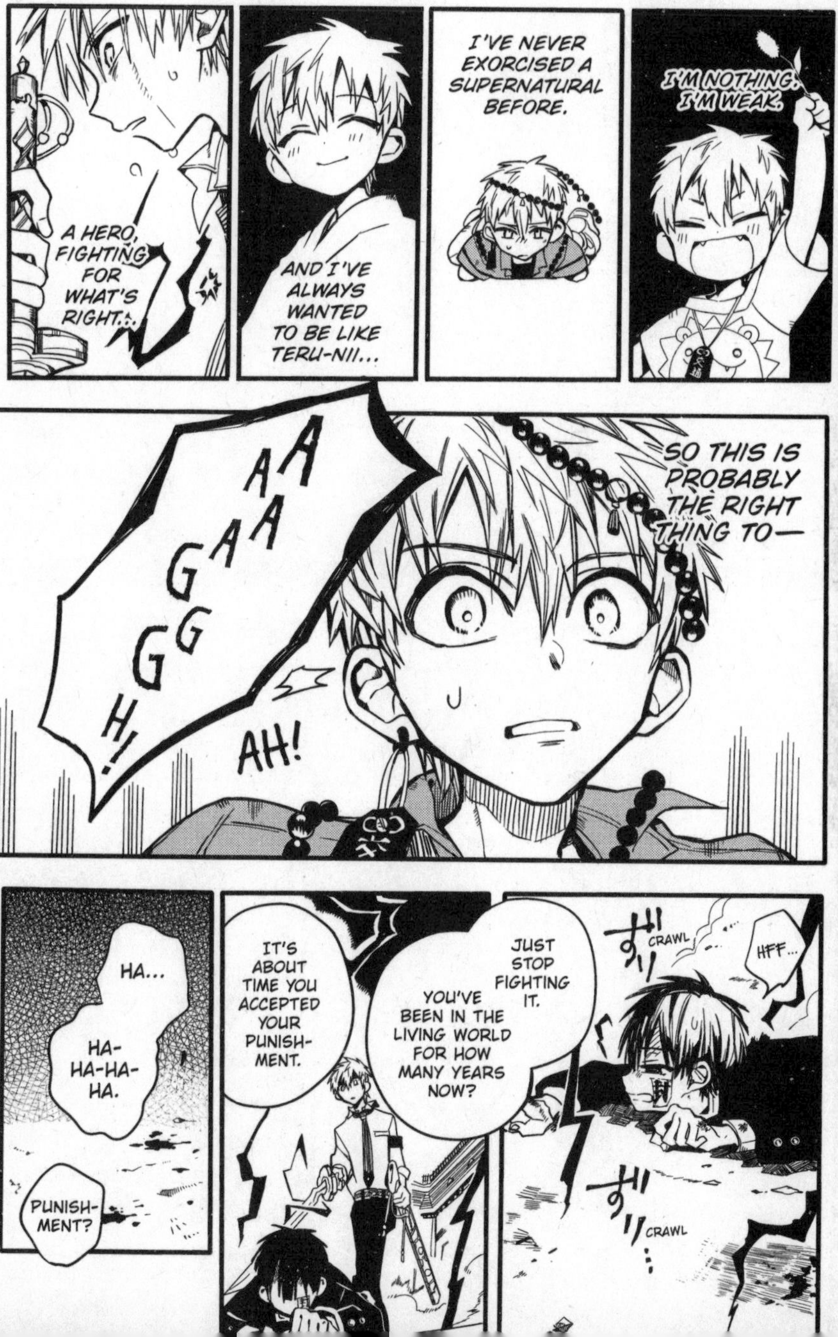
I'M NOTHING. I'M WEAK.
I'VE NEVER EXORCISED A SUPERNATURAL BEFORE.
AND I'VE ALWAYS WANTED TO BE LIKE TERU-NII...
A HERO, FIGHTING FOR WHAT'S RIGHT...
SO THIS IS PROBABLY THE RIGHT THING TO—
AAAAGGGH!
AH!
HFF...
...
CRAWL
CRAWL
JUST STOP FIGHTING IT.
YOU'VE BEEN IN THE LIVING WORLD FOR HOW MANY YEARS NOW?
IT'S ABOUT TIME YOU ACCEPTED YOUR PUNISHMENT.
HA...
HA-HA-HA-HA.
PUNISHMENT?

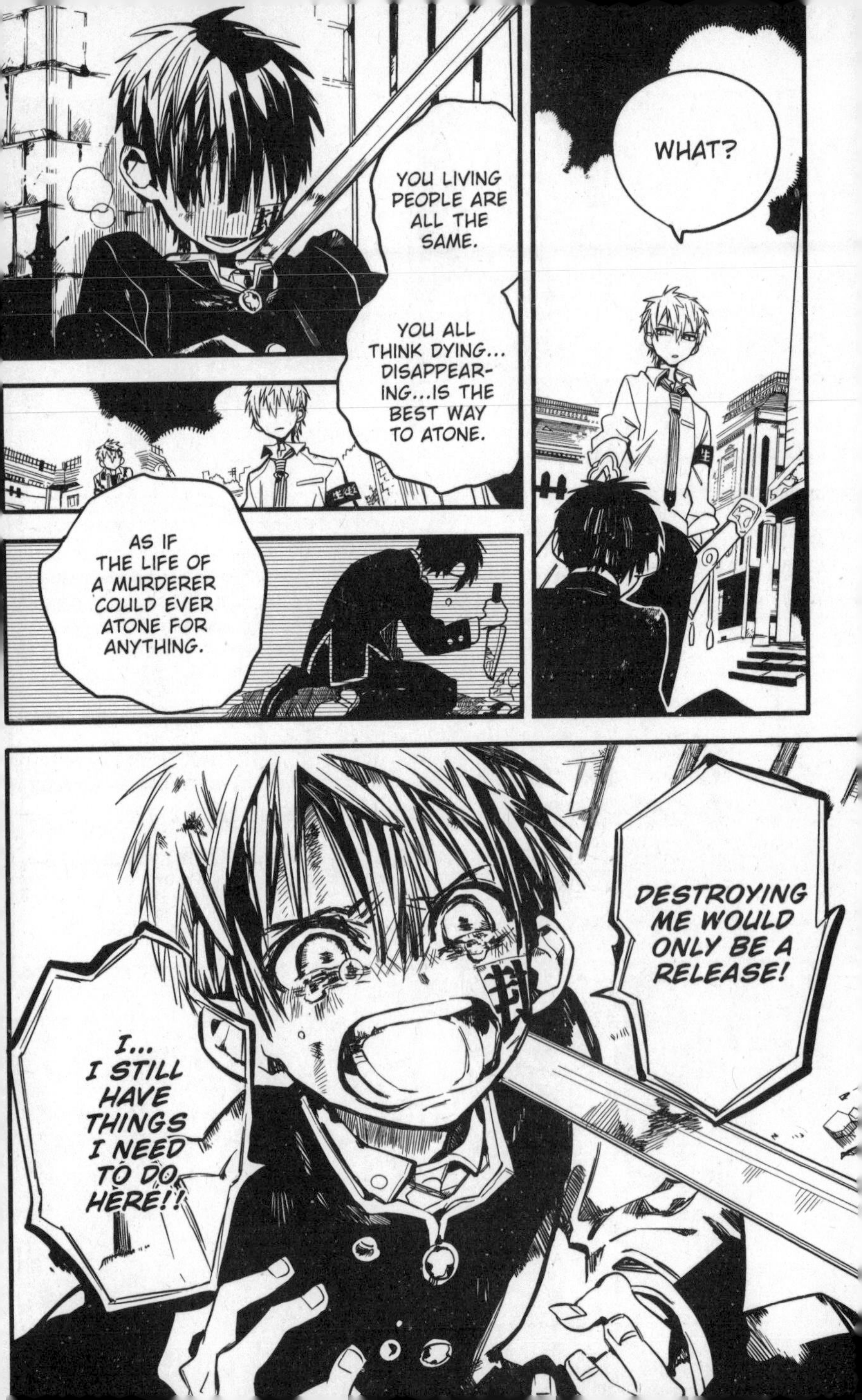
WHAT?
YOU LIVING PEOPLE ARE ALL THE SAME.
YOU ALL THINK DYING... DISAPPEAR-ING...IS THE BEST WAY TO ATONE.
AS IF THE LIFE OF A MURDERER COULD EVER ATONE FOR ANYTHING.
DESTROYING ME WOULD ONLY BE A RELEASE!
I... I STILL HAVE THINGS I NEED TO DO HERE!!

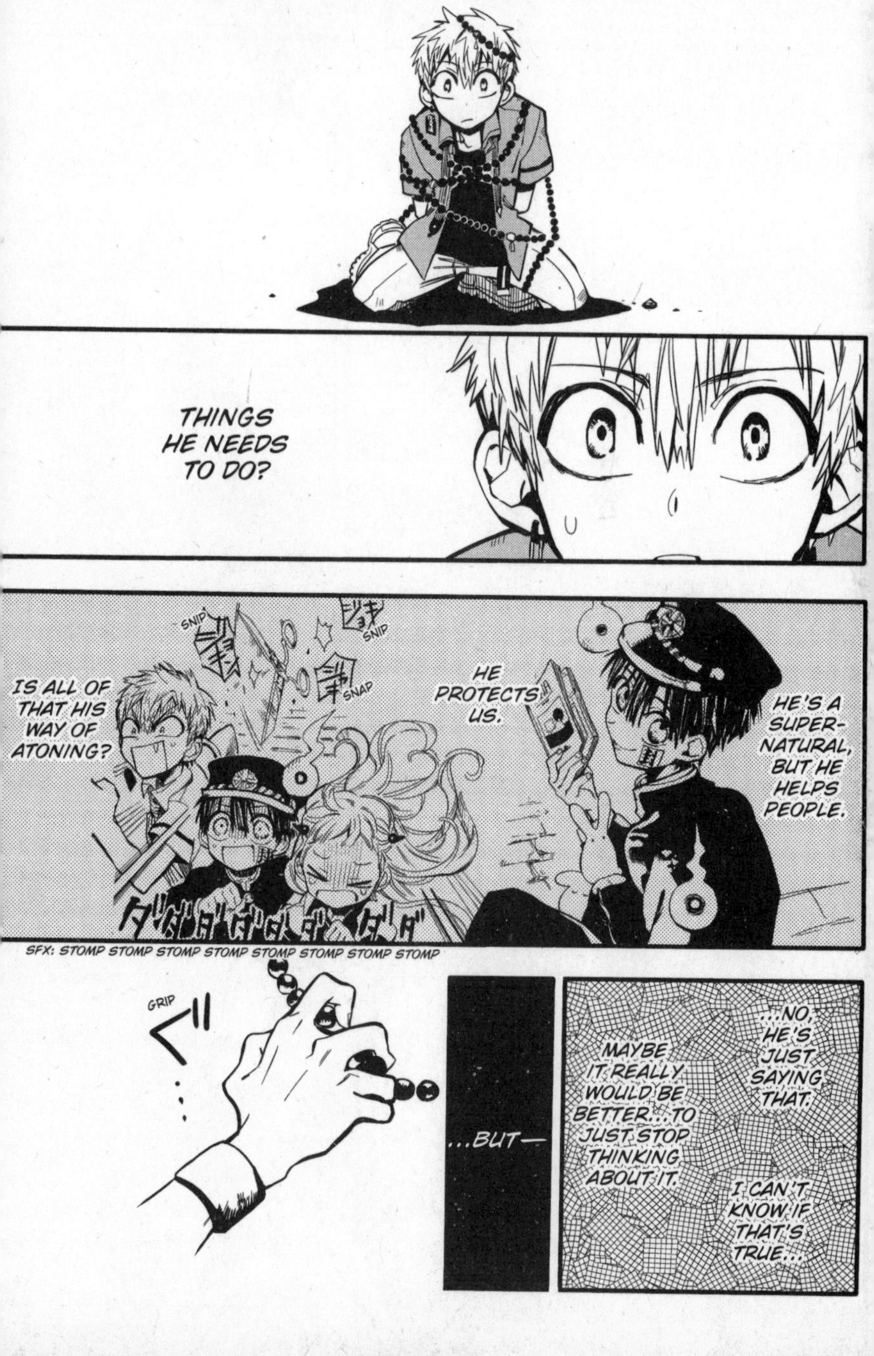
THINGS HE NEEDS TO DO?
HE'S A SUPER-NATURAL, BUT HE HELPS PEOPLE.
HE PROTECTS US.
SNIP
SNIP
SNAP
IS ALL OF THAT HIS WAY OF ATONING?
SFX: STOMP STOMP STOMP STOMP STOMP STOMP STOMP STOMP
...NO, HE'S JUST SAYING THAT.
MAYBE IT REALLY WOULD BE BETTER...TO JUST STOP THINKING ABOUT IT.
I CAN'T KNOW IF THAT'S TRUE...
...BUT—
GRIP

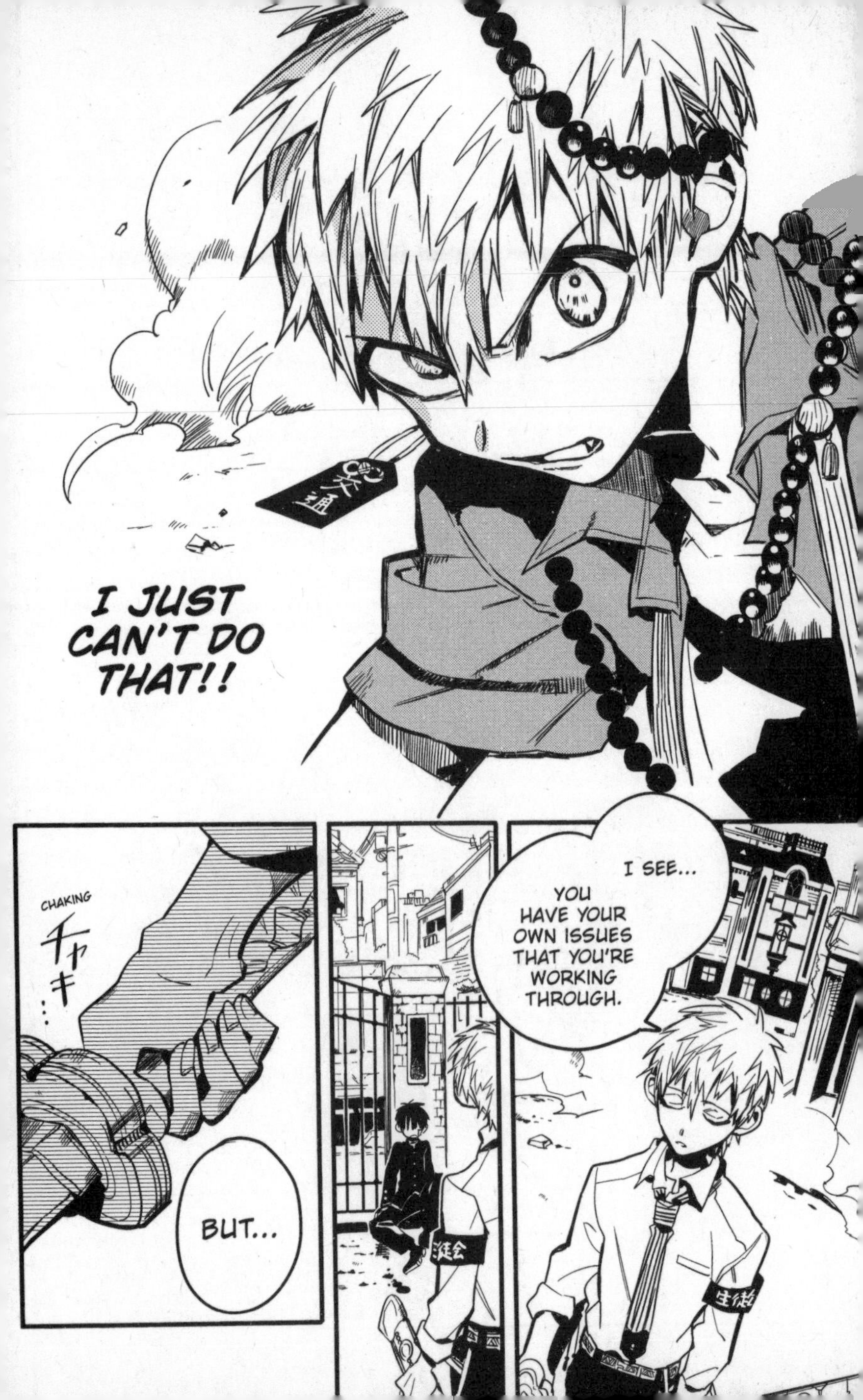
I JUST CAN'T DO THAT!!
I SEE...
YOU HAVE YOUR OWN ISSUES THAT YOU'RE WORKING THROUGH.
CHAKING
チャキ…
BUT...

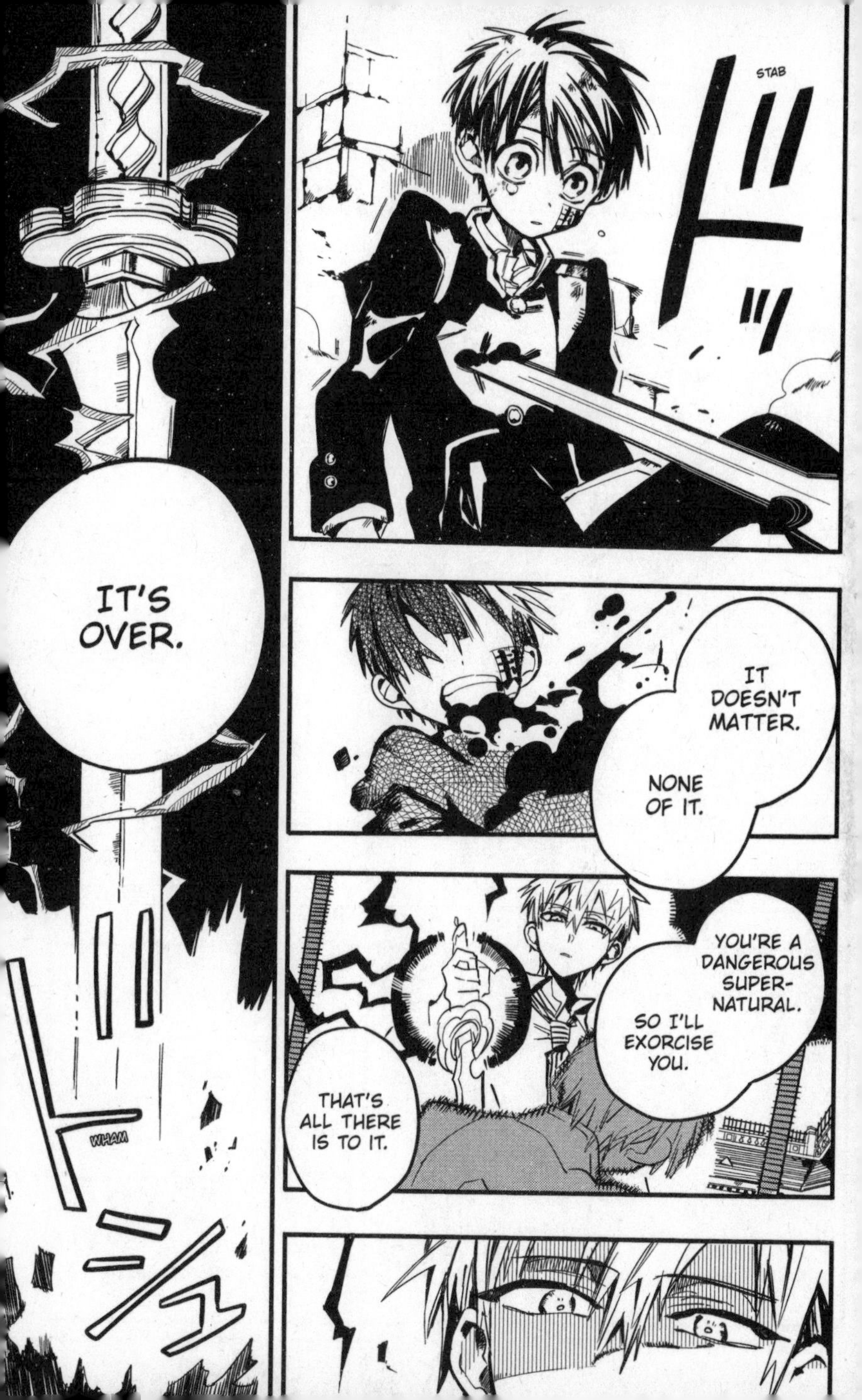
STAB
ドッ
IT DOESN'T MATTER.
NONE OF IT.
YOU'RE A DANGEROUS SUPER-NATURAL.
SO I'LL EXORCISE YOU.
THAT'S ALL THERE IS TO IT.
IT'S OVER.
WHAM

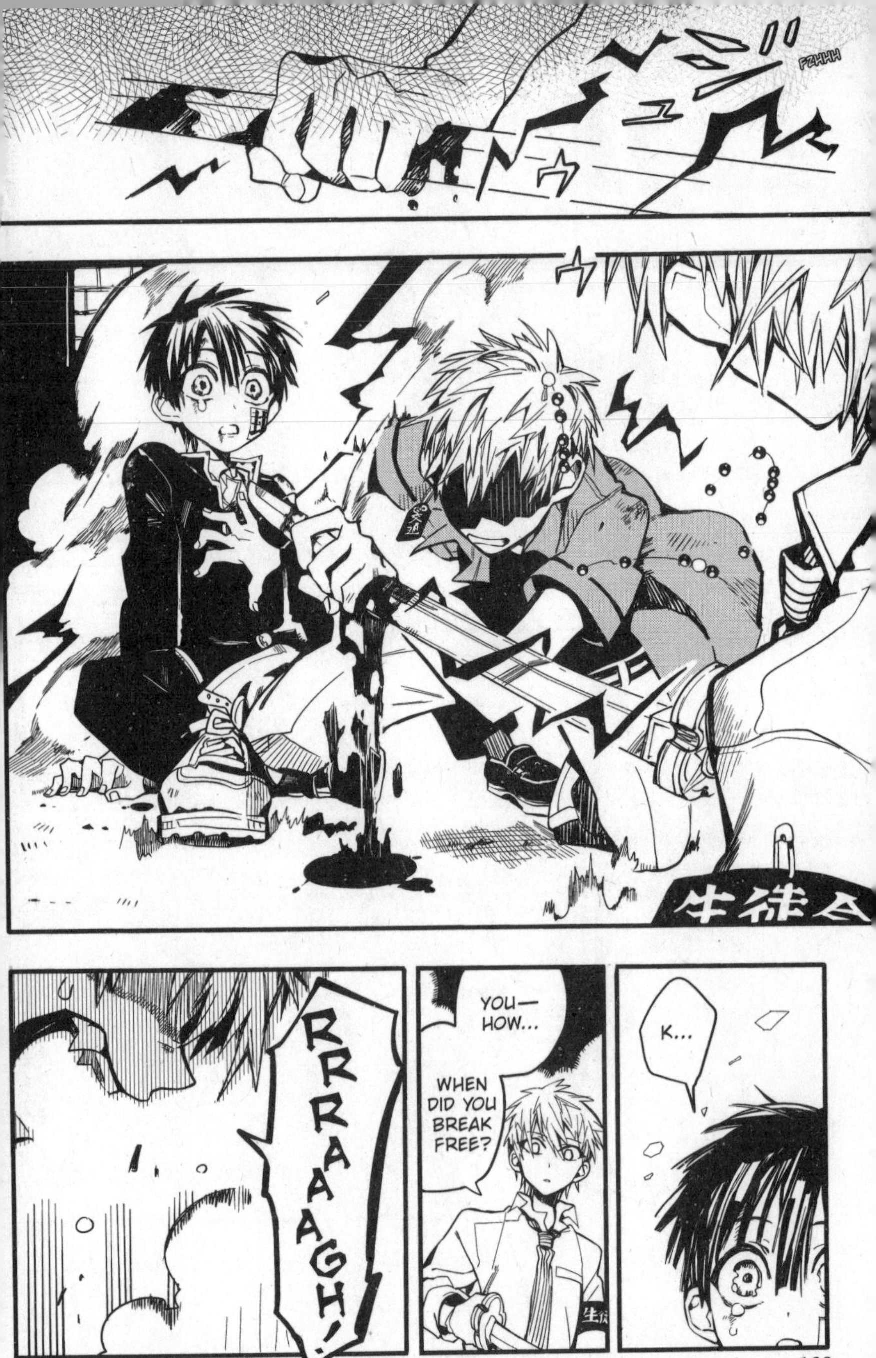
FZHHH
K...
YOU— HOW...
WHEN DID YOU BREAK FREE?
RRRAAAGH!

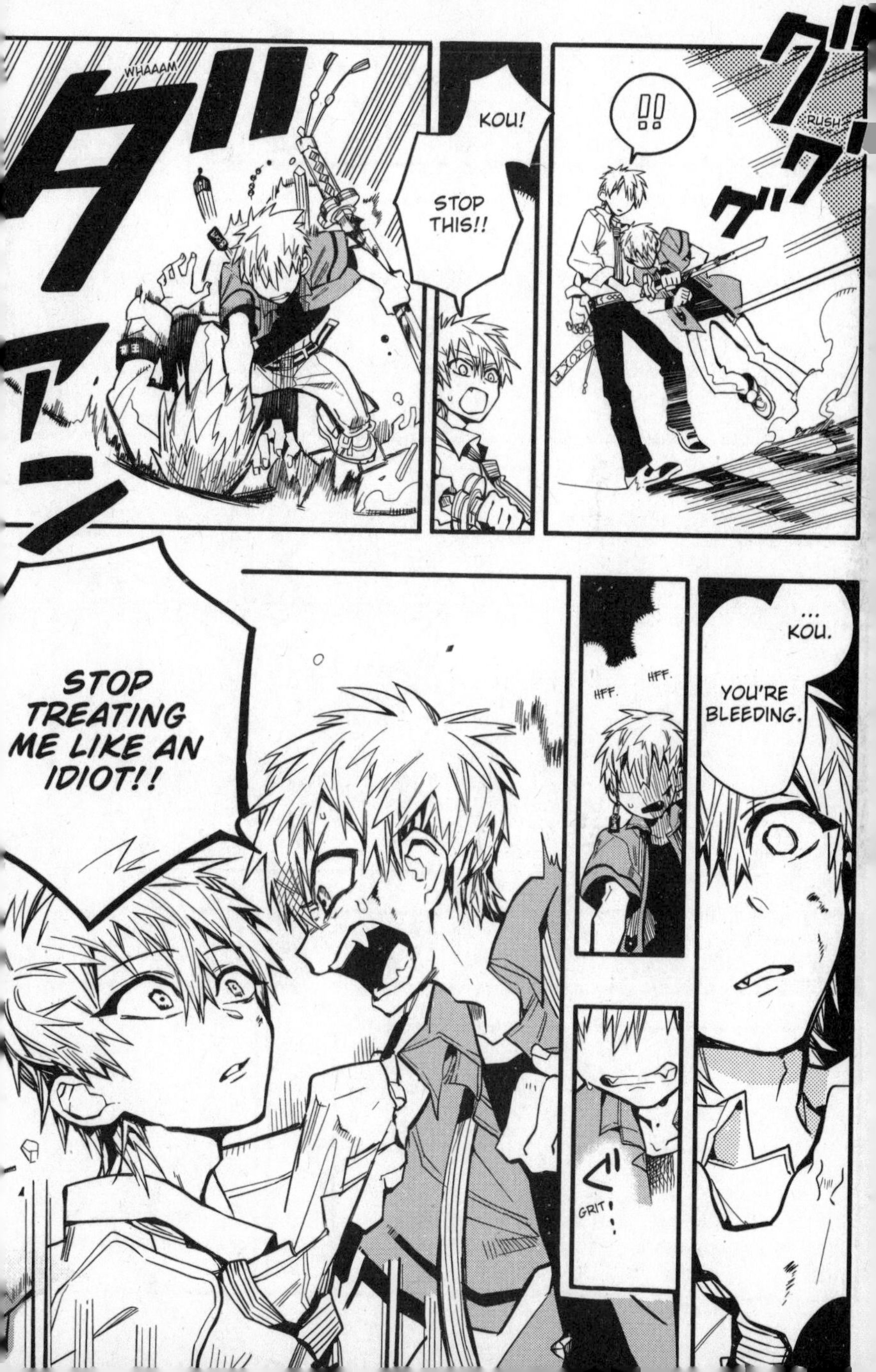
!!
RUSH
KOU!
STOP THIS!!
WHAAAM
... KOU.
YOU'RE BLEEDING.
HFF.
HFF.
GRIT
STOP TREATING ME LIKE AN IDIOT!!

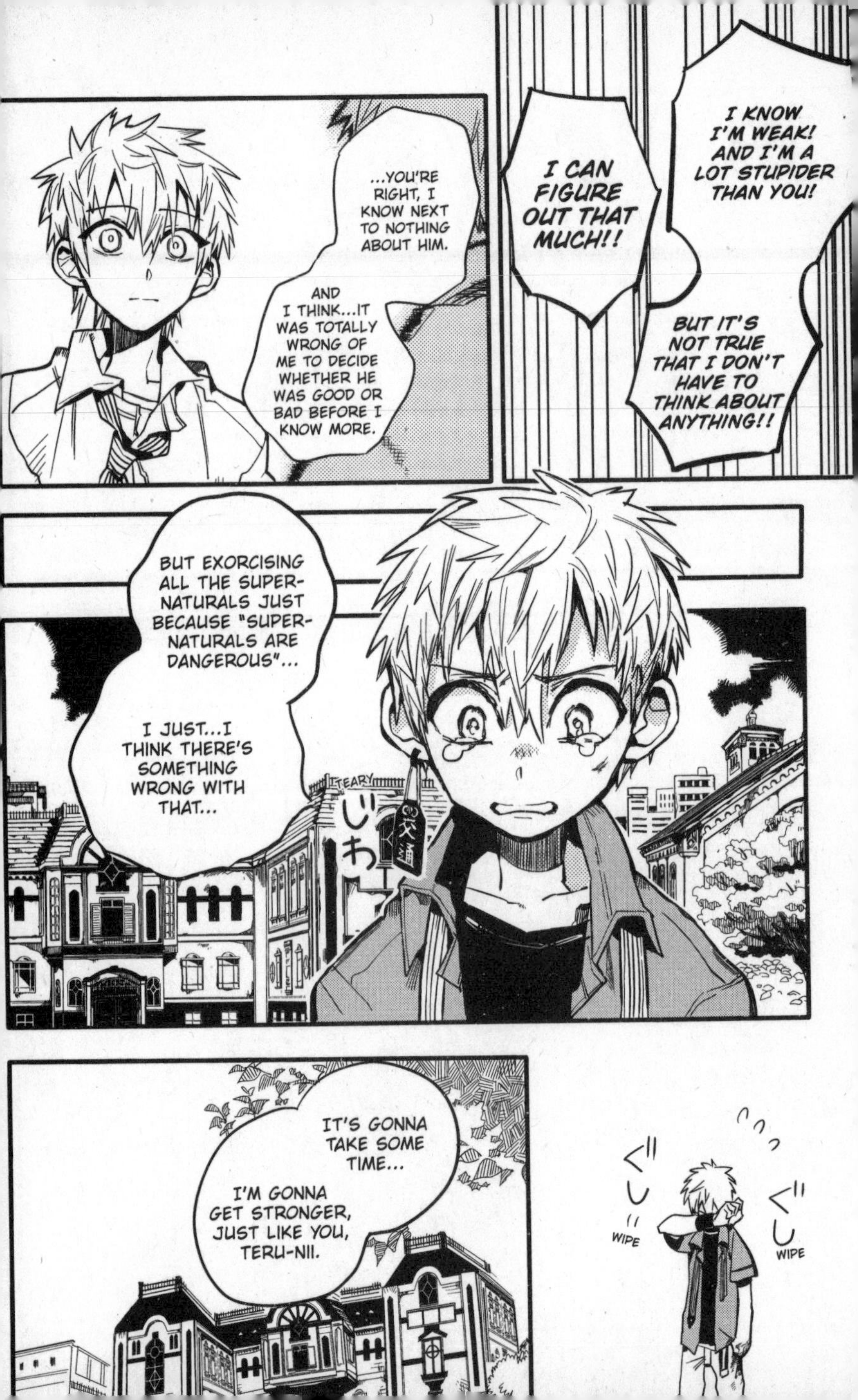
I KNOW I'M WEAK! AND I'M A LOT STUPIDER THAN YOU!
I CAN FIGURE OUT THAT MUCH!!
BUT IT'S NOT TRUE THAT I DON'T HAVE TO THINK ABOUT ANYTHING!!
...YOU'RE RIGHT, I KNOW NEXT TO NOTHING ABOUT HIM.
AND I THINK...IT WAS TOTALLY WRONG OF ME TO DECIDE WHETHER HE WAS GOOD OR BAD BEFORE I KNOW MORE.
BUT EXORCISING ALL THE SUPER-NATURALS JUST BECAUSE "SUPER-NATURALS ARE DANGEROUS"...
I JUST...I THINK THERE'S SOMETHING WRONG WITH THAT...
TEARY
じわ
ぐい
WIPE
ぐい
WIPE
IT'S GONNA TAKE SOME TIME...
I'M GONNA GET STRONGER, JUST LIKE YOU, TERU-NII.

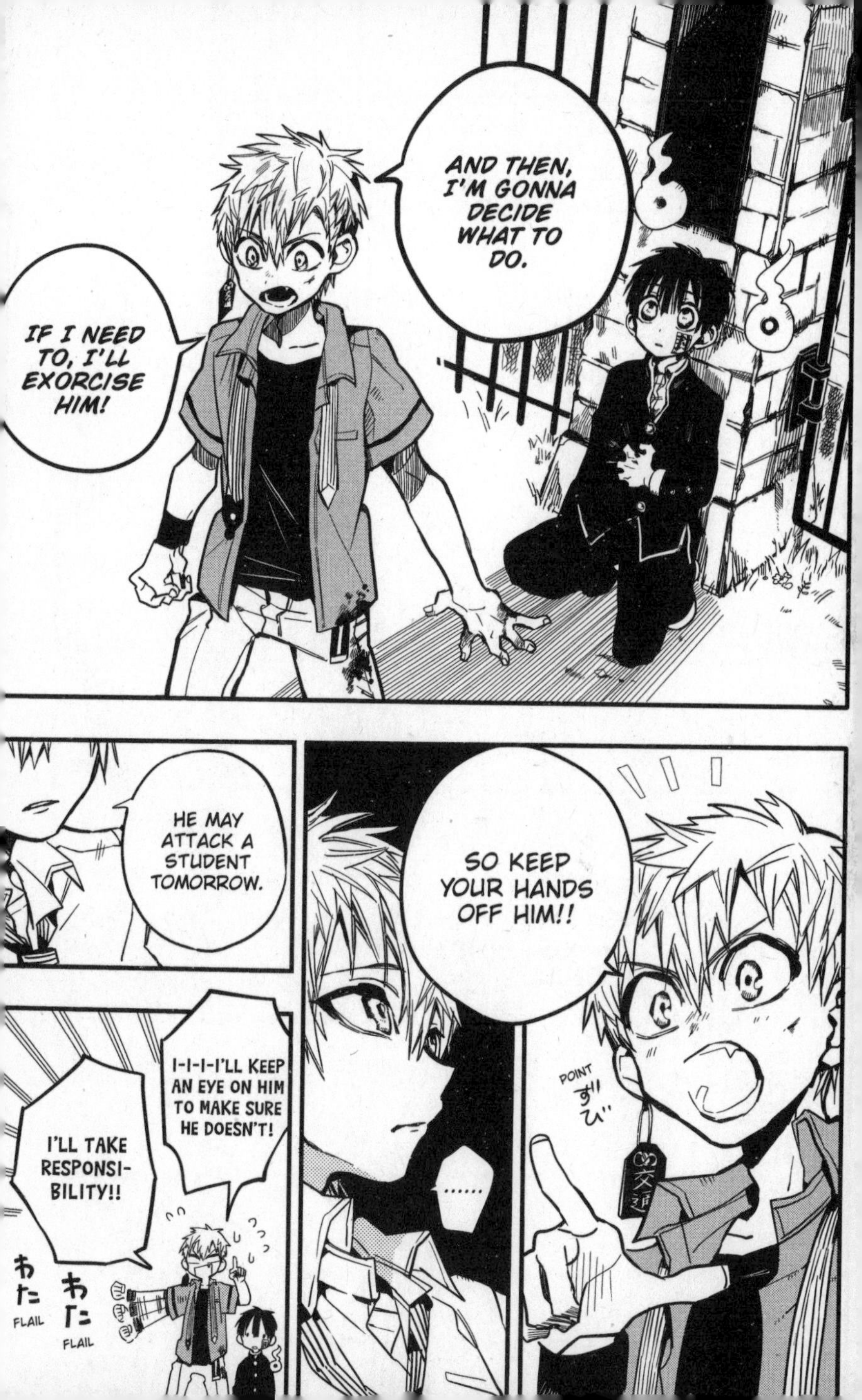

AND THEN, I'M GONNA DECIDE WHAT TO DO.
IF I NEED TO, I'LL EXORCISE HIM!
SO KEEP YOUR HANDS OFF HIM!!
POINT
ずび
......
HE MAY ATTACK A STUDENT TOMORROW.
I-I-I-I'LL KEEP AN EYE ON HIM TO MAKE SURE HE DOESN'T!
I'LL TAKE RESPONSI-BILITY!!
わた
FLAIL
わた
FLAIL

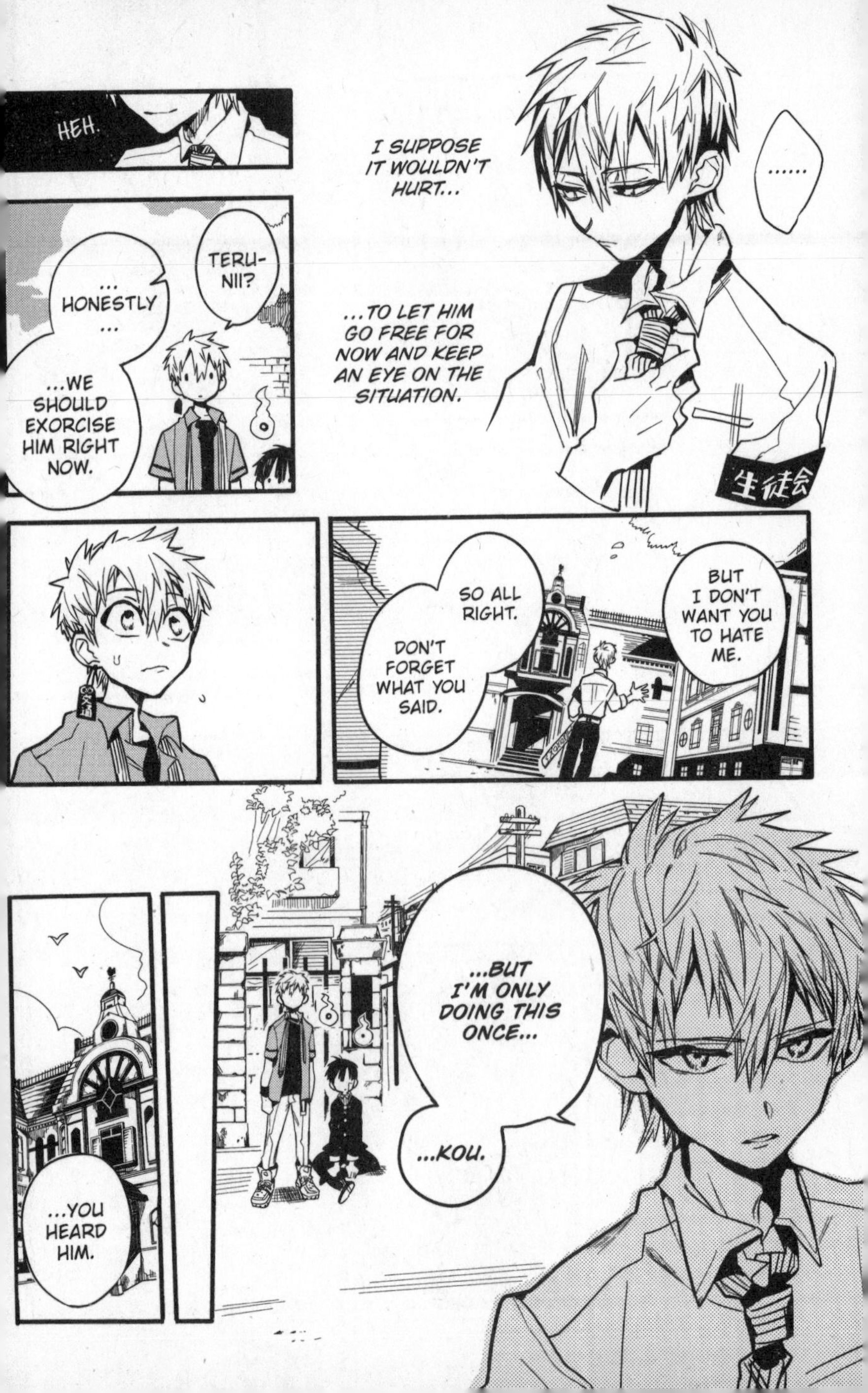
......
I SUPPOSE IT WOULDN'T HURT...
...TO LET HIM GO FREE FOR NOW AND KEEP AN EYE ON THE SITUATION.
生徒会
HEH.
TERU-NII?
...HONESTLY...
...WE SHOULD EXORCISE HIM RIGHT NOW.
BUT I DON'T WANT YOU TO HATE ME.
SO ALL RIGHT.
DON'T FORGET WHAT YOU SAID.
...BUT I'M ONLY DOING THIS ONCE...
...KOU.
...YOU HEARD HIM.

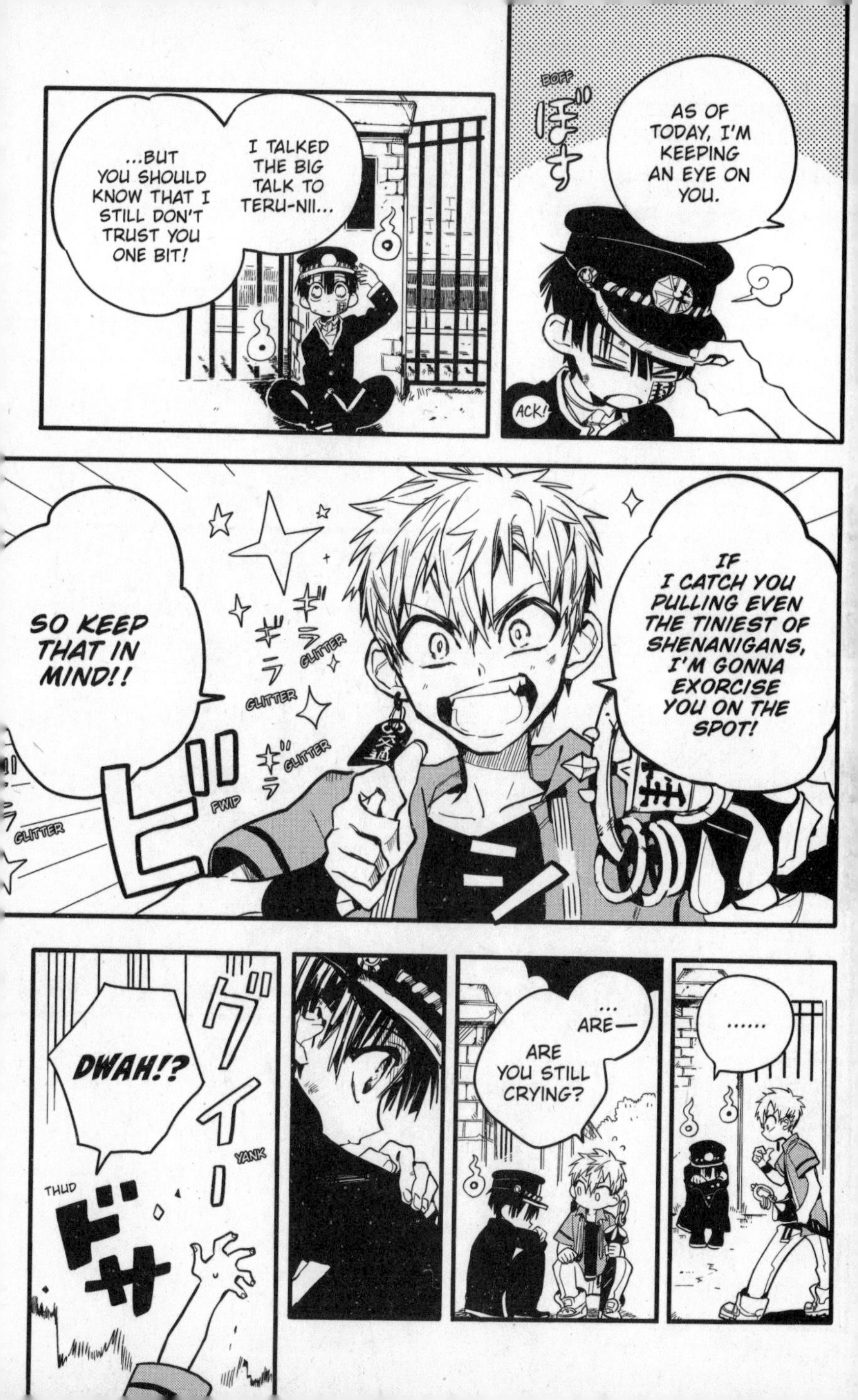
BOFF
AS OF TODAY, I'M KEEPING AN EYE ON YOU.
ACK!
I TALKED THE BIG TALK TO TERU-NII...
...BUT YOU SHOULD KNOW THAT I STILL DON'T TRUST YOU ONE BIT!
IF I CATCH YOU PULLING EVEN THE TINIEST OF SHENANIGANS, I'M GONNA EXORCISE YOU ON THE SPOT!
GLITTER
GLITTER
GLITTER
FWIP
GLITTER
SO KEEP THAT IN MIND!!
......
...ARE—
ARE YOU STILL CRYING?
YANK
DWAH!?
THUD

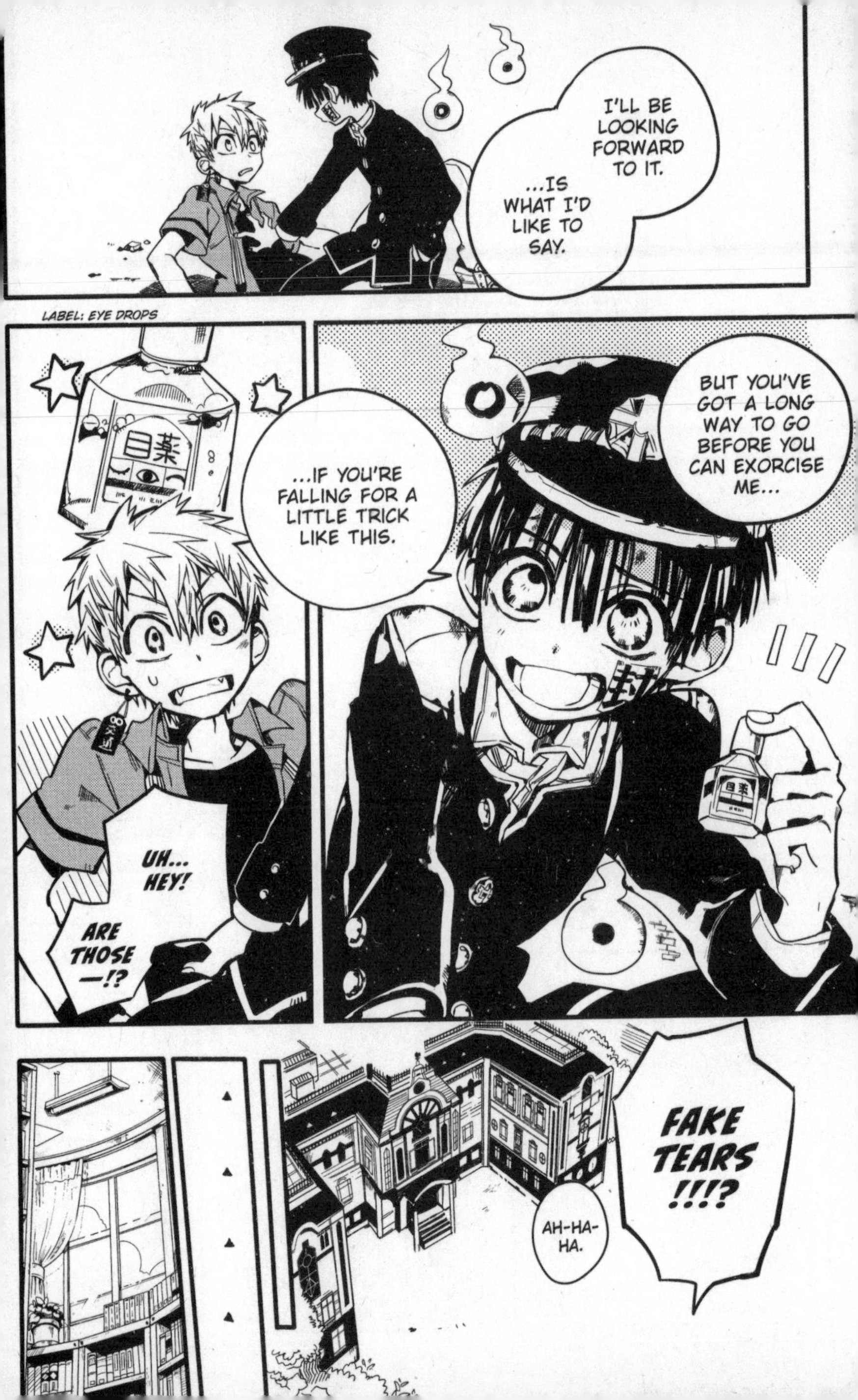
I'LL BE LOOKING FORWARD TO IT.
...IS WHAT I'D LIKE TO SAY.
BUT YOU'VE GOT A LONG WAY TO GO BEFORE YOU CAN EXORCISE ME...
...IF YOU'RE FALLING FOR A LITTLE TRICK LIKE THIS.
LABEL: EYE DROPS
UH... HEY!
ARE THOSE —!?
FAKE TEARS !!!?
AH-HA-HA.

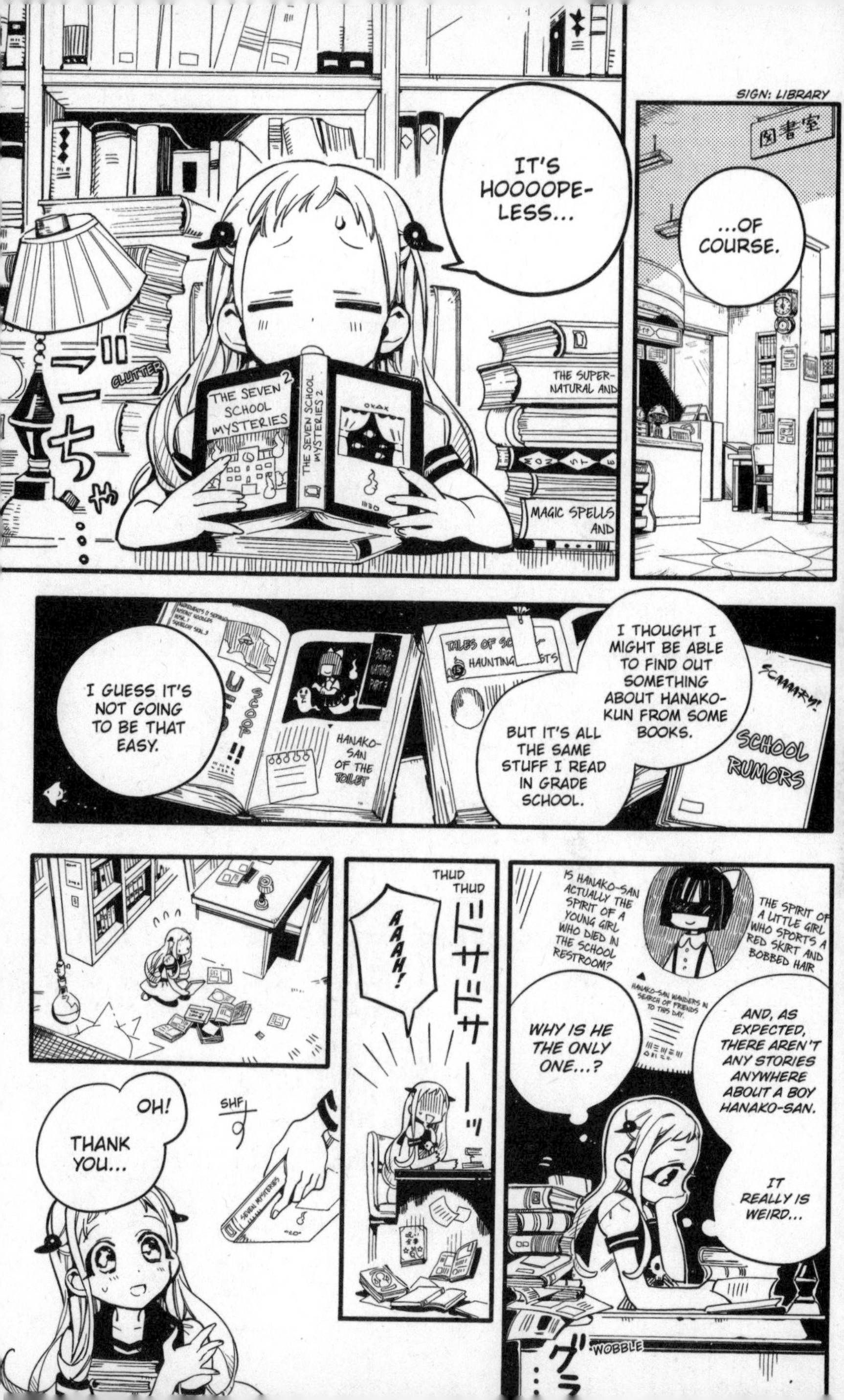
SIGN: LIBRARY
...OF COURSE.
IT'S HOOOOPE-LESS...
THE SEVEN SCHOOL MYSTERIES 2
THE SEVEN SCHOOL MYSTERIES 2
THE SUPER-NATURAL AND
MAGIC SPELLS AND
CLUTTER
I THOUGHT I MIGHT BE ABLE TO FIND OUT SOMETHING ABOUT HANAKO-KUN FROM SOME BOOKS.
BUT IT'S ALL THE SAME STUFF I READ IN GRADE SCHOOL.
SCHOOL RUMORS
HAUNTING
SUPER-NATURAL PART 7
HANAKO-SAN OF THE TOILET
SCOOP!!
I GUESS IT'S NOT GOING TO BE THAT EASY.
IS HANAKO-SAN ACTUALLY THE SPIRIT OF A YOUNG GIRL WHO DIED IN THE SCHOOL RESTROOM?
THE SPIRIT OF A LITTLE GIRL WHO SPORTS A RED SKIRT AND BOBBED HAIR
HANAKO-SAN WANDERS IN SEARCH OF FRIENDS TO THIS DAY.
AND, AS EXPECTED, THERE AREN'T ANY STORIES ANYWHERE ABOUT A BOY HANAKO-SAN.
WHY IS HE THE ONLY ONE...?
IT REALLY IS WEIRD...
WOBBLE
THUD THUD
AAAH!
SHF
OH!
THANK YOU...
SEVEN MYSTERIES

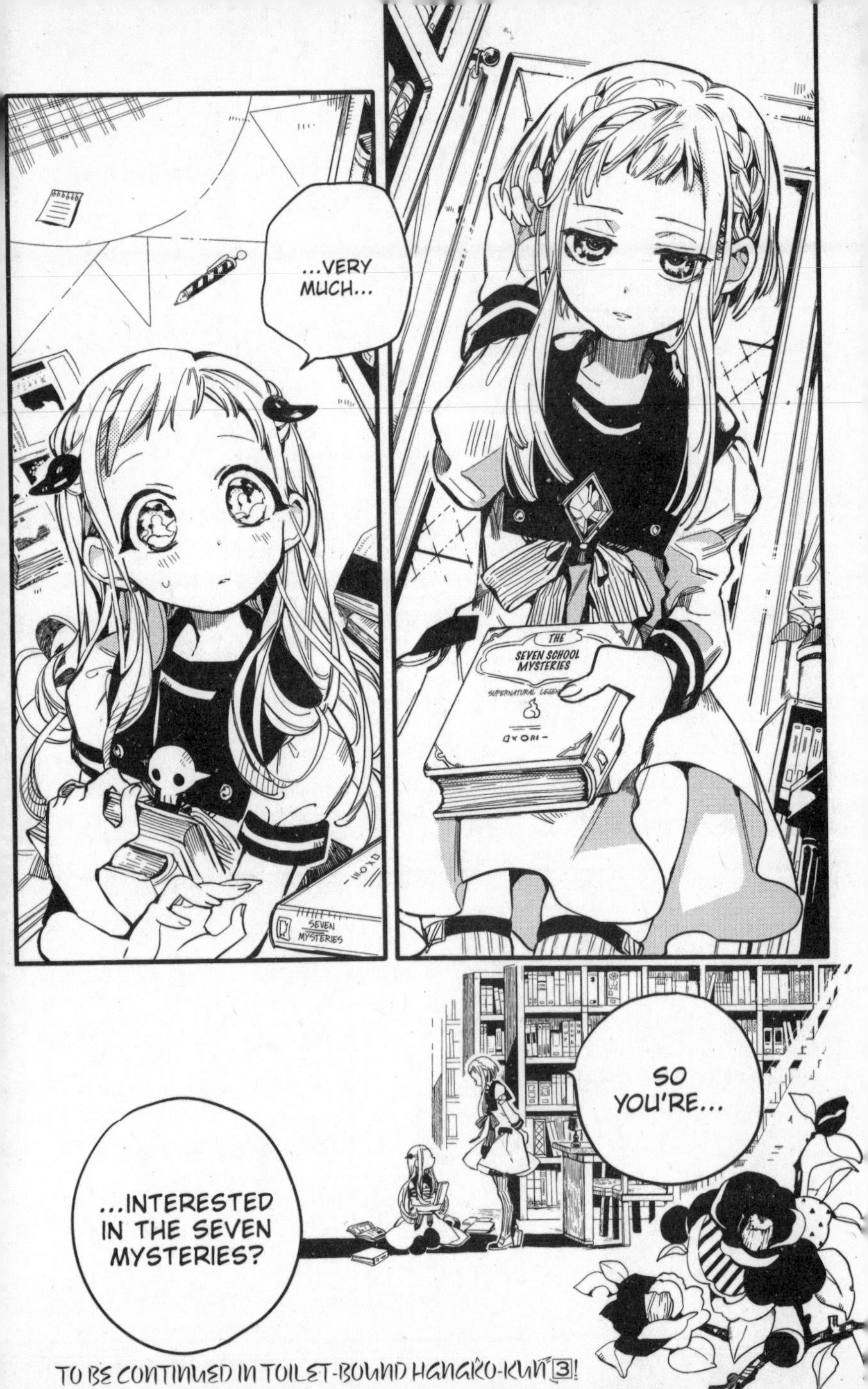
THE SEVEN SCHOOL MYSTERIES
SUPERNATURAL LEGEN
...VERY MUCH...
SEVEN MYSTERIES
SO YOU'RE...
...INTERESTED IN THE SEVEN MYSTERIES?

TO BE CONTINUED IN TOILET-BOUND HANAKO-KUN 3!

TRANSLATION NOTES

Common Honorifics

no honorific: Indicates familiarity or closeness; if used without permission or reason, addressing someone in this manner would constitute an insult.

-san: The Japanese equivalent of Mr./Mrs./Miss. If a situation calls for politeness, this is the fail-safe honorific.

-sama: Conveys great respect; may also indicate that the social status of the speaker is lower than that of the addressee.

-kun: Used most often when referring to boys, this indicates affection or familiarity. Occasionally used by older men among their peers, but it may also be used by anyone referring to a person of lower standing.

-chan: An affectionate honorific indicating familiarity used mostly in reference to girls; also used in reference to cute persons or animals of either gender.

-senpai: A suffix used to address upperclassmen or more experienced coworkers.

-sensei: A respectful term for teachers, artists, or high-level professionals.

Page 15

Yorishiro is a Shinto term referring to an object that first attracts a deity and is where the deity resides during ceremonies, festivals, etc.

Page 70

If Hanako's statement is to be believed, Yako is an Inari statue brought to life. Inari is another name for Uka-no-Mitama, a deity who watches over rice cultivation and is often represented as, or by, a fox. Shrines to Inari are adorned with fox statues wearing red bibs.

Page 70

Kitsune ("fox") *udon* is so called because the main topping for this dish of noodles is *aburaage*, deep-fried tofu. According to Japanese folklore, *aburaage* is a favorite food of foxes. It seems likely Hanako's recipe would replace the tofu with fox meat.

Page 130

A civet is a small, catlike animal of the Viverridae family. This teacher specifically surmises it was a palm civet, which is native to Southeast Asia.

Page 154

Tsueshiro literally means "cane replacement" and refers to someone who serves a god or emperor. The kanji can be pronounced *joudai*, as in *hakujoudai*. (*Haku* means "white," and *koku*, as in the *kokujoudai* possessed by the mysterious girl on page 77, means "black.")

Underjacket

In this short sketch, Hanako teaches Kou how to write the kanji for the "shiro" in *Yashiro*: the top half looks like the characters in the *katakana* syllabary for *yo* and *ero* (casual ways of saying "hi" and "sex"), while the bottom half is the same as the kanji read as *sun*. The kanji itself means a unit of measurement equal to one-tenth of a foot, but *sun* is also a homophone for a casual way of saying "Sure!" While breaking down the kanji this way is surely an effective way of memorizing it, it's easy to see why Nene wouldn't be too pleased with Hanako rendering her last name as "Hey! Wanna screw? Okay!"

Toilet-bound Hanako-Kun 2

AidaIro

Translation: Alethea Nibley and Athena Nibley
Lettering: Jesse Moriarty

This book is a work of fiction. Names, characters, places, and incidents are the product of the author's imagination or are used fictitiously. Any resemblance to actual events, locales, or persons, living or dead, is coincidental.

JIBAKU SHONEN HANAKO-KUN Volume 2 ©2015 AidaIro / SQUARE ENIX CO., LTD.
First published in Japan in 2015 by SQUARE ENIX CO., LTD. English translation rights arranged with SQUARE ENIX CO., LTD. and Yen Press, LLC through Tuttle-Mori Agency, Inc.

English translation © 2017 by SQUARE ENIX CO., LTD.

Yen Press, LLC supports the right to free expression and the value of copyright. The purpose of copyright is to encourage writers and artists to produce the creative works that enrich our culture.

The scanning, uploading, and distribution of this book without permission is a theft of the author's intellectual property. If you would like permission to use material from the book (other than for review purposes), please contact the publisher. Thank you for your support of the author's rights.

Yen Press
150 West 30th Street, 19th Floor
New York, NY 10001

Visit us at yenpress.com • facebook.com/yenpress • twitter.com/yenpress • yenpress.tumblr.com • instagram.com/yenpress

First Yen Press Print Edition: March 2020
Originally published as an ebook in August 2017 by Yen Press.

Yen Press is an imprint of Yen Press, LLC.
The Yen Press name and logo are trademarks of Yen Press, LLC.

The publisher is not responsible for websites (or their content) that are not owned by the publisher.

ISBN: 978-1-9753-9957-3 (paperback)

10 9 8 7 6 5 4

WOR

Printed in the United States of America